THE LIBRARY
ST. MARY
ST. MARY

P9-ASK-595

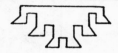

KAROK
MYTHS

Mary Ike, informant for both Kroeber and Gifford. Photographer and date not known. (Courtesy of Mrs. Lucinda Miller)

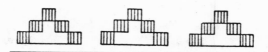

KAROK MYTHS

A.L. KROEBER
E.W. GIFFORD

Edited by Grace Buzaljko

Foreword by Theodora Kroeber

Folkloristic Commentary
by Alan Dundes

Linguistic Index
by William Bright

UNIVERSITY OF CALIFORNIA PRESS
BERKELEY · LOS ANGELES · LONDON

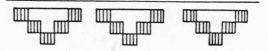

A. L. Kroeber's "Karok Myths" is published
by permission of Mrs. Theodora Kroeber
and the Bancroft Library, University of California, Berkeley.
E. W. Gifford's "Karok Myths and Formulas"
is published by permission of Mrs. Delila Gifford.

University of California Press
Berkeley and Los Angeles, California

University of California Press, Ltd.
London, England

© 1980 by The Regents of the University of California

Printed in the United States of America

Library of Congress Cataloging in Publication Data

Kroeber, Alfred Louis, 1876-1960.
  Karok myths.

  Bibliography: p. 331
  Includes indexes.
  1. Karok Indians—Religion and mythology—
Collected works. 2. Indians of North America—
Northwest Coast of North America—Religion and
mythology—Collected works. I. Gifford, Edward
Winslow, 1887-1959, joint author. II. Buzaljko, Grace,
ed. III. Title.
E99.K25K76 1980   299'.7   78-66022
ISBN 0-520-03870-3

1 2 3 4 5 6 7 8 9

CONTENTS

INFORMANT H.

MRS. BENNETT

ETHNOGRAPHIC NOTES

PART II.

KAROK MYTHS AND FORMULAS

E. W. Gifford (1939-1942)

MYTHS

I. TALES OF IMMORTALS AND HUMANS

II. TALES IN WHICH COYOTE IS A CHARACTER

III. ANIMAL TALES WITHOUT COYOTE AS A CHARACTER

IV. PLANT STORY

V. FORMULAS

ILLUSTRATIONS

MAP

PLATES

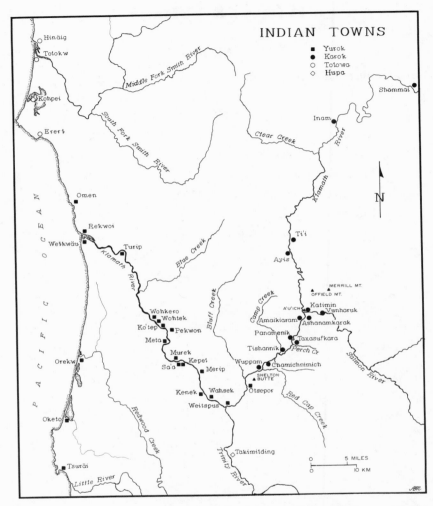

Northwestern California, showing principal Indian towns. Town names shown are those given them by the resident group, except for the Tolowa towns, for which the Yurok forms are used. (Adapted from Spott and Kroeber, Yurok Narratives, frontispiece.)

FOREWORD

About the Authors

Karok Myths is a companion volume to *Yurok Myths* (Kroeber, 1976). It comprises two collections of Karok Indian folklore, one made by Alfred Kroeber in the first decade of this century, the other by Edward Gifford in the fourth decade, and together bringing crucial and heretofore unavailable materials from manuscript archival storage to the light of print. Both collections were made from Karok language-speaking Indian informants, and then translated into English with the help of the original informant or, in most cases, that of a younger bilingual Indian. Kroeber's collection, smaller than Gifford's, constitutes as it were a coda to his definitive *Yurok Myths*, and is the last completed work of his to remain until now unpublished. The physical placement of these two collections side by side within a single binding celebrates a unique association and long friendship between two men of different age, background, and temperament, beginning when Gifford, the younger of them, was fifteen years old and continuing without interruption until his death, a year before Kroeber's. Let us take a brief look at the two men.

Alfred Kroeber (1876–1960) came to California in 1900 to his first anthropological position, which was with the California Academy of Sciences in San Francisco. Within two months of his coming from New York, he made his first California field trip, which took him by fortunate chance to the Klamath River in the northwestern part of the state, the homeland of the Yurok and Karok Indians. Here there began for Kroeber a preoccupation with the languages, literature, and culture of the native Californians which would culminate in the *Handbook of the Indians of California*. (It was written in 1917; publication by the Smithsonian Institution was delayed until 1925 by the First World War and its aftermath.)

In 1900, the Academy was unprepared to finance so avid an ethnographic field man as Kroeber. His brief appointment of some six months was not renewed. However, before the year was out, Kroeber was back in California and San Francisco, having completed his Ph.D. thesis at Columbia, and having been invited by President Benjamin Ide Wheeler of the University of California to come to the University to be a permanent part of a just-to-be-established department and museum of anthropology.

I would like to add here two items of particular interest to the materials of this volume. Kroeber's relations with the Academy staff remained close and viable, which circumstance is presently made manifest in the Academy's new Hall of Man, where a typical Yurok redwood plank house stands, built, furnished, and furbished according to Kroeber's description and measurements as given in his *Handbook* (1925:78–80 and pls. 9, 10, and 12). Members of the Academy's staff examined and photographed the old house timbers and doors collected by Kroeber and stored by the Lowie Museum, and they journeyed to Requa (Yurok Rekwoi) to study a Yurok house, re-erected there around 1910, which Kroeber had also examined. Besides the historic and architectural interest of the Academy's northwest Californian house, I see it as a symbol of the Academy's and Kroeber's own scientific and humane growth, side by side. And it was at the Academy that Kroeber and Gifford first met, in 1903.

Edward Winslow Gifford (1887–1959) was born in Oakland, California. His graduation from one of that city's high schools brought to an end Gifford's formal education. He had been since age 15 a voluntary worker at the Academy of Sciences in San Francisco. In 1903 the Academy sent him with their expedition to Revillagigedo Island, Mexico, as a student conchologist. From 1904 to 1912 he was assistant and then assistant curator to the Academy's Department of Ornithology, during which time (1905–1906) he made his second field trip, as ornithologist this time, for the Academy's expedition on the schooner *Academy* to the Galápagos Islands. Along with the other expedition members he helped work the schooner, thus becoming "one of the very few anthropologists who have literally 'shipped before the mast' " (George M. Foster, "Edward Winslow Gifford," *American Anthropologist* 62:[no. 2]:327).

Kroeber meanwhile had helped to initiate a Department of Anthropology at the University of California, Berkeley, and a Museum of Art and Anthropology, which for many years was located on Parnassus Heights in San Francisco,[1] and in 1912 Gifford accepted Kroeber's offer of an associate curatorship at the Museum, thus beginning their 47-year association. In 1915 Gifford was made assistant curator and in 1925 curator. Over the years Gifford assumed ever greater day-to-day executive responsibility for the running of the museum, and in 1947, upon Kroeber's retirement, Gifford became its director.

More unusual was Gifford's ascent up the succeeding rounds of the University teaching ladder, usually limited to those holding university degrees. Kroeber considered Gifford to have become by his own efforts one of the best educated men he knew. He had a creative and inquiring mind. Witness his introduction into the anthropological vocabulary of the word and concept *acculturation*; of the word *lineage* in its now accepted anthropological sense; his introduction of the technique of weighing instead of counting certain sorts of archaeological sherd materials; his report at age 18 of a tool-using bird, the pallid tree finch of the Galápagos, which, unable to dislodge an insect in the bark of a tree, took in its beak a twig or thorn as a tool to help it remove the insect. This report was not believed in the scientific world until its confirmation in 1940 by way of close-up motion pictures (ibid., pp. 327–329).

Kroeber brought Gifford from the Museum to the Berkeley campus to teach first a single course, then others, in which experience Gifford proved to be a methodical and informed teacher. In 1920 Kroeber succeeded in having him appointed lecturer in anthropology at the University; in 1938 he was made associate professor, and in 1945 he was promoted to the full professorship, thus, says Foster (p. 328), "becoming one of the very few men in this country to achieve such distinction without ever having gone to college." This official recognition came by way of action by Provost Monroe

1. For a fuller history see Theodora Kroeber, *Ishi in Two Worlds* (1961) and *Alfred Kroeber, A Personal Configuration* (1969), both published by the University of California Press, Berkeley and Los Angeles.

E. Deutsch in the first place and President Robert Gordon Sproul in the second. Do we have university administrators today as ready to read the record with a like enlightened appreciation of true scholarly worth and an equal freedom from academic custom and cant?

Gifford's work associations and friendships with men of scientific and personal distinction were a continuing part of his life interest and style; never as disciple to guru but quietly secure in his own accomplishment and capacity, he learned from others as they, in turn, from him. Like Kroeber, Gifford contributed original work in the various areas of anthropological theory and investigation: linguistic, folkloristic, archaeological, social, ethnographic, and physical. Like Kroeber, he went outside California to do archaeology: Gifford to Nayarit, Mexico, and to Oceania (Fiji, New Caledonia, and Yap); Kroeber, to central Mexico and to Peru.

Gifford's bibliography is an impressive one: solid monographs, more than one hundred of them. Besides the Karok materials published here, there remain in the archives other as yet unpublished manuscripts by Gifford which with time and some knowledgeable scholar's attention will, I trust, be added to the long list of his published works.

To anyone who knew "Giff" over the years, an appreciation of him becomes an appreciation of Giff and Delila. Delila, his wife, whom to know is to love, who, all during their married life, accompanied Giff on his field trips and expeditions, not only as amiable, serene, and reliable buffer to the shadow side of every field trip, but as modest but active participant. All peoples love her, from Queen Salote of Tonga to whatever California Indians and whatever anthropologists—and their wives and children—are lucky enough to know her. Giff passed on to Delila, an apt pupil, his expertise in conchology, and she carried on in her own way his early ornithological interest. She smoothed the way to comfortable communication with native women who are usually reserved and shy before a white man. Today those Indians who remember Delila are very old; the old eyes light up, the smile comes, at the mention of her name.

Gifford confined his collecting to the Karok, in part because of Kroeber's earlier concentration on the Yurok, and in part because by the time he got to the Klamath River he found the Karok in their relatively more protected upstream position less dispersed and less disrupted culturally and economically than the Yurok. The Gold

Rush, having put an end to the Yurok-Karok hegemony and autonomy and way of life, moved destructively on to richer fields, leaving behind those of the native population who had survived the holocaust, although they were never again in real possession of their riverline homelands. And never again were they undisturbed or unintruded upon by the white man, an intrusion falling most heavily on the downstream Yurok, whose territory includes, besides the lower reaches of the river and its spreading mouth, the adjacent coastal lands.

About the Indians

The Karok and Yurok Indians alive today occupy, although they can no longer be said to own, the land in fact owned by their ancestors, the watershed of the Klamath River from its mouth upstream a certain distance and including the watersheds of streams immediately tributary to the Klamath. Their villages were built on a land-spit jutting out into the water, or in an oxbow curve or on a high point overlooking the stream, always within ready trail or canoe reach of the main artery of travel and communication, the river itself.

The mouth of the river and along the coast immediately north and south of the mouth and upstream as far as Weitspus was Yurok. Here the Klamath bends sharply northwest, away from its earlier southwest flow, and here its waters and those of the Trinity River conjoin. The Trinity lands belonged to the Hupa, but up-stream from Weitspus as far as Happy Camp the main river was Karok. The Salmon River was the largest tributary along the Karok stretch, and up that remote and beautiful watershed the Karok Indians more and more retreated with the coming of the whites.

In the *Handbook of the Indians of California*, Kroeber's opening sentence on the Karok Indians follows immediately upon his 97-page description of the Yurok, with which he opened his book:

> The Karok . . . are the upriver neighbors of the Yurok. The two peoples are indistinguishable in appearance and customs, except for certain minutiae; but they differ totally in speech. In language, the Yurok are a remote western offshoot of the great Algonquian family, of which the bulk resided east of the Mississippi and even on the Atlantic coast; the Karok, one of the northernmost members of the scattered Hokan group, which

reaches south to Tehuantepec [Mexico]. The nearest kinsmen of the Yurok are the Wiyot, on their south and west; of the Karok, the Chimariko and Shasta, southward and eastward. In spite of the indicated total separateness of origin, the two groups are wholly assimilated culturally.

Except for a few transient bands of Hudson Bay Co. voyagers, the Karok knew nothing of the existence of white men until a swarm of miners and packers burst in upon them in 1850 and 1851. The usual friction, thefts, ambushing, and slaughters followed. . . .The two sacred villages near the mouth of the Salmon, and no doubt others, were burned by the whites in 1852; and a third, at Orleans [Karok Panamenik], was made into a county seat. There were, however, no formal wars; in a few years the small richer placers were worked out; the tide flowed away, leaving only some remnants; and the Karok returned to what was left of their shattered existence. Permanent settlers never came into their land in numbers; the Government established no reservation and left them to their own devices; and they yielded their old customs and their numbers much more slowly than the majority of Californian natives.

The term "Karok," properly *karuk*, means merely "up-stream" in the language of the Karok. It is an adverb, not a designation of a group of people. The Karok have no ethnic name for themselves, contenting themselves, in general Californian custom, by calling themselves "people," *arara*. They will sometimes speak of themselves as Karuk-w-arara in distinction from the Yuruk-w-arara, the "downstreamers" or "Yurok"; but this denomination seems wholly relative. . . .

. . . there were three principal clusters of towns: at the mouths of Camp Creek, Salmon River, and Clear Creek. Other stretches of the river held smaller villages. . . .

Just above the mouth of the Salmon rises an isolated little peak, cut out between the Klamath and an old channel, which can not fail to impress every imagination: A'uich. Adjoining it, on a bluff that overlooks a shallow rapids in which the river ceaselessly roars among its rocks, lay the most sacred spot of the Karok, the center of their world, . . . Katimin. . . . From this district up villages and information become scanter. . . . Then, at the mouth of Clear Creek, Inam is reached: a large town, as shown by its boasting a Deerskin dance, and famous even to the Yurok. . . . Some 8 miles above, at the mouth of Indian Creek, at Happy Camp, was Asisufunuk, the last large Karok village. . . . [Above that the Shasta Indian world began.] Since the American settlement, the Karok have emigrated in some numbers, until now they form the sole Indian population on Salmon River. (Kroeber, *Handbook*, pp. 98–100)

They were less numerous than the Yurok; Kroeber estimates a population of 2,000 souls at the time of the Anglo-American conquest, as against 2,500 Yurok (ibid., pp. 101, 17). Kroeber's figures are always conservative, based on prehistoric village and house-site counts and average size of families in historic times. The riverine peoples of the Klamath were offside the main routes of conquest, and their survivors remained in the homeland. It followed that they transmitted to history fuller and fairer parts and parcels of their culture than could by any means be recovered from the physically and culturally destroyed Indian nations of most of the rest of California.

Kroeber notes the physical alikeness of the Karok and Yurok peoples. They are in fact unlike other California Indians in being slimmer and longer of limb, although median in height; their skin, a paler bronze than most, shows some red in the cheeks; the nose is higher-bridged and narrower than in the more usual serene moon face one comes to expect in California; the mouth generous, mobile; eyes wideset, with an occasional suggestion of epicanthic fold. Their gestures are quick, graceful. They dive to great depths, their diving and swimming form excellent. Their bodies are attuned to maneuver heavy redwood log dugout canoes through river rapids; to steep trail travel, to action and tension, and then to leisure. In manner they are reserved, courteous but formal to each other as to strangers, assured; the customary expression reveals an animation of controlled tension.[2]

Kroeber (ibid., pp. 1–5) characterizes Karok-Yurok social values as being puritanical, legalistic, aristocratic, and wealth-oriented. Settlement of any and all infraction of customary practice and accepted behavior, of feud, murder, or personal or property injury was by money payment, calculated by the elders, who fixed the exact amount down to the last string of dentalium shell money. The amount depended upon the kind and extent of the crime or injury, the precise amount fixed according to the actual and relative wealth of each party to the settlement, the wealthy man paying and receiving more than the poor—how much more depending further upon the extent of his wealth, the degree of distinction of person, family, and aristocratic emoluments.

2. These observations were made by A. L. Kroeber in a discussion in 1955 and were noted by me at that time.

Wealth and position were made visible in the first instance in the ownership of a good family home (houses were built of hand-adzed planks), the house in a sunny and favorable central situation in the village and possessing a name, the name known up and downstream and serving to identify members of the household. The head of a "good" family would own, to begin, many carefully made boxes filled with strings, many strings, of the best-quality dentalium shell money. He would own as well fishing rights at choice spots along the streams, hunting rights on certain hill lands, and rights to stands of preferred acorn oaks and timber. His "treasure" would consist in ownership of old, inherited, and new, much-valued ceremonial regalia such as white deerskins, woodpecker crest headdresses, and huge, carefully worked obsidian blades, too heavy and too precious for any but ceremonial use. He might from his own store outfit a full ten-day dance ceremony.

He would have paid a high price for his wife. The better her family, the higher the price and the greater the honor to him. He would help his sons to pay equally well for their wives, as he would give his daughters in marriage only to families of note and at as high prices as standing and circumstances allowed. At these high prices, the brides *ipso facto* according to Karok ideal would be virgins at the time of marriage, women of rectitude, with beauty and grace as well as wealth and family.

In pointing up these Karok-Yurok customs and traits, it should be said as well that in no instance does their pattern add a contrary configuration to the overall California culture-value design. Like other Californians they did not engage in war as such or have potlatches, nor did they live other than by hunting, fishing, and gathering; and like other Californians they equated the phenomena of the physical world with those of feeling, belief, and mystic consciousness. Rather than moving outside it, the Karok-Yurok culture heightened, exaggerated, sharpened, and defined the familiar pattern, in ways consistent with their fortunate economic and geographic situaton and their temperamental tension of reaction to all aspects of living.

It follows that the Karok-Yurok seasonally repeated ceremonies were specializations on the pan-Californian pattern of seasonal and calendric observances. The Karok word for them has been trans-

lated as "world remaking." The sacred dance rituals of spring
centered around the great spring run of salmon upriver, but in fact
celebrated the reawakening of the world from its winter's sleep
(death); while by contrast the sacred dances of thanksgiving for the
year's abundance were keyed to the fall upriver run of salmon and,
more particularly, to the harvesting of ripe fruits, seeds, and of
course the all-important acorn crop. (See Kroeber and Gifford,
"World Renewal," UC-AR 13:[no. 6]:4–7.) Kroeber and Gifford
list thirteen separate celebrations of world renewal for northwestern
California: four Karok; one Hupa; seven Yurok; one Wiyot. Each
ceremony lasted ten days and was timed to begin with the waning
moon and to conclude with its death and the appearance of the new
moon. The esoteric rites, the dances, the songs, the prayers, and the
recited formulas were directed to the continuing health of the world,
its people and its goods, and to its regular renewal. The word
"renewal" describes more closely than "remaking" the ritual purpose of the dances, which was to give thanksgiving for and to ensure
the continuance of a world unchanged since its creation, whose
people wished beyond other wishing to have it remain unchanged.
Climaxing the Karok and Yurok renewal ceremonies was the ritual
lighting of a New Fire. The fire was made by the Master of Ceremonies; a sacred glowing coal was taken from the fire by the head of
each house for starting the home hearth fire for the New Year.
Nowhere else in California does one find the New Fire rite.

Whether in fact 120 and more days of each year went to these
rites, or whether some of them were biennial or of less significance
and hence less thoroughly observed than the principal ones, is not
known. But they may well have been repeated in full each year:
traffic up and down the river was ubiquitous, life there gave more
leisure than was to be enjoyed in less well endowed worlds, and the
ceremonial dance was the chief social as well as religious outlet for
an otherwise driving, perfectionist, and contentious people.

New archaeological evidence points to occupation of California,
as of the Americas as a whole, over many more years, perhaps
millennia, than we once believed. The Karok and Yurok Indians
have been on their river immemorially long: their most profound
beliefs, embedded in their Creation myths, place them there.
Kroeber notes that the two peoples were become physically totally

alike, and culturally alike in all respects save only that of the language each spoke, which remained distinct and separate and so little changed from its linguistic family beginnings as to be readily placed. This is a phenomenon so rare as to make one pause; it tempts to speculation. How may it have happened that so potent a barrier to the sense and the actuality of cultural identity was in this instance bypassed or overcome?

At the time Kroeber was gathering their myths he may well have asked his Karok or Yurok informants for their answer to the question of the persistence of the two languages. The answer would have been as of something self-evident to the speaker, going more or less to this effect (my source for the extrapolation is a summation of the Creation myths of the two peoples as related to me by Robert Spott, a Yurok Indian, in the 1940s):

> At the Karok center of the world, Katimin, and at Weitspus, the Yurok center, and Creator Gods set about and completed the creation of their respective worlds. When the ground was planted with trees and flowering plants, the air and marshes stocked with birds, the streams with fish, the land with animals, they made the people. Upon the emergence of the people into their world, these same Gods taught them the Way they were to follow, the rules and the customs and beliefs by which the Way should be forever maintained. They taught the people as well the language they were to speak. The Way had proved good, the language intrinsic to it.[3]

To this logical explanation one might add the probability of the Karok and the Yurok having arrived at the river at about the same time, in about the same strength; to have realized more or less simultaneously the advantage of their riverine environment over hill and valley and coast, whose separate and different worlds were "foreign," whose peoples lived and hence thought differently from the river people. The Karok and Yurok may be presumed to have started *unlike but equal* in an equality not to be discovered for any migrant peoples in historic times, and to have grown to look and act alike, as people tend to do when they share equally in the common culture, an alikeness not dependent upon intermarriage, although abetted by it. I suggest that the all-important river, common to both, overcame the barrier to a mutual identity usual between peoples of different tongues, and that the Creator God-givenness of the lan-

3. Here and later in this Foreword I have freely retranslated some of the myths.

guages may well have contributed to the ease of acceptance of a permanent Karok-Yurok bilingualism.

About the Myths

Here, then, are the Karok stories collected by Kroeber as they were told in the 1900s and by Gifford as they were told forty years later, sometimes by the same informant; nearly identical stories as told and retold over no one knows how many hundreds and more than hundreds of years, Karok and Yurok, in the separate languages of the tellers. The possibilities crowd the imagination. Grace Buzaljko (editor of *Yurok Myths* as well as this book) and I were tempted to take the folklore bit between our teeth and run with it, speculating, prognosticating inner literary evidence for economic, social, spiritual change; for alterations in symbolic meaning; for age changes in informants; for signposts of acculturation; for evidence of temperamental and field-technique differences between the two collectors. We have tried to resist the temptation: the field is virgin and open for others.

In English translation, unaided by geographic or other native name cues, the Karok and Yurok oral literary styles are almost indistinguishable. They delineate a like World and Way; take a like moral stance toward persons and events; follow a like pattern of story development; the story recitation is focused, vivid, formal, sure, its character and personality portraits subtle and supple. The possible psychological states are myriad, arising from shame for dishonor brought upon the protagonist by himself or by another. Pride, fallen or risen. Greed. Fear. Blazing anger. Despair. Desire. Nostalgia. In the old world of the Karok, gods, heroes, and living men wept tears, openly, without embarrassment. Mourning tears, tears of shame, tears to bring power and wealth. In Kroeber's myth F1 there is the Creator God, Hakananapmanan, who cries constantly. His tears flow and grow and make Upriver Ocean (Klamath Lake). And in Upriver Ocean appear very tiny dentalia, "things like little fish," which wriggle and grow to become large, even to become the great dentalia. Tears may indeed be *pregnant* tears.

Gifford's collection shows some loss in full expression of these qualities. He was able to elicit fewer of the long, individualized, and exceptional stories than are to be found in the older collection. Some of the later stories suffer from crossings over into another tale of elements and episodes originally belonging elsewhere, and from a blurring or loss of a once clear motivation. The standard tales—of the Creation, of the origin of animal characteristics, natural phenomena, and customs—and the Coyote-trickster cycle stories retain their earlier quality and clarity, these the durable tales remaining in memory from childhood repetition of them and affection for them, the proverbial, the morality tales, the Karok Genesis, Mother Goose, and Struwwelpeter.

Story loss is inevitable with time lapse *cum* nonstop culture erosion such as was suffered by the Karok people. Analysts of these collections should be wary of some temptation to account for the loss as due to the sex and age of Gifford's informants, who were women and in their upper seventies to nineties.

Kroeber's informants were for the most part men, the taboo against any traffic between Indian women and white men being compelling in the first decade of the century. There were of course exceptions, one of them Mary Ike, the wife of Little Ike, a principal Kroeber informant. In the forties Little Ike was dead, but Mary Ike was very much alive and became, in turn, Gifford's principal informant. She was as good a storyteller as her husband, and in old age her sense for myth remained keen and discriminating.

I met Mary Ike in 1939 or '40, the occasion being a canoe trip up the Klamath River with Kroeber, for whom it was a sentimental journey back to once familiar village and ceremonial sites and a renewing of friendships. Among the Old Ones who had known Kroeber earlier were more women survivors than men, Mary Ike one of them—soul-warming and impressive women they were, bright, spontaneous, expressive, humorous. Their outgoingness and naturalness were not the result of changing customs—change brought by the white man was not liberating change—but went back rather to old Karok custom in which many of the restrictions imposed on young women were lifted once a woman was no longer of childbearing capability, the contaminating and potent moon-blood fear no longer attaching to her. I mentioned earlier that high bride price and the institution of the dowry put a young woman in a potentially strong family and community position. Besides which, since beginning Karok time, women were frequently the shamans, serving usually as doctors who "sucked out" pains, while male shamans generally used herbs in their treatments. Shamans held in their hands much power which, as with our doctors, was usually expended for the good of their patients and their own legitimate growing wealth and influence; and with the Karok, as with us, a shaman of experience was more highly regarded—and paid—than a beginner. And, as with us, this great power might sometimes be misused by a spoiled or arrogant shaman, in which event he or she would surely be shunned—and would be murdered if fear and resentment ran high.

That Karok women were responsive to the possibilities inherent in their several areas of family and community and shamanistic power is reflected in Karok literature. Here are two examples of what I mean, one a "recent" tale—at least it is recorded for the first, and so far as we know the only, time by Gifford: "Origin of Men's Use of Sweathouse" (Gifford II.12.). Adumbrated, it tells how in the beginning the sweathouse was the women's house, a place to keep materials for basketry, blankets, robes, and capes; bark for shredding, quills and shells and feathers for elaborate decorating of costume; findings, needles, twine, etc. It was always in a mess, until one day Coyote, tired of its disorder, took the sweathouse away from the women and gave it to the men! So much for the sacrosanct men's sweat lodge.

The other is from Kroeber, "Pleiades and Coyote" (A9). The Pleiades, *atairam tunueich*, "little stars," seven of them, were dancing the Girls' Adolescence Dance across the sky, all the way across to where they set in the west. They were holding hands. Coyote wanted to dance with them. "You cannot dance so far, you will get tired long before." "Oh, I can do it." So they let him, and started on their way. Soon he said, "Stop, I must urinate!" "No, we cannot stop." And they kept holding his hands as they danced. Then he said, "Stop! I want to defecate!" "No, no, we never stop dancing! Defecate as you dance along, if you like." So he began to defecate, but one by one all his parts dropped off until only his anus was left dancing across the sky.

This story and the sweathouse story are among the myths one can all but hear women telling on a long, lazy evening around the fire in the family house with the children, the women weaving their fine baskets or playing a gambling game, or toasting pine nuts in the coals while the men would be in their sweat lodge, excluded from the company of women because of the taboo against female presence or contact for several days before an important undertaking: settlement or embroilment in a feud; hunting, fishing, seeking power.

There is another category of story of particular and serious concern to women, and to children, boys and girls whose sex attitudes were formed by way of such tales: the dire consequences of incest, adultery, any sexual irregularity, any infraction of the female taboo. The Karok, the reader should know, were people who did not permit sexual intercourse within the family house, even between properly married couples—it must be done in private, and out of doors.

Kroeber "Excrement Child" (D7) is one such myth:

> An *ikhareya*[4] girl became pregnant. They thought, "What has happened to her?" Then she had her baby, but no one knew the father; she did not. When the child was old enough to walk about as she sat outdoors, she found out from whom it was. Before, as she was walking, someone had seized her from behind. "You musn't," she cried, and threw him off without looking to see who he was. When she turned back, there was no one there. Then, looking another way, she saw him going across a prairie. It was her own excrement who had done it.

No less a person than a wise Karok shaman, versed as she would be in Karok morality, puritanism, sex beliefs, and fears, could begin to uncover the frightening unconscious depths and meanings within this stark myth.

Buzaljko points out tales in which a woman is the protagonist, monster tales in which the monster is female. Then there are the incest tales; see Gifford I.1, "Yadubi'hi (Widower)," in which the wife commits incest with her father-in-law, glueing shut the eyes of her son and daughter that they should not see and report to their father, her husband, her actions.

Familiar up and down the river are the tales grayed with homesickness. See Kroeber C3 and Gifford I.18: A daughter marries a stranger and goes to live with him far from her childhood

---

4. The Karok predicate a first people, the *ikhareya,* who made ready the world for its people. Upon arrival of the later people from underground, the ikhareya sorrowfully left the world, taking themselves away across Outer Ocean or transforming themselves into a boulder or other natural object. (The *wogé* were the Yurok-equivalent first people.)

home. The husband sees that his wife is homesick for her mother. He loads their boat with gifts for his mother-in-law and, with other members of his family, takes his wife to visit her mother. When the time comes to return home, the man's wife tells her mother she will not be coming again. The mother watches her daughter's departure: she can see only her own child, though she knows there are her son-in-law and the others in the boat. There is a subtlety here the total meaning of which would be apparent, I suspect, only to a Karok. One remembers the reserve observed between mother and son-in-law. It would seem too that for however many days the visit lasted mother and daughter had the time to themselves. A haunting, gentle tale, with a nice feeling toward husband and wife and mother-in-law.

There are the stories in which figure ten brothers and occasionally a sister, the youngest of the family. These are at once intensely Karok in their number symbolism and particular event and feeling, and of a sure progression of plot to a happy ending in accordance with the classic fairytale pattern the world over. In Kroeber's F3 and F5, the ten brothers test the hunters who come to win the hand of the sister, taking them out to hunt in the morning; the hunter who comes in with much game will be the lucky bridegroom. Hunters of great renown come but fail to bring in any game, until, that is, the sister takes a fancy to one of them and confides to him the secret of how to find and recognize the game. In F3 there is an Ariadne and Theseus ending, with the bride abandoned; in F5, a simple, presumably "lived happily ever after" ending.

In Kroeber's F8—modified in Gifford's III.8—the theme is the familiar one of the youngest and weakest brother who, in this story, goes out after the monster who has killed his nine older brothers. A splendid David and Goliath combat ensues between the little brother and the huge monster, ending in the brother whirling the monster by his great toe—the only part of him small enough for the brother to grasp—and throwing him into a lake, where he drowns. Returning home, the brother now sets up the chairs belonging to his nine brothers, laying across each empty chair a hair from the head of the chair's owner. After he recites the proper formula, the brothers are returned to life, to the delight of the nine mourning wives.

In Kroeber F9, the words and word order are as Kroeber translated them; they seem to me to fall into the lines of a prose poem.

Sun was *Imtarashun*—
He said:
"I will be Sun.
When I come up
I shall be fine looking.
All will know me.
All the people born in this world will know me.
I will shine.
I will be handsome
Because I am *Imtarashun!*"

The temptation is to go on—and on. Reluctantly, I turn the book over to you, the reader, with envy of the discoveries lying ahead for you.

It is with gratitude and affection I acknowledge my debt and anthropology's debt to August Frugé, now Director Emeritus of the University of California Press, for his early and faithfully kept interest and his persistence in seeing to it that these folklore materials should at last be in print, and in such good print and binding. Thank you, August.

For the rest I can but repeat here the gratitude I tried to express in the companion volume, *Yurok Myths*, to Grace Buzaljko for her careful and caring editing of these difficult manuscript collections—difficult linguistically, and by way of lacking the crucial finishing work on them which Gifford and Kroeber did not reach. And repeat my thanks to Alan Dundes for his contributions and for the moral as well as practical encouragement needed from him to make the book a reality. And again my thanks to the Bancroft Library and to the University Manuscripts Collections, in the persons most particularly of Marie E. Byrne, James R. K. Kantor, and the Library's committed and helpful Director, James D. Hart.

Theodora Kroeber

Plate 2. Georgia Henry Orcutt, one of Gifford's two major informants, at her home in Orleans (Karok Panamenik). Photograph undated. (Courtesy of Lowie Museum of Anthropology, University of California, Berkeley)

Plate 3. Mamie Offield, a minor informant for Gifford, photographed in 1954. (Photograph courtesy of William Bright)

Plate 4. Left, A. L. Kroeber, 1914. Right, E. W. Gifford, about 1920. (Photographs courtesy of Lowie Museum of Anthropology, University of California, Berkeley)

FOLKLORISTIC COMMENTARY

The publication of two major manuscript collections of Karok folk narratives in a single volume is an important milestone in the study of California Indian cultures. For students of native American folktales, it will prove to be an indispensable source. In 1935, well before Gifford had even made his collection, Anna Gayton, in her remarkably comprehensive overview of the distribution patterns of California Indian folktales, bothered to complain that Kroeber's collection of Karok myths was available only via the footnotes in Du Bois and Demetracopoulou's 1931 monograph on Wintu myths (Gayton 1935:584, n. 7). In effect, it was essentially only graduate students at Berkeley who had access to these valuable primary materials. Permelia Catharine Holt, for example, in her impressive 1942 doctoral dissertation devoted to finding analogues for Shasta folk narratives made extensive use of both the Kroeber and Gifford Karok manuscripts. But aside from these very occasional instances, specialists in American Indian folklore have not been able to take proper advantage of the Karok field data gathered by Kroeber in the first decade and Gifford in the fourth decade of the twentieth century.

Despite the overall title *Karok Myths*, the materials fall mostly under the generic rubric of folktales. In addition, Kroeber's collection ends with some random ethnographic gleanings, not in narrative form at all, while Gifford's collection concludes with a set of formulas or charms intended for medicinal, magical, or ritual purposes. Narratives functioning as charms in native American life have not been collected as often as they might have been (cf. Kilpatrick and Kilpatrick 1965, 1967; Holt 1942:152), and this makes Gifford's

Karok compilation all the more valuable. For example, we can now compare the flood story used as an apotropaic formula when crossing a river in a boat (V.29) with more conventional nonritual narrative versions (F6, I.3).

One indication of the authenticity of the narratives in this combined collection is the absence of European tales. Not that there is anything wrong with reporting native American retellings of European tale types; quite the contrary, inasmuch as such retellings can often provide valuable indices of acculturation. But in this body of narratives there is only one apparent non-native tale (II.52). In this tale, collected in 1940, a turtle stations another turtle at the finish line of a race which enables him to beat a squirrel. This is unquestionably a version of Aarne-Thompson tale type 1074, Race Won by Deception: Relative Helpers. Decades ago, Stith Thompson listed nearly a dozen American Indian retellings of this tale in the published version of his doctoral dissertation (1919:449). He considered the tale to be of European provenience, whereas the thirty-nine versions from Africa listed in the most recent edition of the tale type index make it equally likely that it may be an African tale type. In any case, with the exception of this single tale, the present compilation of Karok tales includes only traditional American Indian tale types. The reader should keep in mind that these narratives are for the most part standard California Indian narratives. Large numbers of cognate tales can easily be found among many California Indian tribal groups, not to mention American Indian groups in the Northwest Coast, Plateau, and Basin culture areas. Thus while readers familiar with classical mythology and Indo-European folklore may be unable to resist seeing what they construe as parallels with "Ariadne and Theseus" or "Hansel and Gretel," they should make a concerted effort to understand Karok narratives in their own terms.

Nearly every single narrative in this book has its own distinct identity and if time and space permitted, one could show the wide geographical range of each tale's distribution in native North America. Editor Grace Buzaljko's valuable index of parallel plot elements in representative Karok and Yurok narrative collections (included as an appendix to this volume) is a step in the right direction, although of course it is no substitute for a full-scale California Indian motif or tale type index. The vast majority of the plot elements are in fact standard motifs, and a researcher familiar with

Thompson's six-volume *Motif-Index of Folk Literature* (1955–58) may wish to consult that source to find additional parallels to a given element.

For example, the story of Coyote and Blowfly (II.21) or Coyote and Fly (II.22) tells how Blowfly obtains meat by entering a deer's rectum and cutting off fat. Coyote, inevitably greedy, tries in his turn to cut off too much and he gets trapped in the deer's anus. This is almost certainly a version of a standard American Indian tale (Motif J2425, The bungling host). Franz Boas discussed this tale type in some detail (1916:694–702), as did Stith Thompson (1929:301, n. 103). Faber's more recent study (1970) was based upon well over two hundred versions of this popular and widespread tale. It turns out that the presence of Fly or Blowfly as host is quite unusual, but the anal source of food is not. Typically, the host cuts fat out of his own anus (or nose, a common anal symbolic substitute), but the dupe fails in his attempt to imitate him (cf. Boas 1916:697–698; Faber 1970:72, 90–93, 105–106). The final riotous scene of Coyote *captivus* being dragged about by Deer while protruding from Deer's anus certainly attests to the importance of this area of the body in Karok thought. This same theme is also evident in the Karok tales (II.15, II.17) in which Coyote plugs up his own rectum with pitch so that he can retain the numerous grasshoppers he eats. Noteworthy is the fact that in both Karok versions of this tale, found also among the Shasta, Hupa, Wintu, and Takelma (Holt 1942:127–129), the narrative begins with Coyote's searching for dentalia or the Karok equivalent of wealth. This strongly suggests the possible symbolic equation of wealth and feces—plugging up the anus to retain or "save" the grasshoppers orally incorporated—an equation which is also common among the Yurok and Northwest Coast peoples (cf. my commentary in Kroeber 1976:xxxv).

Among the more familiar narratives in the collection are versions of the theft of fire (A7, F11; II.7, II.43). The relevant motif is Motif A1415.2, Theft of fire by animals. The theft of fire is a very popular American Indian narrative (cf. Boas 1916:660–663; Thompson 1929:289, n. 63; Gayton and Newman 1940:60–63; Holt 1942: 27–31). Gayton in her 1935 survey essay suggested that the relay-runners form of the narrative constituted a distinct northern California and Basin subtype (1935:590). The consistent occurrence in Karok versions of the frog as final runner in the relay is quite rare elsewhere, although it is also reported in Wintu and Shasta accounts (Holt 1942:30).

Another widespread American Indian tale is the story of the Pleiades (cf. Motif A773, Origin of the Pleiades). The narrative is common enough in California (Gayton and Newman 1940:65–66); the association with dancing is not, although dancing is reported elsewhere. Wycoco in her unpublished tale type index for native North America has isolated one subtype which she described as "A band of dancing children are translated to the sky as the Pleiades as a punishment for disobedience" (Wycoco 1951:43–44), which is found among groups as diverse as the Eskimo, the Paiute, and the Iroquois. In one of the Karok texts (A9, but not II.51) we find once again the already noted preoccupation with the anus.

Other recognizable American Indian tale types in the collection include the Loon Woman (A8, I.9), a classic narrative of sister-brother incest, studied by Dorothy Demetracopoulou (Lee); and Trickster marries his daughter (II.44, II.45), an equally classic tale of father-daughter incest studied by Henrietta Schmerler. For those readers who may not fully appreciate why folklorists are so pleased to have access to additional versions of standard tale types already known to them, let me briefly discuss two separate narratives contained in the present Karok corpus: the stolen brother and the bird-nest seeker.

In the story of Crooked Nose and the Stolen Brother (B3), the protagonist's younger brother violates an interdiction not to cook meat with fat, an act that summons an unidentified mysterious being which proceeds to carry off the younger brother. Crooked Nose forces a bird to reveal the whereabouts of the missing brother. He then organizes a party of animals who ascend to the sky world. Mouse is instructed to make holes in the enemies' boats (to prevent eventual pursuit). Crooked Nose disguises himself as the old woman who fells trees and who ferries people across the river. He passes a test consisting of swallowing hot stones without blinking his eyes. Then he proceeds to where his younger brother is hanging near death and removes him, leaving a mouse in his place. He crosses the river while the pursuers are unable to follow because their boats (with the holes in them) sink. In one of Gifford's formula stories, reportedly used both to encourage rapid tobacco growth and to hasten tree felling by fire (V.33), we find another version of this tale. A younger brother eats the fat meat of a deer. A mysterious "nice little thing" comes and licks up the spit the younger brother put on his hand, a detail also found in the earlier Karok version. The thing begins to eat more and more until finally it devours the entire supply of dried meat. The older brother fails repeatedly to reply to his younger brother's inquiries, and the younger brother disappears. A bird, trapped by the older brother, reveals the younger brother's location. Enroute, the older brother encounters "Day-moon," who advises him to kill the old woman who sits by the fire that is burning down the tree, and don her clothing and cap. (An older Karok version also has the sun-informant motif, according to Holt 1942:80.) He does so, taking moles and mice with him to scuttle the enemy boats. He rescues his brother in the nick of time and the pursuers fail to catch them because of the holes in their boats, which is a standard motif (Motif K636, Holes bored in enemies' boats prevent pursuit) reported in Iceland and Indonesia as well as aboriginal North America.

The narrative of the retrieval of a stolen brother is extremely popular in California (Holt 1942:76–83) as well as in the Northwest Pacific Coast. The reason why it is of particular interest to students of North American Indian folklore stems from a fascinating debate about the possible meanings of the tale. In 1958–1959, Melville Jacobs published tales he had collected in 1929 and 1930 in Oregon from Mrs. Victoria Howard, one of the last speakers of Clackamas Chinook. One of these tales "Seal and her younger brother dwelt there," is a fragment of the stolen brother tale type. Mrs. Howard herself indicated her tale's fragmentary nature by her concluding words "Now I remember only that far" (1959:340–341). In the narrative fragment, Seal's daughter tries to warn her mother that her uncle (Seal's brother) has a peculiar new wife. Specifically, the new wife urinates like a male. Mother Seal ignores her daughter's warnings and is shocked next morning to find that the uncle's head has been cut off by his "wife." Jacobs in his later interpretation of the tale (1960:238–242) suggests that the sexually aberrant "wife" might be a homosexual. However, he can offer no explanation as to why the murderer committed the crime. Dell Hymes, dissatisfied with Jacobs' interpretation, offered an extensive reanalysis of the narrative and suggested that the "wife" was not a murderous transvestite or homosexual but rather a trickster (1968:184). More recently, the tale has been interpreted again by Jarold Ramsey in an article in

PMLA. Ramsey correctly observed that the Clackamas Chinook fragment was in fact part of a longer narrative and cited a 1903 Coos text, "The Revenge Against the Sky People" (Ramsey 1977:12–13). The narrative includes the ferry woman, the boring of holes in the canoes, and other comparable details. In the Coos narrative, it is an older brother who is mysteriously killed by a stranger and who is rescued by a younger brother. It is clear that the killing of the ferry woman and donning of her skin represents a crafty strategem rather than an overt act of homosexuality as Jacobs originally argued. However, even in the Coos text, one finds no real motivation given for the original act of murder by the stranger from the sky world. In this context, it is interesting that in the present Karok versions, we do find motivation, namely the younger brother's violation of an eating interdiction. According to Holt's detailed comparative consideration of the various traits of this tale type, the roast meat or fat taboo is found only among the Wintu, the Hupa, and the Karok (Holt 1942:82). It would be inappropriate to extend the discussion of this tale here. Those readers genuinely interested in the range of interpretations of native American oral literature would do well to read the essays by Jacobs, Hymes, and Ramsey for themselves. The point is simply that the availability of two Karok versions of this fascinating tale type will surely add to our appreciation of the tribal variations and creativity within the framework of a given basic plot.

For similar reasons, we must be grateful for so many Karok versions of the narrative wherein an old man persuades a young man (son, son-in-law) to climb up to a bird's nest to obtain the fledglings, after which the old man removes the poles or ladder, thereby stranding the youth (A10, C2, D3; I.1, III.37, III.38). This narrative is very likely related to either motif K 1616.1, Marooned egg-gatherer, or B31.1, Roc, a giant bird which carries off men in its claws. The old man's motivation is typically that he has amorous designs on the young man's wife. In some versions, while the son is engaged in climbing a tree, the old man magically causes the tree to stretch. Here we certainly have an instance of motif K1113, Abandonment on stretching tree, and motif S11.2, Jealous father sends son to upper world on stretching tree (cf. Thompson 1929:332, n. 199; Gayton 1935:585, n. 15; Holt 1942:45–47, 50). In this battle between old man and young man, or in some cases, father and son, the possible phallic significance of a stretching tree is evident enough. It is the father, not the son, who controls the power of the tree. Ironically, in most versions the son-hero is forced to kill the bird-analogs to himself, namely, the fledglings. Placing the hero in a bird's nest is an attempt, perhaps, to infantilize him, but the hero is finally successful in overcoming his older male adversary.

What makes this narrative of special interest is that the very same tale is found in South America and what is more, Lévi-Strauss has chosen it as the basic or key myth of his elaborate and ambitious four-volume work devoted to mythology. He begins his major mythological opus stating, "I shall take as my starting point *one* myth, originating from one community" and the myth he selects from the Bororo Indians of central Brazil is none other than what he calls "The Bird-Nester's Aria" (1969:35–37). In this narrative, a father discovers that his son has raped his mother. Furious, the father forces the boy to submit to a series of tests, one of which is to capture macaws nesting on top of a cliff. He provides a long pole by means of which the boy ascends. The father then removes the pole thereby stranding his son. At the end of Lévi-Strauss's key myth, the son takes revenge on his father by donning false deer antlers and impaling him on the horns. It is tempting to speculate that the son who originally rose on the erection of his father's pole, that is, served as the victim of phallic aggression (while being punished for his own phallic aggression against his mother) succeeds in turning the tables by penetrating his father in the end! Lévi-Strauss in later volumes discusses additional South American Indian versions (e.g., 1973:334–358), and in the fourth and final volume of his series he considers a number of North American Indian versions of the tale (1971:450–451, 469–478). No doubt he would have appreciated having had access to the Karok versions now being published.

So these two collections of Karok narratives by Kroeber and Gifford will happily be henceforth available to serious students of American Indian folklore. The texts are not only precious native documents in and of themselves, but they will become part of the mainstream of current scholarship dedicated to the exploration of the meaning of Native American oral literature. Future investigations of individual American Indian tale types will be able to draw freely upon the rich store of Karok tradition. For this reason, I am delighted that my initial suggestion that the two manuscripts be combined has, thanks largely to Grace Buzaljko's extraordinary editorial skills, resulted in a single and singular volume truly worthy of standing next to Kroeber's *Yurok Myths* on library shelves. Despite the lack of storytelling performance contexts, the great variety of informants, the different personalities of the two ethnographers, and the forty-year timespan between the two collecting periods, something of the Karok voice survives translation to speak forever not only to Karok and other California Indian descendants but to all of us who take pleasure in the art of traditional narrative.

Alan Dundes

Literature Cited

Aarne, Antti, and Stith Thompson
1961.   The Types of the Folktale. Second Revision. Helsinki: Academia Scientiarum Fennica.
Boas, Franz
1916.   Tsimshian Mythology. Annual Report of the Bureau of American Ethnology, No. 31. Washington, D.C.: Government Printing Office.
Demetracopoulou, Dorothy
1933.   The Loon Woman Myth. Journal of American Folklore 46:101–128.
Du Bois, Cora, and Dorothy Demetracopoulou
1931.   Wintu Myths. UC-PAAE 28:(no.5):279–403.
Faber, Mac Jean
1970.   The Tale of the Bungling Host: A Historic-Geographic Analysis. Unpublished M.A. thesis in anthropology, San Francisco State University.
Gayton, A. H.
1935.   Areal Affiliations of California Folktales. American Anthropologist 37:582–599.
Gayton, A. H., and Stanley S. Newman
1940.   Yokuts and Western Mono Myths. UC-AR 5:(no. 1):1–109.
Holt, Permelia Catharine
1942.   The Relations of Shasta Folk Lore. Unpublished doctoral dissertation in anthropology, University of California, Berkeley.
Hymes, Dell H.
1968.   The "Wife" Who "Goes Out" Like a Man: Reinterpretation of a Clackamas Chinook Myth. Social Science Information 7:173–199. Reprinted in Structural Analysis of Oral Tradition, ed. Pierre Maranda and Elli Köngäs Maranda. University of Pennsylvania Press, Philadelphia, 1971. Pp. 49–80.

Jacobs, Melville
 1959. Clackamas Chinook Texts, Part 2. Indiana University Research Center in Anthropology, Folklore, and Linguistics, Publication 11. Bloomington.
 1960. The People Are Coming Soon: Analyses of Clackamas Chinook Myths and Tales. Seattle: University of Washington Press.
Kilpatrick, Jack F., and Anna G. Kilpatrick
 1965. Walk in Your Soul: Love Incantations of the Oklahoma Cherokees. Dallas: Southern Methodist University Press.
 1967. Run Toward the Nightland: Magic of the Oklahoma Cherokees. Dallas: Southern Methodist University Press.
Kroeber, A. L.
 1976. Yurok Myths. Berkeley and Los Angeles: University of California Press.
Lévi-Strauss, Claude
 1969. The Raw and the Cooked. New York: Harper & Row. Originally published as *Le Cru et le Cuit*, Plon, Paris, 1964.
 1971. *L'Homme Nu*. Paris, Plon.
 1973. From Honey to Ashes. New York: Harper & Row. Originally published as *Du Miel aux Cendres*, Plon, Paris, 1966.
Ramsey, Jarold W.
 1977. The Wife Who Goes Out Like a Man, Comes Back as a Hero: The Art of Two Oregon Indian Narratives. PMLA 92:9–17.
Schmerler, Henrietta
 1931. Trickster Marries His Daughter. Journal of American Folklore 44:196–207.
Thompson, Stith
 1919. European Tales Among the North American Indians: A Study in the Migration of Folk-Tales. Colorado College Publication, Language Series, Vol. II, No. 34, pp. 319–471.
 1929. Tales of the North American Indians. Cambridge: Harvard University Press. Reprinted by Indiana University Press, Bloomington, 1966.
 1955–58. Motif-Index of Folk Literature. 6 vols. Bloomington: Indiana University Press.
Wycoco, Remedios S.
 1951. The Types of North-American Indian Tales. Unpublished doctoral dissertation in English, Indiana University, Bloomington.

EDITOR'S PREFACE

Of the two myth collections that follow, Kroeber's was largely recorded in 1901 and 1902 and Gifford's between 1939 and 1942, roughly forty years later. After Kroeber's death his typescript and his Karok field notebooks were housed in the University Archives in the Bancroft Library of the University of California at Berkeley.[1] His typescript of the myths was obviously a revised version, neatly typed from what must have been one or more earlier drafts, and literate in tone.

Kroeber arranged his collection according to the tales told by his individual informants, as he had for his *Yurok Myths* (published in 1976). Unhappily for us, he did not write personality studies of his Karok informants, of the type which are a rich lode running through the Yurok collection. I have sifted through the tailings of biography given in Kroeber and Gifford's "World Renewal" (1949), and with those we must be content.

Gifford's typescript of Karok myths and formulas was a triple-spaced copy held in the files of the Department of Anthropology in Berkeley.[2] In contrast to Kroeber's, Gifford's typescript appeared to be an exact transcript of the narrators' or interpreters' own Karok English, in which the article "the" was usually omitted, verb tenses

1. Notebooks 8, 10–11, 14, 37–38, and 43 are dated 1901 and 1902; they also contain lesser amounts of Hupa, Yurok, Shasta, Smith River, New River (Shasta), and Wiyot materials. Of three later Karok notebooks, no. 89 appears from internal evidence to be from 1904; no. 90 (undated) ends with 1909 Papago vocabulary material; and no. 207, from 1923, also contains Wiyot data.
2. The University Archives has Gifford's 398-page longhand version of what he then called "Karok Narratives," from which his typescript in the Department of

were nonstandard, and colloquial expressions like "got her in the family way" were used instead of the more elegant "impregnated her." Gifford had written character studies of his two major informants and had made some penciled changes aimed toward a more standardized English in the myths themselves. My own first impulse, as editor of a co-authored work, was to carry Gifford's changes further in order to blend the styles of the two ethnographers. I also felt that it would be fairer to the Karok informants and interpreters, who were recounting the lore of centuries in what was to them a second (or third) language, picked up from one or two generations of contact with American miners and storekeepers and possibly supplemented by some minimal formal education in a one-room country school or at the Hoopa reservation school up on the Trinity.

Alan Dundes, however, argued for the historical approach. He wished to give readers, and especially folklorists, the opportunity to read an unvarnished text just as it was taken down by an anthropologist. Specifically, he wanted readers to be able to identify Gifford's later emendations, as well as my own. After considerable debate, I acceded. The texts, therefore, are as Kroeber and Gifford left them, with the following provisos:

Key to Punctuation

Words in *parentheses* are the authors'. Parentheses in the texts indicate either a brief translation or explanation shown actually typed in parentheses in their typescripts *or* a handwritten change they had made in the typescript. Nearly all of Kroeber's parenthetical words and phrases are of the former type; Gifford had many of both types. In rare instances where one of the authors later revised his own parenthetical wording, I used a slant bar to show the earlier form separated from the latter. For example, in Kroeber's myth Fll*f*, the sentence, "He called, 'Ishawash (sister's/brother's child)!' " indicates that Kroeber first had "sister's" as his typed parenthetical explanation but later changed it in handwriting to "brother's."

Anthropology was made. A note with the longhand version indicates that the typescript was checked against the manuscript.

University Archives are now the depository for unpublished manuscripts and typescripts formerly housed in the Department of Anthropology and the Lowie Museum.

In order not to interrupt the narrative flow, longer parenthetical asides by Gifford—or his informants—which were originally part of his text, have been moved into the footnotes and the parentheses omitted. Unenclosed footnotes are thus Gifford's (or Kroeber's) own material, which I have taken the liberty of editing silently.

Words in *square brackets* in the text are mine, enclosing words added for greater reading ease. Bracketed headnotes at the start of a myth, and bracketed footnotes, both ending with the abbreviation "Ed.," are also mine.

In the authors' texts and footnotes I have silently modernized the punctuation and spelling of English words. I have not attempted to regularize the spellings of Karok words and names except for the names of the half-dozen largest towns, on which the two authors were usually in agreement in any case. Kroeber spells the name of the Karok immortals as ikhareya, Gifford as ixkareya. Where the two ethnographers heard and recorded words differently at different times or from different informants, I have left the spellings as recorded, though I have frequently supplied cross-references to variant spellings elsewhere in the volume.

After the manuscript was edited, William Bright of the Department of Linguistics at the University of California in Los Angeles reviewed it and generously offered to prepare a linguistic index of the Karok words in the texts, giving a brief definition, text references, and a more exact transcription of each word. Scholars will be greatly indebted to William Bright for his contribution to this volume.

Gifford grouped the myths in his collection by subject matter rather than by informants. I left his arrangement, but I gave each of his myths a roman-and-arabic number designation (I.1, I.2, etc.), so that each could be briefly referred to in footnotes and index and would at the same time be readily distinguishable from Kroeber's sequence by informants: A1, A2, etc. For the Gifford texts I adopted Kroeber's system of supplying small italic letters at the start of each new development in a plot, at the beginnings of most paragraphs. Again, the device was useful in index and cross-references.

Karok and Yurok: A Commentary on Style

Alan Dundes observed in his "Folkloristic Commentary" on Kroeber's *Yurok Myths* (pp. xxxiii-xxxiv) that we lack a motif index for aboriginal California myths. As a step in that direction, I have compiled an index of comparative plot elements from Kroeber and Gifford's present collections of *Karok Myths* as well as those from Kroeber's *Yurok Myths* (published in 1976),[3] John P. Harrington's *Karuk Texts* (1930) and *Karuk Indian Myths* (1932a), and William Bright's myth texts in his *Karok Language* (1957), earlier collections not reprinted here. The comparative index is found at the end of the present work.

I have organized the index with emphasis on the action rather than the actor. It is the action which is echoed from one myth to another and from one literature to another. The Karok had no monster-ridder comparable to the noble Pulekukwerek of the Yurok, and thus many of his achievements are ascribed to others, usually to Widower or to Coyote. The philandering Widower appears in the literature of both groups. The Yurok myths have him bestirring himself to undertake such feats as securing salmon and acorns for mankind from the two sisters who guard the sources of these chief foods (Yurok A15x *r-v*); the Karok often assign this honor to the otherwise self-serving Coyote (Karok II.10, II.11).

That stock Californian character, Coyote, has a larger role in Karok than in Yurok literature. In both, he has one episode in which he rises above cowardice and avarice: he slays a monster the second time it appears, having the first time hidden in fear of it (Yurok Q1g-*j*, there with a large assist from the modest Screech Owl; Karok A4c-*d*, II.33a-*f*, and II.47). The Karok collection has one unique and startling story (II.25) in which Coyote, instructed by Wolf, undergoes long privation and learns the incantations necessary to create five sons from arrow-wood sticks, only to lose them by sending them into battle against overwhelming forces.

The Karok, with their love for the animal tale, were decidedly more didactic than the Yurok. Bluejay, like Coyote, is a Karok personification of greed, against which the Karok constantly preached. The Yurok, by contrast, were more interested in the convolutions of plot and subtleties of character. The drama itself absorbed them; the ethical implications of that drama they left to their hearers, who had, after all, been reared in the all-pervading puritanism of northwestern California.

3. Kroeber compiled nearly two hundred pages of detailed summaries of the Yurok myths, which have not been published because of the costs involved. These typescript summaries are in the files of the Bancroft Library and are accessible to scholars.

Most striking of all the differences in persona between Yurok and Karok is the difference in the sex of the leading protagonist in a number of the myths. In two Karok tales (C3, I.18) a girl visits the house of the ten frightening Thunders, a visit strongly reminiscent of one paid them by the Yurok hero Kewetspekw (Yurok A13*d-e*). A long-absent child returns on a brief visit to grieving parents; in Yurok the child is a son (B6*g*, G6*f*, T3*h*), in Karok usually a daughter (C3*g-h*, I.18*j-n*, with C1*g-h* the exception). The evil ones who wear huge, death-dealing ear pendants are male according to the Yurok (A15x *i-j*) but are female in the Karok tellings (A10*f*, III.38*f-j*) — and in one Karok account (D3*c*) the murderess is accused of wearing ear ornaments made of human testicles!

In the Yurok myths the monster-destroyer Pulekukwerek burns down a house containing two blind cannibal sisters (C1*r*). In the Karok tales (I.14) a small girl who has been kidnapped by a cannibal giant burns down his house while he is in it, sleeping off a feast on one of her brothers. Not only does Gretel act without Hansel, but the villain is transformed from a wicked (female) witch into a giant male, who meets his end at the hands of a courageous and indignant girl-child.

In the only Karok account (V.47) of a giant snake or water monster raised as a pet by a human, it is a young woman who raises it. Harboring a serpent was dangerous, and in the numerous Yurok tellings of the myth (A11, B2, U3, and CC1) only men dared to such hubris, in the face of strenuous objections from their wives, mothers, or brothers.

Both the Yurok and Karok have Orpheus themes. In the two Yurok accounts (S3 and X2) a young man goes to the underworld to bring back his dead sweetheart. In all the Karok accounts (Kroeber's two 1946 tellings, extracted from the present collection; Gifford's I.15 and I.16; and one recording by Harrington), a young woman (or two young women) makes the journey in search of her lost lover. Though permitted to see him, she is forced to return without him, being given in compensation a wondrous bit of salmon which, rubbed on the lips of the newly dead, restores them to life. And so, until the salmon is used up, there is no death on the earth.

In two Karok tales women rather than men pray for and secure wealth (V.25 and V.26); in fact, both narratives are wealth formulas specifically to be used by women, which the informant learned from her female relatives. In contrast to the Yurok Widower's finding of salmon and acorns hidden in the house of the two women possessors (see above), two young Karok women (III.3) find water hidden in the house of a handsome young man, for whom they are competing. Californian folklore generally, and Yurok folklore particularly, does not give so active and decisive a role to women. Was this feminine bias a characteristic of traditional Karok mythology or did it come about because most of the later recordings of myths were from women, who might have consciously altered them to conform to their own sexual biases?

I think the reason women played a more active role in Karok literature than in Yurok may be embedded in one facet of the culture which was different in the two groups. The Karok and the neighboring Hupa, but not the Yurok, held a public adolescence dance for their girls at the time of their first menses (Kroeber, Handbook, p. 106).

Kroeber (ibid.; see also this volume, p. 98) describes the Karok girl's adolescence dance as "performed chiefly by men — a distinctly northwestern attitude. . . . The girl herself had on a little visor of jay feathers, and carried a rattle of deer hoofs. . . ." He goes on to say:

> The dance was made at night to keep the girl awake. . . . For 10 days she ate no flesh and drank no water, might not look at the sun or sky, could not touch water to her face. Each morning she carried to the house 10 loads of wood cut by a female relative. On the last day she emerged early and ran back and forth 10 times, motioning at the morning star as if to catch it, and asking it to give her long life and many dentalia. The entire observance was repeated twice subsequently.

The ceremony had a strong element of propitiation in it, for "the potential influence for evil of a girl at the acme of her adolescence is very great. Even her sight blasts, and she is therefore covered or concealed as much as possible" (Kroeber, Elements of Culture in Native California, UC-PAAE 13:[no. 8]:311). But she herself must have had a triumphal feeling of incipient power, and if she acquitted herself well in her long ordeal she must have gained a sure sense of her own self-worth. Yurok girls underwent a period of concealment but were not publicly celebrated at the start of adolescence (ibid.: 311–312). And no similar formal initiation ceremony was held for young boys by either group (ibid.:314).

Theodora Kroeber points out to me that other Californian groups besides the Karok and Hupa who held adolescence dances for their daughters did not engender a correspondingly decisive role for women in their literature. We may never know whether the feminism evidenced in this body of Karok literature is a relatively modern development or an ancient mind-set of the culture. The time may be too late to discover the answer.

In concluding this Preface, I wish to thank several people who gave essential help in the publication of the volume. Mrs. Delila Gifford of Chico, California, generously gave the Department of Anthropology and the University of California Press permission to publish her husband's collection of Karok myths and formulas. Mrs. Theodora Kroeber gave never-failing encouragement and cheer. Jane Taylorson exercised great care in retyping the Gifford typescript for the printer. With the interested help of Eugene R. Prince, senior photographer of the Lowie Museum, University of California, Berkeley, and of Eleanor Brown of the Siskiyou County Historical Society, Yreka, California, I was able to locate photographs of two of the Karok informants. Kim Yerton of the Indian Action Library in Eureka, California, put me in contact with Mrs. Violet Tripp of Eureka, daughter of Jasper and Emily (Ike) Donahue and granddaughter of Little Ike and Mary Ike. Mrs. Tripp provided needed information on her family's genealogy, which in turn led me to Mrs. Lucinda (Ike) Miller of San Francisco, the last survivor of the ten children of Mary Ike and Little Ike. Mrs. Miller kindly provided the photograph of her mother which is reproduced here. For the help of all, I am extremely grateful.

Grace Buzaljko
Editor, Department of Anthropology
University of California, Berkeley

PART I

KAROK
MYTHS

A. L. KROEBER

(1901–1902)

Plate 5. Little Ike, Kroeber's Informant A, wielding a plunge net from a fishing platform at Amaikiaram. Photographed about 1900. (Courtesy of Siskiyou County Museum, Yreka, Calif., Daggett Collection, and Lowie Museum of Anthropology)

LITTLE IKE

[In Kroeber and Gifford's "World Renewal" monograph, Kroeber says that Little Ike was so called because of his stature. "He lived at the great falls of the Klamath, which has gone onto our maps as Ike's Fall. He was about fifty in 1902. He was lively, engaging, amiably adroit, and intelligent" (World Renewal, UC-AR 13:[no. 1]:134). Compared to Informants D and E, Kroeber says, Little Ike "was somewhat older, a person of established status, and was more definite in his personal reactions" (ibid.). It was his father who signed the peace treaty with the whites in 1851 (Siskiyou County Museum, 1971:31). Little Ike was the source of many of Kroeber's Ethnographic Notes, below.–Ed.]

A1. COYOTE AND THE YELLOW JACKETS

a. It was summer. Coyote[1] went to hunt. He shot a large buck. He began to skin it and had partly taken off the hide when he saw something near him. It was pretty and he looked at it a long time. It seemed as if it were painted with black. It was Yellow Jacket (pishpish). Coyote said, "My father's brother (ishawish, also man's brother's son),[2] help me skin it. We will eat when we get on the

---

1. [Gifford, in his Introduction and later, gives the usual Karok name for Coyote as Pinefish (pronounced in three syllables). See also Gifford, II.35, n. 2, for Coyote's descriptive name.—Ed.]

2. [Gifford, Californian Kinship Terminologies, UC-PAAE 18:(no.):31, gives ishavishi as designating the child of a man's brother or of a woman's sister after the death of the sibling.—Ed.]

ridge." Then they skinned it and started. The deer was very fat. Coyote carried it some distance; then he rested. He carried it farther and rested. He carried it again and got halfway up the ridge. Then he said to Yellow Jacket, "Help me now." He thought, "He will not be able to carry it; he is too small; it is too heavy for him." Yellow Jacket said, "Perhaps I shall be unable, but I will try: it is very heavy." He took hold of the deer. Almost he did not get up with it. Coyote laughed; he thought it was too heavy for him.

Yellow Jacket went a little distance with the load. Then he went far. Now he went very fast. He went far ahead. Sometimes Coyote did not see him. He called, "Wait for me on the ridge!" Yellow Jacket flew faster. Coyote gave out and became angry: "Wait for me!" He took his bow and arrow; he wanted to shoot. He reached the top of the ridge, but could not see Yellow Jacket. He shouted. Still he could not see where he had gone. A long time he looked; then he saw him across the creek halfway up the next ridge. Coyote shouted but could not overtake him. Then he followed; he could not see but tracked him.

He found Yellow Jacket's house. He saw many Yellow Jackets. They saw him coming and said, "He has come to get his deer." When he came near, a swarm of them were about to sting him. He said, "Hu hu," and ran off, he did not know where to. He only thought, "I can do nothing, I must run." So he reached his house, very angry. He said, "We will go against those who took away my deer."

b. He asked Bear (wirushur) to help him. Bear said, "I will kill them; I can do it. I like what they have and will eat it." Coyote got many to help him. They all started together. Coyote said, "They are bad, very bad. I am afraid of them." Bear said, "It is best to arrive there in the morning. They are always indoors then. I will go first." Coyote said, "I will go behind." Then they entered, Bear ahead. Coyote stayed in the wood room (just inside the door). Squirrel sat outside. Bear started to kill and eat them. A Yellow Jacket came out as far as where Coyote was. He was buzzing, quivering, and nearly dead. Bear called, "Kill him!" but Coyote jumped out of the wood room, afraid. He said to Bear, "You had better leave one." Then Coyote said to that one, "You will be Yellow Jacket. You will not kill men. You will be only Yellow Jacket."

A2. KINGFISHER SNITCHES FOOD

a. Kingfisher (shahkunishamman) grew across-river from Ti'i, 15 miles above mouth of the Salmon. He thought, "I will marry." So he married. Soon he had plenty of children, two little girls and two little boys. He said, "I am going to fish downstream across the river." He went into his boat, crossed, and went downstream. There he started to fish with his dip net, after dancing a little. He caught a large salmon. He thought, "I will cut off its tail." He threw the tail away. Then he thought of the salmon, "I will eat it by myself." He cooked it, ate, and was satisfied. Then he went upriver again in his boat. When he came near his house, he shouted from the river, "Children, a tail! (ahichip ipumnish)." The children cried, "Goody, goody, goody! (yūtwi)." He came and said, "Too many persons came to where I was fishing. I gave them all some. So I have only the tail left." Soon they ate their supper. "Here, take a piece of the salmon," said his wife. "No, the children will get hungry. I will eat acorns. That will be enough," he said.

b. Not long after, he went fishing again. (The incident repeats verbatim.)

c. Next morning he said, "I will go fish." He went downriver, sang, "tanimuuh," and danced. Then he caught a salmon, and, throwing the tail away, cooked and ate the fish. But his wife had said to the children, "Go and see. Perhaps he eats it alone. Go down and watch from this side of the river what he does." The children went and saw him catch the fish, cook it, and eat it. Then they ran to the house. The woman said, "Let us leave him. We will go somewhere. Make a fire there upriver and make another here up the hill." So the children made a fire by the river and one on the hill. Then they all went off.

d. When Kingfisher called "Ahichip ipumnish," no one answered. He went to the house; he saw nobody. Soon he noticed smoke upriver. He went up, far, but saw no one: there was only a fire. Looking uphill, he saw smoke there. He thought, "Maybe they went uphill," and went, but he did not see them, even though he shouted. He was still carrying the salmon tail. He went back to his house and shouted again. A mouse tittered. When it laughed again, he caught it and said, "I will kill you unless you tell me where they went." The mouse said, "Do not kill me. I know; I will tell you. They took up this acorn-pounding slab and went in underneath." Kingfisher took it up. He saw tracks going into the ground. They led uphill and came out again somewhere. There he shouted again. The woman said to the children, "Do not look back. Leave him." He was still carrying the salmon tail, shouting "Ahichip ipumnish!"

e. Then he overtook them. He wanted to throw the tail into her pack basket. She threw it out again. Picking it up, he tried to throw it back in. Then, becoming angry, he said "Well, then, I let you go." He threw her up and she turned into a yellow pine, and he threw away the children. The woman said to him, "You will eat no more salmon. You will fly up and downriver and eat anything you can. As long as people live they will use me. I will be for their good, and so will my children be. They will be hazel (sharip) and Xerophyllum (panyurar) and five-finger fern (kiritapkir) and Woodwardia fern (tiptip). As long as people live, they will use us (for baskets)." She herself was the yellow pine (whose roots make wefts).[1]

A3. Sieruk-pihiriv Marries at Weitspus

a. Sieruk-pihiriv (Across-Ocean Widower)[1] was at Weitspus (Ansafriki) fishing. Two women, sisters, lived there whom no one ever saw. He watched for them all the time that he fished. He caught no salmon, but kept looking for them. At last he became tired of it. He said, "I cannot see them. I want to bring it about somehow. I think I will make an elk." He went uphill, far up on Trinity Summit. There he said, "What shall I do to make an elk? How shall I make it? I will make it of my semen." Then he made an elk of that. He put on a head and legs, but at first he put no horns on [it]. Then he drove it down to the Trinity River. There, among the logs, he thought a long time. "I think I will put horns on it. Of what shall I make them?" He said to the elk, "Come here, I will put horns on you." Then he made horns for it of crooked sarvis-berry [serviceberry]. He put them on and looked at it to see if they were good. Then he said to it, "I will go

1. [For details on the structure and weaves in basketry, see Lila M. O'Neale, Yurok-Karok Basket Weavers, UC-PAAE 32:(no.1):1–184.]

---

1. [Comparable to the Yurok culture hero Wohpekumeu, whose name means the same as the Karok name.—Ed.]

far behind. You go ahead. Stand just where the rivers flow together. When any one shoots you, do not fall down. When I come I will shoot once at you; then fall right away. After that, no matter how many tug at you, do not let them lift you. Soon I will pull at you with one hand: then you must make yourself be lifted.''

b. Soon all the people at Weitspus shouted, ''An elk comes swimming downriver!'' All went to shoot at it. They shot, but it did not fall: the arrows did not enter it. Then Sieruk-pihiriv came downriver. All said, ''Look at him coming down!'' All looked as he came running with his quiver. When he arrived he shot once: the elk fell over. Everyone there tried to lift it; they could not. Sieruk-pihiriv had sat down and was looking on, smoking. And the two women had come outdoors to see. When he finished smoking, he went to the elk and picked it up with one hand. So all the people had good meat. Then the two women, thinking him a good hunter,[2] married him.

A4. Screech Owl, Coyote, and Giant

a. Screech Owl (or Cat Owl, ipashnavan)[1] constantly snared deer. Every morning he went hunting. He whistled for his two dogs and they came and ran uphill, while he went down to the river to watch for the deer. Then he saw one come swimming downriver. It was a large buck with big horns. Screech Owl watched closely. He jumped on the horns and sat there while the deer swam on down. When they came abreast his house, he caught up the deer and killed him. He found the buck fat. ''Now I will have a good time,'' he said. Then he was skinning his deer. Someone came there. He looked bad. He had a large knife stuck in his belt. He said, ''Let me carry it.'' Then he carried it away. He gave Screech Owl a little piece and carried the deer off. Screech Owl thought, ''That is too bad.'' He went to his house and ate the little he had.

b. In the morning he tried again. He called his dogs and they drove a deer. As it swam, Screech Owl lit on its horns, and then,

2. Rationalized Bowdlerization? [See C2*a*, below, a more typical version in which he impregnates a woman merely by looking at her.—Ed.]

1. [K.'s typescript showed the spelling ipashnawan, but he queried it. I have adopted the spelling given in F5 and H5.—Ed.]

pulling it out of the river, he killed it as before, and skinned it. When he was ready to carry it, the same person came. He was tall, and Screech Owl was afraid. That one gave him a little piece but carried the deer away.

c. Coyote came. He said, "I hear someone always takes away your deer." "Yes, always." "I will kill him," said Coyote. Screech Owl said, "Well, I wish you would." "Where do you kill your deer?" asked Coyote. "Down there. You had better wait for me there." So Coyote waited, and a deer came swimming downriver, with Screech Owl sitting on its antlers. Screech Owl pulled it up on the bank and killed it. Coyote, hiding near by, was waiting for the stranger. Then he said, "Throw me some soft belly meat: I am hungry." Screech Owl gave him all he wanted. He had skinned the deer and was ready to carry it when that one came. Coyote looked at him and was afraid. He had said to Screech Owl, "When you help him get his load on his back, hold him back a little." So now Screech Owl pulled back. The large man said, "Why do you hold me back? Let go!" But Coyote was afraid to come out, and the man carried the deer off. Then Coyote came up to the house and said, "That one is very evil (kemish). Well, I will kill him tomorrow."

d. In the morning Screech Owl killed another deer. Coyote again asked him for meat, and told him to pull back on the man as he was rising with the load. Then the large stranger came, and as he was about to get up, Coyote this time really jumped out, drew his knife, and killed him. He said, "You will not be an evil danger (kemish) at all. You will be Water Dog (or mud puppy, salamander larva, suf-sam). You will live in the water." He threw him in. The stranger's large knife was only a piece of alder bark.

e. Then Coyote said, "Carry your deer up to the house; I will go to see where he came from." He went up the creek, following Water Dog's tracks. Then he saw smoke. He came to a large house. Children were laughing inside. He looked in and saw the children and much meat. He wanted to kill the children. He threw them into the fire, but they did not die. They only laughed. "I will not die in the fire while my heart is hanging up there," they said. Coyote thought, "That is so." So he threw the hearts into the fire, and all the children died at once.

f. Coyote ate, and then carried off the meat from the house. Then he rested, for his load got heavy. He made for himself ear-pendants of meat. "I will go to sleep. When I wake up I will turn my head and snap up the meat," he said. Looking across the river, he saw Bald Eagle (chuufshi) sitting on a dead tree. Coyote, sitting there, said to him, "Eat this, Deep-Eye (yupichnu)," and he held up a piece of meat. Bald Eagle became angry. He thought, "Go to sleep! Go to sleep!" Coyote became sleepy; he slept. Bald Eagle flew down, carried away all his load of meat, took off his ear pendants, and went back across river on [to] the tree again. There he ate. When Coyote awoke, he turned his head, snapped, but got nothing. He snapped toward the other side and again got nothing. Then he saw Bald Eagle, and thought, "Look at him eating! He is the one who took it away from me." He crossed the river, went to Bald Eagle, and said, "Throw me down a piece of meat!" Bald Eagle had eaten everything up, but he threw down the empty pack basket.

g. Coyote thought, "I will go to see Screech Owl." He could not find him in his house. "Where did he go?" he thought. He looked up and saw Screech Owl sitting on a high stump, eating. He shouted to him, "Throw me some meat. I am hungry." Screech Owl continued to eat; he did not look down. Then Coyote said, "It is well. You will not kill deer any more. You can kill lizards."

A5. Dog and Bow

a. At Amaikiaram, in the sweathouse Kiririp, lived an ikhareya[1], Kiririp-a va-ikhareya. He made all kinds of animals in the world. It was just as if he made them. Now he had lived there a long time and knew that human people had nearly grown. His sweathouse, where now there is a large pit, was below the (sacred) sweathouse of these present human beings; there he lived. He thought, "How shall I do, now that people have nearly grown? I will make bows for them." Then he made bows, many of them. "Let us go into the old house,[2] all of us together." There were Dog, Wolf, Mountain Lion, Wildcat, Eagle, Hawk (apuvichiyunu), Chicken Hawk (ikchahwan), Falcon (aikneich), Great [Horned?] Owl (sufkirik), and Coyote. Now the

1. [One of the "supernatural beings who created the world, established its institutions, and then took up their abode" at the Upriver End of the World 'when the people came' " (Drucker, A Karuk World Renewal Ceremony at Panaminik, UC-PAAE 35:[no. 3]:26).—Ed.]

2. Possibly a name for the sacred house, wenaram, as among the Yurok.

ikhareya set bows up all around the house. He said, "Go to sleep. Whoever wakes up first can have the bow he wants to hunt with." Coyote thought, "I will sit here by the door: I will wake up first." He took small sticks to prop up his eyelids. The ikhareya did not sleep at all; he watched, thinking, "Who will wake up first?"

b. Dog was the first one to get up. He took the best bow and went away with it. Mountain Lion woke, took another, and went off. Wolf, Wildcat, Eagle, Falcon, Chicken Hawk, Apuvichiyunu hawk, Great Owl—all woke up and went out with bows. The[n] Coyote awoke: all were already gone. He got the poor bow that was left. So he went to a flat and killed gophers. He sat and watched for them constantly.

c. Now Dog would pursue all the others. He wanted to take away their bows. He went here and there and everywhere, running after them, trying to overtake them. Then he came back to Amaikiaram. Human beings were living there now: they saw him come. Then Dog said to the person, "Be my companion. Take this bow. We will go together. We will hunt together."

d. Wolf came. He said to Dog, "I am no longer your friend. I will eat you when I see you about in the mountains."

e. Dog said to the human beings, "This bow I have given you is not (altogether) good. Sometimes I will die by it. This man to whom I gave it sometimes will also die on account of it: He will be shot at. This bow is not good. As long as people live (on earth) they will die on account of bow, and also will kill food with it."

A6. Screech Owls Marry

a. At Ahoeptini[1] lived ten brothers and their two sisters, ikhareya. They hunted and saw elk, but could never kill them. Then their father told them, "Sing deer songs." They sang all night in the sweathouse, then went up in the hills. Still they had no luck. They saw elk, pursued them, could not kill them. Then their father said, "Whoever kills the elk will marry my two daughters."

b. Coyote came there. The two Screech Owl brothers (ipashnavan),[2] also came to try. There were patches on their quivers and they

1. "Twelve miles above mouth of Salmon." I cannot identify it with any recorded Karok town. The distance mentioned, if in river miles, would put it in the vicinity of Aftaram, Ayiis, or Sufkaro'om. There was a settlement called Atsiptsinik a few miles upriver from Sufkaro'om. Possibly Ahoeptini is a mountain.
2. [See A4, n. 1.—Ed.]

looked poor. All night Coyote danced and sang: "Faugh, I smell your stench. You came in to flatulate. You can't kill anything. You won't marry." In the morning, when all went out to hunt, the two brothers were not asked to come. So they went out by themselves. The older said, "You shoot first, then I'll take on the rest." Now they heard the crowd of hunters driving the elk. "Watch," he said. Then the elk came in a line. The younger brother stepped out, kneeled, shot, and killed the first elk. Then the older shot and killed all the rest with one shot. The ten ikhareya brothers arrived one by one, looked at the elk, and went off home, saying, "My brothers-in-law!"

c. Then Coyote cut himself, and rubbed his bow with the blood to make it appear that he had killed the elk. But when the Screech Owls returned to the house, they had beautiful quivers and were finely dressed. So they married the two girls and took them home with them.

A7. THEFT OF FIRE

a. Coyote grew at Panamenik (Orleans): that was his place; he lived there long. Now others grew elsewhere. Then Coyote said, "Let us get fire." There was no fire here then, only far upriver at Isivsanen ip, world's end. Coyote said, "Those who have the fire are bad: they can run faster than we. Nevertheless, let us try to get it." First he asked Bear to help him, then others. After a while there were many who were going. They asked each other who could run fast. Coyote said, "Let us gather all who can run fast." Eagle said, "I will go." Falcon said, "I will go." Chicken Hawk (ikchahwan) said, "I will go." Hummingbird (hanpuchinishwe) also said he would go. Grouse (timkuru) said, "I am good to run downhill." Measuring Worm (chavanich) said he would go. Bear[1] said, "And I will run downhill." Tortoise (ashahwu) said, "I do not run fast, but I will roll down like a log, having pulled in my head and legs." Frog (hanchifichi) said, "I cannot run fast but I will make one jump into the river, then they will not see me any longer." Buzzard (atipimamuvan) also said he would go. These were the ones that started out.

b. Coyote said, "I will go ahead. I will see their house where

1. [The Karok name is given as wirushur in A1*b*.—Ed.]

they keep fire. I want to be first." It was Yellow Jackets (pishpish) who kept the fire. Coyote came to their house. As they sat around in the house, he marked all their faces with black stripes, with oak bark which he held between his toes, having let it char in the fire. Then he said, "I must go out to relieve myself; when I come back I will paint you up even better." Then he took the glowing oak bark from out between his toes and put it under his arm and he ran. He ran hard.

c. After a long way, when he became tired, he met Eagle. He had left him where he knew he would become tired. He said, "Here it is; I am exhausted." Eagle took it and fled and gave it to Falcon, who gave it to Chicken Hawk when he tired. He gave it to Hummingbird. Now they had gone far, and the pursuing Yellow Jackets were tiring also. They had nearly caught up with each one as he gave the fire to the next. Hummingbird gave it to Grouse. He went uphill very slowly, and the pursuers nearly caught him: then he went down very fast on the other side. When he tired he gave the fire to Bear. Bear also ran down fast, but was nearly caught as he climbed up the next ridge. Then Measuring Worm took it and went over three ridges. He wriggled along slowly; when they nearly caught up with him, he humped himself and stretched over three ridges. Then Tortoise took the fire and, fearing to be hurt, drew in his legs and head and rolled downhill.

d. Now the Yellow Jackets had nearly caught up, when Frog was there with his mouth open. He took the fire in his mouth, made one jump, and was in the river. The Yellow Jackets could not see him. So they went home. Frog emerged and saw alders and willows growing there above him. He spat the fire out into the willow roots: then there was just a little smoke.

e. There are only two trees that make fire well, willow at the river and cedar on the mountains. Cedar grew at the same time: it was Buzzard who made fire on the hill. So there was a little smoke rising up at the river and on the hill. Buzzard had made that on the hill; he had made it with cedar bark rubbed fine. He blew hard on the tinder, it blazed up, and he burned his face (neck) and head and looked as he does now.

A8. Loon Woman[1]

a. At Akhapini, two miles below Cecilville on South Fork of

1. [K. numbered this myth as A9, but his final page numbering contained no

Salmon River, there grew ten brothers, the old man their father, their mother, and a sister called Ishanhihura. The brothers hunted together and killed many deer. Ishanhihura kept falling in love with men, and did not stay at home. She would go somewhere, live with a man, leave him, take up with another. That is how she did. Sometimes she came home, but then she went off somewhere again.

b. Now she found a pakor stick for whipping and drying hair. It had one long hair on it. She stretched the hair: it was long, a fathom long. She thought whose it might be. She thought, "Where is my younger brother that I used to have? I have never seen him since he was a little boy. Perhaps he is somewhere around." When all the brothers were together, she said to one, "Let me louse you." In her hand she held the long hair she had found. As she loused him, she measured the hair against his head, but hers was the longer. Soon she said to another brother, "Let me louse you." She measured again, but his hair too was shorter. Ten times she did this. "It is not that one," she said, as she measured the last one.

c. She thought, "I will not sleep but watch. Perhaps it is his hair, my younger brother's." When it was nearly morning she saw him come in, like a fire. He ran around on the upper ledge inside the house. Then she knew that was the one.

d. In the morning she said to her father, "I want to get a husband. I want to go off." She told her mother, she told her brothers. Then she pounded acorns, to carry the meal (with her). When she had enough, "I want someone to go with me," she said to her father. The old man said, "Go with your oldest brother." Ishanhihura said, "He can do nothing. He cannot talk." "Well, take another, the next one." "He does not know how to talk." Thus she refused all ten. Her mother said, "Well, I will go with you." Ishanhihura said, "You can do nothing: you do not know how to talk." Then the old man said, "I think I will go with you." But she would not have him. He was thinking, "Perhaps she herself will find her youngest brother." He had not let her see him since he was a little boy. She said, "What did you do with the youngest brother I have?" Her father said, "I think he cannot go. He is sick all the time." Then she

gap. Thus I have renumbered this and the succeeding A myths. In A Karok Orpheus Myth, Journal of American Folklore 59:13–19, K. included Karok versions of the Orpheus theme by Little Ike and Informant F. Kroeber and Gifford, World Renewal, AR 13:(1):113–117, contains accounts of the world renewal ceremonies by informants A, B, D, and F.–Ed.]

told her mother, "I am going with him." Her mother said, "He is always sick. He does not go away." Next she told her oldest brother, "I am going with your youngest brother," but none of them consented. Then she said, "Well, I will get him myself." So she went and pulled him out. "I am going with that one," she said. They all sat together by the fireplace to watch them go.

e. Then the two of them went, went far, to find a husband. Her youngest brother's name was Makikiren. Soon she said, "Let us kill a rat." When a rat came out, she said, "My husband, it jumped out!" Then she thought, "Let it rain. Let it begin to be dark." He said, "Let us make camp: I think it will rain." Then it did rain. He made a bark camp. There they made a fire, cooked the rat, and ate it. She almost said again, "My husband." Makikiren had made a tiny hut on one side, a very small shed. When it became dark they went to sleep, one in each hut; his was small, hers was good. Now she tried to push down Makikiren's shed with a stick. "Your hut is leaking; come and sleep with me," she said. But Makikiren said, "No, I will sleep here." Then she went in to him: "Let us sleep in there; you do not want to get wet." Now he was afraid of his sister.

f. After intercourse, she held him fast. When he heard her snore, he spread her legs, crawled out, laid a log on her, and ran away. When he reached home he said to his father, "She wanted me. I left her. Let us all run away. We will go up together, for we shall soon be killed if she comes. But do not look back." They were all afraid and went up a pole. Makikiren went first, the oldest brother after him. Near the last was the old man, and the old woman was behind.

g. Now they heard Ishanhihura shouting: "I have come back." The old woman was sorry and thought, "Let me look back." Makikiren called, "Do not look back; not one of you! She has made a large fire; if you look down, we shall all fall in." She was burning up their house, calling: "Do not leave me! Come back for me!" Then the old woman looked back, and they all fell into the fire. Ishanhihura sang and danced about it. She held a large tray basket (muruk) over the fire: she did not want the ashes to fly up. As she danced, she sang: "Ishanhihura, Ishanhihura!" When the fire burned down, she knew their bones. "This is my father's bone. This is my mother's bone. This is my eldest brother's bone," she said of each one. But she did not see Makikiren's bones. She looked for them long; she did not find them. Makikiren had flown up as a spark, as a flake of ash. He had gone up where his sweethearts lived in the sky, far upriver. That is where he had always been when he came home at night.

h. Now the two girls had heard that he had been burned up. There was a little lake where the grass grew: there they sat making baskets. They were sorry for him. Then they heard singing somewhere in the grass. "Listen, it is like Makikiren's singing. I hear it somewhere." Then they heard the song again, but could not see anything. "It seems that he is singing near us." They looked but could not find him. "It must be he. We heard he was burned, but perhaps he flew up here." Then they saw something very little on the grass. "Perhaps that is he. Let us keep it. Let us carry it into the house." They carried him into the house. Flesh began to grow on him. Then they rubbed deer marrow all over him. After a long time Makikiren was alive again.

i. Then he had two children, a little boy and a little girl. They became large enough to shoot. Makikiren made a bow and arrow for his boy and for the girl too. They had ten quivers each, filled with arrows. Then Makikiren said to them, "Go and see your aunt (miskya)". They went to her house. They had taken their hearts out, holding them between the bow and the hand. Inside the house they heard pounding. It was Ishanhihura: she was pounding her brothers', father's, and mother's bones. The boy and his sister went on top of the house and looked down in. Ishanhihura thought she saw something. She went out, ran around the house twice, but did not see them. She went in and pounded; then she saw their shadows again. She came out, did not see them, went inside again. Then she saw them on top of the house at the smoke hole. "Eh, my brother's children, come in!" she said.

j. She took ten quivers, went out, shot at them. And the boy shot at her. They fought till nearly all their arrows were gone. She shot the boy and his sister all over, but they did not die. She also was shot everywhere, but she did not die. "I fight because you pound those bones," he said. Then they heard someone say, "In the foot, in the foot, shoot her there!" Then they shot her in the heel and she dropped. Her heart was there. Then they threw her in the lake there. Then they went home, having killed their aunt. "We have killed her," they said to their father.

A9. Pleiades and Coyote[1]

The Pleiades (atairam tunueich), "little stars," seven of them, were dancing the girls' Adolescence Dance across the sky, all the way across to where they set in the west, holding hands. Coyote wanted to dance with them. "You cannot dance so far, you will get tired long before." "Oh, I can do it." So they let him, and started on their way. Soon he said, "Stop, I must micturate!" "No, we cannot stop," and they kept holding his hands as they danced. Then, "I want to defecate!" "No, no, we never stop dancing! Defecate as you dance along, if you like." So he began; but one by one every part dropped off until only his anus was left dancing up above.

A10. Anhush[1]

[This is essentially the same myth as the Pulekukwerek monster-ridding cycle given in Kroeber's *Yurok Myths*, A15x, A16x, C1, F1, and J3.—Ed.]

•

a. Anhush[2] lived downriver at Shwufum (Kenek) with his grandmother. He lived there a long time. Then he heard that there were many evil ones (kemish) upriver. He said to his grandmother, "I will go up and see what kind of bad ones there are. I will kill all that I see." He stood up some of his feathers in the house and said, "You can always look at these. Any time that they droop, and then fall, you will know that somewhere upriver, I do not know where, I have died." Then he started upriver.

b. He saw a house. He looked long, but no one seemed to be there. So he went on top of it and looked in and saw two young women sitting there. He thought, "They are good-looking." They had no fire in the fireplace, but sat on opposite sides of it. He looked at them a long time. They could not see: they had eyes, but they were small, and blind. Now they were going to eat: Anhush continued to

---

1. [There is another gap here in K.'s numbering of the myths (see preceding note). K. numbered this as A11.—Ed.]

---

1. [The present myth was numbered A12 by K.: see notes for A8 and A9, above.—Ed.]

2. Weasel, probably. On account of some uncertainty, Anhush has been retained. [Bright confirms this identification; see Linguistic Index, below.—Ed.]

look at them. Each put something in her armpit. He thought, "What do they put in there?" Then one of them took it out and said, "It is beginning to be cooked." The other also took hers out from under her arm and said, "It is nearly done." Then they ate what they had held in their armpits. After a time they cooked some more. When it was done, they said, "Here, it is cooked," and held it out to each other to eat. Then they put in still more, but when one held it out to give to the other, Anhush reached down and took it away from her. He ate it and thought it tasted good. The one who had held it out asked, "Have you got it?" The other one said, "No." "I gave it to you." "No, you did not." Then she in turn held out what she had cooked and again Anhush took it and thought, "It tastes good. I will stay here and marry them both." "Have you got it?" she asked. "No." "But I gave it to you." Then they cried. "Perhaps someone took it from us," they said. "Who can it be? Perhaps it is a man. Perhaps he has run off." Then they went to opposite sides of the house.

c. Then Anhush entered and caught them; they were both crying. With an arrowpoint flaker he opened their eyes. When they looked about, they thought that it was pretty. What they had been cooking under their arms was [were] brodiaea bulbs (tayiis, "Indian potatoes"). Anhush liked the bulbs and wanted to live with them a while so that he could eat that. Now he made fire for them. Then he lived there and they cooked tayiis and other pleasant food for him. They were Moles (ahpuum).

d. Anhush thought, "I will start." He went upriver. He saw a house. Many Yellow Jacket wasps (pishpish) came out. He retreated and they all went back into their house. Then he killed them with a stick, all of them together. "You will be nothing. You will not kill people: you will be only Yellow Jackets," he thought.

e. Then he came to where Spiders (ha) lived. When he went into their house, they tied him with ropes, but he broke them all. He killed all the spiders with a stick.

f. He went on upriver and saw a house: he heard the sound of pounding as of acorns. Then he looked in from above: an old woman was pounding. Seeing his shadow, she came outside, but did not see him. She was wearing large earrings of stone mauls (taknuris). Then she said, "Perhaps I shook my head and saw my ear pendants. Yes, that is what I must have done." So she went inside and began to pound again. Anhush looked in and again she saw his shadow. She came out and saw him under (among) the boards of the roof. "Let us go into the house," she said. Then she said, "Let us gamble." They sat down opposite each other. As they played, she sang "Anhush itura tura, Anhush itura tura." Then he in turn sang, "Keish hach mutiptip aarhishu." Thus as they played, each ridiculed the other. "Why do you say that to me?" she said, and took off one of her ear pendants. "Let us fight with these." She tried to hit him with it; he dodged it. She took the other maul and threw it at him, but again missed him. He picked up the maul and threw it at her. He threw only once, struck her, knocked her over, and killed her. Then he said to her, "You will not be a danger (kemish). Where there is an old house, or a deserted sweathouse, you will live there when no one else lives there. You will be called Yaunakayeishch. And you will be called Taknuris-tenvara, Mauls-for-earrings. Children will we frighten (be frightened) with you. When they are left in the house and told not to eat, they will be told, 'She will throw her maul pendants at you.' "

   g. He started upriver again and came to a sweathouse and house. He looked in and saw an old woman and two young women with long hair and handsome. He thought, "Perhaps they will be my wives." When he went to the sweathouse, an old man was lying there who said, "My son-in-law! I have watched long to see you. I have wanted you to come. Bring me sweathouse wood; I have none left." Then Anhush went uphill and carried down wood. The old man, leaving the sweathouse, said, "Make the fire large for me; make it hot; I am always cold." So Anhush made a fire; but when it began to get hot, pitch dripped down like rain; the whole roof was pitched. So he crawled under the floor planks until the fire was over.

   h. Then he said to the old man, "It is hot enough now; you can go in." But the old man said, "Here, the house, go in there!" Anhush entered; soon he heard something drop. All over in the house things were falling and beginning to rattle: they were rattlesnakes coming to bite him. "You will not be able to kill people: you will only be snakes. From now on you will be flat-headed," he said as he hit them on their heads with the palm of his hand. Some he killed, some he threw outside, and they crawled into a rocky place. Then he took some to the old man in the sweathouse and said, "Here, eat them!" The old man said, "Yes. I will eat them outdoors." But he went out and buried them: they were his children.

i. Now he said to Anhush, "My house is always leaking. I saw a good large log lying up the hill. Let us go there." They took along two wedges and mauls. When they came to the log, the old man said, "Split it in the middle." "Yes, I will do that," said Anhush, and drove in the two wedges. Then the old man said, "Split it so that a man can crawl in. I used to enter the cleft and then pry it apart with my elbows." Now Anhush had large white wood-maggots hidden under his belt. He entered the crack, laid the worms in it, and himself went out through the bottom. Suddenly the old man knocked out the wedges and the log closed. From under the log Anhush made a faint sound as of crying. The old man said, "I am glad he will die," and going off a bit began to dance. Then Anhush was standing there and saying to him, "Why do you say that?" The old man said, "Oh, I was so sorry that you were dead." Then they went back down to the house.

j. Soon the old man said to him, "There is a salmon that I always see in a certain place. I wish you would spear it. I want to eat it. Let us go!" So they went down. "Right there it is," said the old man. Then Anhush saw a very large salmon, and right away he knew that it was a monster (kemish). It looked like a salmon but wasn't. He saw it moving slowly and speared it. The salmon dashed off, and Anhush went with it, his hands sticking to the pole of his harpoon. That was the time the old woman downriver, his grandmother, who was always looking at the feathers he had left, saw them swaying. She said, "He has nearly died now. Some kemish has him." Now Anhush nearly pulled the salmon up on shore, then it nearly dragged him underwater. Sometimes his head was almost submerged, then he succeeded in pulling it back once more. The salmon ran upriver, dragging him along through ten pools where the water flowed still (shiv'ak). Far downriver, the feathers nearly fell over; sometimes they hung far down: that was when Anhush had his head submerged. In the last smooth pool he remained a long time; because of the pitch on the handle he could not let go. Then someone came who cried ä, ä, ä! When he was near he said, "What is the matter with you? I always pull them out with one hand." Anhush said, "Help me and I will give you this dentalium necklace. I am worn out; it has nearly killed me." Then that one lifted the salmon out of the water with one hand. He was Kingfisher (ashkupamuvan). He has a white collar:

that is the dentalium-bead necklace that Anhush gave him. When he took hold of the harpoon and pulled up the kemish it was a "long-snake" (apshunhara, Yurok knewollek). Anhush carried it back downriver to the house and said, "I nearly died from it. You called it salmon, but it was a kemish. Now eat it!" "Yes, I am glad you killed it. I will eat of it outdoors," said the old man. The long-snake was his son. The old woman and two girls had had long hair, but each time Anhush returned they cut some of it. He had thought, "Why do they always do that?" The girls were cutting their hair on account of their brothers' deaths. Now he knew why.

k. Then the old man said, "Let us go uphill. I saw a nest there with fledglings in it. You might bring them for the women; they would like to keep them as pets." So they carried long poles uphill with which to climb the yellow pine the birds were on. Anhush thought, "I know what is in this nest: they are kemish again." He climbed up (by the long poles) and saw the old birds flying about. They were large and fierce "bad eagles" (itinivikya wakar). As he climbed and came to the nest, the two old ones flew past him swiftly to knock him down. Anhush, looking down, saw his father-in-law going away, carrying off the ladder poles and rejoicing. Then the feathers downriver leaned far over, and the old woman thought again, "A kemish has him!" Now before he started, Anhush always thought, "How will I do to escape?" So he had put sinews under his belt. With the sinew he now struck the two eagles and they fell to the ground dead.[3] Then he threw down the young birds.

But the old man said, "Let the tree grow up!" Then it stretched up. He said, "Let the wind begin to blow." Then the wind blew: the yellow pine was bent far over. It leaned this way and that way, and its limbs had broken off, and Anhush thought, "I shall die." Then again the feathers far downriver sank. Soon all the bark had been blown off the tree: only one short broken limb still held, on which Anhush sat, singing medicine. (Song, without words, to abate hard wind.) Then the wind went down. Now he wanted to descend. He climbed to the very tip of the tree, put his hand over the point and pressed down, gently, saying, "Go down, go down!" Then the tree contracted back to its former height. Then Anhush took pitch off the tree, chewed it, stretched it into a string, fastened it to the limb on which he had clung, and made it reach to the ground. So he came

3. As a person emerged from the grave can be disposed of only by stroke of a sinew bowstring, the Yurok say.

down. He took along the young birds that he had killed, came to the house, and said, "I nearly died. You said there were little birds on the tree, but they were dangerous eagles." The old man said, "I am glad you killed them. I want to eat them." "Well, eat them!" said Anhush. "I will eat them outdoors," said the old man. He took the birds out and buried them. The women did not speak. Their hair was cut short to the shoulders now.

l. Then the old man said, "Let us go to where I have a spring-pole (gunashgunash, "seesaw"). When I was young I used to play with it." When they arrived the old man said, "You hold to it there; I will go right here." On the way Anhush had caught a rat (chinaat) and had hidden it in his armpit. When the old man swung, he bore down hard, and when he let go, the end on which Anhush was flew up violently. But he had slid off, leaving the rat in his place, and dropped under the gunashgunash. The rat flew up, and the old man heard "chi!" as it struck the sky. Downriver, the old woman's feathers had sagged far over, then stood up again. "He nearly died then," she thought. Now the old man was dancing, singing, "I am glad you are dead: you killed many of my children." But then Anhush was saying to him, "Now you go on the gunashgunash!" The old man said, "No, I am too old. I only used to go on it when I was young." "Go on it!" Anhush ordered. "No, I cannot do it," the old man continued to protest. He went out on it only a little way. "Further!" said Anhush. "No, I am nearly dead. I cannot go further, I am too old," said the old man. But Anhush only said, "Hurry!" The old man was halfway. "I will stay right here," he said. "No, you will go where I was. If you do not go to the far end, I will kill you." At last the old man went to the end. Anhush asked him, "Are you ready?" and he said, "Yes." Anhush began to teeter him softly. The old man said, "Move it slowly! I am old, I cannot hold fast." Soon Anhush swung him hard, until he flew up through the air. After a long time Anhush heard a noise above. The old man was laughing: "Ehehehehe! You did well to me. I like it here. As long as people live I shall go across here every day, and they will see me," said the old man. He was the moon (kushura).

m. Anhush went down to the house. The women did not speak. In the evening, when it began to be dark, he threw one of the girls in this direction (west). She is the evening star, the large one. In the morning he threw the other one to the east, and she became the morning star.

Informant B

MRS. MARY IKE

[*Mrs. Ike was the wife of Little Ike of Ashanamkarak. Both she and her husband were Kroeber's informants in 1902, and Kroeber said of her, "I consider her, like her husband, superior in general scope of personality" (Kroeber and Gifford, World Renewal, UC-AR 13:[no. 1]:134). In 1939, near the end of her long life, she served as one of two major informants for Sara M. Schenck and E. W. Gifford's study of the Karok uses of plants (Karok Ethnobotany, UC-AR 13: 377–392). In that same year and in 1940 and 1942, Mrs. Ike was a major informant for Gifford in his collecting of Karok myths and formulas; he has provided an affectionate description of her in his Introduction, below. She died in January, 1946, at the age of ninety-three or ninety-four (UC-AR 13:132).—Ed.*]

B1. Bat Smokes

a. Bat (timshukuri) lived where there were many [people]. He thought, "I will marry." There were good girls who were always working: the people said to him, "You cannot marry them; you smoke all the time." "I like to have a good wife," he said. The father of those girls was constantly up in the woods, growing tobacco. That is why Bat wanted to marry them: he thought he would get tobacco from the old man. Then he married one of them and took her with him.

b. After a time the old man came to see his daughter. Back up the hill from where she lived grew sugar pines. The old man liked sugar pine nuts. He told his son-in-law, "I like to eat that kind." Bat said, "Very well, let's go up on the hill." Then the old man and the

22

woman and Bat went up, and Bat climbed a sugar pine. Just under the tree they made a large fire to roast the nuts. Bat went up partway, then said, "I am giving out." The old man said, "Come down if you are exhausted." But Bat said, "I think I can go on." He climbed higher and had nearly reached where the needles began when he fell. He fell into the fire; they could hardly pull him out. They carried him down to the house. His buttocks were burned.

c. Some people said of Bat's wife, "She is no good: she is always sick." The woman had sore eyes and cried constantly. But when it was dark she got up, went out into the woods, gathered acorns, and before daylight came in again. She slept all day: she worked at night; her house was full of food. She was Woodrat (chinati, "long tail").

d. Then the old man her father, who had gone back home, became hungry: he had nothing at all to eat. He heard that his son-in-law killed deer, and thought, "I will go to see him." He went there. He sat down outside the sweathouse. When he had sat there some time, he saw his son-in-law come carrying a deer and bring [take] it into the house. The old man continued to sit outside the sweathouse. Soon the woman came and told him to go into the house. She was cooking acorns. Bat was at the fireplace, cooking a very fat deer. Soon he put some on a platter and gave it to his wife. She thought, "I will eat of it, unless he gives my father nothing." Bat continued to cook but gave the old man nothing. After a time the old man fell over. The woman poured water over her father and he revived. Bat continued to eat. Then the woman gave her father acorn soup and she herself also ate no deer meat.

e. When the old man finished eating his acorns, he reached into his quiver. He had ten baskets of tobacco. He took out his pipe and smoked. Bat looked at him smoking, stopped eating, and shifted. He continued to change his place. The old man continued to smoke. Soon Bat went outside the house and looked down inside so that he might catch the old man's smoke as it floated up. After a while there was a noise on the roof. Bat had fallen over: he desired extremely to smoke; he was crazy for it.

f. Then he came back into the house. "I want someone to give the old man what I have been eating," he said to his wife. She said, "Why do you not give it to him yourself? Just now you would give him nothing. Why do you want me to give it to him now?" Then Bat gave the old man deer meat, and he ate. Then he said to his wife, "That which I smelled a little while ago, do you think it is all gone?'' No one answered him. Then he asked his wife again, "That which I smelled a little while ago, do you think it is all gone?'' No one answered him. Then he asked his wife again, "That which I smelled a little while ago, do you think it is all gone?'' She said to him, "I don't know.'' Then the old man reached into his quiver and took out five baskets of tobacco and handed them to his son-in-law. Then he smoked. He smoked as if he were crazy; he smoked all night. The five baskets were nearly gone when it began to be day. Then he took in his hand what little there was left and threw it into his mouth. It was too slow for him to smoke it up.

B2. GRASS SNAKE SMOKES[1]

a. Grass Snake[2] (apshun-munakich) thought, "I will go up-river.'' He came to a house and heard pounding of acorns. He went in and said, "You are pounding acorns?'' "Yes, I am pounding acorns.'' He looked on. Then he said, "I am going upriver, far up.'' So he went. After a time he thought, "Where shall I go? I have much property. I will go back to it.'' He sat down, rested, took his stone pipe, and smoked. He put it back into its sack and started to return. He went a little distance. He had smoked too much: his foot slipped and he fell downhill. He said, "Oh, I broke my stone pipe. Well, I will not lie here too long. I will get up.'' He went a few steps farther, slipped, and fell downstream. He got up, went, and slipped upriver; got up, went, and slipped uphill; got up, went, and slipped downhill. This time he slid far. There was a big rock and he slid under it. He said, "How will I go about?'' He had no arms and no legs (left). He said, "What will I eat? How shall I live without arms and legs?''

b. He saw a flat rock. "What shall I do with this rock? It is a nice rock. I think I will do something with it.'' He defecated on it. Then he said, "It looks very nice. I think I will taste it. Perhaps I will eat

1. [K. numbered this myth as B3, but his typescript page numbering showed no gap. In Kroeber and Gifford, World Renewal, AR 13:(1):116–117, K. gave Mary Ike's myth of the origin of salmon and of the Amaikiaram New Year.—Ed.]

2. J. P. Harrington, Karuk Indian Myths, Bureau of American Ethnology, Bulletin 107:27, gives the same Karok name and identifies it as the western yellow-bellied racer. [The myth recorded by Harrington from Mrs. Phoebe Maddux is the same as the present one by Kroeber.—Ed.]

it, for I have no arms." Then he tasted it. "It is exceedingly sweet. It tastes just like marrow. I will eat lots. I will live well." There was large flat rock there. He put much on that. He said, "Let me eat some more. I will try it again." He tasted, ate, thought it good. Then he vomited. It did not taste good to him any longer. "Why, it is feces! Well, I will try to go." He slipped and slid around. Then he began to travel all right.

B3. CROOKED NOSE AND THE STOLEN BROTHER[1]

a. Crooked Nose (yufivihasip) lived together with his younger brother. He always went hunting. He would drive five large bucks down near the house and then shoot all five with one arrow. "Watch well, Crooked Nose, my older brother (ichitkin yufivihasip aan)," his younger brother told him. The younger took off their horns and carried the deer into the house. Indoors he would skin them. Next day the older would go hunting again and kill five more. He would shoot once and the five would drop. Then his younger brother skinned them. Thus they did. They had two good houses without a hole (gap), one each, full of meat. Crooked Nose always told his younger brother, "Do not cook meat with fat." Again he told him, "Eat your meat raw; do not cook it. If you do cook, cook only meat. Do not cook the fat."

b. Once the younger brother thought, "I will cook the fat. Why does he tell me not to cook it?" He roasted it. Then he heard someone shout: he did not know where it came from. From inside his own house he said to his brother, "Someone shouted." The older did not answer. The shouting came near. It said, "I smell fat." Then it was very close. "I smell fat," it said. Then it was on top of the house. Crooked Nose was not answering his younger brother. He thought, "My younger brother will die." Then where the younger was, something dropped into the house. He picked up what had fallen and held it in his hand. It was small and hairless. "Where is my older brother?" he called.

c. He spat into his hand and that which had fallen ate the spit. "I will give him a piece of fat. It is exceedingly pretty." He thought, "I will make my older brother talk." But his elder brother did not

1. [K. numbered this myth as B4.—Ed.]

answer: he thought that the younger would die. Then the younger said, "It is a little larger now. I will feed it some more fat. It is eating. Where is my brother?" There was no answer. He said, "It is beginning to be large now. It is eating more fat." Again there was no answer. He said again, "It has nearly eaten up everything. It is very large." Still there was no answer. Then at last the older brother said, "I have long told you not to cook fat." Soon the younger said, "The house is full. It is large!" Soon there was shouting from on top of the house: "Help me!" The shouting went off, the older brother did not know where to. Then there was no shouting any more.

d. Crooked Nose looked for his brother long. He searched everywhere. He cried constantly. As he searched for him he cried. Uhuriv, a small blackish bird,[2] kept flying about him crying, "Yufivihasip lost his younger brother, Yufivihasip lost his younger brother!" Crooked Nose did not like that. He put pitch on his cane, then rested and left the stick standing in the ground. The bird flew about; it lit on the stick. Then it cried: it wanted to fly off but couldn't. Crooked Nose said, "I think I will kill you; you are always saying, 'He lost his brother.'" Uhuriv said, "Do not kill me: I will tell you where your brother is. Tomorrow will be the last day. He is nearly killed. Tomorrow they will make fire again. He is far downriver, across the ocean. He is wrapped up in deerskins over the fire with his head down. At night they cook him. One of them paddles across every night to get fuel and then goes back and makes a fire under your brother to cook him."

e. Crooked Nose got many to come together, Mountain Lion, Coyote, and the rest. They said, "Let us all make string." So they all made it. Coyote made two baskets full. He thought he had enough to reach the sky. He laughed about Ha-wishwantini,[3] the small, flat Spider, that was picking up bits of fiber that were not long enough for the others and was rolling string from them. Coyote said, "You can't make enough. I have two baskets full." Then they agreed that they would shoot the string up with their bows and arrows. Mountain Lion wanted to shoot first. His arrow did not reach the sky. Then Eagle tried. His arrow also did not reach. Coyote thought, "I will shoot last": he had the most string. His arrow flew

2. [K. has a marginal note that this word is defined as a net sack in G*lb.*—Ed.]
3. [K.'s typescript has a marginal query, perhaps questioning whether the name should be written Hāwishwantini.—Ed.]

up a little distance and fell. At last little Spider shot. Then they heard a crack. The rope was hanging straight down as if held fast above.

f. Coyote said, "I will be the first to climb up." He could not do it: he had gone only a little way when he fell and lay there. Then Mountain Lion wanted to try. He went a little farther. Eagle climbed and went farther but could not reach the sky. Coyote said to Spider, "You cannot climb it: I tried but couldn't." Spider started to climb. They could not see him any longer. Then he reached the sky. Then all of them went up, Coyote last.

g. Then Crooked Nose said to Mouse, "Go and see what they do. Make a hole in all their boats; in all ten of their boats. Only in the one at the end, don't make any." Mouse crossed the river. He came back and said, "I have done it: there are holes in all the boats. There is one of them there that has a long nose. With that she strikes and cuts down a tree, puts it in the boat, and carries it across the river. She brings it for the fire; she comes here for it every evening."

h. Then they watched for her to come across. They saw her come. She made a fire against the bottom of the tree (in order to burn it down). Crooked Nose turned himself into an old woman with cropped hair, carrying an old basket. The kemish (evil one) had nearly made the tree fall. Mouse said, "Tonight is the last time they will make a fire. They have nearly killed your younger brother." Crooked Nose wore an old apron, and had made himself female parts, which he let her glimpse under the apron, so that she was sure he was an old woman. Then he came up to the kemish and threw her into the fire.

i. Then he made himself look like her, and crossed the river, and entered the house. When he came in, "Perhaps you are Yufivihasip," they said. He denied it. Now that kemish (had) used to swallow hot stones without blinking her eyes. So they gave him hot stones, thinking that if he were Yufivihasip he could not swallow them without winking. Then he swallowed them without closing an eye.

j. He went to where his younger brother was hanging, wrapped in deerskin, shriveled up and shrunk small. "Perhaps you are my brother Yufivihasip," he said. "Be quiet," his older brother said. He had a mouse hidden under his clothes. He took his brother, put him under his apron, and put the mouse in his place. After a time one of the kemish went there to feel. Touching the mouse he thought

Crooked Nose's younger brother was still there.

k. Then Crooked Nose went out. He had crossed the river when they again felt and touched the mouse. Some of them cried, "Yufivi-hasip has taken his little brother!" They jumped in their boats, but the water ran in through the holes Mouse had made. They took dippers and baskets to bale, but everything they had was full of holes. They could not overtake them. Crooked Nose and all his [group] went down the rope.

l. They thought all had descended and took off the rope. But Coyote was left: he had stayed behind looking about him and had lost his way; when he came to the rope it was gone. He was in the sky a year. He wandered about. He looked down and thought, "It is not far. I can nearly reach it with my hand. I will jump." They were clouds that he saw. When he jumped, he fell a long time. He broke all to pieces. His bones, his hair, his flesh fell scattering everywhere. That is why there are so many coyotes.

Informant C

LITTLE IKE'S MOTHER

[I have no data on this informant, except that she was living in or near Katimin in 1902 (Kroeber and Gifford, World Renewal, UC-AR 13:[no. 1]: 134). If her son was about fifty at that time, as Kroeber says, then she herself must have been seventy or more. Thus she would have spent her girlhood in the years before white contact.–Ed.]

C1. Across-Ocean Dance

a. Patapirihak (Flat-Rocks-on-the-Ground) grew at the mouth of the Klamath.[1] There he constantly carried sweathouse wood and when he had finished making his fire in the sweathouse, he played his flute (kuremia kuvarar). He had grown up, and his hair was very long but he never cared for ("knew") girls. Now there were two girls living on the other side of the river among the people there. He thought, "Let me go over and see them." So he crossed and sat down with them. Looking uphill, to the house there, he saw an old woman on top, drying seaweed (ashahem)[2] on the roof. He said to her, "Cook for me: I should like to eat what you are drying." When he entered, he saw a little girl lying alongside the fire. She was sick:

1. So I understood; but the meaning given fits a place better than a person, and the narrator may have said: "At Patapirihak he grew." My notebook reads: "Raised at mouth of Klamath, Patapirĩhak." I assume the hero grew up at Wełkwäu on the south side of the Klamath, opposite Rekwoi, which I take to be called Yufip, "mouth," in Karok.
2. [Bright says that the identification here as seaweed is incorrect and that it should be moss; the Karok words for the two are related (letter, September 26, 1978).—Ed.]

she had sores all over her, and looked very bad. Then the old woman
cooked for him. He got through eating, went out, and came down to
the two girls. They said, "Where have you been?" He said, "I have
been eating in the house above." Then he crossed to the side of the
river where he lived, carried sweathouse wood again and made his
sweathouse fire, and played on his flute.

b. Then he crossed again to see the two girls. He said to them, "I
want to sleep with you tonight." They said (mockingly), "You don't
want us. You have come on account of that sick girl in the house
above." But after a time they said, "Yes. Come tonight when it is
just dark." So he went back, and when it began to be dark he crossed
again. He was starting to look in the house, when at the door he
heard one of the girls say, "What sort of dress will you wear? What
front apron will you wear?" "I will wear the same, the same as last
night," said the other. Then they both ran outdoors. The young man
tried to catch them but could not. They were carrying paddles and
ran down to the river. He followed them down and saw many men
there: there were ten boats of them. There was also one small boat,
with two young men sitting in it. They told him, "Come with us.
Let's go and see where they dance." He said, "Yes," and hid in the
boat, covered with blankets. Then he saw the two girls jump into one
of the other boats: they had two baskets.

c. Then they all started to paddle out on the ocean. At Shitūm, a
large rock,[3] they stopped and filled them (the baskets) with seaweed.
Then they started again. All of them had smoked and from that the
plants on the rock had been set afire and it was burned all over.

d. They came to the other side of the ocean, to Yurashisiak.
There they danced the Deerskin Dance: Patapirihak saw them
dancing. One man sang wonderfully: all liked his singing. He was
Beaver (shahpīni): he leaped as he danced. Crane (ahwa)[4] jumped in
the middle. He had put a whole basketful of dentalia about his neck;
at that his neck was so long that it looked as if he had not put anything
on it.

Then they began another dance; those who had come in the ten
boats danced now. One girl walked about where they danced, carrying wood and tending fire, in the middle of the dance place. She wore

3. A sea stack, not a shore crag, but the informant did not know how far out.
4. [Bright in the Linguistic Index, below, identifies the bird as Great Blue
Heron.—Ed.]

a blanket all of woodpecker scalp. For a dress she wore dentalia, and at the ends of the dentalium fringes she had woodpecker scalps. Patapirihak said, "Let us go farther down to see that dance better." His two companions said, "That is the sick girl. She came here. That is she." "When I return I will go to see her," he thought.

e. Now they started to go home again, and came to where he lived. When he got out of the boat he ran uphill and got sweathouse wood. Then he made fire in the sweathouse all day; when the sun went down he finished. Then he thought, "I will go to the other side and see that girl." Then he crossed again. He saw the two girls who had deceived him the night before: they were laughing. They said, "Do you think you came to see us? I think you came to see the sick girl up there." He said, "Yes, that is why I came."

He looked up to where her house was. The old woman was still working on the roof, drying seaweed. He said to her, "I wish you would cook for me. I like that food." Then she went indoors to cook. He too went into the house and saw the sick girl lying there. He sat down close to her. She looked very sick. Then he prodded her. The old woman said, "Do not touch her! She is very sick. She is always ill." When he started to pick her up, the old woman said, "You must not!" Then he told the old woman, "You are lying to me. I saw her last night." The old woman said, "Go outdoors and come back." He went out, then came back in, looked at the girl, and saw that now she wore the same clothes that she had had the night before. When he started to go back, the old woman said to him, "You must marry her because you made her get up; because you did that you will surely marry her. She made herself appear very sick, but she was not. It was she that gave herself that appearance." So he returned and married her.

f. Now they were about to start again to see the (across-ocean) dance. Then a man came down from far upriver where he lived alone there. His name was Karuk-pasikiri,[5] and he was the father of the girl that had been sick. Then she said to him, "I am married now." The man said, "To whom are you married? I wish you were married to the young man across the river who plays the flute." "Yes, that is the one; that is the one I am married to." The man said, "I want him to sing well. Let us go and see them dance." Then they all started, ten boats again. They rested at Shitūm, smoked there, and set the

5. [See C2, n. 3, below.—Ed.]

rock on fire: all the grass and brush burned. Next day it had grown again, that which they had burned. So they started again and arrived at the other side.

g. Now they were dancing indoors. The two girls sat down inside to look on. Then the dance began. One of the two girls said, "The singer looks like the young man across the river from where we live"; and the other one said, "Yes, you see that young man here." "Now he will go to see the sick girl." "The one that is singing, I think that is he." The two young men said, "Yes, he is the one who is singing now. He married the sick girl." Then the two girls would not say a word; they were so ashamed. When they stopped dancing, the people said, "Let us start to go back, for we have far to go." They said to the two girls, "Let us go home," but they did not answer. Though they continued to look at them, they would not answer. Both were wearing basketry caps. They started to touch them and there were only two caps there: they could no longer see the girls (who had sunk into the ground from shame). When they picked up the caps, the two of them were lying there rotting, they had become so ashamed.

h. Now they all went back, I do not know where to, but they went very far. His wife went with him and his father-in-law also. Patapirihak had said to his father and mother: "Wait for me ten days." Now they cried all the time; they were sorry for their boy. Then it was ten days and they looked on the ocean and watched, for he had said, "I will come back in ten days." So they saw him far on the ocean, nearly at sunset. He continued to come: they saw a beautiful bird. It came close to the house; he flew around it. He was a bird when he went behind the house. Then they saw him sit down and turn into a young man. "I came after my ten sacks of tobacco and my flute. I must go where my wife is. I shall not come back any more." Then he flew back out on the ocean. They cried for him.

She was Ivharak ifapi, About-the-House Girl.

C2. SIERUK-PIHIRIV

a. Sieruk-pihiriv (Across-Ocean-Widower) grew at Kenek (Anshwufum).[1] He thought, "Let me go to the upriver end of the

1. [The Yurok myths frequently state that Across-Ocean-Widower (Yurok Wohpekumeu) grew at Kenek or lived there. See Yurok Myths, A14a, Hl*a*, Pl*a–b*, and Xl*a*. The Karok name for the town is spelled Ashwufum in Dl*c*, below.—Ed.]

world (Karuk isivsanen ipan).'' He saw a girl there chopping wood. There were many chips about. "She must be chopping a long time," he thought. He continued to look at her. After a time she could hardly move because she had become pregnant. He had made her so by looking. She said to him, "Let us go to the house. Do not go home. Stay as long as you can until I have had a child. Perhaps I cannot give birth and will die. I want you to see what happens to me, whether I die.''

b. She had ten brothers. Then he lived there. After a time, he became tired of staying and ran away. He went far and thought he had escaped. But when he looked around, he was still sitting in the house. He thought, "I do not think I shall escape from her." Each of the brothers had a knife: they intended to kill him if the girl died. He ran away again, thinking, "Let me run off," and thought he had gone far. When he looked around, he was sitting in the house. "I think I cannot run away from here," he thought again. So he stayed.

c. Then that woman became sick: she was going to have her baby. Sieruk-pihiriv thought, "Let me make medicine." All the young men her brothers were in the house. He told them, "Go outside. I will make medicine somehow." They sat down outside on both sides of the door, watching, to kill him if he came out. He had a quiver. "Of what will I make medicine?" he thought. He reached into his quiver and found leaves there. Then he talked to it [the plant] at all corners of the fireplace. When he had talked at every corner he heard a baby cry. Then the young men came in again: the girl had given birth to a boy.

d. Then Sieruk-pihiriv started back (for Kenek). He had gone far, looked back, and saw his son coming. He thought, "I do not want him to come. I do not like him. All the girls will not like me. They will think, 'He has a son.' I wish he would die." He swam across the river where the water was rough. He thought, "Maybe he will be killed this way." He went on. He looked back again. He swam across the river again, whenever he saw a dangerous place. He thought his son would drown. So he went far. Then he looked back and his son was coming. He was continuing to follow his father. The last time that he looked back he saw that his son had a quiver. Then he thought, "I think I will go with him because he has not been killed anywhere."

e. Then they arrived at Kenek. When they were there it began to snow. The snow lay deep. The people who lived elsewhere did not want Sieruk-pihiriv to come to them because he always ran after girls: therefore they made this snow. Then Sieruk-pihiriv made snowshoes for himself, thinking, "Let me go upriver to Wahsek (Hohira, Martin's Ferry) and look for girls." When he arrived where the houses are, the sun was shining and there was no snow; but where he had come from there was much snow.

f. Sieruk-pihiriv told his son, "Do not go about to those who live elsewhere. They all do not like me." He thought, "If he goes about, some girl will fall in love with him." Then the young man went outdoors. He went a short distance, and a sweathouse was there. He went inside. Those who were in the sweathouse were making arrow points. They said to the boy, "Help us make them!" They handed him obsidian. The young man said, "Very well." They gave him the flaker, but he said "No, I do not want to use that." He had a quiver; he put the obsidian in that. After a time he reached into his quiver and took out the obsidian: it was all worked and shaped. They looked at it. They thought, "He is wise." Then they said to him, "You had better smoke." The young man said, "Very well." So he smoked. When he smoked he blew the smoke out. He blew it far across the mountain. Then he went back home.

g. His father said to him, "I want you to marry"; so Sieruk-pihiriv said to his son. Then he married. After a time he had two children. One was a girl, one a boy. Then the old man said, "Up the hill there is a young bird on a tree. I wish you would catch it so that the children may play with it. Let us go catch it." Then they went uphill. They had a long pole for a ladder. Sieruk-pihiriv set it against the tree. His son climbed up, and came to the nestling. He looked down and the ladder was gone: the old man was carrying it away, dragging it downhill. He had done it because he wanted to sleep with the young man's wife. Then the boy thought, "How will I get down?" The tree continued to grow: it grew up to the sky. So he reached the sky and he escaped. He went to the end of the sky ("world"). There he came down to earth and then back downriver to Kenek.

h. He saw a little boy and girl. The girl had a basket on her back, the boy a bow and arrows. They were his own children. But he who had come back did not know "that is my son" when he saw him. The boy heard a woodpecker chattering in a tree, shot, and held out his hand. Then he who was returning held out his hand above the boy's so the woodpecker fell into it. Then the boy cried, "Who are you, you who injured my eyes?" he said. (His father asked,) "To whom do you belong? Who is your father?" "The son of Sieruk-pihiriv: We are his boy and girl." "Yes? I am that one." The boy could see nothing: he was blind; the girl was blind too. The father said, "Who did it to you that you cannot see?" The boy said, "Sieruk-pihiriv did it. When he had intercourse he rubbed his semen on our eyes: that is why we are blind." The young man said, "Oh, that is awfully bad!" He would not go back to his father's house.

i. He went below it, leading his children down to the river. There, among the rocks, he prepared a little hole with water and there he washed his children's eyes. Then they could see again. He took his son away, down to the mouth of the river, and gathered dentalia, woodpecker scalps, deerskins, and all valuables. He took everything. He went everywhere over the world taking all the money (treasure), gathering it together.

j. Sieruk-pihiriv did not know. He slept in the house a long time. He never went outdoors. He was sleeping with the woman. Then nuts fell into the house. Bluejay in carrying them [had] dropped them into the house where the old man was sleeping with the woman. So Sieruk-pihiriv got up and went outdoors. He thought, "I have slept a long time. It has become summer and I am still cohabiting." Then he looked for his son, thinking, "Where has he gone?" He went everywhere in the world but could not find him. He did not know where he had gone.

k. Then he overtook his son at the mouth of the river, as he was climbing the hill there. Sieruk-pihiriv tied fast a small dentalium on the other (south) side of the river and said to it, "Shout, and I will follow my son." Then Dentalium[2] shouted, and the son reached back to the other side to take it along too, for he was leaving (this world). Then it was that Sieruk-pihiriv overtook him. He said, "You have done wrong to take away everything. When people grow, what will they use, when you have taken all wealth? You have done badly." Then he took away from him one basket. It contained every kind. Then he threw them about, everywhere, dentalia and woodpecker scalps and everything else (of value). He said, "When human beings grow they will use these." Then his son's son went across the

2. [For a discussion of Dentalia, see headnote to G4, below.—Ed.]

ocean to stay there; he was called Yuruk-pasikiri. And his (own) son
went upriver to live there; his name is Karuk-pasikiri.[3]

l. Then the old man had no place to go to. He ran about; he did
not know where he was going. He had a cane of oak: with that he
went about. Then Yuruk-pasikiri thought, "I wish the old man
would come here. If he does not come, if he stays on the other side,
they will constantly die here, but over there they will not die. Let
them die on the other side, when people grow. Let them come here
and be immortal."

m. Then Yuruk-pasikiri thought; "The old man always wants
women." So he sent a woman to swim up across the ocean to him.
He told her, "Go bring the old man. I think you can catch him. He is
always wanting women." Then the woman came where Sieruk-
pihiriv was coming along the beach. Then she came up out of the
water naked and spread her legs. Sieruk-pihiriv did not stop: he only
looked a little and went by. But then he came back and leaped
between her legs. Then she went into the water with him. As he was
beginning to enter the ocean, he cried, "Wait, let me throw back my
(herb) medicine, so that when people grow they will have it." Then
he threw back his medicine.

n. When he arrived on the other side of the ocean, Yuruk-
pasikiri was making a Jumping Dance. Sieruk-pihiriv could not see
it; he had become blind. Yuruk-pasikiri thought, "You did wrong to
me. You put something on my eyes. I wish you would be as I was, so
that you cannot see my dance." So when Sieruk-pihiriv came where
they were dancing he cried: "I cannot see, I cannot see!" He had
done it to the boy before; but now the boy was a rich man making a
dance.

C3. Hupa Girl Marries Water Person

a. At Ipupuhwam (Medilding, Captain John's Ranch) in Hupa,
there was a girl who always carried firewood. She would go far uphill
to get wood. When she came down halfway, she rested. Then she
would go on to the house. For a long time she did this. She was
grown up; her hair reached far down.

3. The Yurok reverse their directions. I would suspect confusion in my
note-taking except that at the end it really is the grandson who is across the ocean.
Karuk-pasikiri is named also as the father of the heroine of C1. [There too he is said
to be from far upriver.—Ed.]

b. The last time she went uphill to carry wood, she rested in the same place. Then she went downhill a little, bathed, and looked back to where she had left her basket. "My basket is standing outside a house!" she said. When she went back up to her basket, an old woman came out of the house. She said, "I have wanted you a long time. I have seen when you carried wood. I am glad you have come: I want you to marry my son." The girl said nothing. She saw a sweathouse there; an old man came out of it. He said, "I want you to marry my son." She said nothing. The old woman took her into the house. When she entered the door there were five dogs lying on each side. The girl looked around. There was much deer meat in the house. There were ten seats high up in the house for the ten young men who lived there. When the ten were about to return from the hunt, the seats jumped down on the floor. One seat came close to the girl, the seat of him whom she was to marry.

c. When the young men came back all had deer or other game and threw it down in the house. The girl was sitting very much frightened. Some came back from hunting in the ocean and had "large suckers" (chamuhkichkam). Nine of them had returned. Then the one she was going to marry came. Thunder crashed and fire lightning filled the house when he came. He sat down by his wife. It was nearly sunset; what they were to eat was all prepared. Somewhere there had been a war dance to settle a feud; the one who arrived last had been there and was carrying a quiver. The girl looked at him sidewise. From inside his quiver a man's foot stuck out. Now they cut up the deer and gave half of one to the dogs. The dogs were mountain lions. Then the men also ate. Then the old woman's husband came in, and fought, and they all fought about the house. The girl thought she could not escape, but somehow she got out of the house away from them. She thought they were fighting each other, but she did not know that they were only eating: it looked as if they were fighting.

d. Then she went far north near the ocean, in Tolowa country. Then she saw a woman who said to her, "Those among whom you married are bad. Do not stay there. There is a place here where there is a good man. You had better go and marry him." She went there, and saw a house, and when she was before it, an old woman came out. She said, "I have seen you carrying wood. We hear you chopping all the time. I am glad you have come. Come indoors." In the house she saw a man sitting on a seat; he had long hair. All over his hair were tied dentalia.

e. As she came in, under foot it was covered with sand at the door, for all the floor of the house was of (slippery) flint (or obsidian). All the house was covered (roofed) with flint. Then the Thunder (ishnur) whom she was first to have married came. He thundered; he tried to tear down the house; but he could not get at her.

f. Now the man she had come to, her husband, said to her, "I have a louse on my head. Catch it!" When he said this, his sister took peeled shoots and went outdoors as if to make a basket; but the girl thought she would not make a basket. So she loused her husband. When she found a louse she was about to kill it, but the man said, "Do not kill it; give it to me." He took it in his hand and went outdoors. Soon he came back in carrying a child (in its twined cradle basket). When the boy had grown a little, the man said, "Louse me again." Then he said, "Give me the louse," went outside, and came back in carrying a little girl in a baby basket which his sister had made.

g. After a time he said to his wife, "Your mother is crying all the time." He went all over the earth and knew everything; that is why he knew her mother cried. She thought that her daughter had died somewhere because she had never come back from carrying wood. Then the woman said, "I would like to go home." The man said, "It is good. You can go home and see your mother." Then he took ten (carrying) baskets and filled them with deer meat. On top he laid dentalia and woodpecker scalps and obsidians. Then they started to go by boat. He had ten slaves; he said to them, "Let us go." The woman left her children home. They reached her home town and he said to his wife, "Go on up." Then she was glad to be back and went up to the village. The ten slaves carried the baskets. When she came to the house she heard the old woman crying inside. Then she came in the door and asked, "Why do you cry?" The old woman said, "Who are you to speak to me like that?" "I have come back," said the young woman.

h. Then they brought everything into the house. And her brothers came, and all her relatives. Then they ate. Much water entered where they were sitting, and the fire was put out: it was because her husband belonged to the water; that is why it happened. Then the young woman said, "I will go back tomorrow: I left my children home." Then they pounded acorns all night, so that she could take that food back with her. They filled the boat with acorns.

Then the boat started, but they could not see the others in the boat; they saw only the woman. They had not seen them all the time. After a time they could no longer see her. The last time they heard her, she called, "Good-bye, I shall not come back." So she went back to her husband's home.

He was Sharuk-ashimnaun (Down by the River Living Long-haired); he was not a kemish monster.

Informant D

OAK-BOTTOM-FLAT JACK

[*Oak-Bottom-Flat Jack is identified by Kroeber (in Kroeber and Gifford, World Renewal, UC-AR 13:[no. 1]: 134) as a resident of Katimin, about thirty-eight or forty years of age in 1902. Kroeber says that at that time he rated Jack and Three-Dollar-Bar Billy (Informant E) as "only mediocre informants. But their data are clear and reliable, and I evidently underestimated both men. They did behave somewhat colorlessly, probably because of their relative youth and a certain timidity of what their own people might say about their revealing the native culture to a white man" (ibid.: 133–134).*

Oak Bottom Flat, or Vunharuk, was on the Salmon River, "something over a mile above Somes Bar, about two and a half miles up from the mouth of the Salmon . . ." (Kroeber and Barrett, Fishing Among the Indians of Northwestern California, UC-AR 21:[no. 1]: 20). The town on the flat, or prairie, must have been Jack's original home; it was one of several places where the Karok built fishing weirs.—Ed.]

D1. Sieruk-pihiriv

a. A man grew far upriver at the end of the world. There he had a child. He left it there. He went downriver. He went uphill to a lake. He bathed in this. He bathed in all the lakes about. Then he reached this country. As he went downriver he would swim across again and again. Then he would go uphill again and swim in a lake. When he came to Katimin he entered the river where the bluff is. He came out

40

in a large eddy. From there he followed the path uphill. He piled up rocks along the path like small mountains.

b. He went downriver once more. At Keremia ivnen ("wind-rest," above Orleans) he rested. There were many ikhareya at Panamenik. He thought, "What shall I do? If I go there, I shall be ashamed. Well, I will do thus. Let my hair grow." Then he shut his eyes. When he opened them his hair hung down to the ground. "With what shall I tie my hair? Let me tie it with woodpecker scalps. Let me have on otter skins. Let dogs grow to go with me, and let them have woodpecker scalps on their tails." Then it was thus, and he said, "That is good." He stood up, looked back, and saw some-one coming. That one reached him. It was his son from far upriver. Then he went with him. Far upriver he saw a deer standing shining.

c. Then they went downriver. At Ashwufum (Yurok Kenek) he stayed one night. Then he had a child, a girl. She grew up fast. Now her brother (from upriver) was with her; she went hunting with him. Every morning he killed one woodpecker. Then the boy said, "I want to go back to where I was born." His sister said, "Go upriver to the end of the world. There are many woodpeckers there." The boy did not tell his father. He went upriver with his sister. The man did not know where his son and daughter had gone. He went all over the land looking for them. They went to Karuk isivsanen ip, Upriver the world's end.

The man was Sieruk-pihiriv, Across-the-Water-Widower.

D2. COYOTE'S THIRST

a. Coyote thought, "Let me go upriver." Then he came to where a man was making fire in his sweathouse. Coyote stood outside. He saw water in a basket. He looked at it. He thought, "Let me drink." So he drank it all and went on.[1] The one who had been inside came out. All his water was gone. He looked at the basket. "I wish you would want water, you who drank my water. I wish you would become very thirsty," he said.

b. Coyote went on. He became extremely thirsty. He came near a creek: the water was running in it. He reached it: the water was all

1. ["To make away with the drink set aside by a sweating man to break his thirst is despicable," K. says in Yurok Myths, E2, n. 1.—Ed.]

gone. He went on far to another creek. When he reached it, it too was dried up. He became more thirsty. He went on until he saw another creek and heard the water in it. He was nearly dead now. He took his deerskin blanket and thought, "I will tie it in a bundle and throw it in and then chew it. Perhaps I can suck water from it." So he threw it into the creek, but the creek was dry. Now Coyote ran downhill to the river[2] and drank. He died and rolled in.

D3. ANHUSH

a. Anhush (Weasel?)[1] came to an old woman who was pounding acorns. Her name was Yaunakayeishchi. She had long ear pendants that reached to the ground. Anhush said, "Old woman, you have long ear pendants." Then she got up and caught him. She had a basket in the middle of which a (flint) point stuck up. When she caught a man she always threw him in; so she killed him. She wanted to throw Anhush in, but he threw her in and killed her.

b. Then he went on. He saw where someone lived. There was an old woman. She said, "Climb this tree so that you can get the little birds that are there." She put up long sticks for him as a ladder so that he might get up. Then he climbed up high. The old woman took away the ladder. He could not come down. She thought, "I will make a strong wind; then he will be killed." She was Wind-Old-Woman (Ikeremia kemniikich). Anhush found pitch on the tree, chewed it, then stretched it out from his mouth. Then he descended by that. He entered the house where the old woman was. (Evidently the end is omitted.)

c. Then he went upriver. He saw an old woman pounding acorns. She wore long ear pendants. He said to her, "What kind of ear pendants have you? Are you wearing human testicles (sirihaon)?" Then she caught him. "Why does he talk to me like that?" she said. She had a basket behind her. In this was a long sharp bone; she used to throw people into it. Then Anhush threw her into her own basket.

2. River water is not drunk, ordinarily. [It was regarded as polluted; see Kroeber, Yurok Myths, E2, n. 2.—Ed.]

---

1. Weasel-like as described to me, but J. P. Harrington gives another name for the animal. [Bright confirms the identification of Weasel.—Ed.]

D4. MARUK-ARAR'S MEDICINE

a. Maruk-arar (Hill Person) made this world. He made the mountains. The last he made was a long ridge. He thought, "I will go hunting." He made five ravines. The first time he went hunting, the five ravines became filled with the deer he killed. He came back and stood outside his house. He said, "I killed many. I cannot carry them all." Then he looked downhill. Far below he saw smoke. He thought, "I will go down." Then he went down. He saw a woman living in a house. He said, "I came to get you." She said, "Yes? You have come just at the right time." Then he took her back to his house. Then they carried the deer home: they carried them all into the house. Now he looked at her while she was eating. He thought, "A woman will not eat that kind: a man will eat it. It is not the right kind for a woman to eat."

b. At night the woman could not sleep. She appeared to be sick. "What is the matter with you?" he asked. "I have bellyache," she said. When it was day he said, "I will hunt again." He had a dog; he took him along to hunt. The dog found the deer and drove them. But Maruk-arar could not see them: he killed nothing. Next night when it was nearly day the dog came back. The man thought, "Why is it that I cannot kill deer, and that this woman has bellyache? I think it must be wrong that that woman ate deer." She said: "I am menstruating. That is why you cannot kill deer." "Is that it? Well, I will make medicine." Then he took leaves and made medicine. At daylight he went out. Now he filled eight creeks with the deer he killed. He told the woman to go home. He thought, "When people come to live they will do like this. They will find no deer when a woman menstruates."

D5. MARUK-ARAR (AND) THE GIANT

Maruk-arar saw where a person had been on the hills with snowshoes.[1] He thought, "He has large feet. What kind is he? I should like to see him." Then he measured the tracks. His own feet were small. These tracks reached from his fingertip nearly to his shoulder; his own (snowshoe) tracks reached only to his elbow. Then he was much afraid of that person.

1. Or: A human being saw where a Maruk-arar had been . . . ?

D6. COYOTE AT THE PUBERTY DANCE

a. Coyote cut all his hair and put pitch on his head (like a widow). He put on ear pendants of broken dentalia. They were long and reached to his waist. He had heard that somewhere they were making a girl's puberty dance. He made a small baby basket and put a little baby in it. Then he went to where they were dancing. Many people had come there. Then he was asked, "Will you dance?" Coyote said, "No, I cannot dance. I have no bone *(sic)*." "Can you not dance with that girl for whom the dance is made?" "Well, I will do that," said Coyote. He told a woman, "Hold my baby for me. Take good care of it, for it has no father." Then he went into the middle of where they were dancing (and held the girl). Now that old woman (Coyote) danced hard. Then they said, "He is having intercourse with her with whom he is dancing." At once they threw his baby down the hill. They picked up big sticks and struck Coyote. He said, "Hit me, drive me in!" Then he ran off.

b. They pursued him. He entered a hole in a tree. "Let the hole close," he said. The people could not find him. The tree was smooth: it had no crack; Coyote was inside. He stayed there long. He became very thin. Then he heard someone outside. He said, "Who is outside to make a hole for me?" The birds said, "We will make a hole for him." They could do nothing. Coyote said, "You had better get the great woodpecker. Let him try to make the hole." Then the great woodpecker[1] came. He struck off chips. He made the hole as large as when Coyote went into it. Coyote came out very thin. He said, "All you who tried to help me to come out stay here: I will do something good for you." Then he put red on their heads. At last he said to the great woodpecker, "Sit down by me." Then he put red all over the top of his head.

D7. EXCREMENT CHILD

An ikhareya girl became pregnant. They thought, "What has happened to her?" Then she had her baby, but no one knew the father; she did not. When the child was old enough to walk about as

---

1. [The large pileated woodpecker, *Dryocopus pileatus,* whose pointed crest was worked into dance ornaments and regarded as a precious material (Kroeber, Yurok Myths, A1, n. 9).—Ed.]

she sat outdoors, she found out from whom it was. Before, as she was walking, someone had seized her from behind. "You mustn't," she cried, and threw him off without looking to see who he was. When she turned back, there was no one there. Then, looking another way, she saw him going across a prairie. It was her own excrement who had done it.

D8. SMALL DENTALIUM

Small Dentalium (Hakananapmana)[1] was raised upriver. He listened downriver. Then he heard someone talking. He thought, "Let me go downstream to where they are talking." So he went down. At Shafnaikano[2] he sat down. Then he saw where they were talking. There was something lying which they wanted to lift up. So he went down among them. "What are you going to do?" he asked. "We want to raise this but cannot." Then he raised it: it stood up. He went back upriver. What he had raised was the large rock at the mouth of Salmon River.

D9. WATER

An old man grew on Salmon River. He thought, "What will they live on, when Indians grow?" He went above to the sky. There he saw a man, who asked him, "Why did you come?" He said, "I am looking for water." This one above had water. He told him, "Go back. I will give you water." Then he went back. Then he heard water coming. All the streams began to run. He said, "When people grow, they will drink that."

1. [For a discussion of Dentalia, see the headnote to G4, below. F1 states that Dentalium was raised far downriver, across the ocean.—Ed.]
2. [K.'s typescript has a marginal question mark, seemingly about the spelling or identification of this name.—Ed.]

Informant E

THREE-DOLLAR-BAR BILLY

[*In "World Renewal," Kroeber says that Billy lived at Somes Bar in 1902 and was close to forty years of age (Kroeber and Gifford, World Renewal, UC-AR 13: [no. 1]: 134). Billy is the source of many of the Ethnographic Notes, below. For Kroeber's rating of Billy and of Oak-Bottom-Flat Jack as informants, see the biographical sketch for Informant D, above.*

Kroeber (Karok Towns, UC-PAAE 35: 34) says that E. S. Curtis (The North American Indian 13: 222) identified the American name Three-Dollar Bar as Karok Ishivinnipich, on the left bank of the Salmon between Somes and Oak Bottom. The bars in local place names refer to sandbars in the river.—Ed.]

E1. Lingam and Yoni

A half mile above Somes Bar store (of 1902), where a little creek comes into Salmon River from the north, is Sufaim. Here there is a hole like a house pit. There lived Lingam and Yoni.[1] She asked him, "What are you going to eat? Shall you eat this? Or that?" Lingam did not answer. She asked him about everything. Finally she asked, "Shall you eat Yoni?" Then suddenly he turned to her, tearing the hole in the ground, and caught her. He still eats her.

1. [The names used here are the Sanskrit words for "penis" and "vulva." —Ed.]

E2. FALCON AT A'U'ICH

a. Falcon (Aikneich), who had Grizzly Bear for wife, made himself a dam at the foot of his home on A'u'ich peak,[1] where the rapids are now. He made it with big rocks, and shut off salmon from upriver altogether.

b. Then he went to Scott Valley (Shasta tribe's territory) to get himself another wife. Grizzly Bear suspected him, got jealous, threw down his dam, and went off. That is why there are the rapids there now, instead of a fall. As Falcon, returning, came to the crest of the Salmon Alps ("Scott Valley Mountains"), he did not hear the roar of his dam (fall) and knew that something was wrong. So he hastened, and as he came above Katimin, he saw Grizzly Bear fleeing, and shot her.

1. [K. describes A'u'ich as "a precipitous and striking conical peak around which the Klamath winds just downstream from Katimin (Segwu') and upstream from the mouth of the Salmon" (Yurok Myths, C3, n. 25). In the headnote to that myth he says, "The swift duck hawk or gerfalcon . . . is always associated by the Karok with the peak A'u'ich (Sugarloaf), which overhangs the Klamath . . . in the heart of their territory. A ledge near the summit of the little mountain has been the meeting place of individuals of this species probably from time immemorial. The Karok believe in consequence that the pair of *aikneich* hawks homing on A'u'ich are immortal, and that they go off only to take away their young of the year. The bird has deeply impressed their mythologic consciousness. It is of significance that Stone, the narrator of this tale, was half Karok in ancestry, and in fact that his father was from Segwu' . . . "

See also the Ethnographic Note on Aikneich, p. 96, below, which was supplied by the present Karok informant, Three-Dollar-Bar Billy.—Ed.]

Informant F

DICK RICHARD'S FATHER-IN-LAW

[*In "World Renewal," Kroeber says that this appellation is the only one he has "for a man of seventy-five or more who lived upstream across the Klamath from Katimin a few miles, near Ten Eyck creek or mine, and with whom I spent most of two days. He knew or would speak no English, and appears to have escaped an English name; native names one did not then ask for, if they were not volunteered; it was not good form" (Kroeber and Gifford, World Renewal, UC-AR 13:[no. 1]: 134).—Ed.*]

F1. Hakananap-manan at Upriver Ocean[1]

a. Hakananap-manan[2] grew far downriver across the ocean at Yuruk-i-siaruk.[3] He cried constantly. He thought, "I will go to the upstream ocean across, to Kayurash." So he came to this world. He camped at the middle of the world here (oku sivsanên āchip okuêshirihan). He thought, "When people live here they will remember my tears (yupashtaran) as long as anyone is alive." He went on and camped at the lower end of the (future) upriver ocean; he was still crying. Then he went to the other side of that ocean, still crying. His tears began to make a little lake there. He looked at it. He said,

1. [The F myths have been renumbered. K.'s manuscript as originally numbered did not contain an F1 or an F9. The myth now numbered F1 was his F2, etc; the myth now numbered F8 was his F10, etc. For an explanation, see A8, n. 1, above.—Ed.]
2. [Small Dentalium. See the discussion of this personification in the headnote to G4.—Ed.]
3. [Spelled Yurashisiak in C1*d*.—Ed.]

"I cry because I want to know how dentalia are to come into being."
Then there were things like little fish jumping in the water: they were
dentalia; Hakananap-manan had made them. His tears made the
upriver ocean Kayurash.

b. When he had made it good there, he thought, "How shall I go
downriver?" Then he followed the river. When he came to where it
flows through the rocky ridge Keichivikyuripa at Hayward's Bar, he
left the river. He did not want to go further that way but widened the
rocky chasm and went up the ridge on the mountains to the right, to
Sihaviitka, where all the ridges meet and the streams flow down in
ten directions. He made these streams by crying there. Then he said,
"They will remember me by this. They will call them creeks." Then
he went on down to Sufip, to the mouth of the river, and from there
he went on back to Yuruk-i-siaruk from which he had started when
he crossed the ocean.

F2. SUHURIVISH-KURU

a. Suhurivish-kuru was the one who made this water to flow
down. He began at the head of the river. At the time he grew, this
earth was nearly level; there were only little hills. Then he was born.
After two days he had grown up. He looked about. He thought, "I
think persons have not grown anywhere. I was the first one born.
This world is level now."

b. After two days, hills and mountains had grown up all around.
But they were only sand; there was no brush, nor anything growing.
Then he made it that water ran down from all the hills. He said, "All
people when they are born will use this water to drink." He knew
that he would not always be alone, that others (human beings) would
come soon. Then he looked up on the hills and now deer had grown,
and leaves and grass and brush. After a time small trees grew. Then
this river began to run down. Suhurivish-kuru made it all.

c. Then all the earth, green earth, red earth, and all colors,
washed off. There was too much water, and it kept running down
and washed away the sand and earth. Suhurivish-kuru thought,
"How shall I do?" Then he made rock. He made rocks to lie all
about, down along the river, as far as down to the mouth. So he
stopped the hills from being washed down and running off with the
river. Now he had made everything, and the mountains were all

rock. Then he thought and knew that he had made it right. He had done everything, and stopped.

F3. ASHAHEVARA ITS IKHAREYA

a. Ten men lived at the mouth of the river. They had one sister. All of them continually hunted. They did nothing but look for game. The ten had grown up together; after them was born their sister. Many people came to where they lived. Almost every night a crowd went into the sweathouse and sang for deer, but no one ever killed anything, and all came back and were ashamed. Whoever succeeded in killing the game was to marry their sister, but no one succeeded, though many came and hunting was constantly going on. It was told everywhere that no one could kill the game in that place. All good hunters had gone there and had come back and told everywhere that they had failed.

b. Now there was a good hunter at a little mossy (ashahem) hill near the head of Clear Creek at Ashahevara.[1] He said, "I will go to the mouth of the river." Then he started to go uphill from where he lived and went along the ridge of the Siskiyou Mountains and down to the mouth. "I am glad you have come down to see us," said the ten ikhareya brothers to him. "I wish you would go hunting with us. We start early in the morning." Then he slept in the sweathouse with them. When he awoke, all had already gone hunting and he was alone in the sweathouse. He went out, looked, went up the hill, and hunted by himself. He looked everywhere but saw nothing. In the evening he came back to the house; he had got nothing.

c. The girl said to him, "What did you see? Anything?" Ashahevara its ikhareya said, "No, I saw nothing." "Did you not see a little fog?" she asked. "Yes, I saw a little fog move." "What else did you see? Did you see any ants?" "Yes, I saw ants." "Well, those ants are the game. That is what my brothers shoot. That fog is deer; the ants are bears. When you see them again, shoot."

d. In the morning they all went off hunting. Ashahevara its ikhareya waked up and saw nobody. He went out; all had gone away. He stood there thinking. He thought, "I will make

1. Astexewa in Kroeber and Gifford, World Renewal, UC-AR 13:(no. 1):11 ff. [There it is described as the sacred mountain which the priest faces as he constructs the stone wall for the Inam world renewal ceremony.—Ed.]

medicine." So he began to make it. With his fire drill he made fine wood dust. Then he spat on it and rubbed himself over his body with it. He started, went a way, and looked. Then he saw fog. Then he shot into the fog, and deer came rolling downhill. He had shot ten deer. He saw ants, and shot ten of them; then they were bears.

e. After he had killed them all he thought, "How will I carry them? I am unable." Then he cut off the feet from the deer and the bears, and went down and left them behind the house. He left his moccasins there also. Then he entered the house and sat down. The girl thought, "Why did not (didn't) he kill them? What [Why] did not he not (didn't he) shoot as I told him?" Ashahevara its ikhareya sat a while, then said to the girl, "Get my moccasins. I left them behind the house." So she went out. Behind the house she began to drag at something but could not move it. She pulled and tugged. She called, "My load is too heavy; I cannot carry it in." Then her ten brothers came out. All saw what he had killed: they were glad and jumped about. All of them said, "My brother-in-law, my brother-in-law, you have done well." Then they carried all the feet indoors. They knew he had killed the deer and the bears. Thus Ashahevara its ikhareya did.

f. Then he said, "Tomorrow morning I will start home." The girl got ready. She thought, "I will go with him," because it had been said that whoever killed the game would marry her, and now he had married her. So she went with him. He went up along the mountain the same way he had come. When he came to the head of Rock Creek, he was thinking, "I did not do well. I married too far away. I do not like it. I will leave her. I wish I knew how to abandon her. I think I will say that I am thirsty. It is a dry mountain and water is hard to get." Then he said to her, "I am thirsty. Go downhill and bring me water." He thought, "As soon as she goes away, I will leave her."

g. The woman started for water. She thought, "He will deceive me, I think. I know that somehow he will leave me." Then she went only over a little elevation, and behind a tree she put her elbow into the ground and water came out. Then, not having gone far, she came back. But that man was already gone. He had deserted her. She wanted to overtake him but did not know how. So she went back again to her old home, and he went on up to where he lived.

h. But he had forgotten his pipe on top of the mountain where he abandoned her. He was carrying it in his belt, and when he sat down, he had taken it out, but when he got up he forgot it. That is why that place is called Ahuram usaniirak, "Pipe-Left-Behind."

She was Sufip ifapi, River-Mouth-Girl.

F4. Origin of Bow and Dog

a. Deer grew first. After that other animals grew: Mountain Lion, Wolf, Wildcat, and all the others. Then they [the animals] made (bows of) five kinds: of yew, alder, white oak, and so on. Then they said, "Tomorrow morning we will all go to hunt. Let all start early." Now they were all living in one house. Dog was there too: he seemed to know nothing. He lay at the entrance; as they came in, they stepped over him. Coyote said to Dog, "Ah! you cannot take the best bow." Whoever got up first (and killed Deer) was to have the best bow. Coyote thought, "I will not go to sleep! Then I can take the best bow for myself." He set little sharp sticks between his upper and lower eyelids to keep himself awake. He thought, "I cannot see Deer, but when it jumps out from its place I will see it and can follow it." Deer was sleeping in the middle of the house. Whoever caught him would always have the best bow.

b. Now Dog had a little black-oak bark. When it became nearly daylight, Dog thought, "It must be nearly time he will run out." He put the bark into the fire, then burned Deer with it between his hoofs. And he put sweet-smelling root in that same spot. Just about the first day (light), Deer went out. No one heard him: they were all asleep. Only Dog was awake; he got up and followed Deer by his tracks: he could smell where he had gone.

c. Deer had gone far; he had gone all over the earth. He thought, "I have gone far enough. I will lie down here." When he lay there a little while, he heard barking; Dog was coming. He got up again, ran, ran far. He ran all over the world. Again he lay down on a hill, thinking, "It is far," but again Dog came baying, and Deer ran. Sometimes he doubled back on his tracks. He was thinking, "No one will ever take and kill me." He went in every direction, to the ocean, then back. Then he became tired and lay down. He thought, "You can no longer catch me and eat me." But Dog, scenting his tracks, came on, barking.

d. Then Deer thought, "He will eat me. Well, I have become tired in this world. Let me go where the water comes from and flows down: there I will jump into the sky.'' So he ran to the head of the world. His way crossed the head of the river. He was going to jump over this, then into the sky, and run along that. So he jumped, but fell short, and dropped into the river. Dog was close behind, jumped, seized him, pulled him out of the water and killed him. He said, ''I shall be able to eat you always. I shall always catch you. This is how I did it: I burned that medicine on your hooves: that is how I can always follow you.''

e. At last Coyote awoke and got up. He still had the little sticks in his eyelids. The sun was high, and all had left. He took a bow of alder, the worst one, which all of them (had) left. Dog had taken the bow of yew. Coyote was hungry; but he could do nothing with his bow. So he went on a flat and hunted gophers. They said to him, ''This is the poorest bow. You will kill gophers. You won't be able to catch anything else.''

f. This is the beginning of the bow. Dog said, ''I give this bow to the human beings who will come into existence. Whoever will remember me, to him I give this bow.'' Thus men obtained bows. Dog is still as he was at first, good at tracking.

It happened in ''this middle world'' here.

F5. Ipashnavan Owls Marry

a. Ten men and a woman, their sister, grew at Sufip, the mouth of the river. They were good hunters. Many people started from everywhere to go there: they had heard that the woman was to be married to him who could kill elk there. When they arrived, the ten said to them, ''I am glad you have come. In the morning I should like you to hunt with me. Whoever can kill the elk will marry my sister.'' So they said to all who came, from here and there and everywhere. In the morning they would try, but none killed elk. Then they gave up and returned home. Some, after they had started, never went back to the house of the ten, but went home, ashamed. They were good hunters who had thought that they would marry the woman. So it was told all over the river that no one was successful there.

b. Now there were two here in this middle of this world, two brothers. They said, ''My brother, let us go to Sufip. Perhaps we shall get the woman; perhaps we shall kill the elk.'' ''Well, let us go downriver.'' So they started and arrived at Sufip, after supper, nearly at dark. They sat there outside the sweathouse. Inside, many people were laughing. The two took off their clothes: these were old and dirty. They had old quivers of stiff deerskin, so rotten that pieces were falling off. They laid these on top of the sweathouse. Then they went into the sweathouse and lay down at the end. When they had lain there a while, Coyote went outside and said, ''Hi-i-i-i-i-i-i! Whose funny clothes are these, falling to pieces? They must have picked them up on the way.'' He went back in; they all smoked. Then Coyote started to sing a deer song. It was not a deer song: he just made it up. The two brothers did not join in the song; they only cried, for they thought, ''We can kill nothing. Many have been here and failed.'' Then Coyote said to them, ''You stink from flatulating. You will just sleep here, that is all you will do. You can't kill game.''

c. Early in the morning Coyote ran out quickly. All the others came out, and the ten also. But the two brothers still lay there. Then the youngest of the ten said to them, ''You had better go into the house.'' They said, ''No, we will stay here.'' He said to them, ''Go on into the house and eat acorn soup,'' but they said, ''No.'' So they started, with their stiff, dirty, rotten clothing and their quivers so badly dressed that the fat still clung to the hide. The youngest of the ten went ahead to show the way. He (had) told the other ten ikhareya, ''Go ahead, we will follow you.'' He was looking at them and thinking, ''Their clothes are bad. Why do they not wear better clothes?'' When he looked around he no longer saw them and thought, ''They are ashamed and have gone home.'' But after awhile they came up, wearing yellowhammer and eagle feathers and net headdresses and carrying fine otterskin quivers. Then that ikhareya thought, ''They know something, after all. They are real people.''

d. He said, ''This is the place to wait for them.'' So they waited. They made a little fire to straighten and dry the arrows and their bows. The ikhareya said, ''I hear them! Now they will come down.'' They were close to a creek; soon they heard the noise near by. He said quietly, ''There they come.'' The two did not answer. He said, ''Shoot! Shoot!'' They sat still. Ten elk were coming. ''Shoot!'' said the ikhareya. ''No, don't,'' said the elder of the two brothers. ''Shoot! they are nearly past,'' said the ikhareya. ''No, don't.'' The elk had already passed by them when the older brother said, ''I will shoot them from behind. Let all of them fall. I will shoot the last one first and then the next, and so all ten." Then he shot: ten elk dropped together. Thus they got all of them.

e. Now the oldest of the ten ikhareya came. "Who did this?" he said. "These two have done it," said the youngest; "they are our brothers-in-law." "Oh, I am glad, my brothers-in-law," said the oldest of the ten. Then the next one of the ten asked, "Who has done this?" All nine came, one after the other, and asked whose bow and arrow had shot the elk; and all of them said, "My brothers-in-law."

f. Last of all, far behind, came Coyote. As he approached he said, "When a man is old he can do nothing, it does not matter how good a shot he is. I have killed many in my time. I shot these elk but did not kill them." He showed his arrow, bloody up to a certain point. "It must have dropped off them," he said. But he had cut himself on his leg and then rubbed his arrow in his own blood. The ten brothers said, "You did not shoot the elk. These two are the ones that hit them." They did not believe Coyote. Then Coyote went away; he did not even return to the house.

g. And the two brothers married there. They were Ipashnavan (Screech Owls):[1] The spots on their heads now are the netted head-dresses they wore. They are the ones that were married at the mouth of the Klamath.

F6. The Flood

a. In the middle of the world (ok isivsanen achip) in this land here, there grew two people. They knew that the water would spread out here (paura isha chupisrihesh) and cover the world, and that all the people would die. They took a shipnuk storage basket, and getting pitch, they rubbed it over the basket, covering all its stitches until it would not leak, and on top they had a cover. But one of them came too late and did not get into it and was left behind. The other jumped into the basket, and his dog jumped with him. When he heard the water about him, he drew the cover over the top.

b. With a deer-bone awl (ipiskipishii) he prepared to make a small hole, holding pitch ready in his hand to stop the hole if water entered; he wanted to see if the water had stopped rising. Finally no

1. [It is also the modest Screech Owl who shoots the giant bird on Shelton Butte in Kroeber, *Yurok Myths*, A8*c*.—Ed.]

water came in at the hole. Then he made the hole larger, and larger. He could see nothing but endless sand hills (yuuh wītkiri kaura). He uncovered the basket and looked around. The water had gone. All people were dead. Not a single person was left; only the man and his dog were saved. He looked in all directions. Down at the river the water was running off. Where there had been many people not one was left now. There were hills and this man and the dog; that was all in the world.

c. Then he went downriver with his dog. He wanted to find if anyone was still alive. He came to the mouth of the Salmon and looked everywhere: all were gone. He came at last to the mouth of the Klamath, having looked everywhere that people had lived. But there was only sand, and he could see nothing. So he went back. He came back here and made a little house for himself; there he lived.

d. He thought, "Well, what can I do? I am living here alone. I must have someone with me. I do not know how people will grow again." Finally he thought, "Well, I will cohabit with my dog (tahu-ravuripki chishi)." After a time the bitch had young. Some were half dog and half human; some were nearly human. Those that were most like dogs the man killed; the others he saved. Then he did so again. So people grew once more. From here they went everywhere; some here, some there, to every town, until at last the world was full again from the mouth of the river to far up at the end of the world, and all the towns had people, men and women. Wherever he went he left people. Then he came back to where he lived and stayed there.

e. One night, starting again, he went downriver to Katimin: there he left a man and a woman. Then he went on to Ashanamkarak and left a man and a woman behind. He went on to Chamikiniinich near Orleans, and then on to Weitspus. Again he stayed one night and left a man and a woman. In the morning he went on down to Aavunai, Kepel. The last place he reached was the mouth of the river. There, too, he left a man and a woman. Then he looked about him. He said, "Every place is full now. From me the people that will be will grow." Yāsh-ara means real human beings—it also means rich people; they are all from him and his female dog.

F7. AHSAI SQUIRREL SAVES FIRE

After the water was gone and people had grown again, they had no fire. They ate their food raw. They looked everywhere but could find no fire. They could cook nothing. While the water was still high, the ground-squirrel (ahsai)[1] was swimming about with a little fire on his back. He was looking for a peak above the water. At last he saw one just projecting. It was Kichiim (Siskiyou), the highest mountain (kipihan taapash) in the world. There he swam, and on it he left the fire; but his back was burned black. After the water had gone down and people were in want, he threw his fire to them. Then he said, "I will always live here now. I will remain away from my own country." He pitied the people because they ate their meat raw. If he had not thrown them the fire that he had saved, we should now be eating our food uncooked. This (master, head) squirrel was large, as large as a dog. From him grew many young ones. They were small. They came down from the mountains and went all over the world, but they all were black on their back.

F8. Kunācha'a and Maruk-arar

a. In the middle of this world there grew ten men. The youngest one was called Kunācha'a. They thought they would hunt; the oldest one started out. He was told, "When you go hunting do not go over this ridge." It became dark but he did not return; he never returned. Next morning the next oldest went up the hill. At night he did not come back. Next morning the third one said, "I will look for them." The sun went down, but he did not return. In the morning the next one went up; in the evening he did not return. Next day another one went up but did not come back. They were talking about those who were lost. They said, "I wonder where they have gone." In the morning another went to look but did not return. Next day again one went but did not come back. Another one said, "Well, I will look for them," and went up, but it became dark and he did not come back. In the morning another, the ninth one, went out to look for them. He also did not return.

b. In the house sat nine women, their widows, with their hair cut short.[1] The youngest brother, Kunācha'a, was crying. A (mourning?) fire was burning in the house. The nine widows told Kunācha'a, "Why do you cry? Go and bring wood. Why do you always

---

1. [K. queries this identification, noting "Identify by vocab. or by black on back." Bright confirms the translation.—Ed.]

---

1. [In mourning.—Ed.]

cry, sitting by the fire?'' He picked up his lost brothers' carved stools. ''Do not take those seats,'' said the women. ''Why do you cry?'' For he was always crying, ''Kunācha'a! Kunācha'a!'' And he was picking up shreds of deer sinew that were about. From these he tried to make a bow and arrows and a pipe. The women asked, ''Why do you make a sinew pipe? That kind is not made. Why are you doing it?'' But he did not answer, he only cried, ''Kunācha'a!'' So he began to make a bow of sinews. They said to him, ''Make your bow of wood! Why do you make a sinew bow?'' He cried, ''Kunācha'a!'' He said no other word.

c. When he had made everything, his bow, his arrows, his pipe of sinews, he went out, on top of a tree, and sang: ''Hovena hanina, Hadikman chimini.'' Then he pushed down the tree. He broke it up for firewood. He was thinking, ''I shall have to be strong.'' That is why he pushed it over. Now the nine women all came out to look at the tree that he had crushed. Then Kunācha'a, still crying, came out of the brush and said, ''You told me to get wood. You said, 'Why do you cry? Go and get wood.' ''

d. He thought, ''If I find the one that killed my brothers I will try to overcome him; that is why I must become strong. I must train.'' In the morning he took his bow and arrows and pipe. ''Where are you going?'' asked one of the widows. ''Do not go anywhere!'' But he did not answer: he only kept crying, ''Kunācha'a!'' Then he went uphill looking about. When he was far up the ridge he saw the tracks of his brothers; and he saw a deer (carcass) hanging. He thought, ''Perhaps one of my brothers killed it and hung it up. I will go to the very top. Before they started out they were told not to go to the very top.'' Then he reached the summit. It was level and there was a lake there. He thought about it. He thought, ''That is why they said not to go to the summit. This is the danger.'' He looked at the end of the lake. His nine brothers were floating in the water.

e. Then a man came; he was immensely large; he was (a) Maruk-arar.[2] ''That is how he (who?) killed my brothers.'' He knew him and looked frightened. That one called, ''Kunācha'a, are you here too?'' ''Yes,'' said Kunācha'a. He thought, ''He will beat me.'' ''Let us shoot at a target,'' said Maruk-arar. ''No,'' said Kunācha'a, ''I am too little. I am afraid.'' Maruk-arar had a bow made of a tree, of a split tree. For arrows he had young trees. He

2. [This name is translated as Hill Person in D4a.—Ed.]

shoved his bow and arrows at Kunācha'a. He said, "Don't refuse: let's enjoy ourselves shooting (at the mark)." Then Kunācha'a took Maruk-arar's bow, lifted it to shoot, drew, and broke it in two, thinking, "That is how all my brothers were killed; it was this they were overcome by." Maruk-arar said, "Kunācha'a, I begin to be afraid of you," but Kunācha'a only thought, "They were all killed by him."

f. Then Maruk-arar took out his pipe. It was a whole tree, a heavy tree. Kunācha'a thought again, "My brothers could do nothing against him. That is how they were killed." Maruk-arar said, "You had better smoke my pipe." Then Kunācha'a smoked it: he split the pipe.

g. Then he said to Maruk-arar, "Take my bow to shoot with!" The bow was very tiny, and Maruk-arar thought, "I will break it all to bits." He tried to pull it: he could do nothing with it. He rested, then tried again. He strained with all his might, but he could not break it. Then Kunācha'a said, "Smoke my pipe," and Marukarar consented. He thought, "It will be nothing. I will chew up the whole pipe. It is soft." He bit the pipe and tried to break it. He could not do so. He said, "I cannot. Kunācha'a, I am afraid of you." Kunācha'a, looking around at the open level ground, thought, "It was by means of this that my brothers were killed here. He overcame them and threw them into the lake."

h. Maruk-arar said, "Let us wrestle." Kunācha'a answered, "No, I am afraid of you. I can do nothing to you. Your legs are too large around. I cannot even grasp them. I cannot hold you." "You can hold my toe," said Maruk-arar. "No, I cannot wrestle with you." "Come on, let us enjoy ourselves, let us wrestle," said Maruk-arar. Again Kunācha'a refused and again Maruk-arar urged him, thinking, "I will throw him into the lake." Then Kunācha'a said, "Very well, I will hold you by your toe; but I am afraid. I am unable to compete with you." So they began, Kunācha'a holding on to his toe. They came near the lake, but then Kunācha'a pulled him back. He knew that Maruk-arar wanted to throw him in the lake as he had done to his nine brothers. Again they approached the lake, and again (Kunācha'a) drew away from it. Thus they moved about wrestling for a long time, back and forth. Then Kunācha'a seized his thigh. Maruk-arar thought, "He will beat me." But he said, "Let us wrestle again." Kunācha'a said nothing, but he thought, "I will throw him in." Then he did lift him up and threw him into the water. There was a great noise as he fell: it was heard all over the world. People said, "Kunācha'a is killing the one who killed his brothers."

i. Then Kunācha'a went where his brothers had been left floating. From each he pulled off a hair. He thought, "I can do nothing unless I take only one hair from each." Then he went home. He arrived very late, having the nine hairs with him, and went into the sweathouse. The women were all in the house; they did not know that he had returned. In every sweathouse place where one of his brothers had used to sleep he laid that one's hair, each in its place. Then he made a fire. He came out, covered the entrance to the sweathouse, and went into the house. The widows said, "Where have you been, Kunācha'a, where have you been?" But he did not answer. He took the nine seats that he had put away before, and set them around the house as they had been before. The nine women were listening. They were hearing something like crying. It sounded as though there were crying in the sweathouse. The women thought nothing of it, but Kunācha'a knew that his brothers had come back. Then they came in, all nine, and each sat in his seat, the oldest first, and then the others.

That is what Kunācha'a did; that is how he beat Maruk-arar. He is a little bird that tweets sadly, "chi, chi."

F9. Sun and Moon

a. Sun was imtarashun: he had no father (was a bastard). He said, "I will be Sun." He said, "When I come up I shall be fine looking (nawura yawuhesh). All will know me. All the people born in this world will know me. I will shine. I will be handsome, because I am imtarashun." He is Painanu-avahkam ahooti, "the one walking above." At night he passes under the earth; in the morning he comes up again. He shines because he wanted all that are born on the earth to remember him.

He is called Kuushura. He is also called Shupa-hak-kuush, "daylight-moon" (*sic*), but Kharam-kuush is "night-sun," the moon.

b. Moon is imahka, one whom nobody likes. He had Rattlesnake (apshun-mukuroo) for his wife; he had Grizzly Bear (pirishkarim).

He had only disgusting ones for wives. He married them because no one (else) liked him. He also had Frog as his wife. Many kinds of animals went there. Large Lizard (havuram-tīkivên) is he who is always eating Moon (at eclipses). He eats him until he is nearly gone. Then Frog his wife comes up, and from his blood, what Lizard has left of it, makes Moon over until he is large again. Frog, Grizzly Bear, and Rattlesnake are now all to be seen on Moon.

F10. COYOTE STEALS LIGHT

a. An ikhareya lived in the middle of the world, at Katimin. Coyote was running about, doing nothing; he had no sense. He thought, "I do not like the world where we live: it is too dark." Then he came back to Katimin after he had been away long. He said, "In one place I saw something like light. Every little while it lit up. It is very far away. I went and went and then I saw it. I do not like it like this. I should like to bring that light here. Let us plan for it. Let us see who are the best runners; then let us take away the light that I saw far on the other side of the (eastern) ocean." Then the best runners came: Eagle, Chicken Hawk, Mountain Lion, Grizzly Bear, Black Bear, Fox, and Hummingbird. Many of them came and prepared to start to take away the light (shupā). As they went, they left one of them at each place. Coyote said, "I am he who will seize the light. When they are asleep I will take it from them."

b. He went ahead. He came to where the people were that had the light. They did not think that anyone would ever come to take it away from them. They did not fear Coyote, who was always roaming about. He took their light and tied it up in a bundle. He took it and ran with it. Then he gave it to the next runner, and when he was tired and his breath became short he gave it to the next one, and he ran with it until the next one took it from him. Then Hummingbird took it and pi-m-m-m! he was gone. The people were pursuing Coyote. They called him bad names and dirty names: they abused him. "Coyote is the one who did it," they said. Then he ran over the last ridge, and they said, "Well, let him go." They knew that they could never get light (back). When the people came here to the middle of the world, they broke that in which light was tied. Then it was light all over the world. That is how Coyote stole light.

F11. Coyote's Theft of Fire and Adventures

a. Coyote went about everywhere. He was looking for fire. The ikhareya had none; they only had white quartz rocks which they called fire. Coyote said, "It is too bad we have no fire." He went off. Coming to Katimin he said, "I have found fire. Let us steal it. It is far off." So all of them gathered. There were Horsefly (ananāmvan yupeiton), Bear, Mountain Lion, Eagle (wahar), Chicken Hawk (ikchahwan), Wolf (xāmnam) and Hummingbird. Then they started. They posted themselves to run in relays. Coyote was going to steal the fire. Horsefly was next to him, and then Hummingbird. All the fastest runners were at that end. The last one was Tortoise; he said, "I will roll downhill." He thought that was the only way he could help. Frog said, "I will stay close to the river. When Tortoise comes to me, I will take the fire in my mouth."

b. Then Coyote went into the house where the fire was. The people watched him, for they knew that he did foolish things; but as he did nothing, soon they no longer watched him closely. He had slow-burning bark hidden under his belt. When all were asleep he held it in the fire. It was nearly the end of the night. He felt the bark, and saw that it was glowing. Looking about, he saw all asleep. He said, "I will go and take away all of it." So he gathered up all the fire and went off. He had said to Horsefly, "I am not a good runner; you must stay near the house. When I come, I will throw you the fire and you must run with it." He had gone only a little way when the people in the house awoke and began to abuse him. As he ran, he drew back his prepuce and a heavy fog came, so that they could see nothing. They could not follow him and he escaped with the fire, but his prepuce got dry and he could not get it back.

c. Then he gave the fire to Horsefly. The next who carried it was Niiknikits (Sparrow Hawk?). Then Hummingbird carried it. He flew over a mountain ridge and now was nearly on this side of the world (sky). Each one in turn took the fire and became tired and gave it to the next: Mountain Lion, Grizzly Bear, Black Bear, all carried it. Coyote was running far behind with his penis dry. The pursuers were close and nearly caught him. Now when they were nearly here in this world, the fire was almost taken away from them again. But then Tortoise received it: they had nearly seized him when he rolled himself downhill. When he reached the river, Frog was there, and

Tortoise threw the fire in Frog's mouth, and Frog jumped into the water.

d. They who kept the fire came there. All the runners who had fled with it arrived too. The owners of fire said, "What did you do with it? Give it back to us." The others said, "No, we cannot return it." Frog jumped into the river with it and was drowned. "It cannot be helped. We have worked for nothing." Tortoise said, "I threw it into his mouth and he jumped into the water. He must be drowned."

e. After the fire owners left, the others said to Frog, "We have done our work in vain. If you do not give us back the fire we will kill you. You put it out by leaping with it into the river." Frog sat there saying nothing. "We have gone far, all for nothing," said the others. "We will kill you unless you tell us what you have done with it." Frog still sat and said nothing: he only moved his throat. Then he said, "Take willow roots. Cut dry ones, and make one a little wide, and one small and sharp at the end. Cut them that way and make holes in the wide one. Then turn the other one in the hole and perhaps it will burn. Then you will have fire. I did not hide it away." They were all angry and ready to cut Frog up to recover the fire. But they did what he told them, and when the wood dust came from the turning, they put a little dry moss (tinder) on it and blew on it, and taking it into their hand, waved the hand back and forth. Then it blazed up and they had fire, and all were glad. Thus they stole fire, Coyote and his companions.

f. Then Coyote remained here in the middle of this world. He twisted a long cord; he made a net sack full of it. Then he started; he went upriver with his sack full of string. He was going to the end of the world to get dentalia. Berries and everything were ripe. He came to where a smoke was thick. Coyote tried to look in. He called, "Ishawash (sister's/brother's child)!"[1] He always called everyone ishawash. He called again into the sweathouse, "Ishawash! Ishawash!" There was no answer. The man inside only went on singing. He sang, "Aanina kuvakiinya." Again Coyote called and called and got no answer. At last the one inside said, "Faatyaha (be quiet)!" Then Coyote looked about him. "What sort of things has he?" he thought. He looked at the entrance of the sweathouse. There he saw a basket.

1. [K. has a marginal note: "see ante"; the term is spelled ishawish in A1*a*, and explained more fully there.—Ed.]

In it was gooseberry pudding (aharat hushashit). The one inside was still singing. "I will taste it," Coyote said. "Ah! it is good." And he ate it all, both basket and contents, he liked it so well. Then he went on his way to the (upriver ocean) lake where the dentalia grew.

g. Then the one inside came out of the sweathouse. "Where is my sauce that I was going to drink? Coyote has eaten it," he said. Then he called him everything bad. He thought, "I wish he would fail. I wish he will get no dentalia. He has drunk my gooseberries, he who is going upriver. I wish he will obtain nothing. I wish the country would burn over far ahead of where he goes."

h. Then Coyote came to a place where it had burned over. He saw grasshoppers lying singed and ready to eat. "I cannot eat you. I am (fasting because I am) on my way to get money (wīshini aweyishap)," he sang. He went on and came to more burned-over places. Everywhere roasted grasshoppers were lying about. Again he sang, "I cannot eat you. I am going to get dentalia." Then he began to call the grasshoppers bad names because he could not eat them. He thought, "I want to be rich: I must not eat." He went on. Then he thought, "Well, I will taste them." Then he seized them with both his hands and ate. He took more and more and swallowed them. Then his tail began to burn. He heard something, "Tutututututu," and listened. "It must be the wind blowing," he thought, and went on eating greedily. Once more he listened and said, "Perhaps there is thunder somewhere in the distance." Then he heard the noise right behind him and looking around saw that his tail (fur) was burned off and that the hair on his legs was on fire. In his greed he had thought the roaring of the flames to be the noise of water or wind or thunder.

i. Then he became very thirsty. He knew there was a creek ahead upriver. He went on, came near, and heard a large creek running. He said, "I am glad: now I will drink creek water; I will not drink river water." He reached the creek, but it was dried up. He thought, "Well, there used to be a creek here. There will be another one with water running in it." He went on and came near another, and again he heard water running, but came there and found it empty. He thought, "What made this dry up? I heard it running." He scratched in the bottom and tried to suck the dampness out of the ground. "Well, let it be," he said, "there is one farther on: I will drink there."

j. He started and went until again he heard running water. He thought, "I will take off my blanket and throw it into the stream: I am very thirsty." He took his (deerskin) blanket (yarihivash), threw it, and then ran fast to the stream. Seizing his blanket, he put his mouth to it to suck the wet from it, but like the stream it had become dry. He went on and came to another creek. Again he bundled up his blanket and threw it, running as fast as he could. When he reached the creek the blanket was dry. He had nearly reached the lake where the dentalia grow, but now he said, "Well, I cannot get to it; I am too thirsty."

k. So he turned downhill to the river and saw drift logs piled on the bank. He thought, "I cannot reach the lake, so I will have a drink anyway. But I will not drink at the shore, I will drink from the very middle of the river." He went out on one of the logs, out to the middle of the river, and drank there. He drank a long time. He raised his head and took breath and drank again. He continued to drink. At last he raised his head again and tried to rise. He began to lift up very slowly. Then the log rolled over, Coyote dropped into the river, and drowned.

l. In the fall the river rose and much wood floated down. Coyote came down with it. He arrived in this country here. Two women were by the river taking out firewood. Coyote said, "I will be wood. I wish I were a good plank." The two women were young and pretty. "That will be my board," both said at the same time. They pulled it out with crooked sticks. "It must be Coyote! Throw it back! I hear he was drowned upriver. Throw it away," they said, but they were already pregnant. Then Coyote floated downstream all the way to the mouth of the river. Everybody said, "That is Coyote," when they saw the board, for they had heard of the girls getting pregnant. No one would take up the plank.

m. Coyote floated across the ocean to the other side. There he came out of the water after sundown, just as it was beginning to be dark. He went cautiously. He came to houses. "I think my sister's (dead brother's) children must live here. I will go into the sweathouse," he said to himself. He went in the sweathouse and lay down. In the living house everybody was eating supper. "I smell grease," Coyote said. "I should like to go into the house." He picked up the wooden headrest pillows in the sweathouse and sniffed at them. "They smell like grease. Let me bite it." Then he nibbled one; bit again, ate, and ate it up. He ate another and another, until he had eaten them all.[2] Then he ate the ladder in the sweathouse, and nearly ate the center post through.

n. Now the men all came out of the house to go into the sweathouse for the night. As each one entered (and stepped) where the ladder had been, he fell. Coyote thought, "I wish I could get out! Anyhow, I will hide," and he crept into the woodpile. These men were Ducks, and they called lakes their sweathouses. Now they said, "Let us sing." As they sang they named all their lakes, one after the other, in turn, and then Ukunamhanach, the small lake at Orleans. This was where Coyote was born, and when they mentioned it he was sorry. He was sorry for his country and that he could not go back to it. Then they sang about Spohokuran, the little pond at Katimin. Each place the Ducks named in their songs. Then, as Coyote kept crying, they found him. They said, "Every night we go to Ukunamhanach and to the others; we have a boat in which we go. Every day we come back here." Coyote said, "I am sorry (homesick) for Ukunamhanach. I wish you would take me with you. If you take me there I will do something good for you."

o. The Ducks agreed. They put him in their boat and covered him up, telling him, when they started, "Do not look out. If you take off the blanket you will wake up where you are now." "Well, I will not look," said Coyote. "You will hear the boat grating on the gravel. Then you will think, 'I have reached home; we must be nearly there,' but do not look out from under your blanket." So they started. Then Coyote heard the boat grating on the gravel bar. He secretly drew off his blanket to look out. Then he was lying alone in the sweathouse. He lay there and cried. He said, "My sister's (dead brother's) sons will return in the morning." He cried all the time. He wanted so much to get back.

p. The Ducks came home and said, "We will start again this evening." They gave him the same warning. Coyote was weeping for his land, he was so sorry for it. This time he did not look. When they landed, he rolled out of the boat. He did not walk but rolled. He rolled about and stretched and kicked his legs. He said, "My country, my country." He kicked out his foot and pushed the bar with it

2. In Kroeber, Yurok Myths, J5c, Coyote, hiding in Sun and Moon's sweathouse, also eats the headrest pillows, but there they are made of whale meat.—Ed.]

and made it wide and flat. Farther up there is a prairie: there also he rolled and made it flat as it is now. That is Coyote's place: he made it as it is. The small gravel mound was his place particularly: it is never covered by high water.

q. In the morning all the Ducks came to him. Coyote had ceased crying for his country. They all thought, "What will he do for us?" Then he painted them all with semen from under his prepuce. He painted some under their eyes, some down the forehead, some on the throat, some on the cheeks. That is all he did to keep his promise when he said, "I will do something good for you."

INFORMANT G

SWEET WILLIAM OF ISHIPISHI

[*Kroeber in his account of the Katimin world renewal ceremony notes that Sweet William was an old man who was one of several possible ikxarey-arar, or formulists, for the ceremony. Kroeber continues, "One man may officiate for a good many years in succession, but sometimes they relieve each other. The formula or prayers are not bought and sold or transmitted by inheritance from father to son as property is. The older men try out the young ones and when they find one who is interested and has a good memory, they teach him what he needs to know as ikxarey-arar so that the ritual will not die out" (Kroeber and Gifford, World Renewal, UC-AR 13: [no. 1]: 34). Gifford gives Sweet William's Karok name as Ikūv, meaning "silver-gray fox" (ibid.: 26).*

Sweet William's trained memory served him well when he acted as Kroeber's informant; in the Ethnographic Notes, below, K. summarizes the data he obtained from the four origin myths told him by Sweet William. —Ed.]

G1. A'U'ICH, SALMON, AND STURGEON

a. The mountain A'u'ich (Sugar Loaf) at Katimin was a man, an immortal (ikhareya). His children were rocks. He made salmon in a little pool: there he kept them while they were small. When they grew, he turned them into the river; the salmon went down, stayed in the ocean, and when they were larger came upriver again. They were nearly full grown but not quite, so A'u'ich told them to go downriver again. When they came up the next time he made a lifting

68

net and a scoop net and a scaffolding to fish from and everything needed to catch them. "Ukunii," he said.

b. When he caught salmon, he made a net sack (uhuriv)[1] and put them into it, and carried them to the house. And he made a basketry cap (aphan) to be used with the scoop net,[2] and a wooden club with which to kill the salmon (while still) in the net. Then he made the suckers (chamohich) and the ashkuu (hook-fish) in the creeks by causing wood to fall into the streams and turning into these smaller fish.

c. At first he had no knife: he could do nothing with his salmon except to put a whole fish into the fire to cook. Then Fish Hawk (Chukchuk) said, "I am the one who will use rock. I will make a knife of stone." He split cobbles to a sharp edge. Then he cut salmon with them; he cut up suckers too. Then many people came to him. He cut up their fish for them. He gave each one a piece of rock.

d. Then A'u'ich said, "Ukunii," and made sturgeon (ishihikir). He made them small. After a time he looked at them again and they had grown. The ikhareya said to each other, "We shall have sturgeon for food." Then A'u'ich said, "Sturgeon will come back upriver. But when it comes up the river as far as here and people eat it, they will die. Whoever eats it when it is caught here where I made it (at A'u'ich) will die." Then he took ten little sticks, each as long as two joints of a finger, and put them into the river. They swam downstream, and over the fall at Amaikiaram (Ike's Fall).[3] They swam in the large eddy there, around and around. After a while they had turned into sturgeon. Then they grew large. Then A'u'ich told them, "Come upriver as far as this place (Amaikiaram). Do not come farther. If you are caught and eaten here at the mountain, people will die."

e. Sturgeon said, "I will do this. No one will see me, but I will go into the mountains and eat grass and whatever herbs smell good: I

1. [K. has a marginal query: "Also name of a bird in B4?" K.'s B4 is now B3. Bright confirms the present translation. He is unable to identify a uhuriv bird and thinks that an initial consonant was lost by mishearing or miscopying (letter, September 26, 1978).—Ed.]

2. Men wear a woman's cap to protect the head when it steadies this net. See Kroeber, Handbook, pl. 6.

3. "Sturgeon rarely get up Ike's Fall. One was caught in a salmon net above the fall. A man who ate of it died." To the Karok and Yurok, everything has its ordained bounds. Any transgression of these is a portentous evil.

will be like a deer. When they kill me they will treat me like a deer. They will do everything cleanly. They will wash me and cut off my tail and pull out my spinal marrow. They will not just throw my bones outdoors. They will have to keep my bones together, and when they have finished they will have to throw them into the river, and the bones will turn to sturgeon again. They must throw them all in. And they will take my eggs and pound them on a flat rock. The eggs that stick to the rock they will put into the fire and cook and eat them off the rock. The other eggs they will wrap in maple leaves and put them into a hole by the fire, and when they are cooked they will take them out and eat them. But some men will not eat my eggs: they will throw my eggs into the river so that there may be more sturgeon. If only my head is left lying in the house, and my body is hanging up to dry, or has already been eaten, yet if a man that has slept with a woman comes into the house I will know it and my mouth will open of itself. When a man has eaten me he will wash his hands. He will treat me well: he will use a clean (basket) plate for me. If he is not a good man, if he has slept with a woman, he will not be able to take me, but a clean man will take me."

G2. SALMON AND FIRE AT SHAMMAI

G2 and G3 were told by the informant as one narrative. They show some connections, but more repetitions or conflicts of substance, and so I have separated them. G4 is similar in character but is concerned with what is wealth, how it is got, and how it is used, whereas G1-G3 deal with the origin of food and the tools, techniques, and taboos of subsistence, though there are three separate instituters.

•

a. Far upriver at Seiad (Shammai above Happy Camp), an (ikhareya) man thought, "I will make salmon." He took gravel that looked like salmon eggs. When he looked at it again they were fingerlings (tivaak); soon there were many. Then he rolled twine on his thigh to make a net; with this he thought he would catch them. The fish became large and grew to be many. Then he made his net and caught them. Then everyone ate salmon.

b. When human beings first grew they were to have no fire. They were unable to make it and could cook nothing. Then another(?) immortal (ikhareya) said to the people (arar), "You will do like this. Take willow roots, like these, and use them so. As soon as they begin to get hot, fire will come out. Where the smoke comes, put dry grass there." Then they tried (twirling) it and when they saw smoke coming from the wood they laid dry grass there and (it) caught fire. Then all human beings began to do this way. All had fire drills, and whenever they traveled they kept them in their quiver.

c. Then this ikhareya at Shammai gave names to all kinds of salmon. He called them āma (grown salmon), ashkup-an (six inches long); tivaak (finger length); chiipich (eight to nine inches long); (a)shkup-hiit (finger length, shiny); yufkumuru (small salmon). He made it that if a man ate ashkup-hiit after sleeping with a woman, he would be injured. A stick would hurt him, or something else. He made it that when the salmon trout (sha'ap, steelhead?)[1] come upriver and a man eats a fresh one he is injured; and a man who has (recently) buried someone, or a woman, do [does] not even touch it. The ikhareya said to Sha'ap, "I will make you the kind of salmon that he will not touch who does not at all wash his body (a mourner); and that one also will not touch you who wears a hat (a woman). That is the kind of salmon I will make you (to be) when you first come upriver. For a month after you come up no one will yet touch you; but when two months are gone they will touch you and eat you. Such I make you. If anyone thinks, 'It is nothing, I can eat it,' you will kill him. You will think, 'That man thinks I am nothing. I will kill him.' "

d. When he had made the salmon, this ikhareya made what the Indians use: he made the scaffolding to fish from. He made it of long poles. He bruised grapevines with which to tie the poles, and made it all good. He thought, "This they will do when they fish." He laid a plank on the poles to fish from, and on this he put a little stool so that they could sit while they fished. He thought he had made everything. Then after a time he thought, "It is not quite right as I have made it." He had put a screen of brush at his fishing place. He concluded, "It

1. [Bright confirms this translation. A. L. Kroeber and S. A. Barrett, in Fishing Among the Indians of Northwestern California, UC-AR 21:(no. 1):4–5, say that of the five species of Pacific salmon only two regularly frequent the Klamath: *Oncorhynchus tschawytscha*, the king or Chinook, and *O. kisutch*, the coho or silver salmon. "The steelheads are sea-running trouts or Salmonidae, and do not die on spawning. The usual species is *Salmo gairdnerii (irideus)*, the rainbow trout."— Ed.]

is not right like that. It is too far out in the stream. Let it move back a little toward the shore." Then he thought, "It is not right yet. I do not think it will be good if I use brush. I do not want the salmon to go through: I want them to go right to where I am fishing with the net. Let me make something flat and even." So he made a weir ("dam") of sticks and tied them together with pounded twigs (into a mat). Then he thought, "Now I think it is good as I have made it. Now when the people grow they will do that. It is a good way I have made it now." So now the people do like that. When they grew they saw what he had made.[2]

G3. Fish Hawk Invents Implements
[For the background of this version, see the headnote to G2.—Ed.]

•

a. Fish Hawk (or Eagle, Chukchuk)[1] thought of another way to kill salmon. He took a long stick. At the end of it he fastened two small ones. He thought, "I will spear salmon. Let me make that kind. Let me make it so that if a man has no fishing place and he sees salmon he can catch them. If he has no net he will kill them in this way." So now if people own no fishing place they spear salmon. Chukchuk was the one who made it thus.

b. And that was the time when he made a flint knife (yuhirim) with a flint flaker (taharatar). He took a stone[2] point, set it to a stick, and tied it. He thought, "When that knife becomes dull, then they will take up this flaker to make it sharp. That is the way people will do when they come into being. They will use a flint knife and a flaker."

c. Then Fish Eagle made a stone pot (of steatite). He thought, "Let me make a stone pot." He made everything for the people. He arranged how they would treat their acorns, how they would pound them. He made pestles and mortar baskets and a way of cooking. "If

2. Kroeber and Barrett (see n. 1) comment that among the Karok the weir seemingly became "a rather simple type of barrier (little more than a guide fence) running straight across the river" (p. 21).—Ed.]

1. [K. identifies Chukchuk as Osprey in the Ethnographic Notes, p. 87—Ed.]
2. [K. queries "sic?" in his typescript.—Ed.]

they boil acorns, how will they do?'' he thought. Then he thought, "Let me do it with hot rocks (stones). I will put them in the fire." Then he took a cooking basket (aship), and put water into it, cut up fish and put it in, and then put in the hot stones also. Then the water boiled. He thought, "If they put the basket into the fire it would burn. It will not burn when the hot rocks are put inside it. So they will cook (boil) salmon." And now the people do that way.

d. Now they had no spoons. Fish Hawk thought, "How can they eat acorns without a spoon? I will make a spoon of leaves." Then he made it of that. "I do not think it is the right way, the way I have made the spoon. It will not last long. I will make it of wood. I think it will be better." Then he thought, "How shall I make it? I will make it with mussel shell." Then he used mussel shell to cut it with, and made a spoon of wood. Then he thought, "I do not think it is right. That spoon will break easily. Many elk grow on the hills: I will make a spoon of elkhorn. I think it will be better." Then he went on the hill looking for elk antlers. He thought, "I think somewhere I will find horns that have been dropped by elk; from them I can make spoons." He found antlers and brought them down. "Now I will make a spoon. That is the kind to use. That is the kind to make a spoon from with mussel shell." Then the mussel shells broke every little while, and he thought, "Let me make it with white rock." He saw white rock (quartzite) outdoors and cracked some of it: it was very sharp. Then he began to work with it. Now he made the elkhorn spoon right and it was good. Then elkhorn spoons were to be seen: that is why human beings now make them.

e. Then he thought, "Let me make an arrow. Let me make something with which they can hunt and kill." There was no arrow then, nor anything to kill with. So he made an arrow. He took a stick, made a hole through it, and then, putting the arrow through the hole, straightened it. Then he made an arrow point and put it on. He thought, "I will make a bow. I will go on the hill and get wood." He went up, found wood, and came down again. Then he split the wood. He had no knife. He used mussel shell to work the bow and arrow.[3]

3. [Yew was the preferred wood for bows, as it was in many cultures, because of its resiliency. K. says that the bow was "short, broad, and so thin that only the sinew backing kept it from breaking at the first pull. . . . Only that side of the tree which faces away from the river was used for bow wood. . . . The arrow is of *Philadelphus lewisii*, a syringa, foreshafted with a hard wood, and tipped with stone" (Kroeber, Handbook, p. 89).—Ed.]

Then he finished it. He tried to shoot. It shot well. Then he thought, "I will hunt." He killed a deer. After a while he had killed many.

Then he thought, "How will I finish the human beings' bow?" He thought, "I will finish it with that which comes from the back of the deer. I think it will be good if I put deer sinew on the bow. If I put on sinew, I think it will not break." So he made the sinew backing. He made it well. He tried to put it on; but it did not stay on the bow. Then he thought, "How will I put it on the bow so that it will stay?" He thought about that; then he found a way. He thought, "I will do it with salmon skin." So he cleaned a salmon skin and chewed it; he chewed it up thoroughly. Then he took maple leaves and spat on them. He thought, "Let me cook it." He thought, "Now perhaps it will be well to take it out of the fire." He took little sticks to rub the glue on the bow. Then he thought, "Now I will put it on." So he glued the sinew on the bow. He put it all on so that it would not come off. He thought, "And I will tie it on with string. Then it will not come off." Then he thought, "I will dry it." After a while he thought, "I think it must be dry. I will take the string off." Then he took off the string and held the sinew; and he tried to put the bowstring on the bow. He thought, "I think it will be well. It is hard to string the bow." Then he got the bowstring on. He thought, "What I have made is good. When human people grow they will do that way. They will use everything that I use. They will make human bows like this." If he had not made it, there would be no human bows. That is the way they make them now.

G4. DENTALIUM'S CREATION

[In Kroeber's unpublished summaries of the Yurok myths (on file in the Bancroft Library of the University of California, Berkeley), he includes an analysis of the Karok personifications of dentalia. Three of the four versions in his "moderate-sized" Karok myth collection are about Small Dentalium, he says: C2*k*, D8, and F1*a, b* (above). In this last, SD "grows across the ocean, travels upriver, weeping, finally makes the Upriver Ocean with his tears; money shells leap in it; he then returns to where he grew." Kroeber then discusses the present myth, as follows.—Ed.]

G4*a-x* exalts lone or Great Dentalium as a veritable creator. He originates in Upriver Ocean, travels down to the mouth, and returns. He not only makes, decorates, names, and values money shells, but creates human beings, towns, sweathouses, dress, acorns, babies and cradles, wife buying, settlements for killings, gambling, world renewal dances, treasures, and rich men. He probably creates or originates more different specified things in this one story than the Karok counterparts of [Yurok] Wohpekumeu and Pulekukwerek originate in the several versions devoted to them. And he is not associated with them: he operates in solitary majesty. Like Pulekukwerek, he never eats (nor has intercourse, we may suspect). And while he devises utilitarian objects, there is usually an afterthought of wealth: he makes baskets for men, but also treasure baskets; women's fringed dresses but also shells hanging on them; nose perforations for money shells; sweathouses so men can become wealthy; snowshoes so they can sweat and get rich even in winter—everywhere money creeps in.

It will be noted that these four Karok tales that make dentalia into persons are from as many different informants, four out of eight or nine—a higher proportion than among the Yurok.

There seem to be no personifications of either Great Dentalium or Wetska'ak [Yurok Small Dentalium] in the recorded Hupa narratives. I doubt that they would be wholly lacking from a full collection; but they would probably be proportionally few.

●

a. At first there grew in Upriver Ocean (Kahiyurash or Pasurak) (Large) Dentalium Shell (Pisivava). He was alone. After a while he had young; then there came to be many. They continued to grow. Then Dentalium began. He thought, "How will there be money?" He thought, "I will make money from these little shells." Then he made money from them. He made it that long ones were worth so much. Those a little longer were called shishareitiroopaop. Those a little longer still were called pichvava afishni. Those still a little longer were the longest of all: they were called pisivava. Then he made string from fibers in the leaves of small iris. He thought, "I will put them on the cord so that the dentalia will be strung." He put the longest one at the head; the last one he put on was the shortest. That is why people do it that way now.[1] Then he made the small (broken) dentalia (ishpuk atunueich) into necklaces. He thought, "People will hang them on their necks when they assemble to enjoy them-

1. [The Yurok, however, named five sizes of dentalia and strung each size separately (Kroeber, Handbook, p. 23).—Ed.]

selves." So now people do that. Then he made the very small ones, the smallest of all (apmaananich): they were the last to grow. Thus he made all the kinds of dentalia. They grew in the water and swam around.

b. He thought, "How will human beings catch them when they come into existence?" He thought, "Let me make it so that they will know how to take them." Then he made a string; at the end he tied on a grasshopper with a hair he pulled from his head. Then he fished with it in the water for the dentalia to bite. So he thought, "That is how they will catch human beings' money. When people come into existence they will fish for them like this.[2] Thus they will have peoples' money."

c. Then he went downriver, he that made money, and there he made towns. He thought, "There will be people here." Where he made a human settlement, there he put his hairs to turn into people. And he put hair where he had been fishing for dentalia. "Then when people grow they will see those dentalia," he thought. So he went downriver through the whole world. When he had gone on, then at the place where he had made a human village, his hair turned into people. That is from what the people grew: from this man's hair.

d. Then he thought, "It is not right what I have made (for money). I have put nothing on it. It is nothing but (like) a little bone." Now he saw a little snake, red on the belly. Then he drew off its skin from the neck down. He did not kill it, but let it go when he had taken the skin off. Then he pulled that red snakeskin on the dentalia: "Now they look different." He thought, "What I made looks better now." Now people do this. When they catch that snake, they draw off its skin and put it over their money shells.

e. Then he thought, "What I have made is not yet complete. I will make everything. I will make a purse also." Then he made an elkhorn purse. He thought, "That is the place into which they will put their shell money so that it will not break." Then he made another one: he made it of deerskin. He thought, "They will use this kind of purse also." He made another purse. He made it of the shell of the small black water turtle.[3] So now they use these kinds of

2. This account of dentalium catching is of course wholly apocryphal and imaginary.

3. This kind of purse has not been described heretofore, apparently.

purses. When they buy a wife they open the cover, and perhaps there are ten strings of dentalia.

f. No one knew that this man had made money. He looked at it again and thought, "It is not yet quite right the way I have made it." So he put pitch on some of the dentalia. That kind are called ahvahahi wurukur.

g. No one saw what he did; they did not know what he had made. He was a little way from where he had made the people's town; then he wanted to see how it (that thing) looked. He thought, "I will put a little bit of woodpecker crest on its end." So he put (a tiny piece of) woodpecker crest on the end of the dentalium (string). That was the last time he did anything to the dentalia: human beings' money was all made.

h. He continued to go downriver. Wherever he rested he made a town. He made everything that people would use, what we use now: cooking baskets, storage baskets, basket plates. Then he thought, "In what will they keep their valuables? I will make a basket for that." Then he made a storage-shape sipnuk basket.

i. Then he came here, right here (opposite Ishipishi, at Katimin), and called the place isivsanen aach, the middle of the world. He thought, "I will make them so they look pretty. On the deer's ears I will put woodpecker crest and around the legs I will put woodpecker crest, and I will put some too on the deer's mouth." So he made them like that. He thought, "When people dance they will have a hole in their ear(lobe) so that they can hang things in it: they will hang haliotis ornaments (yuhsaraniyuunupus) in their ears. In their nose they will make a hole too, and when they dance they will put a dentalium there so that everyone can see it."[4] That is how he made it.

j. Then he took ahchunupich, the small black (univalve) shells that live in the water (olivellas?). He thought, "People will use that kind. When they make a woman's dress they will put them on it. They will put woodpecker crest on it. That is the kind that women will use."

k. Then he thought, "It is not enough what I have made." He thought, "I will make a circular (sausage-like) headband with wood-

4. Karok practice; Yurok and Hupa pierce the septum and insert a dentalium only after death.

pecker scalps on it (furah iruhap).'' Then he thought, ''Let me make
what they stick up on their heads when they dance the Deerskin
Dance,'' and he made the (triple) thin rods of sinews covered with
woodpecker crest (furah pikivash). He thought, ''Let me also make
what (else) they will put in the same place,'' and he made long eagle
feathers with woodpecker scalps on them (iskahar).

l. Then he thought, ''It is not enough: let me make another.'' He
took buckskin and thought, ''I will make (four to five foot) long ones.
I will put small woodpecker scalps (marar) on them. They will tie
them around their heads and the end will hang down.'' Then he
thought, ''It is not enough. I will make another kind.'' He took
another piece of buckskin. He thought, ''I will put them on differently: I will put them on so that they do not touch.'' Then he put on
large woodpecker scalps a little distance apart.[5] Then he thought,
''They will come here to the middle of the world and they will use the
kind that I have made here. They will use all these at this town to
which I have come.''[6] Then he thought, ''I will make a tortoise shell
as they will use it when they dance.'' The men that carry obsidian
blades in the Deerskin Dance hold a turtle shell (paisharuk) against
the quiver that they carry.[7]

m. Then he decided to go downriver. He came to the mouth:
there he made things too. He made women's dresses and other
things; he made small (clam) shells (shapru) and haliotis (yuhsarani,
abalone) for people to put on women's dresses. Then he said,
''There will also be a dress made of maple bark. If they have no
deerskin, they will make a dress of maple bark.'' And he made oaks
for the people to eat the acorns. When people grew, the acorns
would fall and they would eat them; everything that they would do
he made. He thought, ''If they (shamans) dance in the sweathouse,
they will wear this kind, the dress of maple bark''; and he made it
how people would pound acorns in a mortar basket with a pestle. He
showed them how they would do and they saw it; now they do it that

    5. Ichaprimvar; the scalps are about two inches apart; the band is three and a
half feet long.
    6. None of these woodpecker headdresses are the full, standard, most valuable
forehead bands of large woodpecker scalps that are worn in the Jumping Dance; but
then this is not made at Katimin, which performs the Deerskin Dance. [For the
association of towns with particular dances, see Kroeber, Yurok Myths, A23*l* and
the accompanying notes. For a description of the Katimin dances, see Kroeber and
Gifford, World Renewal, UC-AR 13:(no. 1):19–34.—Ed.]
    7. This use of turtle shell also seems unreported.

way. Then he made shoes (one-piece moccasins). He thought, "They must have shoes too."

n. Then he thought, "What I made is not right": he had made a house. He thought, "How will they get their money? It cannot be that they will all live together. It cannot be that they will all sleep indoors, men and women. I will make a sweathouse, so all the men will sleep in that. They cannot sleep in the house: let them stay in the sweathouse." Then he thought, "I will (make it that they) carry sweathouse wood. If a man brings down wood for the sweathouse, he will get money. Money will like that man. It will like him if he carries wood (ihseira ahup) and cries." So now they do that. A man who carries wood for the sweathouse is always lucky, because it was made that way.

o. Then a heavy snow came. He thought, "How will they go about when there is snow? Let me make snowshoes for them to use." Then he made snowshoes, and they were able to get sweathouse wood even when there was snow. So at last he found how to make the sweathouse and everything to go with it, so that people could get money. He thought, "It is good now, I think. All who (ceremonially) carry sweathouse wood become rich." Before he made the sweathouse, he found that money would not come; so he knew that it was not right. When he had made the sweathouse, he saw many dentalia coming. So he found that he had made it right.

p. Then everyone had no blankets, and nothing to wear except maple-bark dresses. Then he thought, "I will show the people. I will make a baby and a cradle for it." So he made a cradle, and everything with it, complete. He thought, "You people will do this way. You are the ones who will do this when you have a baby." He put the baby into the basket and made everything for it. He cut off its navel string and hung it on the side of the cradle. With it he hung up a dentalium, a piece of the smallest size. He thought, "You will do like this when you have babies. If it is four years and the baby remains (alive), take his navel string up on the hill. Find a little fir on the hill, split it, and put the navel string into it. Leave it there and come back. Do this and the baby will be well. If you do not do it, the baby will not be very strong. It will be too soft, and it may die quickly. But if you do what I am doing, the baby will be well and strong." Now people always do that.

q. This first Dentalium ate nothing. He who made people's

money thought, "That will be their food, money's food, which grows outdoors, whatever kind of brush smells good." He told the people, "Rub in your hands that kind of outdoors brush that smells good; those money dentalia, that is their food. If you do that they will like you, those dentalia, because you rubbed their food on your hands. They will smell it and they will think, 'He has my food,' and they will like you. Do that."

r. And he made it that the baby, when it was first born, would not drink from its mother (for five days). He thought, "It will not do like that, the baby; it can do nothing. Let it eat pine nuts (ahayuush)." Then he worked pine nuts with rocks: he crushed them and put water on. Now they were just like milk. So now they do that way: when a baby is born, they (first) give it that with a mussel shell.

s. Then he thought, "How will they do to get themselves a woman? Let me make it. They will not get her for nothing. I will buy a woman and see how it is." Then he bought a woman. Now he thought, "I think it will be good. You will have to buy them. Then it will be well. If you do not buy the woman you will not have a good name. If you buy a woman you will get a good name. Everyone will know: 'He paid so much.' "

t. Then he thought, "Let me do something else. I do not think it will be right if he who kills a man does not pay for him. If he does that, if he kills a man and does not pay for him, I think that will be wrong. I think he will always have trouble. I will make it that he will pay." Then he made it that they paid for whom they had killed. Then it was well, and he thought, "It is good now," and was satisfied. So now they do that.[8]

u. Then he was thinking, "Let me make gambling. I will try it. I will see how it is." So he told them, "Let me see you gamble." Then they played and bet dentalia, and one man won. Then he thought, "I think this is right. I think this is the way in which some will get money." So now they do that and some people win money. They bet dentalia or woodpecker scalps or any kind of property. He made eleven sticks for the gambling. If they win the eleven they win (the stakes).

v. Then one gambler had lost everything. He lost everything he had in his house, his baskets, his arrows, and all. He had a

8. [For a list of valuations for such payments, see the Ethnographic Notes, p. 99, below.—Ed.]

grandmother. Then he bet her dress and lost it. The last time he lost his grandmother. Then he stopped gambling and cried. He turned into a bird: he would not remain a human being, he was so sorry. He is called Pinnanih-tanakan.[9]

w. When Large Dentalium (Pisivava) got to the mouth of the river, he made dentalia there: so some dentalia come up from downriver. Part of them come from there, and there are rich people there, for he made many valuables there. On coming downriver he had thought at some towns, "A rich man will live here" and he made much wealth there. When he reached the mouth, he listened back upriver. He listened to everything he had made, the dancing and the gambling. Everywhere they were doing that. Then he turned back and saw that everything was good. He went to every town and wherever he had made anything it was good. So he returned to where he had grown.

x. There he thought, "I will make another kind of people here." Then he made those with sharp mouths who eat dentalia. He thought, "You will eat these for food, the meat of dentalia." So he made those that fish for dentalia in the ocean at the upriver end of the world.[10]

9. [K. has a marginal note on his typescript: "Cf. Hupa bird?"—Ed.]
10. [See a similar statement in K.'s Ethnographic Notes, p. 97, below.—Ed.]

MRS. BENNETT

[I have no data on this informant, except that she was living in or near Katimin in 1902 (Kroeber and Gifford, World Renewal, UC-AR 13:[no. 1]: 134). —Ed.]

H1. Mountain Lion Remarries

a. Mountain Lion lived with his mother on Salmon River. Every morning he went out to hunt and in the evening came back carrying deer. Thus he continued to do. Then his mother told him, "Get married." So he married and after a time had a child. All this time his mother said to him, "Never look over the top of the hill." Now he began to think, "Why does she tell me not to look over?" Then again he went to hunt and returned carrying deer. Again he went out. Now he thought, "This time I will look over. Why does she always tell me, 'Do not'?"

b. Then he looked over and was so astonished that his eyes almost were turned out. The valley was full of girls digging roots. He thought, "I will shoot among them." When he shot they all rushed to the arrow, and the one who seized it said, "My husband!" When Mountain Lion came down to them he asked, "Where is my arrow?" Then a girl was standing there carrying a white basket.[1] "This is my wife," he said. Then they went to her home. Now the people there were careless how they handled the deer they ate.

c. Mountain Lion lived there a long time. He stayed there ten

1.[K. queries this word on his typescript.—Ed.]

years. Then he thought, "Oh, my wife and my mother! I left them so long ago! I will go back to them and see them." Then he started. When he arrived at his old home his mother was dragging a flat basket. She was turned to stone. "Oh, my mother! I have returned," he said, but she did not answer. Then he became angry and stabbed her and struck his wife with a stone. Now they turned into rock. "You will be hostile to all," they said. "Everyone will hate you." That is what Mountain Lion did.

His mother and wife are rocks now. The flat basket which his mother was dragging when he arrived she threw into Woollen Creek, where it is now an eddy in the stream.

H2. KINGFISHER SNITCHES FOOD

a. In the morning Kingfisher went to fish. He sang: "Taniminok! Taniminok! Taniminok!" Then he caught a salmon and drew it out and made a fire. He cut off the tail and tossed it to one side. Then he cooked the fish and ate it. When he went home he carried the fish tail. He called out: "Children, a tail!" "Hurrah! Hurrah! Hurrah!" they cried. "Many came to me to beg," he said. Then his family ate the tail.

b. In the morning he went to fish again and sang: "Taniminok! Taniminok! Taniminok!" Again he caught a salmon and drew it out and made a fire and cooked it, but tossed the tail aside. He ate the fish. Then he went home. "Children, a tail!" he cried. "Many came to me and begged." "Hurrah! Hurrah! Hurrah!" they cried.

c. In the morning he went again. Then the children's mother said: "Let us go and see, to make sure that there are many who beg." When they saw him she said: "There he is, fishing." He was singing: "Taniminok! Taniminok! Taniminok!" Then he drew out a fish, made a fire, and threw the tail to one side. Then he cooked the fish and ate it. The woman said: "Come, we will go away. He is eating the salmon alone." Then they returned to the house. They turned over the flat rock on which acorns are pounded and entered the ground.

d. Now he came back. "Children, a tail!" he cried. Nobody answered. "Children, a tail!" he cried again, but no one answered. Then he rushed angrily into the house. The mice laughed at him as he found no one. He drew aside the baskets and threw everything about, but found no one. Now some brush was lying there. Seizing it he said: "Where have my children gone?" "I do not know," said the brush. "Quick! Tell me! Or I will throw you into the fire," he said. Then the brush said: "Well then, they turned over this mortar slab here and entered the ground."

e. Then he jumped in there too and went a long way, until he came to where they were. He struck the youngest and it turned into Woodwardia fern (used for red basket designs). He struck another child and it turned into Xerophyllum (used for white). He struck another and it turned into pine root (used for plain weft). He struck another and it turned into Adiantum fern (used for black designs). Another turned into hazel shoots (basketry warp).[1] Then they said: "You who killed us will also be something else. You will eat mud, but we will sit about in front of people and they will prize us." That is the end of what the "water wren" (literally, "mud-eater") did.

H3. GRASS SNAKE SMOKES

Apshun-munukich (a small yellow snake) was going upstream. "Oh, how pretty the world is!" he said. "I will look at it." Then he sat down. "Well, I will smoke," he thought. Then he puffed out the smoke. He puffed it out and puffed it out. Now he became dizzy. He rushed downhill and uphill and upstream and downstream. Then he rushed under a rock. From there he peeped out. Then he thought, "Oh, is not this a pretty stone lying here? I will taste it. Ah! It tastes good. I will try some more." He continued to taste it until at last he said, "Ah, it tastes bad now." That is the end of what Snake did.

H4. BLUEJAY DOCTORS

a. Ukni! People were living there (the Chipmunks); always they picked hazel nuts,[1] their young girls did. And Bluejay lived there with her daughter's children. "E, we are hungry! A person looking around at the river might see something," she said. Then, after a

1. [For a discussion of basketry materials and techniques, see Lila M. O'Neale, Yurok-Karok Basket Weavers, UC-PAAE 32:(no. 1):1–184.—Ed.]

1. Asis-kunta'pan.

while, ha, something poisonous[2] was lying downstream from her by the river. "Let me look at it! Oh, good!" Then she cooked it: "That's what I like! Let me have lots of my food." So she came home. "Well, get to sleep!" Then (the children) all went to sleep; and Bluejay started out. Then she threw a pebble up (on the roof of Chipmunk, with poison on it to bewitch his people). "Someone is throwing a pebble up on us." Then she ran back home: "Quick! Blow ashes over me!" So they blew them on her.

   b. Soon someone arrived. "I have come for you: one of us is sick." "Ih![3] I cannot go, I am sick myself, very sick."[4] "Dentalia I offer you." "No!" "Well, human treasures."[5] "No." "Well then, one basket of hazel nuts."[6] "Well, yes,[7] I might be able to go for that." So she went, and got there. Now there were two of them dancing.[8] "Up, hanging, I want it! Up, hanging, I want it"[9] (sang Hankit).[10] Then she, another one,[11], said, "She can't do anything: her mouth is too tiny!"[12] Now Bluejay too dances. "Bluejay's crest is pointing up,"[13] she sang. Then she got well, the girl. So Bluejay carried home a basketful. "That is what I like," and she ate her hazelnuts.[14]

   c. After a while they were all gone. So again she threw up a pebble. "E! Someone threw up a pebble!" "Quick, blow ashes over me!" Again someone arrived. "I have come for you." "Oh, I am sick!" "Dentalia I offer you." "No." "Well, once more a basket of nuts." "Well, yes." And she went; there were two of them dancing. "Up, hanging, I want it." But of the one, her mouth was very small.

   2. Kemish, poison, monster, evil. It was a dead dog.
   3. A groan.
   4. Usual procedure of doctors, to raise the fee.
   5. Arara'op: obsidians, woodpecker scalp, deerskins—valuables other than dentalia.
   6. Shunyisa, here translated "wild chestnuts," which would be chinquapin.
   7. Chêm.
   8. Two doctors working themselves into trance. Bluejay and another? Or there were two before her?
   9. A varirīhivan kanapish-shāfsip. [Bright in the Linguistic Index translates the words as "high" and "they pay me a doctor's fee."—Ed.]
   10. A small fish, "with a broad head and a mouth like a frog"; a catfish? [Bright, below, identifies it as a bullhead.—Ed.]
   11. The other one, that is, Bluejay?
   12. Too small to suck out the disease object or "pain," apurōn.
   13. Kāchakāche kiririhurā yan'āh.
   14. Asis-hunta'pan again, but here translated chestnuts. [Cf. n. 1.—Ed.]

"E! She is the one who will extract it."[15] So she danced: "Bluejay's crest is pointing up." "There is no hope," she said. Then the little doctor said, "It is your own pain[16] which you pretend not to know!" So they rushed on her, and killed her, that Bluejay.

H5. Ipashnavan Owl

a. Ipashnavan living there, again in the morning went to hunt. Then he killed his deer and dragged it downhill to the river, and, alighting gently on its antlers, swam it downstream. Now he pulled it out and began to skin it. Then he met a man there: on one side of his face a spring was running down, but down the other side was brush.[1] And that one took the deer: only the kidney he threw at Ipashnavan. So he went home and cooked that kidney and ate it.

b. And in the morning he went hunting again. (Several repetitions of the incident follow.) Then (Coyote) came there. "E, my cousin, here I come! We will kill him who always takes your deer away." So Coyote make an ax[2] with pine gum. Then they went to hunt, and killed a deer, and swam it down again, and drew it ashore and skinned it. Then Coyote ate the fat. Then again that man came and took the deer and threw away the kidney. Then he said, "Load it on my back!" So now Coyote hit him on the head with the ax and killed him. Then he said, "It's all right."[3] Then they cooked. That is the end of what Ipashnavan did.

15. Bluejay will suck the sickness out.
16. Apurōn. She had caused it when she tossed the poisoned pebble on the roof, in order to earn the nuts as fee. [For an explanation of northwest Californian doctors and doctoring, see Spott and Kroeber, Yurok Narratives, UC-PAAE 35:(no. 9):155–157.—Ed.]

---

1. Pa mū-aw apap ū-awash huniva, hash apap ū-pirish huniva.
2. Akôra. The Karok had no hafted axes.
3. Pūya pāiōmah.

ETHNOGRAPHIC NOTES

ETHNOGRAPHY IN FOUR KAROK ORIGIN MYTHS
TOLD BY SWEET WILLIAM

A. Fishing

G1*a*. A'u'ich Mountain (Sugar Loaf) near Katimin makes salmon. When they come upriver grown, he makes lifting net, scoop net, scaffold staging.

G1*b*. He makes net sack (uhuriv) to carry salmon in; *basketry cap* (aphan) to use with scoop net; wooden salmon club. [He also makes suckers and hook-fish.—Ed.]

G1*c*. Fish Hawk (Chukchuk) helps by *splitting cobbles to cut up* salmon and suckers.

G1*d*. A'u'ich makes sturgeon, but ordains that if one eats them at A'u'ich or anywhere above Ike's Fall (Ashanamkarak) he will die.

G1*e*. Sturgeon says he will go to mountains and eat good-smelling herbs and *be like a deer,* and be treated like one, cleanly and with respect. He will be washed, tail cut off, spinal cord pulled out, *bones* not cast about but *put in river* to become sturgeon again; eggs pounded, cooked on flat rock they stick to, or cooked in maple leaves by fire. When Sturgeon's body is hung up to dry, or is already eaten, and only head is left in house, if a man enters after intercourse, Sturgeon's mouth will open. Men will eat Sturgeon off a clean basket plate, treat him respectfully, and *wash hands afterward* (as they do with Deer). And he will be caught only by men who have not been having intercourse.

G2*c*. Shammai (Seiad) immortal makes all kinds of salmon:
āma, grown

87

ashkup-an, 6 inches long
tivaak, finger length
chiipich, 8–9 inches long
ashkup-hiit, finger length, shiny; may not be eaten after inter-
    course
yufkumuru, small salmon
sha'ap, salmon trout, steelhead

For a month after beginning of run, sha'ap may not be eaten fresh,
else will kill eater; nor be touched by women or mourners. (This seems
reference to first-salmon ceremony at Amaikiaram.)

G2*d*. Shammai immortal makes *fishing platform of long poles,
bruised grapevine to lash them, a plank, and a stool.* Then adds a
screen of brush in water, then moves it nearer inshore, then *replaces by
an even (flat) screen or weir of sticks* tied together.

G3*a*. Chukchuk, Fish Hawk (Osprey), makes *salmon harpoon for
people who own no fishing places.*

G3*c*. He devises stone boiling to *boil acorns* and *salmon.*

B. Other Material Culture

G3*d*. Osprey (Chukchuk) tries spoon of leaves, then *cuts* one of
wood by means of *mussel shell.* It breaks easily, so he looks for
dropped elk antlers. These spoons are good, but he breaks many
mussels [in working them], and so he *cracks quartzite to work antlers.*

G3*e*. He straightens arrow in a hole [in a stick], splits bow wood,
works bow and arrow *with mussel shell.* He adds deer back *sinew so
bow won't break,* but it comes off. Then he *chews salmon skin,* spits it
onto maple leaves, *cooks it into glue,* puts it on bow with little stick,
ties sinew on with string, lets dry. It sticks; and bow is (now good and)
hard to string.

C. Social Creations by Pisivava (Largest Dentalium) from Upriver Ocean

[I have somewhat expanded the wording of this list in order to make the
style less telegraphic.—Ed.]

•

G4   *a*. Names sizes of dentalia.
       b. Institutes fishing for dentalia.
       c. Makes towns and people.
       d. Adds snakeskin ornament for dentalia.
       e. Makes purses of elkhorn, deerskin, and water turtle.

 f. Adds pitch decoration to dentalia.

 g. And adds a fluff of woodpecker crest.

 h. Makes sipnuk basket to store wealth in, and other types of baskets.

 i. At Katimin makes decorated deerskins for dancing at this center of the world; and holes in people's ears and nose to put in haliotis and dentalia.

 j. Uses olivella (?) shells to decorate women's dresses.

 k. Makes woodpecker head rings and triple sinew rods, and long eagle feathers decorated with woodpecker crest for the Deerskin Dance.

 l. Makes woodpecker bandoliers, and turtle shell held by obsidian carriers in the dance.

 m. Decorates women's dresses with clamshells or haliotis; ordains dresses of maple bark when they have no buckskin or when they dance in the sweathouse; shows people how to pound acorns with pestle; makes moccasins.

 n. Makes houses and adds sweathouses for men to sleep in separately; tells them how to carry sweathouse wood and be lucky, so money will come.

 o. Makes snowshoes so men can carry sweathouse wood in winter.

 p. Makes cradle, hangs up baby's navel string with small dentalium for four years, then puts string into small split fir, so child will be strong.

 q. Ordains that dentalia eat only fragrant brush, which people should rub on hands.

 r. Orders that for first five days baby is to be fed pine-nut milk from mussel shell.

 s,t. Institutes bride purchase, wergild.

 u. Institutes guessing gambling for eleven counters.

 w. At mouth of river makes dentalia and rich people.

 x. Returns to Upriver Ocean, makes sharpmouths who eat dentalia.

OTHER ETHNOGRAPHIC DATA

[*Most of the data below were collected from Little Ike and Three-Dollar-Bar Billy, according to K.'s jottings in the corners of many of his typescript pages. Billy was the larger contributor.*

 K.'s typescript had these data arranged in seemingly random order; I have regrouped them by subject matter. The headings shown are mine.–Ed.]

Hunting and Fishing

Grizzly bears were hunted with bows after a medicine had been spoken or sung at a little distance. Some men would hunt them alone, so they would have to hit a grizzly a number of times before they killed him. When a grizzly was badly hurt and thought he was going to die, he would run off. Some would growl and run away when the medicine was spoken at them.[1]

For taking deer there is a medicine which is spoken or sung, but for taking salmon there is only vegetable medicine.[2]

When there are many snakes at the river there will be many lamprey eels[3] that night. Otters sometimes get caught in the dip nets at the river.

Lamprey eels were sometimes caught with the hands at Ashanamkarak as they clung to the rocks, being thrown into a little net on a kite-shaped hoop which the gatherer carried in one hand.

When the Karok built a fish weir it ran straight across the river, rather than being V-shaped as among the Yurok. There was no gate or pen in the dam, but the fish were caught on its lower side with dip nets, from scaffolds built out from the dam. A part of the catch was given away. Each man's family dried its own fish. There was no dance or special ritual with such a weir. At present (May 19, 1902), there is said to be a dam at Katimin. The spring salmon are already running.

If several men owned a fishing place jointly, the one who was using it would not have to divide his catch with the other owners, but he generally gave away something to whoever might come. If three men all owned a fishing place together but the largest share of it belonged to *A*, he would use it for perhaps two days and nights beginning in the early afternoon. Then *B* would use it for a day and a night until the early afternoon, and then *C*. Each man kept all the salmon he wanted to, but if the fishing place were good and the salmon running, people might come from some distance away and he usually gave away a good part of his catch. But if the fishing place

---

1. [Gifford's V.30, below, is a medicine for killing bears, though grizzlies are not specifically mentioned in it.—Ed.]

2. [For deer medicines, see Gifford's V.31, V.32, and V.42. G. seemingly did not record a medicine for taking salmon.—Ed.]

3. ["Lampreys, customarily known as eels, much prized . . . for their rich greasiness, . . . ascend the river in great numbers" (Kroeber, Handbook, p. 85).—Ed.]

belonged to *B* and he let *A* fish on it, it was as if *A* were working for him, and the salmon belonged to *B* except for such as he chose to give *A*. If only one salmon was caught, it was divided, the owner getting the larger, head end.

(Contradicting the statement of the previous informant): If a fishing place had two owners, each one got half of the catch no matter who took the salmon. All fishing places have names. I (Ike) once bought a fishing place for $5. I won another one at gambling, betting $5 against it.

Clothing

Mountain lion skins were made into blankets. Deer hides used to sleep on in winter were not bought and sold. Carefully prepared deerskins for wearing were worth from four to seven to ten pieces of shell money, or if the skins were large, a whole string of short shells. An otter skin was worth from four to seven shells.

Dresses of shredded maple bark were worn by women doctors dancing in the sweathouse. They are said not to have been worn by girls at their Adolescence Dance, nor were they worn at work in the rain or brush. Women wore buckskin dresses either in the woods or at work. A buckskin dress that became wet could always be softened again.

Foods

Turtles, frogs, and snakes were not eaten, but lizards sometimes were. They were caught in the hands or with a snare.

The Scott River Indians (Shasta) ate honey with the larvae in it. This is probably bumblebee honey, since it was described as honey in the ground, not honey in trees. The larvae were considered good food.

In times of famine the large yellow slugs might be eaten. It is told by legend how a starving man might make a grab for one, but if he missed, it would escape from him: he was too weak to follow as it crawled off.

Sickness, Death, and Burial

Sickness is of two kinds, according to its cause, either by poison, ipshanmaskarav, or by pains, aratanwa. Pains are kept by certain people who send them into their victims. Such men are called apuruwan, or Indian devil, though this name is also said to be applied to poisoners. Pain sensations are caused by pains moving in one's body; therefore they are aratanwa-tôkên or aratanwa-tanakên, meaning the pain moves.

Pains are about an inch long and pointed at both ends. Some are black and some are red. The apuruwan buys them from the Waiyat [Wiyot] Indians or those of Trinidad or Redwood Creek or the south fork of the Eel River.[1] If he sends them into the heart, his victim dies quickly. Perhaps he is envious of another man's wealth and sends his pains into him. Then that man has to spend much of his wealth in payment of doctors. A doctor who is also apuruwan may make people sick in order to earn fees from them. The apuruwan can call back his pains to himself. Formerly, sometimes when a man was apuruwan he and his whole family might be killed, everybody joining in the extermination so that no settlement was made after the killing.

I do not think pains ever enter bodies voluntarily.[2] They are always sent by someone. A man leaving his house may see a large dog. After this has traveled a little way, it turns into a human being. Then the man who has seen it becomes sick, has a pain in his heart, and soon dies. Doctors often find a pain and suck it out, but they cannot tell who sent it, at any rate, not those here. The doctors at Weitspus, below, are able to tell who caused the sickness.

Poisons are of various kinds. They are made of animals such as frogs or snakes, or partly of a dead human body. They are administered with food; I think there is no other way of giving them to a person. If one eats frog poison, a frog grows in him, and a doctor sometimes will suck out a frog. In the same way, a snake gradually grows in the body from snake poison. If it is still small, a doctor may suck it out. It might then be two inches long, but has the eyes and all the parts of a snake. Poisons do not act immediately, but only after some months does the victim begin to be sick.

Human body poisons consist of flesh or a piece of rotten bone. Those poisons cause the sickness called tuwahara, or "dry," when one becomes very thin and at death is only skin and bones. This disease is incurable and is the same as consumption.

1. [The Hupa, the Chilula, and the Huchnom of the Yuki are the other groups referred to here. For the last, see Kroeber, Languages of the Coast of California North of San Francisco, UC-PAAE 9:(no. 3): 348.—Ed.]

2. [Three-Dollar-Bar Billy is identified as the speaker here.—Ed.]

Another disease due to poisons is ikshupkire. This is caused by deer, and a deer grows in one. A man may get this who has used medicine for deer hunting and slept with a woman, or a woman who has eaten deer meat while menstruating.[3] Such people have a deer growing in their belly which swells out enormously. After the person is dead a deer can be seen inside of him, like showing through the belly. It is spotted like a fawn and sometimes it moves. Then it is clubbed inside the belly until killed, and buried with the man.

While he is still alive the deer eats the man's food; [he] is always hungry. He particularly craves venison. There is a medicine for this illness. This is a plant which is boiled in a basket with hot stones. The sufferer may drink of the water, but usually lies close to the steam.

Another kind of poison is obsidian pounded into a fine powder. This acts quickly; perhaps in two, three, or five days the man is sick. The little particles of the stone have gone all over his body and he has pain everywhere.

For five days after a burial one man stayed by himself in the house and ate separately and used medicine.[4] After the interment, all who were present bathed and then went home, but he made a little fire for himself off to one side. Each evening they built a fire close to the grave. The dead were always buried with their head upriver. If they were buried head downriver, bugs called irupurav would come and cause sickness such as smallpox, irupurav-ākāmsh. This epidemic came here once and many Indians died of it. Now there are mere house pits in all sorts of places where formerly there were houses and towns. A single irupurav would break out on a person's body. The swelling would extend over the whole of that side, then all over the body, and then he would die. Very few ever recovered. They could not bury them all: there were too many. Some were just thrown away into bad places. If they had no friends they might be thrown into the river. My father saw this sickness twice, the first time when he was a small boy.[5]

Dead people go to the sky. Some good people are said to go up the ridge called "Ashauyīkura," which begins to run uphill just

3. [See Gifford's V.32, below.—Ed.]
4. [See Gifford's V.36 and V.37, below, for death purification formulas.—Ed.]
5. [The informant for this paragraph was Little Ike. K. has a marginal query: "Smallpox?"—Ed.]

north of my (Ike's) home. It is not good to dream of walking up this ridge: one will die soon, before a year is out, especially if one dreams of going up that ridge on a big trail.

Widows formerly shortened their hair by burning it with pitch. If the hair blazed up too much, they would clap a hand on it and put it out. Boys sometimes had their hair cut the same way.

Houses and Sweathouses

Living houses appear to average somewhat higher than among the Yurok and Hupa. Some of them had stone platforms along the front. Two-pitch roofs with a longer ridgepole are commoner than among the Yurok. A type not observed among the Yurok is a two-pitch roof with a double ridgepole. The two ridgepoles are close together, and each supports the ends of one set of planks. The common Yurok type of dwelling, with a three-pitch roof supported by two well-separated ridgepoles, is regarded as a rich man's house. For instance, at Katimin, Henry, the owner of the Deerskin Dance, lived in such a house, but Hitcherry, who appears to have been a substantial citizen, lived in a double-ridgepole, two-pitch-roof house.[1]

The native house still standing at Ashanamkarak in 1902 was 20 to 22 feet square. The center of the roof was quite high, 9 to 10 feet above the ground. (The reference to a "center" suggests, without quite proving, that the house had a single ridge and a two-pitch roof.) Some of the roof boards were sawn lumber; others had been split and then trimmed off with an ax or adz. The two plates were beams built[2] 3 inches thick and 14 inches wide. In front they projected a foot or two beyond the wall and roof. The side walls were set or leaned up against these plates. The kind of wood used was not noted, but an adjacent house consisted partly of split-out planks of white cedar. The plates and poles across the front wall were lashed with grapevine. The door was at the right front corner as one faced the house, and to the left of the door the partitioned "woodshed" extended along the inside of the front. There were two ladders into the excavated pit: one at the right front corner and the other at the left rear. The fireplace was framed by five stones.

1. [K. indicates in a marginal jotting that this paragraph was based on observation.—Ed.]

2. [K. on his typescript queries whether this should be "split," as seems likely.—Ed.]

The sweathouse at Ashanamkarak, which was no longer in use in 1902, did not face the river, but upriver. This is contrary to custom; for instance, the sweathouse at Katimin had its door on the side toward the river. But then most of the old town at Ashanamkarak seems to have started[3] downhill and upriver from the sweathouse.

Implements

A pair of snowshoes obtained at Katimin was made of hazel withes and was said to be a little too small for satisfactory use. The cross lashings on snowshoes might be made of strips of skin instead of hazel.

Obsidian does not grow in this country. Chunks of it are brought in. Many men know how to make arrow points, but few know how to make the large dance obsidians. There was one near Orleans who knew how, but he died not long since. Some of the large obsidians and flints were made among us;[1] others were brought in already finished. Arrow points are flaked with a rounded, blunt point with pressure.

Stone mortars have been found along the Salmon River from just below the surface to depths of ten or fifteen feet. They are of a light gray granite-like rock, from 8 to 14 inches high, with nearly flat bottoms, so that they will sit without rocking.

Also turned up in the course of mining are cylinders of smooth dark rock 2 or 3 inches in diameter and 3 or 4 inches long, with flat bases. The Indians do not know what they were used for.

Language and Myths

At Inam and Happy Camp the Karok is spoken a little differently from downriver. Above Happy Camp a different and unintelligible language is spoken. This is called Karakuka.[1]

Willis[2] Creek, on Salmon River, was not inhabited, but people went there to camp and hunt. Further up the Salmon around Grants

---

3. [K. queries whether this should be "sloped."—Ed.]

---

1. [Three-Dollar-Bar Billy is the speaker here.—Ed.]

---

1. [See also Kroeber, Karok Towns, UC-PAAE 35:(no.4):29–38.—Ed.]
2. [K. queries whether this should be Woollen. The name given on modern maps is Wooley Creek.—Ed.]

there were no permanent settlements. In fact, there were no villages until Nordhammer [Nordheimer], where the Salmon Indians began.

The Yurok from Weitspus down were called Yuruk-v-ārar. The corresponding term Karuk-v-ārar, upriver people, is applied to those who live upstream, as at Inam. They, however, would call the people around Katimin Yuruk-v-ārar. More often, the specific place name would be used. Yuruk-v-ārar thus has the double meaning of a fellow Karok who lives downstream from one, and is also a specific tribal designation of the Yurok.

Myths were told in the sweathouse on winter evenings, not for amusement, but by old men who told them to instruct.

At the top of A'u'ich there is a sweathouse of stone where it is lucky to make the smoke of a fire arise.

The duck hawk, called Aikneich or Aikiren, lives just below the top of the summit in a cavity or ridge, the white spot below. If anyone kills this bird he will die in a year. This has happened when a man by mistake has shot one, thinking it was a chicken hawk. That year before leaving, the Aikneich flew around looking at all the towns and houses here and there, and sitting on the houses as if to inspect them.[3]

East of A'u'ich there are ten rock piles, each a few feet high. They were begun by the spirits so that when Indian people came they too would each put a stone on the pile as they passed on their way to Katimin. (The informant[4] said that stones were put on only going to or coming from Katimin, but I failed to note the direction.) Subsequently I[5] inspected these heaps of stones and found them to number eighteen, a large one at Auyuhūmun and seventeen smaller ones at Yuyeich. Auyuhūmun is in the woods south of Katimin in what looks like an ancient stream channel between it and A'u'ich. The pile here is perhaps 30 feet long, 5 by 7 feet broad, and varying from 2 to 5 feet in height. It contains a good many large rocks weighing 25 to 50 pounds.

The 17 smaller heaps are conical and only three or four feet high. They are strewn along both sides of a trail for perhaps 150 yards. This trail leads from Katimin toward the Salmon River and up it past Donahue's. This is some distance from A'u'ich. These heaps con-

---

3. [See E2, above.—Ed.]

4. [Probably Three-Dollar-Bar Billy, cited by K. as the source of many of the preceding and following notes in the original pagination.—Ed.]

5. [Kroeber.—Ed.]

tain mostly small stones, with some large as a man's hand. Most of them have sharp angles and look broken. The surrounding area is rocky and covered with small live oaks.

The informant was surprised that the number of heaps actually was greater than ten, and another informant who came by also assumed them to number ten.

There is water in a bit of a pond at Katimin. At the beginning of the world they were going to make this an ocean, but they changed their mind and made the ocean upriver. This upriver ocean is where money shells come from. They do not come from the ocean to the west. The upriver ocean is to the east, not to the north. People live there who have long, pointed, protruding mouths. With these they suck the meat out of the dentalia, then throw the shells away. That is where our money shells come from.[6]

Music

Flutes, keremia, are made of elder (alder was recorded but was probably a mishearing.) They might be so long as to reach from the fingers nearly to the point of the shoulder.[1] The distance between the stops was measured between the creases of the middle finger and was the same for both intervals. It was said that if the flute was measured like this it would sound good.

The flute was held so that the mouth end was pressed into the corner of the lips, with the instrument extending a little to the left of the player's face. Thus the free edge of the opening was about opposite the middle of the player's mouth.

There are flute songs named after Coyote, Acorn, Lizard, Lamprey Eel, Grizzly Bear, and still others. Snatches of several of these were heard. Some, like the Lizard song, seem more imitative than actually melodic.

It is said that men sometimes played the flute in competition in front of a girl's house and that the best player was supposed to marry her. Endurance of breath appears to have played a large part in these competitions. A man might also play the flute for himself in the sweathouse. To the northeast of Katimin are two mountains who, once upon a time when they were human, played the flute in competition.

6. [The speaker is Three-Dollar-Bar Billy.—Ed.]

---

1. [K. has a marginal notation to check this length.—Ed.]

The Adolescence Dance

At the [Karok] girls' puberty dance they first stand in line in one spot, with the singer in the middle. The girl is in front of the line dancing back and forth. After that the girl is put in the middle and they dance around her clockwise, holding hands. The men do this; the women stand behind them. One man comes into the circle with the girl and takes hold of her from behind, turning her around as they dance. After a while another one replaces him. The last dance of all, just before stopping, is the War Dance, with the young men standing in line. All this is performed out of doors, day and night.

The girl wears a band of bluejay feathers over her forehead and eyes, visor-like, held in place with a basketry cap set on top of it. She also wears a maple-bark dress and carries a rattle of deer hoofs. The men do not wear any of the headdresses of the Deerskin or Jumping dances, except that a few of them may put on headbands of sea-lion teeth, and some carry bows and arrows.

There are three kinds of singing in this dance; the first is a half-singing when they stand in line; the next is round, when they dance in the circle, and the last is the War Dance.

The Ghost Dance

About 25 years ago (actually rather 30)[1] a man announced that if they would dance in a certain way the dead would come back. They were to dance in a circle and paint red, and wear any kind of feathers. The dance could be held anywhere. It would go on all night without sleeping. This dance came from far away, from the direction of Yreka.[2] It first appeared at Happy Camp. Then the people from here at Amaikiaram and Katimin were going upriver to see it, and on returning some of them would want to make it here too. It was a woman who made it here at Katimin. They started in a ring and danced around her. She told them to look down, not up. After a while one after another got out of their minds until there were about twenty. After a time they began to dream of their dead relatives. Camp Creek Sam at Orleans dreamed this way and still believes it. They say he still makes the dance along with his wife.

1. [Thirty years before 1902, or about 1872. See also the account in Kroeber, Handbook, pp. 62–63.—Ed.]

2. [Yreka is about 50 air miles to the northeast, near the Oregon border, in Shasta territory.—Ed.]

Many people came from downriver, even from as far away as Rekvoi at the mouth of the [Klamath] river, carrying their woodpecker beads [bands] and other valuables, but they were told that these treasures would be nothing (disappear) when the dead people came back. Then a big dance was made at Katimin and kept up for a while. After a time the Yurok got tired of it and went home. A few of them started dancing there. The Hupa did not take it up, but the Tolowa did.[3]

Valuations

Killing a man	15 strings of money
Marrying a woman	10 to 15 strings
Half-marriage[1]	A very little, and the young man has to get food for the household
Getting a woman with [illegitimate] child	2 or 3 strings
Buying such a child and taking it home after it is old enough to leave its mother	47 strings
A boat[2]	2 strings of not very good shells

There are certain songs which are sung to sell a basket, cap, or boat at a good price or for buying oneself a boat cheaply. The song would be sung when the basket is first started.

A man wanting to buy a certain boat might first borrow it and then come back and announce that he had broken or damaged it, but the owner was likely to know that this was only a ruse for getting it more cheaply.

Formerly a doctor whose patient died returned the whole of her

---

3. [Stephen Powers in Chapter 3 of his Tribes of California (1877) includes a brief account of the Ghost Dance among the Karok.—Ed.]

---

1. [Kroeber and Waterman in Yurok Marriages, UC-PAAE 35:(no. 1):1, explain that in half-marriage a poor man pays less for his wife and goes to live in or near his father-in-law's house and is more or less under his direction. The children are then regarded as belonging to the wife's family rather than the husband's.—Ed.]

2. [The Yurok (and Tolowa and Wiyot) type of boat was a dugout canoe made from half a redwood log. Boats were sometimes sold to the Karok and Hupa (Kroeber, Handbook, p. 82).—Ed.]

fee. Nowadays she keeps part of it because she has had the time and trouble of the trip, but this is recognized as modern. A doctor refusing a call had to pay all that she was offered in case the patient died; sometimes she was even expected to pay somewhat more. If she did not make settlement she might be killed. But if she had any legitimate reason for not heeding the summons, such as being ill herself, or having to treat another patient, she was not liable for damages.

A doctor is called anekiavan. Doctors are now distinguished, in English, as sucking and herb or root doctors; to these they correspond the terms patunukôt and anavukiyêhe. The former sucked out pains; the latter prepared a medicine and formula. Neither class was regarded as superior. A patient might have one of each kind working on him, or three or four together. Sometimes they might all say that they could do nothing.[3]

On killing a slave, payment is made to his master, not to his relatives. If the slave's owner was a rich man, payment for the slave would be high. In all settlements a wealthy man received greater damages than others for the same hurt.

A man might buy his slave a wife; then the children belonged to him because he had paid for them. Slaves were sold. They worked for their owners and slept in the same house. People became slaves because they were unable to pay damages. If one spoke bad words about a dead man, a fine was due his son. If one had no property to settle with, there was only the choice of slavery or death.[4]

Men who quarreled did not speak. If one of them called across the river to be ferried over, his enemy would go to fetch him if there was no one else available, because whoever refused to ferry a person who called had to pay a fine. In that case, he would put him across without speaking. A person who refused to heed the call to ferry was called tanapāsirip. He was liable to have to pay three, four, five, or six short dentalium shells of the sizes now worth 25 or 50 cents. An enemy was called iniwāshan, and washāratuva meant that people met without speaking.

3. [See also under "Sickness, Death, and Burial," above, and Gifford's Introduction to the formulas, pp. 262–69, below.—Ed.]

4. [Kroeber in his Handbook, pp. 32–33, says that the Yurok too had only debt slavery and that the slave population was small, probably not over one-twentieth of the total. Men were not taken prisoner in war.—Ed.]

Hitcherry and I[5] do not speak. Once when he always had headaches he accused my mother of having poisoned him. He said this to a brother. Then when [my?] relatives offered to settle with him they offered him three strings of dentalia. But Hitcherry refused. So my relatives said, "Well, if he won't take the pay, and wants to be on non-speaking terms, let it be that way." After a while Hitcherry got well again without any treatment.

I[6] once saw a fight in the northern part of Katimin. Two men from there and two from Ishipishi[7] had met to settle a quarrel. When they could not agree, the old man from Ishipishi said, "All right, if you won't settle, let's fight." He had a young man supporting him. One of the two opponents, who was from Orleans,[8] had a gun. The others only had bows. The man with the gun came nearer several times, taking aim, but was shot in the side of the throat. They took out the arrow, but he died a month or two later. His companion was shot in the upper arm. The two men from Ishipishi started to run uphill, evidently fearing the relations or neighbors of their opponents. As they were running, one of them was shot at with a pistol and killed.

Settlement was finally made for this affair, but only after a year or more.

Relations with Neighboring Groups

The Tolowa once came to make war. They crossed the mountains from the west to near Inam and then came down the river, taking away anything they came across. At Katimin the Karok, having had word, assembled, and there was a fight; but not many were killed on either side. When they had all shot away their arrows they stopped fighting. The Tolowa went home over the mountains.

The Scott and Salmon River Indians visited the Karok to arrange their dance, but made no big dance themselves. They were mean, poor, quarrelsome, always shifting residence. Mostly the two groups shot each other on sight. They would kill men and steal women, and return a little later on to steal other women. Usually

5. [Three-Dollar-Bar Billy is the speaker here.—Ed.]
6. [Probably Billy.—Ed.]
7. [Opposite Katimin (G4*i*).—Ed.]
8. [Probably meaning that he was originally from downstream at Orleans (Panamenik) but currently living in Katimin.—Ed.]

they did not settle up for their killings but continued to feud. That is why there are so few of them alive. If they killed a Karok they might settle for him or they might not. Mostly they had nothing to settle with. Anything they owned they would have received as presents.

There used to be some living on the Salmon at Grants, but from Nordhammer [Nordheimer] up, the Salmon Indians did not live. But originally the Indians at Bennett's, or Forks of Salmon, were a different lot and spoke another language. This was so long ago that my father[1] never saw them. Then they all came to take the Scott River language; that is Shasta, and the original language from Forks of Salmon was kept up only at Somerville. The latter, Salmon Indians, make no baskets; if they had any they bought them here on the Klamath. They had a few acorns and dried a little salmon, so little that it would seem to us like none at all. That is because they were always moving here and there. They did not make acorn bread and lived on deer.

The Salmon and Scott River Indians were descended from a woman and a wolf, it was said; that is how the Salmon Indians have long teeth.

The people of Trinity and New River also were vicious. That is how they were called pishpish, yellow jackets. They once attacked Hupa, but they never attacked here. Those of Red Cedar Creek, another fighting lot, were descended from grizzly bears; the Tolowa from dogs. But the Hupa and Yurok were like ourselves, not given to fighting.

The Salmon Indians were so constantly at war that they used to tie deer leg bones to the wrists of their children as they played about. This was so that they could snatch them up and throw them on their backs to run off with them if an attack came.

The Scott and Salmon River Indians had only the girls' Adolescence Dance and the War Dance. They did not make our big dance,[2] nor even the Brush Dance.

Extract from a letter to Mr. A. B. Lewis written by Anna M. Mann of 441 -3d St., Portland, Ore., Feb. 19, 1906:

1. [Little Ike is the speaker here.—Ed.]
2. [Probably the Deerskin Dance is meant. At Katimin it followed the ten-day world renewal ceremony (Kroeber, Handbook, pp. 103–104).—Ed.]

A Mr. Bryson had charge of the Reservation (Smith River)[3] for many years—was greatly respected by all whites and Indians. By and by he left the service and opened a trading post near Fort . . . on the Klamath river near the mouth. A canoe loaded with government stores from C [Crescent?] City to the Fort was lost and several Indians drowned. The Indians demanded pay for the lives lost, and whether the government refused or was too slow I do not remember, but a band murdered Bryson—an innocent party. He was the most prominent party they could reach, so took their revenge on him; but of course the government retaliated.

3. [This would have been in Tolowa territory.—Ed.]

PART II

KAROK
MYTHS
AND
FORMULAS

E. W. GIFFORD

(1939-1942)

INTRODUCTION

The threefold segregation of stories in this paper is on the basis of native classification: myths (pikuava), formulas (anava), and confessions (bigishtu'u).[1] The formulas are usually myths dealing with the immortals or prehuman race (ixkareya) and are used as medicines to accomplish like results today. They do not differ essentially from the myths dealing with the adventures of the immortals, which are not used as medicine formulas.

The confessions recount the doings of earlier members of living families and are believed to have supernatural potency, like the medicine formulas. In other words, they are recounted to achieve results today. Thus, they really constitute recent additions to the stock of medicine formulas, but deal with known human beings and not with the immortals. They are used especially to cure illness in infants and children. Wrongdoing of adults causes illness in infants; confession has potentialities for curing. Even the confessed misdeeds of ancestors are potent for cures today.

1. [After Gifford wrote this draft Introduction, he decided to publish the confessions separately under the title Karok Confessions in the festschrift collection, Miscellanea Paul Rivet, Octogenario Dicata, XXXI Congreso Internacional de Americanistas, Universidad Nacional Autonoma de Mexico, 1958, Vol. I. The confessions are not included in the present volume. Thus Gifford's draft title for the present collection has been changed from "Karok Myths, Formulas, and Confessions" to "Karok Myths and Formulas." Also, his original dates for the manuscript, 1939–1940, have been extended to 1939–1942 to match the information Gifford gives in his section on "Informants," below, and in his typescript for the texts. The myths are indeed dated 1939 and 1940, but some of the formulas are dated 1942.—Ed.]

Informants agreed as to certain ancient beliefs concerning the recounting of myths, though they did not adhere to these in telling me the tales, as my visits were in the summer months. Stories were told during long winter nights by both men and women. Children were instructed in them at that time. Myths were not to be told in summer, lest a snake bite the raconteur. Also, if a story were not told in full, the teller might become hunchbacked. At the close of a story the word "Kupanakanakan," meaning "Finished," was uttered. Sometimes was added the statement: "Mai wasa tineyas," meaning "My back will be straight." Also might be added: "I am not going to be humpbacked." This carried the connotation that the person would not be doubled up with hunger in the winter when food was not abundant. Dreams, likewise, were to be recounted only during the winter months. Months one (istahan) to four constituted the myth-telling period. Month one corresponded roughly with . . .[2]

Every story in the native tongue started with the word "ukni'i," the meaning of which was not learned. "Pinefish su kupanik," "Coyote did," might end a story, preceded by the word "Kupanakanakan," if the main character were Coyote. If the main character were someone else, such as Weasel (anixus), then it would run, "Anixus su kupanik."

Additional prayerlike, conventional utterances sometimes followed the termination of a myth: "Lily bulbs" (taichuka), you must grow quickly in the spring." "Small white flowers" (asmammikan), look downriver for early salmon." The latter utterance too was said to have a connotative reference to the backbone of the raconteur, implying that hunger would not double him up.

Stories were often interspersed with songs sung by the characters. Mary Ike embroidered many of her stories in this fashion, though I recorded none of her songs. Places were constantly named, thus bearing out the localization which is so outstanding a feature of northwest Californian culture; these were especially important in formulas.

Certain absences from the collection of tales should be noted. Thus, although Offield Mountain is the great sacred peak in ceremonies at Katimin in particular, there were no tales concerning the

2. [Sentence unfinished in Gifford's manuscript. Month one began in December, according to Mary Ike in Kroeber and Gifford, World Renewal, UC-AR 13:(no. 1):8–9. There were thirteen months in the Karok calendar.—Ed.]

mountain. Although a flood tale was recounted, no earth-diver episode was known. Dentalium shell money played an important part in Karok life, and yet the money shell was not personified as in the Yurok story about Great Dentalium.[3] The monster-slaying, conspicuous in Yurok and Hupa mythology as the exploits of the leader of the immortals, was attributed to Weasel and Coyote in Karok mythology.

Certain tales were admittedly of foreign origin. Thus, the gambling by Eel and Sucker which resulted in the very bony Sucker's getting all of Eel's bones was said to be either a Yurok or Hupa story, not an original Karok tale.[4]

In 1877 Stephen Powers, in "Tribes of California," pp. 35–40, published four Karok myths, all of which are represented in my recordings of 1939–1942: "How People Got the Bow and Arrow" [II.3] (Powers' "Fable of the Animals"); "Coyote Releases Salmon" [II.10 and II.11] (Powers' "Origin of Salmon"); "How People Got Fire" [II.7 and II.43] (Powers' "Origin of Fire"); and "Coyote Dances with the Stars" [II.50 and II.51] (Powers' "The Coyotes Dancing with the Stars").

E. W. Gifford

3. [But see Kroeber's G4, above.—Ed.]
4. [It is not in Kroeber's Yurok Myths; it may be a Hupa myth.—Ed.]

INFORMANTS

The myths, formulas, and confessions[1] recorded in this collection were obtained chiefly from two women informants: Mrs. Georgia Henry Orcutt[2] of Panamenik, a former village slightly downstream from the modern town of Orleans, Humboldt County, on the Klamath River; and Mrs. Mary Ike, who resided at the site of the former village of Ashanamkarak, downstream from the post office of Somes Bar, Siskiyou County. Mrs. Orcutt was about 70 and Mrs. Ike about 90 in 1942.

From Mrs. Orcutt stories were obtained without an interpreter. She was interviewed in 1940 and 1942. With Mrs. Ike, Mrs. Mamie Offield served as interpreter in 1939, and Mrs. Emily Donahue (Mary Ike's daughter) in 1940 and 1942.

Mrs. Orcutt, though living in a very comfortable modern house, was a firm believer in the "good old days" and frequently bemoaned the spoiling of the old way of life, especially by the products of miscegenation. She contrasted the careful rearing of the children of well-to-do families in the past with present-day bringing-up. To some of the tales she recited she added a moral of the old days. This gives a fine sidelight on her views. Constantly, she thought about the old way of living as drilled into her by her relatives; constantly, she

1. [See n. 1 to Gifford's Introduction, above—Ed.]
2. [Gifford in Kroeber and Gifford, World Renewal, UC-AR 13:(no. 1):132, says that Georgia's first husband was named Henry. After his death she married Ira Orcutt, who was still living at the time G. interviewed her.—Ed.]

contrasted this with the acculturated, and hence to her, demoralized, life of today.[3]

Mary Ike, on the other hand, was a mischievous soul, in whose eyes dwelt a constant twinkle. She had seen enough of life, both of the old and the new, not to take life too seriously. Fear of any supernatural vengeance for imparting information seemed not to trouble her.

A good sidelight on her character and also that of the Karok male shaman who attended her was cast by the events connected with her attack of excessive nose bleeding in 1942. When it proved pretty continuous, her daughter and I went for the shaman. After his diagnosis, he took her to the Indian Service Hospital at Hoopa. She seemed to take both the shaman's dancing and smoking, on the one hand, and the ministrations of the hospital staff, on the other hand, all as a matter of course. She came back from Hoopa feeling much better.[4]

It is perhaps unfortunate that I obtained from no male informant an extensive collection of tales.[5] The tales recorded from informants other than Mrs. Orcutt and Mrs. Ike are few in number.[6] Men knew the tales well enough formerly, as attested by the fact that most of those told by Mrs. Orcutt were learned from the father of Red Cap Tom, a man of Wuppam. Red Cap Tom married Mrs. Orcutt's half-breed [half-] sister. Mrs. Orcutt also learned some stories from

3. [Mrs. Delila Gifford says that E. W. Gifford was the only person whom Georgia Orcutt permitted to smoke in her house (letter to Theodora Kroeber, dated June 13, 1978).—Ed.]

4. [Mrs. Ike lived until January, 1946, to the age of ninety-three or ninety-four (Kroeber and Gifford, World Renewal, p. 132).—Ed.]

5. [Gifford did collect a few myths and formulas from Shan Davis, Sr., whom he describes as "seventy-one in 1939. Born in Scott Valley, Siskiyou County. His mother was a Karok, born at Xavishtimi, a house or section in Katimin. His father was half-white, born of a Karok mother at Ipunvaram, near or part of Ayis. Shan was mother's brother of the late James Davis, district attorney of Siskiyou County" (ibid.). Shan served three times as priest in the world renewal ceremonies at Katimin and gave Gifford a detailed account of the priest's duties (ibid., pp. 19 and 21–26).—Ed.]

6. [Gifford says of Mrs. Mamie Offield, another minor informant, that she was a "widow, residing on the slopes of Offield Mountain. Acted as Gifford's interpreter in 1939. In her own right she was well versed in her people's culture" (ibid, p. 132). Mt. Offield was the sacred mountain at Katimin, focal point of the world renewal ceremony there (ibid., p. 19).—Ed.]

Red Cap Tom himself after his father's death. This collection seems to indicate that probably both sexes knew the tales equally well in former times. An exception to this statement pertains to formulas, which were more or less the secret possessions of formulists but might, however, be imparted to close relatives or sold to others.

E. W. G.

MYTHS

I. TALES OF IMMORTALS AND HUMANS

In recording the first four tales, which are about Widower, I heard the name of the principal character in four different ways: Yadubi'hi, Ixyarukbitsi, and Ixyarukbishii from Mary Ike in 1940, and Cherupbixi'i from Georgia Orcutt, also in 1940. These four names refer to the same character or at least to similar characters.

I.1. GIANT STORY (YADUBI'HI/WIDOWER)

MARY IKE (1940)

a. The giant (Yadubi'hi/Widower)[1] lived way down the river at Aswufam (Martin's Ferry) with his son (Karukbatsakidehi=rich man above all).

They (the people) [there] were making arrows. The son thought (decided) he would go to sleep in a different sweathouse. The people (there had) told him his father was no good because he was chasing women all the time. The people told the giant's son he'd (he had) better make some arrows. He said, "No, I have my own." He took their things and put them in his bag. He took some obsidian and put it

---

1. [Gifford's typescript originally showed this name translated as "Giant"; he changed it in handwriting to "Widower." Kroeber gives Widower's Karok name as Sieruk-pihiriv. For more information on the names appearing in I.1 to I.4 and elsewhere, see William Bright's Linguistic Index, below.—Ed.]

in his bag. When he reached in and pulled (the) material out again, it was already formed into arrowpoints.

b. The people told him to take a smoke. He smoked the pipe with tobacco in it, that they offered him. He said, "Well, I guess I'd better go home." The old giant (Widower) had told his son that, when he got ready to go home, he should tell the people it is (was) snowing outside. The people urged him to stay and make arrowpoints with them.

c. He [the giant/Widower] heard a lot of (many) Steller's Jays outside. The Jays were carrying around hazelnuts. One Jay dropped one through (the) smokehole of the (his) house. It was snowing where the giant (Widower) lived. In order to keep him from running around so much, the people had made it snow there. The Jay had dropped a hazelnut through the smokehole of his (the giant's/ Widower's) house. The giant (He) saw the nut and began to wonder what the people were doing to him. So he went outside and discovered that the snow was only at his house.

d. The son said (to the people), "I think my father has learned what you are doing. He went outside."

e. The son went home. The giant (Widower) said to him, "You'd better get married, so you don't go too far away. I know a girl down here who will make you a good wife."

f. The giant (Widower then) said, "I'll go up the river and look for another woman, so you'll have two wives." The old man (He) set out, but he did not go very far. He came back (returned). The son had already begot(ten) a son and (a) daughter from (by) his first wife.

The old man (Widower) said to his son, "There is a nest up on that tree. You'd better go get it, so as to have pets for the children. Let's go up. I'll show you where it is."

They made a ladder to climb the tree. The old man kept telling the tree to grow higher and higher, until finally it reached the sky. It grew to the sky, so the son could not climb down at once. He knew his father was up to something, so he came down. The old man (Widower) had told him to get married, but he (giant/Widower) was the one who was interested in the women.

g. The son traveled and traveled as he came home. "I wonder what my father is up to," he said.

The giant (Widower) did not want the two small children to see him making love to their mother, so he covered their eyes with mud.

The young man (Karukbatsakidehi) arrived home. He sneaked

up behind his house. He saw his son and daughter, the latter with a basket on her back, coming along. They were holding hand(s) and sort of feeling their way. He (They) heard a woodpecker on the hill. The little boy, giant's (Widower's) grandson, shot an arrow in the direction of the sound. His father was watching him. After he shot, he reached in that direction and bird flew right into his hand. The little boy took the bird and threw it into his little sister's basket. Then the little boy and girl went on, holding hands. He did the same thing again. This time when he reached out for the bird, his father put his hand on his. They both cried.

He [Karukbatsakidehi] said to his son, "I came home. What is the matter with your eyes?" "Grandfather locked our eyes with mud, so we can (could) not see while he is (was) making love to our mother."

h. He (Karukbatsakidehi) took his two children down to (the) river and washed them, cleaned out their eyes. "It is a dirty shame," he said. "That is the reason why he wanted me to get married."

i. He decided to have a dance for (his) two children, because of the shame he felt for what had been done to them. He sent the girl north. He sent the boy south.

He (Widower's son, Karukbatsakidehi) assembled all things for a dance. The giant had already left and gone north. He (the giant's son) took a number of large covered baskets (which he) filled with all sorts of dance ornaments.

j. The giant (Widower) came home, and (the) people told him his son had gathered up all the dance regalia because he was ashamed of what the giant (Widower) had done. Therefore he had sent his children away.

The old giant (Widower) ran around like crazy, look(ing) for things (the dance ornaments), but found none. All he could find was (except) some short dentalia. He put these on the end of a string, and went downstream to (the) mouth of Klamath. There he went up the hill. On the other side of the river he saw his son and grandson going up the hill there.

k. The old man (the giant/Widower) put his cane in the ground with the short dentalia attached to it. He told the money (dentalia) to be sure to holler (shout), "Don't leave me behind! Take me with you!" "Now holler (shout)," he said. "Let me hear you holler (shout)."

The young man (Karukbatsakidehi) and his son heard the cry,

"Don't leave me behind!" The little boy reached over and tried to pull it (the dentalia) off the cane but could not. The giant (Widower) chased him. Both he and his son heard the money talking.

The giant (Widower) caught up with his son and asked, "Why did you take everything away? What will the people play with hereafter?" He opened his son's basket and took the things out and scattered them—money, feather ornaments, white deerskins, etc.

l. The giant (Widower) said, "You can go now, I'm going back." After the giant (Widower) got back to his home at Aswufam, he kept running around, not knowing what to do.

m. One young man at the mouth of the Klamath always sweated. After sweating, he sang and played the mouth flute. He sang and played for luck, as someone had told him to do.

n. When he looked across the river he saw an old woman hobbling around. There were two young girls living next door to the old lady (woman). He saw the old lady (woman) day after day. The young man thought he would go over and eat some seaweed, which the old lady (woman) was drying. In the old lady's (woman's) house was (lay) a sick girl lying. The two young girls said he had come to see the sick girl.

Next day he came again. Then he went to the old lady's (woman's) house and got some more food. They (the two girls) taunted him again about coming to see the sick girl. Then he went back down (to the shore) to go home. He saw two young fellows (men) at the river bank. They said to him, "You'd better go to the Jump(ing) Dance with us tonight. We('ll) let no one see you or bother you."

o. He went (decided to go) with them. When ready to go, the two young girls came down. They were going too. The young man noticed a girl in pretty attire in another boat. Everybody in the boats suggested stopping and smoking. Again he noticed the young girl, who got out and gathered two basketsful of seaweed. They all smoked and then went on again, finally arriving at (the) dance place. (The) dance (was) just starting.

p. Some of the people said they knew there was a stranger present. The two young fellows (men) said, "It is us (we) who are strangers from up the river." They had the young man hidden from view.

There was an old blind man who could not see the dance, but who came to listen. There was a young girl leader who was making fire for the dance. She is (was) the prettily dressed girl already mentioned.

q. They all left and went back. It was the giant's (Widower's) grandson who gave the dance. He said, "I wish that young fellow from the mouth of Klamath would sing me a song." When they got back to Rekwoi, the pretty girl took two baskets out of the boat and went up to the house, as did also the two girls who always teased him (the young man). They went up to their house, too.

r. The young man went up the hill for wood and took a sweat-bath. Then he thought to himself, "Tonight I'll go by myself to that dance. I know where they go." Then he thought he would go eat some more food. He went to the two girls' house first, and they made fun of him again. "You've come over to see that crippled girl," they said.

s. Then he went to the old lady's (woman's) house to eat sea-weed. The young man asked the old lady (woman) who the girl was who was dressed so handsomely the night before. "Don't bother her. She is sick and crippled," the old lady [woman] said. "If you want to marry her, I'll see that she takes a bath and cleans up, but you go outside and wait."

He went out and waited. Meantime the two young girls said, "If you want to go to the dance, go with us tonight." He said he would.

The old lady (woman) said, "Come in. She is all ready." He entered. She was dressed up as he had seen her the night before. She had been only feigning sickness, so no one would bother her.

t. They all went to the dance again. The two young girls went. The young man went with the supposed cripple. They all rested and smoked. They all arrived and danced the Jump(ing) Dance indoors. The two young girls sat in (the) front row, as were (did the) two young men who first took the young man to the dance. One of the young girls said, "I think that young man who plays the flute is singing now." One young man replied, "Sure, that is he. He got married to the crippled girl, and she is making the fire now."[2]

The blind old man who was sitting at the dance was the giant (Widower).

u. When the dance was over they all got ready to go home. When ready someone asked, "Where are the two young girls?" They

2. The reason the young man married the girl was that people always made fun of her.

looked and could see only the two hats the girls had worn. They lifted up the two hats and found only maggots under them. They (The two girls) [had] turned into maggots for shame of making fun of the supposed[ly] cripple[d] girl.[3]

I.2. Story About Ixyarukbitsi, a Giant (Widower)

MARY IKE (1940)

a. He (Ixyarukbitsi/Widower)[1] was running around the world. He did not know where to go. He had a son (sons) who lived on the other side of the ocean (Yuras). They [on the other side] were looking at (watching) the old man running around. They did not know what to do. They had left him on this (the far) side[2] of the ocean. They said, "Let's try to get (him) over to this (our) side of the ocean. If he gets on (comes to) this side, why, we would (shall) not die." On whatever side of the ocean he would stay, there people would not die ([would] be immortal).

b. Ixyarukbitsi was supposed to be kind of crazy after (much attracted to) women. On the other side of the ocean was a big fat woman. "We'll tell that woman to get (entice) him." They said for (told) her to go down by the shore on this side of [the] ocean and lie down so that he could see her legs, and he would come. They were trying to get him on (over to) their side of the ocean.

She went down there and they watched her. (As) they watched, and they seen (saw) him coming. He just looked at her and went on and did not stop. They got (were) fooled. They told her to keep on (continue) lying there. He would come back after a while. (The)

3. Yadubi'hi was the name of the giant. This word means [Across-the-Ocean] Widower." Karuk-batsakidehi was the name of the giant's son. It means [He was] "rich man above all."

---

1. [See headnote preceding tale I.1. Preceding the present tale Gifford's typescript had a headnote, later deleted, which read "Ixyarubitsi=widower; Marukarara=top of mountain person=giant." The latter etymology agrees with Kroeber's D4 for a different myth, but G. did not use Marukarara elsewhere in I.2.—Ed.]

2. [G.'s typescript first had "on this side," later changed to "on the far side" here and below. The original wording shows the seduction episode (*b*) as happening on this side of the ocean rather than across it, and thus it conforms to other Yurok and Karok versions of the Skate story.—Ed.]

second time he came, he kind of slowed up (passed her slowly). The third time, he stopped and lay down with her. She grabbed him and took him over to the other (kept him on her) side of the ocean.

His sons said. "I told you he liked women and that you would get him by lying down there." They were glad. They said, "We will not die now. People will die on the other side."

c. He (Widower) stayed over there a long time, and he got married again (not to the big woman). His wife died and he was (a) widower again. They told him not to go back to Karok country where he belonged. But he told them, "No, I am going to go. I heard they are going to start that ixkareyawen (wenaram)[3] at Amaikiaram. I used to like my wife. Now what am I going to do? Well, I guess I'll just have to cut it (her genitals) off and take it (them) with me. I'm not going to leave it (them here)."

d. He started out carrying his wife's private (genitals) on his back. He passed Aswufam (below Martin's Ferry), where his first wife used to live. He rested there a long time, packing his load.

He reached Panamenik, and went around behind it next to the hills. He did not want to carry his load through the ixkareya village at Panamenik, so he swing (swung) around in back at the foot of the hills. He went around the bluff to (Taxasufkarayuskam) Sandy Bar (opposite Karok village of Taxasufkara).[4] He went on up(stream) and rested above there.

e. He went on up packing his load. When he got to Iputash (Knutsen's ranch, no village there), he was getting pretty warm. He lay down there and went to sleep, putting his load down first. When he woke up (awoke), he heard kind of a noise like flies buzzing around. He looked at his load and found [that] the yellow jackets were eating it. He left it there and went on without it. Right there you can now see a rock full of holes, there beside the road.

f. Then he came (went) on up a ways and rested. He looked up the trail and saw three girls. These girls all had big loads on their backs. (He said,) "Gee (Oh), I like them (those) girls! I'd like to go with them." He made a thin ridge with his hands so he could get close to the girls who were sitting there resting. After that he walked by them and talked to them.

The girls said, "I wonder what (has) happened to us? We were

3. [Translated as the "sacred house" by Kroeber in his A5, above.—Ed.]
4. [G.'s typescript had a deleted note which read "yuskam means 'opposite side or across from.'"—Ed.]

all right a while ago. Now we are so heavy we can't (cannot) walk.''

g. Then he went on up the river to (a) place above Amaikiaram. He heard people hollering some place (shouting) on both sides of [the] river. He looked over. "Oh, so many people down by the river! So many girls!'' They were fixing a dam for salmon. The one making the dam was (an) ixkareya named Kakana'apmana (mouth on/at both ends).

He (Ixyarukbitsi) told the ixkareya to have big trees out in front, so as to have the dam in the shade all the time.[5] "When the trees get old, don't bother about them; others will grow in their places,'' the giant Widower (Ixyarukbitsi) said.

The girls on the Ashanamkarak side (of the river) did not like him and would not answer him, but the girls on the Amaikiaram side talked with him. He made the flat place on the Amaikiaram side because the girls were nice to him. On the Ashanamkarak side he left it rough because the girls ignored him.

h. Then he went on up the west side of (the) river, to above the (present) Forest Service bridge. He look down and he saw everybody working there making a dam at the falls at Katimin. The same people who had been making (the) dam at Amaikiaram were making it (one) at Katimin. The girls were all nice to him there. He made a rock pile above the bridge for people to make wishes, and one on A'u'ich, now spoiled by (the) road. When people put (a) stick or stone on (it), they wish (pray): "May I live a long time.'' The people going back and forth to ceremonies and dances make a wish on (pray at) that rock pile, putting (a) stick, stone, or anything they wish [like] on it.

i. At Katimin he made the place kind of nice and flat, because some of the girls went with him. When the dam was finished (completed) according to his advice and he had finished making Katimin nice, he went on up the river. He was now traveling on (the) east side of (the) river.

At Cottage Grove he made a wishing (another prayer) rock pile. He went on. He made all the flat places wherever the girls talked nicely to him.

j. He went way up to Hamburg (Imvirakam), where non-Karok live. He said, "Well, you'd better make (a) fish dam.'' When they

5. The tree on the huge rock opposite Ashanamkarak is now the only one left. Mary saw others formerly.

finished he went on, finally arriving at Etna in Scott Valley.[6] There he fell in love with one girl. She liked him, so he made the valley.

Then he went up Yreka Mountain. "Hereafter people will think about me. I've done lots (much), made everything. Whatever they talk about, they'll mention my name." He was sitting on top of Yreka Mountain, facing this way (toward Katimin). He turned into rock there.

I.3. STORY ABOUT CHERUPBIXI'I (WIDOWER)

GEORGIA ORCUTT (1940)

a. (A) man from across (the) ocean came with (a boy) baby, which he put in [the] ground at Panamenik. Nobody saw him do it. Tiger lily (lilies) (?) called xavits[1] grew back of Panamenik, and women (two sisters) went frequently to dig (them). They were cooked before eating. In digging these they found the baby in the ground. (The) younger sister said to [the] older, "Don't take that baby home. I don't like it." But (the) older one took (the) baby home and raised it. After a while he grew up. His name was Cherupbixi'i.[2]

b. Afterwards as (the) boy grew up, he was always playing on (at the) river making boats. He kept fixing them over. Nobody showed him how to make them. He learned by himself.

After a while grew up that boy (the boy grew up) to manhood. He was always thinking about what his foster mother's younger sister had advised as to throwing him away. He did not like that.

c. That boy make (made a) boat because he know (knew there was) going to be water all over [the] world. He knew it would rain and water would cover everything. He told his (foster) mother, "You'd better get in (the) boat. There is going to be water all over.

6. [On Etna, see II.38, n. 1, below.—Ed.]

1. [Schenck and Gifford, *Karok Ethnobotany,* UC-AR 13:(no. 6):380, identify xavin as *Calochortus pulchellus,* golden lantern. In one Yurok version of the myth, Kroeber's J8, the magical baby is found when brodiaea bulbs are dug. Four of the five Yurok versions are also set in Karok Panamenik, called Ko'men by the Yurok.—Ed.]

2. [See headnote preceding tale I.1.—Ed.] Georgia thought his father was named the same way. The unmarried woman who adopted the baby was called Panamenik ifabi = Panamenik girl.

We can't stay here. We'll have to move, because there is going to be water all over.'' The girl who [had] wanted to throw him away said, "I'm going too.''

"No,'' he said, "you can't go with me. You did not like me. You wanted to throw me away. You'll have to stay.''

d. They filled the boat with provisions. The water came. Just the young man and his (foster) mother entered the boat. All the rest remained and were drowned. Lots of (Many) birds flew over the face of the water, but could find no place to alight, as (the) whole earth was covered.

e. After a while the waters subsided. The young man and his mother brought their boat back to Panamenik, but everything look like (was covered with) mud all over. He said, "Mother, this is your home. I am going down across the ocean to where my father is. Now I am going, but this place here is my home and it is always to be called Cherubipbixi muwapuits.'' Then he got in his boat and went home across the ocean.

I.4. Story About Fertility Rock at Forks of Salmon

MARY IKE (1940)

a. Ixyarukbishii moas is [the] name of (the) rock.[1]

The giant (Widower) thought he would take a trip to Forks of Salmon. On his way up he heard someone (yell) from across the river. He answered, "You stay there. Don't come over, because people over here are sick.'' The one who hollered (shouted) over was Measles (Iduparaup). Then he (the giant/Widower) went up over the hill; he sat down to take a rest. Then he went on. Then he went over another hill. Again he rested on top of the hill. He heard someone talking above him up the ridge. The voice said, "Come up here and we'll play.''

He started to leave, but the other called again: "Come on, we'll play.'' Then Giant got mad (Widower became angry) and went to see what was wanted. He looked around and could see nothing except some little insects which live on trees. They were getting manzanita berries. He picked up a lot of the insects and put (them)

1. Ixyarukbishii was the name of the giant (Widower); mo, his; as, rock. [See also headnote preceding tale I.1.—Ed.]

on (the) end of his penis. He said, "This is what you get for teasing me." Then he went down the hill, mad (angry).

b. He went way up another hill. Then he descended the other side. He wanted to go to toilet (urinate), but he did not stop. He went on anyway. He arrived at Samnannax.[2] He went on up the river a little way and sat down with his legs downhill. His penis was hurting him. He got white quartz flakes and cut off his penis. He threw it in (the) river. That is the rock that is sticking up there now.

c. Then he went on up the river. He went up to (the) fish dam. He stopped, looked down (the) river, and saw a lot of (many) eels. He thought, "I'll catch some eels and cook them. I'm getting hungry." So he got some eels and went uphill a little ways and built a big fire and cooked (the) eels and ate.

d. Then he thought, "I'll go back. I'll not go any further." While he was eating he heard someone laughing up on the hill a little ways. He heard someone say, "He ought to be ashamed of himself. He is eating his own penis." They kept teasing him about his eating his own penis. He thought, "It must be so, because I cut it off and threw it in the river." It kind of (The thought) made him sick.

He said, "Hereafter people will eat this eel. I ate it, and everybody else must eat it." He returned downriver. He saw many eels. Someone told him, "You'd better go down and get some eels." He replied, "No, I've had some."

e. So he returned, following the same trail back. He took a rest on top of a hill and sang a song. (Song) He sang about what he had done with his penis. He climbed another little (hill) and sat looking back upstream. Then he went down to Red Cap (Wuppam). He was hollering (shouting) on top of the hill, saying he could see where the people (Indians) were beginning to appear.[3]

I.5. STORY ABOUT LOST BOY FRIEND

GEORGIA ORCUTT (1940)

a. A girl was staying far up the Klamath. She knew Indians were coming. "I want to go with (my) young man and stay with him." [But] she lost the young man. She never knew which way he went.

2. "Where the store is now at Forks of Salmon."
3. See II.5 for story of the Fertility Rock at Orleans.

She looked all over for him, all over. She looked all along the Klamath to the ocean. She could find him no place.

b. "It will be too bad if I have to stay alone, if I can't find that boy. Where will I find him? I can't find him no (any) place. I'm going up to the sky to look for him."

She went up there. She look[ed] all over, but could not find him in the sky. Afterwards she came down halfway and heard (a) dog barking. She say (said) to herself, "The Indians are coming." The ixkareya had no dogs. "We'll have to go away now, for the Indians are coming."

c. When she came down she saw ixkareya people standing right there. "Where did you come from?" they asked. "Did you lose your boy friend?" "Yes," she said, "I lost him."

"What (have) you been doing? Did you run away?" they asked her. "It looks like I lost him," she said every little while.

d. A woman said to her, "I knew you were going to come down from (the) sky. I know where that man is now. You go down to Sufip (Rekwoi), and you can stand right there and you can look over and see that man on (the) other side of (the) ocean."

Afterwards the wind was blowing. When (the) wind blowing (blew), it looks (looked) like the man was jumping into (a) boat. The girl is standing (stood) at (the) mouth of (the) river and see (saw) the boat. She knew that (the) boat (was) coming over.

When the boy got out (to sea) in (the) boat he could see that girl. When the boat landed, the girl say (said), "I've been looking for you all over. I can't (could not) find you."

e. The young man said, "Now we have to go. We have to go where we can stay in Kayuras (upstream ocean), because we came from up there. Beginning different people (Different people are beginning) to come. We have to go."

They walked up the Klamath, stopping at various places overnight. When they arrived at Kayuras, the girl said, "I've got a good medicine, because I found my boy friend. I have to stay with him, because turn out different people (have come) now (the Indians)." They stay(ed) at Kayuras. The girl is called Kayuras ifabi; the man is called Kayuras afishi.[1]

1. [Kayuras girl and Kayuras young man.—Ed.]

I.6. Ixkareya Story

GEORGIA ORCUTT (1940)

a. (A) man and wife (were) living at Panamenik. All the womenfolks went back toward (the) hills to dig Indian potatoes.[1] The man was left alone, as his wife went with (the) other women. When the woman came home she was empty-handed, though [the] other women brought plenty. They dug Indian potatoes with digging sticks.

That man said, "Why [do] you never bring anything home with you? You got nothing." The man made a chisel end to his wife's digging stick. The others were pointed. She tried this one, but still she got nothing. When she came home she had no potatoes. "Why (do) you never bring home anything, when the other women bring lots (many) of them?" the man asked.

So the man made the end of the digging stick hooked for her to dig with, because she never got anything with (the) regular digging stick or (the) chisel-ended one. "Why [do] you never get nothing [anything]? The others pack them down, but you never get nothing (a thing)."

b. Next day when she went with the womenfolk to get bulbs, she still brought back none. The man thought, "What's the matter? I'm going to look and see what is the matter."

The man went up there and saw all the women digging potatoes. His wife was sitting there calling all kinds of names all day long. She was not digging. She walked around and watched [the] others dig and talked to them, but never got anything herself. She did not see her husband there. She just walked around and looked at (the) others and called out all kinds of names.

c. When she got home, he said, "Why (do) you never get nothing (anything)?" He did not say he was up there. She did not answer him. Then he asked the other women what was (the) matter with his wife. They said, "She walks around and talks all day, but never digs. She can tell anything she thinks about. That's the kind of wife you have. She will be that way all her life."

1. [Indian potatoes are taiyiis, brodiaea bulbs (see II.46, n. 2 below).—Ed.]

The bird tulukwichi (a yellow-breasted bird, almost as big as a flicker) was what the woman turned into.[2]

I.7. Across-Ocean Ixkareya

GEORGIA ORCUTT (1940)

a. In (On the) lower Klamath they never made Indian money. They made it only in (on the) upper Klamath toward Kahayuras.[1] That man pack(ed) him down sweathouse wood to make (a) fire in (the) sweathouse. He made that iris-fiber string for stringing Indian money. All day he made that string. In the evening he would go up and pack wood to make (the) fire in (the) sweathouse; in the morning too. All day he would make string. He put his string in his sukrif.[2]

b. Then he started to go upriver carrying his sukrif full of string.

A girl at Panamenik knew that he was coming. She said, "A Yurok boy[3] has been making string and is coming upriver with his sukrif full, on his way to Kahayuras to make money. He never looks at girls at any time, because he does not want to have bad luck."

c. Afterwards when he come up (As he came upstream) he come (went) down to (the) river at (the little bluff called) Xaipanipa (upstream from Camp Creek and visible from Georgia's house). Then he came (went) to (the) oak tree below Georgia's house. He heard someone singing some place. He said, "I'm going to listen to the singing. It sounds awful (very) nice." The girls were singing to make bad luck for that man.

He said, "Now I've been working hard, but I can't go up there, I can't make money." The song was making bad luck for him. "It will always be that way. I was working hard. Now they have spoiled my luck." He meant it would be [the] same way with others.

---

2. Georgia says it seems almost as though she can tell what the bird says when it talks. [Bright in the Linguistic Index identifies it as the meadowlark.—Ed.]

---

1. [The upstream ocean (I.5*e*). Gifford spells the name as Kahayuras here, but usually spells it as Kayuras in both Georgia's and Mary's stories. See II.25, n. 3 below.—Ed.]

2. [A woven bag carried by men, according to II.1, below.—Ed.]

3. [Perhaps meaning not an actual Yurok speaker, but a Karok boy who lived downstream from the girl's home at Panamenik, as K. explains in his Handbook, pp. 98–99.—Ed.]

I.8. Ixkareya Story

GEORGIA ORCUTT (1940)

Doctor Nancy, an eim (shaman) of Katimin, told Georgia this story.

•

a. Two womenfolks [were] staying at [a] house in Amaikiaram near the sweathouse. They said [to each other], "It looks as if we should try to be somebody." Look like after a while [It seemed that] somebody was trying to make bad luck for those two women. It look as though the other people in Amaikiaram were making bad luck for these two women.

b. After a while the two women said, "Let's get away from here." "Which way shall we go?" one asked. "We'll go over on the 'east' side of the river. The people walking on the 'west' side can look over and see us there." They discussed how they would dress.

They dressed in nice new dress[es] and ornaments. One asked the other, "What are we going to do?" The other one said, "When people see us, they'll feel sorry."

c. They crossed the river and went upslope. When they sat down, they sang. People could hear them singing and asked, "Where is the singing coming from?" "They'll always remember when they look up and see us." The two women turned into rock—two white rocks on [the] slope high up opposite Amaikiaram. The rocks were called Makēs ("back up the hill").

I.9. Story About Sanhiluvra, an Ixkareya Girl

MARY IKE (1940)

[It is most interesting to compare this version of the Loon Woman story with Kroeber's A8, above, told by Mary Ike's husband nearly forty years earlier. Few details have been lost with the passage of time, but the later ending is much attenuated.—Ed.]

•

a. Sanhiluvra, her mother, her father, and two grown (older) brothers lived together. She had a little (younger) brother (named Kumats), whom she never saw (had never seen). She wondered about him, where he is (was). She finally asked her mother, and she replied, "I don't know; he went some place."

One night Sanhiluvra made (prepared) a lot of acorns; (she) pounded it (them) up (into meal). She made a load of things for her basket: acorns, fish, etc. Her father said, "I'm awfully sorry. I think she has seen the boy."

b. The girl said, "I'd like to get married. You can't take care of me. I'd like to have a man to take care of me. I'm going some place." The old lady said, "I'll go with you." The girl said, "You can't say much for me." The old man (Her father) said, "I'll go with you." The girl said, "You can't do much for me. You can't go with me." The oldest brother said, "I'll go with you." The girl said, "You can't go. You can't talk." The other (older) brother said, "I'll go with you. Let me go." "No, you can't go. You can't talk."

The old lady said, "I think she seen (saw) her little (younger) brother." The girl jumped up and pulled her brother (him) out from behind some baskets. She said, "You go with me."

c. The little (younger) brother went with her. On the way the girl prayed: "I wish it would rain. Let it get dark." It started to rain, so they started to build (built) a house (shelter) right there. The little boy (younger brother) was kind of scared (was afraid) of her. They just put madrone bark over (the spot) where they were sleeping (to sleep).

The reason she had never seen her little (younger) brother before was because he was married in the sky and had two kids (children) there, a boy and a girl.

d. She kept praying that it would rain on her brother, and she moved the bark "boards" so it would rain on him. He was scared (afraid) of her when it rained on him. Then she went over and picked him up and put him behind her so he would not get wet. She told him, "Put your arms around me; snuggle close to me." The girl went to sleep and snored. She had a stick of wood for (a) pillow. She had made him put his legs between hers. While she slept he put a stick of wood in place of his legs. Then he got up and ran home.

e. He got home. He made a ladder up to the sky. He said, "Let's all leave. She is going to kill us all." The girl had ten quivers (akawaki) for arrows. They all climbed up to the sky. They put the old lady in the lead and told her not to look back. The girl returned and started hollering (shouting), "Don't leave me! Wait for me!"

f. The old lady said, "I feel sorry for my daughter. I don't want to leave her." The boys told her not to look back. The girl was running around, singing. They had (There was) a big fire under the ladder, and the old lady looked back and they all fell back down into this fire.

g. The girl had one tinwaap (acorn winnower). Her family was all burning. She kept knocking the ashes back (with it), so they would not fly away. She sang as she did this: "Sanhiluvra fell in love with her own brother!" One piece of ashes got away, the ashes of her little brother. It went clear up to the sky, where there was a big lake. On the shores grew a kind of tall grass (bunch grass?).

h. The little brother's wife in the sky asked her children, "Did you hear somebody singing some place?" "Yes, we heard it all the morning." The woman said, "It sounds like Kumats" (the name of the little brother). The ashes were singing a lucky song: "Kumats, here I am!"

His wife and children took a leaf and put grease on it and put the ashes on it. Then (they) got some earth and put the leaf and ashes on the earth. They covered it.

i. Pretty soon they said, "Let's look." It had turned into a human being. Then he (Kumats) told his wife what had happened. Then he returned to earth to see his sister. He found her pounding acorns. She was pounding her parents' and brothers' bones. She said (was saying), "This is my mother and this is my father." He did not let her see him.

j. Then he went back up to [the] sky. He told his kids (children), "You'd better go down and see her, but don't let her see you. She is kind of crazy. Sneak up on her." The two went down and peered in through the smoke hole. She was grinding bones. She had stone mauls for ear pendants. She saw their shadows and said, "Oh, someone is bothering me. Maybe I'll do this way," and she moved around a bit. Pretty soon she got mad (angry) and went outside with (her) bow and arrows. She saw the boy and girl. Their father had told them not to talk to her. "My niece and my nephew, come in! I am so glad to see you," she said. They went in. They talked with her. Then they left.

Sanhiluvra ran outside and said, "Whenever you get mad (angry), you sing my song." She sang it for them: "Sanhiluvra fell in love with her own brother."

I.10. ORIGIN OF BRUSH DANCE

GEORGIA ORCUTT (1940)

a. [The] Brush Dance [is] arara ivwuna. (The) Brush Dance doctor is called pe'sara and is always a woman. (This is the) story of how (the) ixkareya first make (made) it.

A child was crying all the time. After a while (the) ixkareya said, "What's the matter with that baby? ('') He always cries (cried). Can't (They could not) stop it. They make [made] medicine, but it never [did not] stop. They never make (made the) right kind of medicine."

b. "You better try to make medicine." "Yes, maybe I can stop it," one said. "All right, maybe (we) can have that kind." She was going to try. She never drink (She drank no) water all day; she never eat (she fasted) all day. "In the evening I can go up with a girl and get (the) medicine."

Then they went for (the) medicine. All the people waited, sitting down outside the house where the mother and baby were sitting down by (the) fire inside the house.

c. The medicine woman came back, packing [the] medicine. They were [It was] spruce twigs peeled below, but with leaves at (the) top. The medicine woman and the xaxanan ("go with," girl companion) go (went) inside (the) house and sit (sat) down. They take (took a) slab mortar, basket hopper, and pestle and mashed it (the medicine) on (the) mortar. (The) medicine woman sang as she mashed it. Then she got two acorn cooking baskets. She put in two of them in that medicine (the medicine in both of them). Then she put them away. After all (was) fixed, she put (more) medicine in the baskets.

d. After a while she got (a) brush (cylindrical, tied with buckskin and called tetaxnehan, about one foot long). She got (a) string and tied (it) to the brush.

Then the medicine woman stand (stood) up. When she stand [stood] up by (the) fire in (the) square rock (stone) fire pit (box), she stuck her cane in (the) ground at one corner of (the) fire pit (box). Then she put on (her) wood basket with (the) pack strap over her head. She danced around (the) fireplace to (the) left, dragging (the) brush by (the) string in (her) left hand and planting her cane at each corner of (the) firepit, starting with (the) one nearest [the] entrance of (the) house.

After a while she started (again) at (the) same corner of (the) house pit, packing (the) basket and dragging (the) brush, dancing around to her starting point. Then (the) menfolks and girls from outside came in and danced on (the) house platform.

The medicine woman put hot rocks (stones) in (the) baskets of medicine and then steamed the baby by covering it and (the) baskets with (a) deer hide. (The) medicine woman sat down while (the) girls and boys danced. Sometimes she got up and danced with her cane.

Menfolks (The men) go (went) outside to rest a little while. Then (they) came in again and danced all night. In (the) morning (about 4 A.M.) they [the men] put on all the nice ornaments and paint. When morning came they quit, and everyone went out. The girl assistant held up the two baskets of medicine and danced with them when (the) men were dancing. She holds (held) each [basket] in (the) palm of (her) hand, dancing alone near [the] fire.

e. When all went out, after a time the men came in (returned) and played (the) many-stick game (stidjwuni),[1] so everyone (was) happy and (the) baby (would) be sick no more. (On the) first night they danced only a portion of (the) night. The second night they danced all night.

f. In the (Next) morning the people danced (the) Jump(ing) Dance[2] without feathers inside the house. (The) roof (was) taken off by someone who is (was) directed to do so by (the) medicine woman.

g. After a time the medicine woman put (the) brush on (the) end of (her) cane and passed (it) to (a) man on (the) roof beams. Medicine woman (She) told everyone to stand up while she passed her cane and brush to (the) man on (the) roof. As (the) cane is (was) being passed up, everyone shouted that (the) sickness was going out with the cane, not to return. This was done at (the) last.

[The] medicine woman has (had) eaten nothing all day. Only

---

1. [For a description of the many-stick game, and a different name for it in Karok, see V.24, below.—Ed.]

2. [The Jumping Dance was one of the two great ritual dances of the Karok, the other being the Deerskin Dance. For details, see Kroeber and Gifford, World Renewal, UC-AR 13:(no. 1), esp. pp. 40–47.—Ed.]

girls and men, no married women, danced. It would be spoiled if married women danced it.[3]

I.11. Story About Chinas Rock

GEORGIA ORCUTT (1940)

A little boy cried all the time, and finally his mother struck him and said, "Go outside. I don't like you always crying in [the] house here." He went out. After a time she did not hear him crying. He was going away. He climbed up to (Chinas) Rock. His mother came (went) after him. He turned to (into a) rock, which used to be perched on top of Chinas Rock, but which some white man pushed off or destroyed.

Moral: One should never order a crying child out and shove or slap him toward the door, for something may come and get him. If one must slap, slap downward, not sidewise. A mother must never say to her child, "I don't like you," for somebody will come and take it [him] (as in death).

I.12. Deer Story

GEORGIA ORCUTT (1940)

a. One ixkareya man named Witcha stayed at Wītcha (about 2½ miles up from Orleans Bridge on the east side of the Klamath). He hunted for deer all the time, but he never got nothing (any). Every night (he) come (came) home empty-handed. After a while he felt too bad, because he never saw deer or anything. After a while he got (became) half-crazy, because he hunted and never saw anything.

b. His wife always stayed home. Other ixkareya heard something stamping in (the) open place when he come [came] home. Kind of crazy, that man. (That man was sort of crazy.) He cut off one of his legs and was packing it. When he came in, his wife was scared to see him with only one leg. The woman went outside and told the other people, "I think there is going to be something. It looks as though my husband is kind of crazy (yuniyon)."

3. [See also III.15, n. 1, below, on the Brush Dance.—Ed.]

After a while his nephew (brother's son) came in. The woman said to him, "We'll have to do something. We'll have to stop him because I think he is going to turn out (into) something."

The man with one leg was dancing outside near (the) sweat-house. He told his nephew, "My nephew, I am dancing now." When singing, he was saying this: "My nephew, I dance right here. I am dancing here."

c. The woman and the man's nephew can't (could) do nothing. The one-legged man sang, "I'm going to move up to Assawei ("rocks stick on," two peaks on a high ridge visible upstream from Georgia's house below Orleans). That is going to be my home." He moved up there, leaving his wife behind. "If you folks want to kill deer, you must sing my song. I never see (saw) [a] deer, so that is why I move(d) up there. Deer will like it when I move up there. Now I'm going to move up there. If you know my song, you will kill deer."

The folks never answered him. It looked like (seemed that) he was crazy when he went up there. They can't (could) do nothing with him. They gave up. Very few people know this good luck song for deer.

I.13. FIRST MENSES STORY

GEORGIA ORCUTT (1940)

The following story was told to Georgia by her mother's mother, a Forks of Salmon woman.

•

a. An ixkareya girl got (was having) her first menses. Her mother warned her, "Don't touch nothing (anything). Don't eat nothing (anything) outside while you have (your) first menses. You can eat in (the) house; that is all. You can't eat nothing (anything) outside."

b. "Let's everybody (all females) go pick hazelnuts up on (the) hills," the girl's mother suggested. The girl went with all the women and girls. That woman warned her daughter not to eat hazelnuts. "They'll make you sick," she said.[1]

c. Everybody picked the hazelnuts in a nice open space. The girl

1. [On the strictures connected with the first menses, see III.23, n. 2, below.—Ed.]

went up further by herself. After a while, the women who were picking looked up in the direction the girl had gone, and they saw move all the brush (saw all the brush moving). It looked as though (a) white bear were eating hazelnuts.

"I told my daughter don't (not to) eat hazelnuts. (I told her,) 'When you come home you can eat hazelnuts, but don't eat them off the bushes.' " All looked up and saw the bushes (all) waving around. The girl stood up and looked down at [the] people. She had turned into (a) bear except for her face. She said, "If you folks see (a) white bear, don't kill it, for it is me (I)." Her mother said, "I told her not to eat them hazelnuts off of trees (off the bushes), but to eat them when she (you) came home and sat down."

The white bear was singing as it went along, "I'm going up on the hill. I'm always going to stay up there. Don't kill me when you see me." The old lady, her mother, could not say anything any more.

I.14. GIANT STORY (THE CANNIBAL GIANT)

MARY IKE (1940)

a. The story is about the giant Madukarahat[1] who lived way up [the] Salmon River. He lived far up the river. Down the river a ways lived one little girl with a lot of (many) brothers. Every time they ate she would cry. She had a lot of (many) brothers. About suppertime she would cry, and they would throw [put] her outside.

b. They had a lot of (many) dogs, and they (these) heard something always fooling around (warned that someone was) outside.

They put the girl out and she was crying. Pretty soon they did not hear her (the girl) crying any more. The giant had come and taken her brains out and put frogs and a big toad in [their] place. The mother came (went) out. She felt of the girl's head and felt the frogs. She took her back in the house and fed her acorn mush (and) deer meat. After she finished (these), she gave her manzanita berries and pine nuts.

c. Pretty soon they heard someone hollering (calling), getting closer and closer. He was saying, "I found her. She is mine." The neighbors were so scared they all got into one house, where they had a big fire going.

1. [See I.2, n. 1, above.—Ed.]

The giant was running around outside. Every time he hollered (shouted), the fire went out. The people were scared to death (very frightened). They tried to throw (put) the dogs outside, but (immediately) they would come right back in (again). They were scared (frightened) too. For a long time they were just scared (everyone was fearful). The little girl was crying; the mother was crying. The people told her: "You'd better throw that baby outside, so the giant will not come in." One of the brothers took the baby and threw it outside. The people followed him out.

d. The giant put the baby under his arm and ran home with it. When he got home, he asked the little girl, "Are you hungry?" She said, "No, I had my supper." The giant told her, "I'll cook for you." And he got a plate. Human hands were sticking out from it. "Did you ever eat this kind?" he asked. She said, "No, we always eat salmon and deer meat." He ate the whole human body. The little girl would not eat it.

e. The giant went outside and looked up the hill. She was watching him. Pretty soon a whole dead deer came down. He merely put up his hand with fingers spread to get [it]. He cooked the whole deer. Then the girl ate it. The giant went to sleep. He snored loudly. [Then] the girl went to sleep.

f. The giant was nice to her. He did not bother her. She told the giant, "I like acorns and salmon." Then he went to where women were soaking acorns by the river and took them away from them. He took the acorns home to her. They put the acorns in his hands. They were afraid of him.

g. Every day he would go after one of them for food. The girl knew the people he was killing. He would not eat the acorn soup. He ate only people. The little girl said, "I am going to pack wood. I want a basket." He went down and took one away from somebody (some woman) and brought it home. So the little girl packed wood and pitch. The giant would ask, "What are you going to do with that?" She said, "We burn it," and she put a little in the fire and it blazed up. He told the girl to get lots for winter. "We'll burn that in winter," he said.

She had pitch all over the house and outside. Pretty soon she got some oak bark (xansip, "black oak"). She made coals of fire from the bark and put them in his armpits while he slept, but he did not even feel them.

h. One day he came home carrying her brother. He cooked his whole body and ate it. She thought now, "I'm going to kill him." She made a fire and set the house afire inside. She had a lot of pitch on the outside. The house was burning down before the giant woke up. He was hollering (shouting), telling the girl to run (come) outside and put water on it. She was already outside. The sizzling of the pitch sounded like water. He was just running around inside, telling the little girl to run out. "Our house is on fire!"

Pretty soon he fell down and the whole earth shook. The people said, "Now our enemy is gone." The girl, who had grown up, ran home and told her mother the giant was good to her.

I.15. STORY ABOUT OTHER WORLD

MARY IKE (1940)

a. Two sisters living at Katimin lost their sweethearts. They looked all over for them. They met a man who asked them why they were crying and what they were looking for. They said they had lost their best friends.

He said, "You come with me. I'll take you where they are." They climbed up (the) ridge just upstream from Ike's place. On the ridge they found a road which led to [the] other world. Finally they came to two old women, who asked, "What are you doing? Why did you come here?" They said they were looking for their boy friends.

b. The old women said, "They are here, but you shall not see them or take them away." Then the old women asked the girls, "How is Katimin? Do you still have the pikiawish?[1] Is the old oak tree still standing there, where we used to put the wood when we went after it on the hill? Do they still fix the acorns for the fatawenan?"[2]

The girls replied, "Yes, everything is still there." "Do they still go down and get the fresh sand for the fatawenan?" "Yes, they still get it."

1. [Translated as the "refixing of the world" by Gifford in Kroeber and Gifford, World Renewal, UC-AR 13:(no.1):6. The ceremony was performed at Panamenik, Katimin, and Inam, with certain variations at the three sites. G. describes the Karok rites in detail in the above work (ibid., pp. 6–55).—Ed.]
2. [The fatawenan was the priest who performed the rites, assisted by two young priestesses (ibid., p. 7). On the tenth day of the ceremonies, the young women gathered wood from a specified area and brought it to the ritual site. There they cooked acorn meal ceremonially and made "a miniature figure of sacred Mt. Offield with damp sand from the leaching basin" (ibid.).—Ed.]

c. The old women said, "You'd better go back. Don't stay here."
The old women said, "Now you go back and take all this salmon with
you." They returned with the salmon to Katimin. "After you get
home, if you hear of anyone dying, rub this salmon on the dead
person's lips."

d. After that (no) one died, and (for) they rubbed on salmon, and
the person came to life. No one died after that. The country became
overcrowded with people. After the salmon was gone, people began
to die off as formerly. The two girls became aged women, their skins
soft as buckskin. They never recovered their boy friends, who
remained in (the) other world.

I.16. VISIT TO HEAVEN

GEORGIA ORCUTT (1940)

Told to Georgia by Red Cap Tom's father.[1]

•

a. [A] young Katimin woman (human, but close to ixkareya
times) had a lover [—she was] not yet married to him—who died.
She was so grief-stricken that she refused to eat. Her intention was
to starve herself to death.

b. After a while looked like [it seemed that] she went up to [the]
same place her lover's soul had gone. After a while (she) see (saw)
that boy up there. There was one old lady (woman) up there. She
said to [the] girl, "It looks like I always hear it when that ikiyawan
go[es] through Astuwisa (a narrow rocky place through which [the]
ikiyawan passes and against which her shell dress ornaments
strike).[2] I can hear it way up in heaven." This old woman had been a

1. [Red Cap Creek flows into the Klamath opposite the town of Wuppam.
Tom's father was from this town, which was the furthest downstream of the Karok
villages (Gifford, "Informants," p. 111, above, and Kroeber, Handbook, p.
99)—Ed.]

2. [The ikiyawan were the two girl assistants to the priest in the world renewal
ceremony (Kroeber and Gifford, World Renewal, UC-AR 13:[no.1]:7). Gifford
(ibid., p. 27) says that they were barefoot and wore "two-piece buckskin dresses
with shell pendants. People, hearing the jangling of the shells, know the ikiyavan
are on their way and avoid seeing them for fear of becoming unlucky."—Ed.]

pikiawish woman[3] during her life on earth. The girl saw her lover, but could not bring him back to earth.

c. The old woman told the girl, "You can't stay here. You never died. This is only for the souls of the dead. You can take this spring salmon home with you. If anybody dies, rub the salmon on his lips. Don't put [it] on when [he is] sick. Wait till the person dies. He will come to life again."

d. When the young woman came back[4] she had the fish, which they used for a long time to revive people. When it was gone, people began dying permanently again.

I.17. ROLLING HEAD

MARY IKE (1939)

a. A person came from Namkarak (near Oak Bottom). This person thought he would bathe in a lake called Ara-ipamwanati (the person who ate himself). He and his brother went up to the lake (above New Diggings, on the mountains). He told his brother, "You'd better build a fire, so I can warm myself after I bathe." The one building the fire told his brother, "Don't touch your body when you come out."

b. The swimmer went into the lake. His brother, building the fire, watched him from the shore. The man on shore saw that his brother's body was loaded with worms and snakes as he came out of the lake. He wiped his body with his hands and ate the worms and the snakes.

c. The fire builder started to run away. When he got to Ikurowak (a ridge) he heard his brother hollering (shouting). He said, "Now he is eating himself." Then he came to the creek Bahipyanakamichsuuf (one-pepperwood-bush creek). Then he looked back and thought his brother was coming, but it was only his brother's head. He kept running and looking back and saw the head still coming. At Ma'anaixwunam (where they dig mountain medicine), he thought

3. [A young woman assistant in the pikiawish, or world renewal, ceremony. See also notes to Gifford's I.15, above.—Ed.]

4. In the story above it was the whole body of the girl that traveled to the sky, Georgia says, not just her spirit. The girl thought she was gone only a day, but it was a year.

his brother was going to eat him. Then he climbed up the ridge Tamxanach (scorched), thinking his brother could not get up there. Then he came on, getting on the ridge Ohera'rona (to go along smoking). There he stopped to smoke. Then he went down to the creek Asitumutvividak (where the chips are piled up). Then he went atop the ridge Nirik. Then he hollered (called) down to his folks, "Hurry up, he ate himself up!"

d. They heard him hollering (shouting), and took out a basketry salmon trap (bisimvari, used overnight in river for salmon) and packed it up. They set it in the trail. They heard the head hollering (calling) in the distance. It came rolling along. It would roll partway up a ridge, then roll back, then a little higher, and so on until he (it) reached (the) top.

e. The head rolled into (the) basket trap. The people seized it, but they could hardly hold it. They intended to put it in (the) river, [and] so (had) placed a rock in it. As they were about to throw it in the river, the head said, "Wait! Where you throw me grass will grow on the bottom of the river. People can dive in for it. Those who get it will be lucky." Arareiyunkuri (where they poke a person in) is (the) place they put the head in. This is on Salmon River just above Oak Bottom on (the) left bank as one goes upstream. The water can be heard roaring always at this place.

I.18. STORY ABOUT THUNDERS

MARY IKE (1940)

[This story closely parallels Kroeber's C3, above.—Ed.]

•

a. There was a young girl who always carried wood at Hostler Rancheria (in Hupa territory). Every morning she went early and carried wood. She went up on the hill to get the wood.

b. One morning when she put her basket of wood on her back, someone took hold of her right hand. She looked around and there was a house, and an old lady (woman) came out. "I always see you packing wood and I (have) heard lots (much) about you," the old lady (woman) said.

c. The girl was so scared (frightened), [but] the old lady (woman) said, "I am glad you are going to be my daughter-in-law. I have a son. Come in." The girl entered the house and looked around to see the man.

The old lady (woman) had ten sons. Some of them had gone up the river to a War Dance (sivichap). Some had gone to (the) mouth of (the) Klamath to fish for whales. "They will soon be home. Don't get scared," the old lady (woman) said. The girl just sat there and did not say a word. She was wondering why the old lady (woman) told her not to be scared. She looked around and saw a lot of (many) wooden stools. She also saw a lot of (many) basket plates (hasip-nada) for salmon.

d. Pretty soon she heard a loud noise. She heard (a) noise. "Now they are coming home. Don't get scared (be frightened)," the old lady (woman) said. One of the stools jumped down from the platform into the pit right by her. Then the rest jumped down. One fell by the old lady (woman).

Five of the young men who returned from the War Dance had legs and arms protruding from their quivers (akawaki). Five who came from Rekwoi were carrying pieces of whale (ipbara).

e. The old lady (woman) started cooking the whale meat they had brought home. She put (it) in the basket plates. The young men all started fighting. One seized her (the girl); he was to be her husband. She looked over and saw the old lady (woman) and her husband fighting in one corner. She ran out. She ran down till she came to a house. She saw two or three young men in there. (They said,) "Don't come in. We are scared (afraid) of your husband. We heard you got married." Then she ran on again. She did not stay there.

f. She came to another house and ran into it. The people said, "You'd better not come in here. We heard you got married." She ran to five different homes and they all told her the same: not to come in. She arrived at (the) sixth house and they told her to come in. The man said, "Make yourself at home. I'm not afraid of your husband." There was one old lady (woman), a girl, and a man. (The man said,) "I'll marry you. I'm not scared (afraid) of your man. I'll take you." She stayed there one year.

g. She noticed that the girl had some sticks, as though getting ready to make baskets. Pretty soon she saw her making a baby basket. The man asked his sister if she had got through with (finished) the basket. He told her to put (a) blanket in (the) basket cradle and to take the basket cradle (it) down to where they get (got) their water.

h. He told his wife, "Let's go outside. Look for lice (a louse) on my head. Don't kill it, whatever you do." He sat down and held his hand out. "As soon as you find one, put it in my hand." He took the louse down to the baby basket. "You go back into the house," he told his wife. She went into (the) house.

The wife heard a noise outside like (a) footfall. The old lady (woman) said, "Let me be the first to take the baby." It was a little boy.

i. The baby got old enough to walk around. The man said, "You (had) better look for another louse on my head. Take the baby basket down to the spring again." She found a louse and gave it to him. He told her to go back into the house. This time the baby was a little girl.

j. He told his wife, "Your mother and father and brother[s] are worrying about you and can't sleep. You'd better go home. I'll take you home." "All right," she said. "We'll go home." The man said, "Your folks at home don't even dance any more for worrying about you. They think you are dead."

The man took ten strings of eleven-string money[1] in a baby basket. "I don't want my babies to be poor. I want them to have a lot (plenty) of money," he said.

k. They went with the two babies down to the river and saw nine boats ready for them. The boats were loaded down with provisions. They all set out, one person in each boat. They went to the girl's home at Hostler Rancheria. They entered the house. She told her mother, "Take my babies." The old lady said, "Who's fooling me like that? My daughter is dead." She fell down in a faint.

l. The girl said, "I came home. I got married." Her mother got up. The girl's brothers had already got married and had different houses. All her brothers were happy and laughing. They had never done that before; they were always sad. The girl said to tell all her brothers to come back to their parents' house. She said, "I've come home." All her brothers (nine of them) came home. She said to her brothers, "Take the babies." Each took a string of money from the

---

1. [The largest and most valuable size of shell money. Dentalia of this size "were exceedingly scarce. A string of them might now and then be paid for a wife by a man of great prominence; but never two strings. Possession of a pair of such strings was sufficient to make a man well known" (Kroeber, Handbook, p. 24)—Ed.]

baby basket. They all went back to their own houses with (a) string of money each. They all had supper together at their parents' house.

m. Pretty soon everything got dark and it looked like a heavy fog in the house. While they were eating, it looked as though there was water in the house. They (the men) went to the sweathouse (the men only). All the brothers' wives stayed in the house and also her female relatives stayed. Then she told them all about herself, what had happened to her. "The first man I had, I thought they were fighting, but it is just the way they live."[2] She told of her running away and of how many houses turned her out. "The last house," she said, "took me in. I got down to the mouth of the river. At one side there is a rancheria there (Sufip, Rekwoi). From now on they'll have dances here.[3] Tomorrow morning when the sun rises, have ten baskets full of things for me. I'm leaving. I'll never come back again. This is the last time."

n. They left the next morning. "After this think about me when you have the dance. I'll never come back any more." Her little boy was hollering (calling) to his grandmother, telling her goodbye. The little boy said, "This place belongs to me and the dance belongs to me." He sang a song. "You folks must sing this song and you'll be lucky hereafter."[4]

I.19. Weitspus Story Used by Karok in Advising Young Men

GEORGIA ORCUTT

This story about Samchaka was told to young men to stimulate them to accumulate wealth. [The plot resembles Spott and Kroeber, Yurok Narra-

2. The thunder was made by the noisy people in the first house where the girl married.

3. [Hostler Rancheria, the girl's old home, is Takimilding, site of the Hupa world renewal ceremonies, and thus there is a natural linkage between it and Rekwoi, one of the Yurok ritual centers (Goddard, Life and Culture of the Hupa, UC-PAAE 1:[no.1]:12, and Kroeber and Gifford, World Renewal, UC-AR 13:[no.1]:56–65 and 91–98).—Ed.]

4. Mary sang the song that went with the above story. When boys are four or five years old, one sings a good-luck song over them and puts water all over them. Mary did this for her grandson Bruce, but Leland said he would not have it done for him and wanted Mary to make a love medicine for him instead. [Bruce and Leland were sons of Emily (Ike) and Jasper Donahue and thus grandsons of Mary Ike (letter from Violet Tripp, dated August 3, 1978).—Ed.]

tives, no. 35, UC-PAAE 35:(no. 9):244-249, on the origin of the legendary White Deerskin Dance at Welkwaü.—Ed.]

•

a. They were having [the] Deerskin Dance at Weitspus (human beings, not ixkareya). When they start[ed] in to make [the] fire, everyone had to dance, putting on Deerskin Dance regalia. And after a while all put it on. After a while that poor boy (Samchaka) put on that wolf-hair headband. After a while someone chided him for having it on, he being poor. So he took it off. Afterwards sit [he sat] down by [the] fire.

b. After a while somebody saw him crying and said, "You cry." After a while they were dancing [the] Deerskin Dance, and he was just sitting there. After a while he was thinking, "I wish I had something too. I'm just like nobody because I ain't got [have] nothing." The old men were in the sweathouse. When talking to younger men, the old ones advised, "Do this way, do that way." The boy did not go in[to the] sweathouse at first. He cried many times, thinking about himself and his poverty.

c. And after a while the boy make [made a] net and put [it] on [a] long stick and string to draw [the] mouth of [the] bag net tight. He put it over [a] woodpecker nest in [the] evening by means of [a] long pole. In [the] morning he found he had lots of [many] woodpeckers.[1] Every evening he did [the] same thing. He made lots of [many] net bags and he caught lots of woodpeckers. He made lots of iris-fiber rope for snaring deer. Looked like [It seemed] he was always making something. After a while he see [saw] two vultures flying around, and he found [a] dead wolf. He skinned it and he made many wolf-fur headbands.

d. He was working a long time, so he got everything. He told his folks [people], "You better get ready for [a] Deerskin Dance." He made buckskin robes for [the] men to wear in the dance. After a while he made net head ornaments.[2] In time he had everything ready for the Deerskin Dance. He was getting to be yasara.[3]

1. There was no tree climbing to get woodpeckers, but they were taken by a net on the end of a long pole; shridioni was the bag net for woodpeckers. "Don't call net."

2. They were tied entirely with the fingers.

3. [Gifford defines yasara as "human being" in V.15*i*. Here it probably means "a real man," since Samchaka was accumulating wealth.—Ed.]

e. Maybe it was two years after he started when he made the dance. Two years before he [had] told his womenfolks they must make baskets because they were going to have a big feast.[4] All these two years he had cut sweathouse wood, crying as he did so, and brought it in to sweat himself.

After a while the womenfolks were making acorn baskets, all kinds of baskets, that [those] womenfolks. He never tell [told] anybody, "I got [have] that kind, I got [have] this kind." He never tell [told] anybody what he is [was] doing. Nobody knew he had lots of [many] things. He hid the things in the house where he lived with his parents and sister.

f. And afterwards [the] Weitspus people give [gave the] Deerskin Dance. And after a while that boy [was] going to have [a] Deerskin Dance, and they go [went to] camp on [the] bar. Then his dancers came down in [a] boat with their deerskins. People were surprised. They knew nothing of the boy's intentions to take part. After a while the people all coming [came] down by the river. Then they all put (on) the new wolf(-fur) headbands he had made. He had sea-lion headbands and netted head ornaments. He had big obsidians. The people were excited because everything was new which the boy brought.

g. The dance lasted ten days at Weitspus.[5] Some days after that the people go [went] up Weitspus Mountain[6] and dance[d the] Jump[ing] Dance. The boy had woodpecker headbands ready for this.[7.]

[They] dance [the] Jump[ing] Dance at different places as they go up. [They] never do [the] Deerskin Dance up there. They stay all night and dance [the] next morning. They quit about two P.M. [and] return down [the] mountain to eat. [They] never eat up there.

Samchaka was [the] name of [the] boy in Karok. It means "bar in river which divides it into two streams." It was [the] name of his home place, this side of Weitspus a short way.

---

4. "Everything free, never charge anything."
5. The ixkareya ordained only two days for the Karok Deerskin Dances.
6. Numen, the same place Bluejay spilled acorns. [See II.2a–c.—Ed.]
7. Usually there was some interval between the Deerskin and Jumping dances to allow time to prepare acorns for the feast after the Jumping Dance.

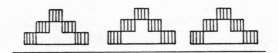

II. Tales in Which Coyote Is a Character

II.1. Story About Hawk of A'u'ich (Ixkareya and Coyote)

MARY IKE (1940)

a. This hawk catches all kinds of birds—ducks on [the] wing, for instance. It is white underneath, brown on top. [It] live[s] at Sugarloaf (A'u'ich). [It is] about [the] size of [a] wild pigeon. Aixnexshan is [its] name. Aixnexshan means "living up high." They go [It goes] away in the fall.

b. The animals were once people, but the ixkareya were the head of everything. When [the] Indians came, the ixkareya became rocks, trees, etc. At Forks of Salmon the ixkareya turned into wolves (ixhamnamich); that is why [the] Karok at Forks of Salmon are kind of mean people. Coyote and this Hawk were ixkareya. [The] ixkareya stayed here and turned into something; they did not go away across the ocean. Sukrivishkuruhan was [the] principal ixkareya. He said if [whether] there would be lots of acorns, etc. The name means [is from] sukriv (woven bag for men) [and] iskuruhan (to carry). Some years he predicted famine: no acorns, no fish, no manzanita berries; and sure enough it was so.[1]

1. There were no stories about him that Mary remembered. [The description sounds like that of Yurok Megwomets, the food-giver. See Kroeber, Yurok Myths, A16x *f.* See also Kroeber, F2, above, in which Suhurivish-kuru is shown as the creator of all things: mountains, rocks, trees, water, and deer.—Ed.]

II.2. How Birds Got Feathers

MARY IKE (1940)

a. There was an ixkareya living at [on] Shelton Butte (Israma-ka.uus). No one had anything to wear except this one man. There was another ixkareya living on (a) big mountain on [the] upstream (Klamath) side of Bluff Creek. The mountain is called Ixnumen. There was the camp of the people. Everybody passing saw the big bird (ixkareya) sitting on Shelton Butte wearing a nice blanket of feathers.

They all got together to discuss how to kill that fellow. "We've got to have blankets. We've got to have something to wear," they said.

b. Pinef (Coyote) said, "I'll be the first one to shoot him." They were all there trying to kill him. Steller's Jay was cooking. They asked him (her), "What are you going to cook? You ain't got (have) nothing." Jay replied, "Never mind me. I'll find something."

c. Coyote gathered the wood and built the fire. Jay flew up on a tree and pulled one acorn from a hole and cooked it. While she was boiling this one, which kept bobbing up and down, Coyote was trying to take it out. "How are we going to get enough from one acorn?" Coyote asked.

There was a little flat [prairie] there, and Jay dumped the acorn on it and it was immediately covered with acorns.[1] She told Coyote, "Now eat this up." They all ate. There were far more than Coyote alone could eat.

d. Coyote said he would be the first to take a shot at the fellow [giant bird] on the mountain. Coyote shot first. Everybody shot (except Wren) a small bird called rain bird (aksimsaxsaxkwen= wren). Coyote told this bird (Wren) not to shoot. "What can you do? I did not hit him." When Wren shot, they heard [the] arrow hit the big bird (ixkareya). Down he came, and a slide is visible now where his body slid down.

e. All the people (birds) went to work at getting the feathers from his blanket for themselves. Wren made the prettiest one. They all went to bed, placing their blankets in a row. "Whoever wakes up first may have the prettiest blanket." Jay was the first to awaken.

1. Now there are little stones in this place which are called Jay's acorns. [See also II.30, n. 1, below.—Ed.]

Everyone else awoke and each put on a blanket. Wren was the last to awaken and there was nothing left. He picked up little pieces here and there all over the ground and made himself a blanket. That is the reason he has such an ugly-looking blanket now. Kupanakanak.

II.3. How People Got the Bow and Arrow

MARY IKE (1939)

a. The story starts close to Ikriripan (still a hole there where it started), at Amaikiara sweathouse. They said (all the hunters), "How are [we] going to live?" Coyote said, "I know how we are going to live." One of the ixkareya said, "You folks better stay here, while I go make what we are going to live on." He brought some xawich (arrow wood)[1] [and] some xuparich (bow yew wood).

b. The rest started to make bows and arrows, while he watched them. After they had the bows made, they put an arrow with each bow. After they had finished, he picked out [the] best bow and arrow and put them a little above the steps of the living house pit. Then the house was filled with bows and arrows placed all around, made by the people.

c. The people were named for all sorts of animals. Dog and Wolf lay by the steps. Coyote came and sat beside Dog. All faced the best bow and arrow. Coyote said, "I am going to be the one to pick up the best." Then Coyote propped his eyes open with sticks so he would not go to sleep before morning. All sat around the fire in the living house for the night. Then Dog beat them all. He woke up earliest, grabbed the best bow and arrows, and ran.

d. When [the] rest woke up, they found the best bow and arrow gone. Coyote overslept with the rest. Wolf was mad because he [had] missed [out]. Panther said to him, "You slept too long. That is all. I'm going to take the second best."

e. The sun was shining before Coyote woke up. He looked around. Everybody was gone, and all the bows except a poor one made of arrow wood (instead of yew). He took this bow and some arrows and went up on the flat called Irivshavak[2] to hunt gophers.

f. The Dog ran. Behind him was Panther. Behind him was Wolf.

1. [Spelled xawish in II.25*b*, below, and identified as syringa.—Ed.]
2. On the flat above Perry Keaton's place on the west side of the river.

The Dog came back to the middle of the earth (the starting place at Amaikiara). Dog saw a person (ara) at Amaikiara. Panther had almost caught up with Dog, as he wanted to take the bow and arrows from him. Dog gave the bow and arrows to the man, saying, "This is what we are going to live with. It is going to kill you and going to kill me." This is the end of the story. This is how man got the bow and arrows.

II.4. Dog and Deer

SHAN DAVIS

[Shan Davis in the year 1939 served as one of Gifford's informants on the World Renewal ceremonies (Kroeber and Gifford, World Renewal, UC-AR 13:[no. 1]:132. See also "Informants," p. 111, no. 5, above.—Ed.]

•

a. [The] ixkareya, Dog and Deer, were in [the] sweathouse with Coyote, Wolf, Panther, and Bobcat. They had bows and arrows. Coyote did not go after Deer when he sneaked (out).

b. Dog had a little stick which he stuck in [the] sweathouse fire. Then he marked Deer's hind leg with it, while Deer slept. Dog did this so he could smell it when he pursued Deer.

c. Deer sneaked out about [the] middle of [the] night and ran off. Dog was awake. He took [a] bow and arrow and followed Deer. Deer jumped in [the] ocean just as Dog caught him and dragged him back. Dog killed him. That was all right, because Deer had said to Dog, "You can kill me any time you want and it will be all right."

d. Wolf was angry at Dog because of this. Wolf was mad all the time and will kill Dog on [the] mountain any time he see[s] it [him].

II.5. Story About Fertility Rock at Orleans

MARY IKE (1940)

a. There were two young girls living in a house at Panamenik. There were many young men hanging around to see the girls.

b. The fisherman[1] said, "I'd like to go with those two girls." He went home and got a big basket (shibnuk, acorn storage basket). He took it down to his fishery at the rock. He talked to the basket and said, "You sit there and fish, so people will think I am fishing there." He told the basket, and said, "Now you sing this so as to make people think it is an old man fishing." (Song)

c. Then he went and got his moccasins and put them on. The shoes were all painted up red. He went around looking for a hollow tree. He found one and pissed (urinated) in it. A lot of little birds came out. He told these birds to tell the Panamenik people that a strange man was coming. The Panamenik people were dancing the War Dance (sivstap). Someone said, "You'd better go see if that old man is dancing. Maybe he is here dancing with us." Someone went up and reported back, "He is there. He is fishing. We saw him." That [reassurance] made the girls come out.

d. Coyote(?) prayed while he danced: "When the girls come out, you make them stand at each end of the row of dancers."[2] When Coyote(?) did this he danced back and forth, and when in front of each girl, he danced very close to her.

e. Someone went again to see if the fisherman was still fishing and reported back, "It is only a basket sitting there fishing." The girls started to go back to [the] house, but could hardly walk, they were so fat.

f. Some of the people said, "We'd better kill that man." He ran off and went way back where the highway is now. He went clean (way) down to Bluff Creek. He said, "Let it get foggy." Then he went way over the mountains and arrived far down the Klamath. Then he went [all the] way down to Afam (in Yurok territory).[3] There he put up a sweathouse right (very) quick(ly). He entered and lay down and made himself look old.

g. Pretty soon a lot of (many) people came, who had been following him. One went in and asked this old man if he had seen anyone come by. He kind of rolled over, just laying there. One said,

1. Mary was not sure if it was Ixyerobixlivi (the Giant) or Pinefish (Coyote) who had the fishery at the rock in Orleans. The rock is named Pavatanshununam. [On the identity of Ixyerobixlivi or Ixyarukbitsi, cf. Gifford's headnote to tales I.1–I.4, above.—Ed.]

2. When the War Dance is done, one steps out and dances back and forth in front of the row.

3. [Identified as a place on the west side of the Klamath, below Martin's Ferry, in II.30*a*.—Ed.]

"Maybe he did not hear. You'd better talk louder." Then he (the old man) tried to talk Yurok, (but) he made his own language (Karok). It kind of sounded half-Yurok and half-Karok.

h. They went on. One of them said, "It did not sound right. It sounded like our language. He is trying to make up his own language." So they returned and called him. There was no answer. He was gone. One said, "I told you that was him! He went back upstream." They followed him back up, but he got to Orleans first.

i. [When] the people got back to Orleans, they saw an old man approaching with two canes. They asked him if he knew any medicine for the two girls who were sick. "Yes, I know a medicine." They told him to come inside, then. He said, "Give me a cup to hold." They gave it to him. "You make the medicine right here. Don't go out," they told him. "Where will I get my medicine, then, if I don't go out?" One said, "You are an ixkareya. You can find your medicine here." He said, "Get a little piece of wood off the doorway and I'll make medicine with that." They got it for him, and he talked to this little piece of wood. He said, "Let me rub the medicine on her leg."

j. One of the women said, "I can rub it on myself." Then they rubbed the medicine on the legs of the two women and heard babies cry. Then he ran outside and he got by with that.[4]

II.6. THE FERTILITY ROCK AT ORLEANS

GEORGIA ORCUTT (1940)

Below Gent's store and on the river bank in Orleans is a fertility rock, which has what look like footprints. The woman seeking fertility walks up the rock in the footprints. The ixkareya arranged this. The rock was formerly Coyote's fishery. Pinefas ("Coyote fix it") is the name of the rock.[1] Coyote was no ixkareya. The story follows.

●

4. This was all that Mary knew; she was not sure this was the end. The creek in Orleans (Orleans Creek) is called Pinefas (Coyote) Creek. Mary was not sure how Fertility Rock was used; she only knew it had a reputation for baby producing. [See a similar version, II.6, by Georgia Orcutt, following.—Ed.]

1. [Mary Ike gives a different name for the rock in II.5, n. 1.—Ed.]

a. Coyote had [a] fishery at this rock. Two ixkareya sisters (were) staying at Panamenik. No one saw the girls because [they] never went out of (the) house. Coyote came to Panamenik and said, "People are coming from way off to have [the] War Dance (sivchap) right here. Makasururup is where people are coming from to dance."

b. Coyote knew the girls were here, even though they never went anywhere. Afterwards Coyote went up on [the] hill and asked small birds of one species (pinefsui) to dress up for (the) War Dance. Coyote covered himself with Indian money and a pair of moccasins with porcupine quills (non-Karok type). All (the) pinefsui birds dressed for (the) War Dance.

c. The girls had been trained to stay in house (indoors, the) ixkareya thus setting (the) pattern for proper behavior of girls. People at Panamenik heard people shouting and said, "We hear somebody hollering (calling)." They looked up toward (the) mountains upstream and saw lots of (many) people coming down the mountains. They approached Panamenik. They danced (the) War Dance at Panamenik. Everybody (was) excited and said [that] these people had come from far off. The two girls still (remained) inside.

d. Then Coyote danced in front of their house. The girls went (came) out and sat at opposite ends of (the) house watching [the] dance. Coyote danced in front of the row of dancers. He danced in front of each girl particularly and made them pregnant.

e. [The] ixkareya people were suspicious. One said, "It looks funny, looks like Coyote. Somebody [had] better go to his fishery and see if he is there." Someone went up to the fishery and saw someone sitting there with (a) blanket over him. (The) man came back and reported Coyote there.

f. Some were not satisfied, so (they) sent another messenger to see and discovered it was (a) deerskin blanket over (a) basket. He returned and said it was [a] shipnuk (acorn storage basket).

g. The people started after Coyote, who ran downriver to Bluff Creek, then over (a) hill and on (a) ridge, with everybody chasing him. He came down to (the) river at a Yurok village at Martin's Ferry (Kôkiriki in Karok) and entered (the) sweathouse there. He was dusty all over. He heard people running outside, so he lay down and (made) himself (an) old man. Someone looked in and asked, "Did you see someone here a while ago?" "Yes, someone ran down a while ago," he said (Coyote replied) in imitation Yurok. So away they went in pursuit.

h. Coyote came out now and crossed (the) river to the east side. The pursurers failed to see tracks. Some were looking back and saw him cross. So they turned back but could not cross [the] river because Coyote had taken the boat. Then the people gave up and returned to Panamenik. Coyote went to Hupa, descending at Bald Hill.

i. The two girls were already in family way (pregnant) when [the] Panamenik people returned. Because Coyote had the rock for (a) fishery and because he made the girls pregnant just by dancing in front of them, the rock is regarded as a baby rock.

II.7. Origin of Fire

GEORGIA ORCUTT (1940)

a. Only one ixkareya (oxswixkareya=right here ixkareya) had fire, but nobody knew it. He was hiding it. Coyote discovered he had it, for he went around everywhere and he visited with this Old Man. Coyote told the people, "That man's got fire."

b. All the people said, "What are we going to do? We'll have to try to get that fire." The Old Man kept his fire in (a) small stone square fireplace in his house. The people talked it over a long time. "How [are] we going to take it (get) that fire?" After a while they discussed who were the fastest runners. Now everybody was getting ready to see who could run fastest.

c. Coyote said, "I can go inside and visit with (the) Old Man. You folks can stand outside. I can sit down by the fire, because I ain't got (have) no shoes on. I can put a coal between my toes and then run outside."

d. Coyote went to Old Man's house and entered. The others waited outside. When Coyote ran outside, the Old Man pursued him, but he passed the coal to Small Chicken Hawk. The other people ran ahead when Coyote came out. The coal was passed to Big Chicken Hawk. Then Eagle took it. Various birds took it one after another. Old Man was chasing them and they nearly give (gave) up. Eagle knew he was about to be overtaken. The Old Man was pretty close to him. Frog was (the) last one, sitting on a ridge. He took the coal in his mouth and jumped into (the) river. Later he put it in (a) willow root.

e. Frog got out of [the] water after he had done this. All ran after him to see if Old Man would get (the) fire. He could not find it. The Old Man give (gave) up because he could not find it. Frog had hidden it (in a) willow root. When Frog came out his mouth looked all red, from having had fire in his mouth (it). The people asked him what he had done with it. Frog said, "I put it in the root."

f. After a while he took out that root. The people then sat down to discuss how they would make fire. They decided to make it with (a) fire drill of willow root, both drill and hearth of [the] same material. Eagle made the fire drill. Now when they rotate(d the) fire drill in (the hearth) all the birds (people) received fire so they will (would) never be cold in winter. It looks like the birds have fire, but at the same time they never have any real fire.

g. Flicker (suk) said he could get along without fire, so he never got anything. Flickers often die in winter in consequence. Kupanakanak.[1]

II.8. Story About Tan(bark) Oak (Kunyeip)

GEORGIA ORCUTT (1940)

[William Bright points out that midway through this myth Widower changes to Coyote, confirming a feeling Bright has always had, that these are really the same personage, as is suggested by the etymology of Coyote's name: *pinefish* seems to be *pihriv* "widower" plus *af* "excrement" plus *ish* "diminutive" (letter, September 26, 1978).—Ed.]

•

a. Yeruxbihi,[1] an ixkareya man whose name means Widower, was living across (the) ocean. At Asisuftisiram above Happy Camp lots of (many) girls were living. Yeruxbihi said, "I'm going to go up

1. [Gifford's typescript had a handwritten cross-reference to another fire story under the Coyote tales. It is II.43, below.—Ed.]

---

1. [See Gifford's headnote to tales I.1–I.4, above.—Ed.]

and see those girls up there. I hear there are lots of (many) girls at Asisuftisiram.''

b. He made himself some acorn bread by cooking it on hot rocks (stones). When [it was] cooked on one side, he turned it over and cooked (it) on (the) other side. He put this in his sukrif[2] and started out. He came up on (the) Orleans [Panamenik] side of (the) river. When he got tired he sat down and ate acorn bread. He threw away (the) scraps. From these, by and by, oak trees grew.

c. He walked up to Panamenik. There he saw many nice girls. The girls were singing. ''I'm going over there, too,'' he said. When the girls saw him they turned their heads and spat, because they did not like his coming up. Yeruxbihi said, ''I'm not going to stay here to see you folks. I'm going on up to Asisuftisiram.''

d. When the girls turned to look, he was already well up the river from Panamenik. The girls sang, ''Yeruxbihi is going up to Asisuftisiram.'' Above Sandy Bar he stop[ped] at Ispunwedap (resting place). There he ate more of his acorn bread. He threw the scraps away, and where they fell oaks grew.

He kept on going upstream, kept on going up. He stopped at Ishiptakra (trail in gap), this side of Happy Camp. He ate bread and tossed away (the) scraps. Then he smoked his pipe. Then he walked on to Asisuftisiram.

e. When he looked in there, he saw lots of (many) girls. They were digging Indian potatoes. He stayed all night. It looked like he could not sleep. He did not care about the girls there. This (was the) farthest point upstream that he ate acorn bread. Beyond Asisuftisiram there are no tan oak trees in consequence.[3]

f. In the morning when he wake (woke) up, he thought to himself, ''I believe I'll go home. I feel better if I am in my own home.'' The singing of the girls at Panamenik had made bad luck for him, so he never got a girl at Asisuftisiram. In the morning he started back. ''I'll not stop at Panamenik again, because those girls don't like me. They looked away when I came.'' When he came to Panamenik, he never look (did not look) back toward the foot of the hills where the

---

2. [Or sukriv, a woven bag carried by men.—Ed.]

3. [Tanbark acorns were preferred for food by the Hupa and presumably by the Yurok, according to Kroeber, Handbook, p. 88. ''Acorns were gathered, dried, stored, cracked, pulverized, sifted, leached, and usually boiled with hot stones in a basket,'' providing the ''chief daily food of more than three-fourths of native California'' (ibid., p. 87). If Asisuftisiram was above Happy Camp (see paragraph *a*), then it was near the northern boundary of Karok territory (Kroeber, Karok Towns, pp. 35–36).—Ed.]

girls were. The girls knew he was coming, and they were playing in (the) same place. Yeruxbihi said, "I'll not go up there." That is the way the tan(bark) oak got distributed, but it never grew further upstream than Asisuftisiram (Asisuf, hazel bush; tisiram, lots of).

g. Yeruxbihi kept on downstream and then crossed [the] ocean to his home in his boat.

h. Ixkareya pinits (Ixkareya Old Man) was living somewhere in (the) Karok country. Coyote know (knew) everything. Old Man had (a) house and sweathouse. Coyote came (went there) and stayed all night.

i. Old Man said, "Let's go into (the) house and eat something." This was in (the) evening. When he go in (was indoors) he got out his acorn bread and soaked it in water. He just soaked it in water to eat it. Afterwards Coyote said, "Amayûp (this is good)." They ate up all the acorn bread.

j. "How do you get it when you ain't got (have) no wife?" asked Coyote. Old Man never say (said) nothing. After a while Coyote asked him again, "How (do) you get it?" Old Man don't (did not) answer. Again Coyote asked him. Then Old Man replied, "I just go up on (the) hill and I lay (lie) down and I holler (shout) and tell the bread to come down. And I shut my eyes and never look up."

Coyote said, "I'm going to do the same way. I like it. Maybe I can get it." Old Man said, "You can get a few [chunks], not much (many)."

k. Coyote went up on (the) hill and lay down. When he hollered (shouted), the bread fell down already cooked. It is called araraix-sara. Coyote think (thought), "Maybe I have not got enough. Maybe I'll ask for more." So he hollered (called), "When you come down, you can come down more big ones." After a while when he lay down and shut his eyes, he thought he heard something rolling. All the rocks were rolling down and hit him every place as he lay there.

l. Afterwards Coyote got up all bloody on his face and every place. Then he walked slowly to (the) Old Man's house. He was sore all over. Coyote came in (entered) and say (said), "Pretty near I die. (I pretty nearly died.) Pretty near the rocks mashed me up. (The rocks pretty nearly mashed me.)" Afterward[s], the Old Man said, "I told you to ask (for) only a few." "But," said Coyote, "I could not get enough, so I asked for more." Coyote can't (can) get no bread. Kupanakanak.

II.9. COYOTE AND ACORNS

GEORGIA ORCUTT (1940)

Georgia heard this story from Red Cap Tom and others.

•

a. Coyote went from Panamenik [Orleans] down to Sufip [Rekwoi]. Acorns were all kept in tightly closed baskets by [the] ixkareya people there. No one else had acorns yet. Coyote said, "We'll have to have acorns all the year around." The people said, "No, we'll have them only in the fall." Coyote insisted on having them right away and all the year around. The ixkareya said, "No, we'll have them in the fall, lots of them, so people can get enough to last until next fall." Coyote failed to arrange it as he wanted it. He was afraid people would starve if they could get them only once a year. [The] ixkareya assured him there would be enough so people could collect [a] large enough quantity to last one year.

b. Coyote threatened to cut open the baskets so as to have acorns the year around on trees, but he never did. He returned empty-handed. Already there were oak trees in the world, but no acorns on them. The acorns were released by the ixkareya at Sufip.

II.10. HOW COYOTE FREED SALMON FOR PEOPLE

GEORGIA ORCUTT (1940)

•

a. Nobody got fish. (There were) no fish in [the] river. After a while Coyote knew that two girls at Amaikiara(m) had fish. He had been thinking about (that). "How am I going to fix it?" He took some alder bark. He make [made] it look like (the) backbone of (a) fish; he fixed it all nice so it looked like (the) backbone of (a) fish. The he put on deer marrow (put deer marrow on his imitation fish). When he [had] fixed it up nice, that was the time he went up to Amaikiaram. Coyote came from right here (Panamenik).

b. When he go up (arrived) there, he go (went) to the house where the two ixkareya girls (were) living. He talked with them (the) girls. They were cooking acorns. They gave Coyote acorns to eat. When they give (gave) him the acorns, he took his imitation fish from his quiver (kavaki) and said, "I'm going to cook fish." It look(ed) like them (the) girls look[ed] at each other and ask(ed), "Where (did) he get fish? Nobody's got fish." They thought this as they looked at each other. When Coyote cooked it, it looked like grease was dripping from it. It was the deer marrow. He never offered them any to eat. He pretended to eat it all himself.

c. Late in [the] evening the girls ate acorns. They never (did not) eat fish. They had no sweathouse, so they had to let Coyote sleep by the fire in their house. Coyote just lay there, making believe he was asleep. After a while it looked like the girls were talking to see if he was asleep. He kept snoring away, but heard them all the time, for he was only pretending [to] sleep. After a while, one girl said, "I think he is asleep now," for they heard him snoring away.

d. The girls got up and went outside. Coyote lay there snoring away. Coyote went outside. He know where the fish were. He had expected the girls would go out sometime during the night and he would have his chance to release (the) fish, which the girls had impounded in a pond in a cave in the mountainside. Coyote released the fish, and they swam down creek to (the) river. Then Coyote ran away.

Everybody thought he did right in releasing fish for people. Usually everybody runs down (berates) Coyote, but this time he did right. (The) girls were excited when they came back. One said to (the) other, "I told you he was not sleeping." Coyote came back (returned) to Panamenik.

II.11. COYOTE RELEASES SALMON

MAMIE OFFIELD (1939)

Mamie Offield learned the following version from her mother, a Karok woman of Saxvuram.[1]

1. [Karok Saxvuram was the town the Yurok called Operger. It was on the south side of the Klamath below the mouth of Camp Creek, and thus it was one of the most southerly of Karok settlements (Kroeber, Handbook, p. 99, and Kroeber, Yurok Myths, map 2).—Ed.]

Coyote released salmon by going to [the] house of [the] two women owners. They had no salmon around, as they did not want him to know they had salmon. He sat in a dark corner of the house and took from his bag a piece of alder bark which he began eating. The women saw it and thought it was salmon. They said to one another, "He already has salmon. We might as well get some of ours." So they did, and in that way Coyote learned where they kept the salmon. Subsequently, Coyote released the salmon so they came up the Klamath for mankind to catch.

II.12. ORIGIN OF MEN'S USE OF SWEATHOUSE

MAMIE OFFIELD

This story was also related to Mamie by her mother.

●

Originally, in ixkareya times, Coyote insisted that the sweathouse was to be for women, the living house for men. The women had such a mess of basketry trash, etc., in the sweathouse that it was decided that they would have to vacate and give the men the sweathouse, since they kept it neat and clean.

II.13. IXKAREYA STORY (COYOTE SPOILS WORLD)

GEORGIA ORCUTT (1940)

This story was told to Georgia by Red Cap Tom.

●

a. Some ixkareya women living on [the] river went up the hill. [The] ixkareya make [made] it that way, that women were to go uphill and put wood in baskets, and the baskets full of wood would walk down by themselves. [The] ixkareya said the same thing about baskets full of acorns: they would come down by themselves, so the women would not have to pack it [them].

b. [The] ixkareya said, "Let's make the river so that on one side you will go up that way, and come down the other. Let's make it that way so as not to have to work hard going up the river. It will be nice when we make it that way. We shall not have to work hard. It will be easy that way." Then [they] talked it over and decided it would be nice to fix it that way.

c. After a while Coyote come around. Coyote said, "You folks think you are going to fix it a nice way. Menfolk will have to pay lots of ishpuk[1] before he gets [they get a] wife. I think man, if he but buy woman, will have her work. She will carry baskets of wood and acorn(s). It will not be the nice way you fixed it so they would [will] not have to carry anything. When a man marries he will have to work hard. You think it a nice way if a man sit[s] down on [in a] boat and do [does] nothing. It will not be nice to have the river running two ways. It will be better for men to use [a] paddle to propel [a] boat."

That's the way Coyote spoiled things for the people.

II.14. SNAKE STORY (COYOTE'S HOME AT PANAMENIK)

MARY IKE (1939)

[This and the next three myths relate the story of Coyote's thirst after he has committed the unpardonable sin of drinking the gooseberry juice a sweating man has set out for himself. Three of the four versions are by Mary Ike. Her present version and Georgia Orcutt's single version (II.15) are the most coherent and complete tellings, as they easily and naturally join the Coyote's thirst story to that of Coyote's upstream journey to Panamenik with the Ducks.

Mary Ike's first variant version (II.16) contains elements usually told as separate stories: Coyote's shooting at the bobcat and Coyote's sleeping with his divorced wife. In II.17 Mary confirms details supplied by Georgia in II.15 or repeats elements from her own first version. William Bright, in The Travels of Coyote, Kroeber Anthropological Society Papers, no. 11, pp. 1–16, carefully analyzes versions of Coyote's journeys as told by several Karok informants.—Ed.]

•

1. [Dentalia, identified in II.15*a*.—Ed.]

a. Absummunukich (a small brown racer? snake) always was sweating himself in [the] sweathouse. Coyote came along and saw a lot of food in basket cups outside the sweathouse. "What a lot of drink someone has!" He drank it all. It was gooseberry juice.

b. Coyote had on a coat called ixturui (of buckskin).[1] The snake said, "You had no business drinking up all my water! I hope you get thirsty. I hope you do not reach your destination."

c. Coyote sang as he walked along, saying, "I am going to Kayuras (upper ocean) to make some money!" He began to get thirsty. He saw a creek and said, "Now I'm going to get a drink." When he put his mouth down, there was no more water. He went on. He found another creek. He tried again, and [the] water turned to dust. He took his coat off and bundled it. "Next water I come to," he said, "I'm going to throw my coat in and get some water out of it." He threw it into [the] next spring; it fell into nothing but dust. Next time he tried to sneak up to [the] water and again threw his coat. Dust only. He went on. He could hardly walk. He decided to roll down to [the] river. There he drank and drank. He got up and looked around. He "drowned" and floated back downstream.

d. He saw five young girls hooking sticks out of [the] river. He said, "See if you can't hook me out." They did. After they got him out, they said, "It may be Coyote. We heard he drowned. Let's throw him back."

They threw him into [the] middle of [the] river, and he floated down. He said, "I want to become a pretty stick." He did. More young girls were hooking sticks, and they hooked him out [but] they threw him in again.

e. He floated [down] to [the] mouth [of the] river. [There] he got ashore and walked up to [the] sweathouse. When people came out, he went in [to the] sweathouse. He was hungry, but he saw only greasy wooden pillows. He ate one. It tasted good, so he ate them all. The sweathouse people came back, and Coyote hid behind the piled-up property at one side. They said, "Coyote has been here. They said he was drowned on his way to Kahayuras."

f. Then they all began to talk. Coyote listened. One asked, "Where are you going to sweat tonight?" The other replied, "At Aspaukram (the little lake at Katimin)." Another said, "I'm going

1. The buckskin was ripped up to the neck with a piece sewed on each end. It was worn in winter as a cape tied about the neck.

to sweat at Uknamxanak ('long lake,' below Orleans).'' All at once the sticks began to rattle where Coyote was hiding. Coyote rolled out and began to shout, "That's my land! That's my land! You'd better let me go along. I'll put all kinds of pretty marks on your feathers[2] if you'll let me go along." "All right, but don't open your eyes when you are in the boat until we tell. If you hear a noise fifteen times you can open your eyes." "All right, I'll do that," said Coyote.

g. He kept his eyes shut. He heard noises and finally decided to peek, although they had told him that if he disobeyed he would find himself back in the sweathouse. He did.

h. The Ducks came [went] on up. After a time they returned home. They told about the lakes they had visited. "At Uknamxanak there were lots of people. At Aspaukram there were lots of people." Coyote wished he could go there. "I'll keep my eyes shut if you'll take me next time. I want to go home. I want to go up there. Those are my people."

i. The Ducks took him along again. "Don't open your eyes this time. Even when you hear ten noises you must still keep your eyes shut."

j. At Orleans they told him to open his eyes. He did. He was so happy he kept kicking out dirt so it formed the big bar this side of Camp Creek. He kicked up the large ridge between Chamichnimich and Xatsipirak on [the] east side of [the] river.

II.15. Coyote's Home at Panamenik

GEORGIA ORCUTT (1940)

a. Coyote decided he want[ed] to go to Kayuras for ispuk or dentalia. He stayed in (the) sweathouse ten days. [Then] he start(ed) off. He was carrying his quiver with [his] bow and arrows. On the way he come [came] to [a] place where someone was making fire in (a) sweathouse. He look(ed) in the telpak (entrance)[1] as he stood outside. At the exit he saw two acorn dishes outside the house with

---

2. The people were Ducks.

---

1. The exit at floor level is called sununum.

gooseberry juice in them. It was Lizard who was making fire in (the) sweathouse. He was going to drink the gooseberry juice when he came out. He was singing in the sweathouse.

b. Coyote thought, "I'll taste it." It tasted so nice (that) he drank it all. Then he went on his way. When Lizard came out he said, "Somebody's been drinking my juice. I wish (the person) who drank my juice will [would] dry up and not be able to drink water."

c. [Coyote walked along.] "I am going to walk and try for water. I am dry for (want of) water." He should not be [have been] eating or drinking while going for shell money. After a while he said, "I'm going to drink water." He knew where there was a little creek coming down. "I am going to drink water." He tried to scoop it up with his hands, but got no water. Then he walked a little further to another creek. "How am I going to drink water? I['ll] try with my buckskin cape." When he threw it in, there was only dust where he had seen water.

d. He went on. At another creek he tried shooting his arrow into (the) water and licking it off. Again nothing but dust. Lizard had made it this way because Coyote had drunk his gooseberry juice. Lizard had wished that whoever drank his gooseberry juice would go thirsty.

e. Coyote went on. He see [saw] another creek. He heard the water coming down. All dried up that creek, so he can't get it that water. He took off his moccasins and threw them in, hoping he could catch some water. It looked like they were floating down when he threw in the shoes. When he picked them up to lick [them] off, nothing but dust ran out of them. (The creek had dried up, so he could get no water.)

f. Coyote walked along. "Oh, I wish I had a drink of water." Further up someone had set a fire. He saw lots of (many) scorched grasshoppers.[2] Coyote sang, "I won't (am not) going to eat you. I am going to Kayuras for money." Normally Coyote ate grasshoppers.[3] Then he changed his mind and ate grasshoppers. They tasted

2. [Gifford's typescript showed the section now labeled *f* as preceding *c*, but he had added the notation, "Grasshopper episode should follow water." I have made this transposition for the printed version.—Ed.]

3. [An indication of his low status. The northwestern Californians "ordinarily did not have to condescend to the grasshoppers, angleworms, and yellow-jacket larvae whose nourishing qualities other tribes of the State exploited" (Kroeber, Handbook, p. 84).—Ed.]

nice. He ate and ate, but he could not get enough. "I eat and eat, but I never get enough." He looked back and he saw the grasshoppers were going right through him. Then he took some pitch and plugged his rectum, so he would get enough.

As Coyote went along he could hear the Kayuras ocean roar. He said, "Now I'm getting near the ocean." But he was really hearing the sound of burning pitch on his rear end. He ran down to the river and jumped in. He got (was) drowned. He never reached Kayuras.

g. His body floated down the river. He saw at one place girls hooking out driftwood. He said, "I'm going to be nice driftwood so the girls will hook me out." When one of the girls hook[ed] out the piece she threw it back in the river, saying, "It might be Coyote." He drifted downstream further to where some other girls were hooking driftwood. "I'm going to be a nice-looking piece of driftwood," Coyote thought. A girl hooked him out, but threw him back, saying, "It may be Coyote."

h. After a while he drifted to Sufip (Rekwoi). It was late in [the] evening and everyone was in dwellings (indoors) eating acorns. No one (was) in the sweathouse. Coyote had eaten nothing for a long time. When he went into (the) sweathouse, he saw all the wooden pillows and steps. He ate them and said, "My, it is so nice!"

i. When he heard the men coming he hid behind the woodpile in the sweathouse. The first man to come in was Mallard (ⁱstaa). Another came and another. The first one said, "We ain't got (have) no stuff. Where is all our stuff gone?"

"We are going upriver to Uknamkana (a pool this side [east] of Camp Creek),"[4] the Ducks sang in the sweathouse. When Coyote heard this he jumped out from behind the woodpile, shouting, "That is my place! That is my place! I am going to go up with you!" The Ducks said they would not take him. Coyote said, "I am going to go up there. Panamenik is my home."

j. The Ducks said, "All right, you can go. You can lie in [the] boat, but don't look up, don't look around. Just sleep." When Coyote lay in [the] boat the Ducks covered him with a taprara[5] mat. "Don't look around," the Ducks said. "When we are ready to land, that is the time you can get up."

k. Halfway up Coyote decided to peek out by lifting (the) cover

4. There are always many ducks in this pool in summertime. They breed there.
5. A kind of ocean grass, of which the Yurok made mats.

slightly. When he looked he found he was still in (the) sweathouse at Sufip.

l. When the Ducks returned from Uknamkana, Coyote begged again for them to take him. They took him and told him to be sure not to look out. "If you want to go up there," the Ducks said, "be sure you shut your eyes."

m. This time Coyote did not look out. He was afraid. He arrived at Panamenik all right. When he jumped out, he said, "My home! This is my home!" He ran down to Camp Creek when he got off the boat. He lay down and rolled around in all directions at Camp Creek. Then he came up to Panamenik and rolled around on the bar on (the) Panamenik side of (the) river. First he made (the) Camp Creek bar when he first got off (the) boat. Then he made (the) bar below Panamenik and upstream from Camp Creek.

n. Coyote said, "As long as this world be (is) here, this is my home here at Panamenik. People will come from other places and play (the) stick game (double-ball shinny) at Panamenik. They will always go away ashamed because they will be beaten at the game." Coyote said, "They would (will) always be beaten by the Panamenik people, whenever they come here to play." They played the game near (the) oak tree just below Panamenik.[6]

II.16. STORY ABOUT COYOTE

MARY IKE (1940)

a. Coyote said, "I think I'll go way up and see the dance at Kayuras (upstream ocean). I heard that there is dancing going on up there." The people told him not to go so far, but to go to a dance close by.

He went on up. "I might see my divorced wife," Coyote said. "It would be too bad if I see her."

b. They had told him not to stop at a Lizard's (djimuit) sweathouse way upcountry. Lizard had some gooseberry juice. Coyote said, "I'm going to drink the gooseberry juice, it looks so good." He drank it all, every bit of it. Then he went on. Lizard came out of [the] sweathouse and saw someone had drunk his gooseberry juice. He said, "I did not know Coyote was around here. I just wish he would get good and thirsty."

6. [For more details on the stick game, see V.34 and V.46, above.—Ed.]

c. Coyote was going along and began to get thirsty. "Oh! I want a drink of water." He heard a creek. "Now here is where I am going to get some water." He lay down to drink, but stuck his nose in the dust. Then he went on. "Oh! I do want water so badly."

d. He was packing a quiver (akavaki). He thought, "I'll take an arrow and shoot it into the water and lick it off." He shot, but when he picked up the arrow it was just dry.

e. He came to another creek and took off his cape of deerhide. "Now," he thought, "I'll throw it into the water." When he threw it a cloud of dust arose.

Then he went on. He looked up the trail and he saw a bobcat (akwi) sitting on a tree. He said, "I'm not going to wear this cape any more. I'm going to get me a new one." So he tore it up and threw it down the hill.

f. He shot at the bobcat. "I missed him," but the bobcat jumped down. He took a shot at another one, and he jumped down. They all got away from him. "Now what am I going to wear?" he asked himself. Then he went down the hill and picked up the pieces and sewed them together again.

g. He went on. He looked over the hill and seen (saw) where they were dancing. Everybody was dancing the ihuk (First Menses Dance).[1] They told him, "You'd better dance with them." He said, "No, I'm going in the middle." He had seen his former wife. She was all dressed up, decorated with abalone shell. His ex-wife was Frog.

h. Night came. "Now where am I going to sleep?" Coyote asked himself. Somebody said, "This man wants to drink." So they gave him some water and he drank just lots. Coyote crawled in bed with some lady [a woman]. In the morning when he woke up he looked at her. "Why, that's my ex-wife!" he said. He was just ashamed. He said, "Hereafter people will do this. They will go with their wives after they are divorced, because I done (did) that." Kupanakana.

II.17. Coyote's Trip to Kayuras for Money

MARY IKE (1940)

a. Coyote was making a lot of twine. He said, "I am going to string money (ispuk) with it." He was walking up the trail (impā)

1. [See II.19, n. 1, below.—Ed.]

singing these words. He was packing the twine on his back. He sang as he walked. He said, "I'm going to Kayuras to make some money." Then he went way [far] up.

b. He saw a fire there. He looked around and he saw a lot of (many) grasshoppers, cooked ones. He thought he would taste one. He ate and ate and ate, and could not get enough, they tasted so good. He looked around and said, "I wonder why I don't get filled up." Come to find out [Then he found out] they just went right through him; they never stopped.

c. He looked around. "What am I going to do? I want to get filled up." He saw a bull pine tree. So he went and got some pitch and plugged his rectum. "Now," he said, "I'll get filled up," and he started eating again. Then he heard a noise. "Now, I hear the ocean roaring. I must be getting close to where I was going." When he looked around, he found he was on fire; the pitch was burning. He ran down to the river and jumped in. Then he floated down the river. He went way [far] down and saw girls hooking out wood from the river.

d. He prayed, "Let me be the prettiest, nicest piece of wood." He became wood, and the girls tried hard to hook it out. Finally, one got it out and packed it up the hill. She said, "It must be Coyote. I feel funny. I'm getting heavy." So they took the wood and threw it back in the river.

e. He floated on down the river to where another lot of girls were hooking driftwood. They tried a long while to hook him out with [a] lashed-on hook (takurada). Finally one hooked him out. "We'll keep him this time. It may make bad luck for us to throw him back." They had heard of Coyote being drowned way [far] up the river. Three girls got fat and pregnant.

II.18. Coyote Story (Coyote's Trip to Kayuras)

GEORGIA ORCUTT (1940)

a. On [the] hill above Yuduksuv (Bluff Creek) Coyote went way [far] up on (the) hill, where lots of (many) people stayed on (the) ridge Apahaisuripa. Coyote hollowed a syringa stick and used (the) pith for imitation dentalia. He put this in his kavaki (quiver).

b. He went up on (the) hill and saw (an) old man there. After a while the old man said, "Let's go in the house and eat acorns." They went into (the) house. The old man said, "It is nice you came to see me. I like to talk with somebody." The old man's name was Apahai-suripa pinits (Apahaisuripa old man).

c. Coyote said, "I've (been) thinking about coming to see you for a long time, but I never started." After a while they both went into (the) sweathouse. When he go(t) in, Coyote said, "Akich (friend), you've got to see my money." He took it out and showed it to the old man. The old man said, "That's not money. It is not ispuk." Coyote insisted, "It is money." The old man said, "That ain't (is not) ispuk." "Isn't it?" said Coyote. "You'd better show me some real money. I thought this was money." Coyote knew the old man had a lot of (much) money. Only the old man had money.

d. After a while, when Coyote kept on asking, the old man brought out his money. "This is money," the old man said. "Where do you get it?" asked Coyote. "I get (it) up at Kayuras," the old man said. "How do you go up there?" Coyote asked. "It is awfully hard," the old man said (replied). Coyote said, "I'd like to get the money too."

"There are awfully mean people up at Kayuras, where we get that money. You can't go there except [unless] you [first] sleep in (the) sweathouse for ten days and every morning carry wood from (the) forest to [the] sweathouse. In the evening you'll have to carry wood, too. You cannot drink water for ten days." Coyote said, "I can do it. I can pack wood early in the morning for sweathouse wood, and in the evening, and not drink water for ten days."

The old man said, "I can go up with you, when you go to Kayuras." The old man knew the way, because he always went there. The old man said, "There are mean people up there. Them (Those) folks fish for that Indian (dentalium) money. They make (a) fire by the ocean. After midnight is the time they fish. We can wait until they go to bed. That is the time we'll go in. The people suck the dentalia to clean it of [the] animal inside. These people have sharp mouths from sucking so much. You can carry a netting bag (sukrif)."

e. Then they started to go up to Kayuras. They did not follow the river, but took a shortcut over the ridges back of Panamenik. After long walking (number of days uncertain) they arrived at Kayuras

Mountain (Kayuras ivre). That old man said, "We can sit down right here and wait a while." From there they could look down to Kayuras.

f. "Let's go down a ways and stop again," said the old man. Late in the evening the Kayuras people were just coming to fish for money. "We have to sit here until midnight, when those folks go home," the old man said. The Kayuras people had a good time while fishing, laughing and hollering (shouting).

Coyote got tired of waiting and wanted to go on down. "We can't do that," said the old man, "for those people will kill us. They are mean."

After a while the Kayuras people were going home. That old man, he said, "We have to get not much, just a little bit. If we take much, maybe those people will find out and kill us. In going back we must follow this trail. Them (Those) folks never come over to it. They can't get over here. Don't put too much money in your sukrif. Put in just a little, then we'll go," the old man said to Coyote.

g. The Kayuras (people) never (did not) hear it when the two carried off the money. They [the Old Man and Coyote] did not fish with a net which (was) cast into the water and drawn in, as the Kayuras people did, but they merely picked up the shells they found on the beach.

Coyote said, "I'm going to get some more. I ain't got (have not) enough." The old man said, "No. Maybe the people (will) find out, if you take more." "Oh, they can't hear when I go back," said Coyote. "I'm going to get some more. You wait for me right here."

h. The old man waited while Coyote went back for more. After a while he heard somebody holler (shout). The old man said, "I told him not to go again. Now I bet they are going to kill Coyote." After a while he heard somebody cry. "Now Coyote got killed," he said. Then the old man ran away. He come [came] home. Somebody asked him, "Where is Coyote?" "He got killed. I heard him cry out."

i. About ten days afterwards Coyote came back. The old man said, "I thought you got killed and never would come back here." Coyote said, "I just made it. When I knew they were about to catch me, I threw the sukrif over the boundary beyond which the Kayuras people would not go." The Kayuras people killed Coyote, but he came to life again. He brought home all the money. "You better keep my money here," Coyote told the old man.

j. Then [Later] Coyote went up to the old man's house again. He asked for his money. That old man said, "Don't show that money to anybody. You must keep it, hide it." Coyote brought his money down. Then he went over to Hupa, where he went into sweathouse at Kicherak (Takimilding). There were many people in the macharam (sweathouse).

k. Coyote said, "I'll show you people the money." They had never seen that kind before. "How did you get that money?" they asked. After a while somebody took the money from beside Coyote and ran out with it. Coyote ran after him, but could (not) find him. Coyote could not do anything. He just sat down. He ain't got (had) no money. He returned to Panamenik. Then he went up to see the old man after a while. "Somebody took my money." "I told you you must not show anybody, that you must keep it, you must hide it."

Coyote said, "Let's go up and get some more." That old man said, "No, we cannot go up again. As long as this world is here, you will always be nobody. You spoil[ed] it." Kupanakanak.

II.19. Coyote Story

MARY IKE (1940)

a. Coyote said, "We'd better have the ihuk (First Menses) dance." There were two girls. One was at her first menses; the other was staying with her. They danced over the one with the first menses.[1]

Elk (ishyu) was going to sing for the dance. He sang, "Mokumoku, mokumoku."[2] Wolf (ixhavnam) sang. Pileated Woodpecker (ixtaktakahen) sang. Flicker (suuk) sang. Woodpecker and Flicker (were) "high toned."[3]

b. They all danced, everybody. When [they] finished dancing they were all to run to (a) lake and took bath (bathe). The girls ran.

1. [For Kroeber's description of the Karok adolescence dance for girls, see the Editor's Preface, above.—Ed.]

2.[The meaning is given in III.4*b*, in a variant of this tale.—Ed.]

3. [Perhaps its literal meaning. Kroeber, in Handbook, p. 96, says that the northwest California Indian, "particularly in the music of his great dances, loves to leap upward an octave or more to a long, powerful note, and then sink back from this by a series of slides, often of a continuous tonal transition. The accompanists at times chant a rhythmic bass without definite melodic relation to the strain."—Ed.]

Whoever could catch up with either one of them could marry her.

c. They all stood in (a) row in line ready to run. There was one old man whom they thought too old to run, and he won the race. Coyote was left way [far] behind. He did not get even halfway. The old man (Wolf) married the girls. He was the one who sang, mentioned above.

II.20. Coyote and Spider

MARY IKE (1940)

a. Coyote was living up in the sky (painonuavakam, above us). Spider was living close by. Coyote was looking down on earth. "I'm going down there. They'll have to do whatever I want them to do." He commenced twisting twine. Spider said, "I'll go with you." Coyote asked Spider, "What are you going to travel on?" "Here is what I am going to travel on," said Spider, and he showed Coyote a lot of twine he had on his chest.

They both landed on earth at the same time.

b. Spider asked, "How are you going to get back? You can't get back." Coyote tried but could not make it. Coyote asked Spider, "How are you going to get back?" "I'll show you how I am going to get back." There were many people watching them.

c. Coyote said, "I'm going to stay down here." Spider said, "I'm not going to stay here. I'll come down every once in a while." Spider said, "You all watch me now. I am going home." He climbed back up on the twine. Spider said, "Whenever you see me come down, you'll know you are going to have visitors."[1] "I'll come down every once in a while," said Spider.

II.21. Coyote (and Blowfly) Story

GEORGIA ORCUTT (1940)

Georgia learned this story from Red Cap Tom's father.

●

1. Descent of a spider is an omen of visitors.

a. Coyote one time went up on [the] hill and went into somebody's house. It was Blowfly's house. When he went in he said, "My, [it] looks like you got [have] lots of deer meat!" After a while the man of the house said, "You better eat some deer meat." Coyote took some and cooked it by [the] fire. This was fresh deer meat.

b. "How do you get it?" Coyote inquired. The man never answered. After a while [But] Coyote never [did not] give up asking him. Finally the man told him, "I go way [far] up on [the] hill. The deer are lying sleeping at [the] bottom of a bluff after running around all night. I walk all over the deer, beginning at [the] head. After a while I go in [the] rectum. I just cut it off that fat. Then I come out. That deer just lay [lies] there. He never [doesn't] feel it."

Coyote said he wanted to try it. Fly said, "You go in kind of slow."

c. So Coyote set out, carrying his yuhidim (flint knife). Coyote cut off the fat while Deer was sleeping. After a while Coyote thought to himself, "I haven't got enough." So he cut off more. After a while, when Coyote [was] ready to go out, that Deer jump[ed] up and ran. Coyote can't [couldn't] get out. The Deer ran everywhere, with Coyote's head hanging out of Deer's rectum. As Deer ran, Coyote's head [was] hanging out and bumping against trees and getting bloodier all the time. After a while Coyote fell out and lay there with blood [all] over his face and head. He never get nothing [had not gotten anything].

d. In the evening start[ed] off walking that Coyote. He walked a little ways and sat down again. He walked all night. Blowfly thought something had happened because he never [hadn't] showed up. Finally Coyote arrived at Blowfly's house.

Blowfly asked, "What's the matter with you that you did not come back in morning [yesterday]?" "Chawash (brother's son)," Coyote said, "oh, chawash, I can't [didn't] get nothing [anything]." Blowfly said, "I never cut it off much. Deer cannot feel it when I cut off small pieces. I told you you must not cut it off big pieces." Coyote say [said], "I thought maybe I can't [didn't] get enough. That's why when [I was] ready to go out I cut off [a] big piece. At that time the Deer jump[ed] up and run [ran] with me, so I hit my head on trees and rocks as he ran." "Spoil everything, Coyote."

"Aw, chawash, I can't [couldn't] get enough to eat. I cut it off in small pieces, but I can't [couldn't] get enough." Kupanakanak.

II.22. Coyote (and Fly) Story

MARY IKE (1940)

a. Blowfly was living in a house and had lots of [much] deer meat. He was drying it and smoking it and had lots [a great deal] of fat. Coyote came along and saw Fly packing the deer.

b. Then Coyote went to Fly's house and said, "I heard you got [have] a lot of meat. I want to get some." Fly gave him some, and he ate and ate. Then they went to [the] sweathouse. Coyote took a piece of meat for [a] pillow, so he could bite off a piece if he awoke in (the) middle of [the] night. Coyote said, "We'll sing all night [the] deer song in [the] sweathouse." Coyote sang. (Song.)

c. Next day Fly went hunting and left Coyote [at] home. Coyote said, "I'll follow him now and see where he gets his deer." Coyote watched Fly. He looked way up (the) mountain and he saw Fly. He seen (saw a) big old buck standing there. Fly hollered at (called to) the old deer to open up his rectum. Then he went up there, crawled in, and cut the fat out. He got a big load of fat.

Coyote was watching, and he said to himself, "I am going to do the same." Fly brought his load of deer fat home. Coyote ran home ahead of him.

d. Coyote said to Fly, "Why not let me go deer hunting?" Fly said, "No, I am going to go." Fly said, "You can go [too]. But when you get inside the deer you'll find a big ball of fat hanging there. Do not touch that."

e. Coyote went up the mountain and hollered (shouted) for the deer. A deer came and let Coyote into his rectum. Coyote (cut) all the fat out. "Now," he said, "I'm going to cut that big one off. I have one of my legs out, so I can jump out quick[ly]."

f. He cut it off. The deer closed his rectum so quickly Coyote was trapped. Deer ran over the hill, up the mountains, and ran around the world with Coyote inside of him with his leg sticking out. He finally fell down.

g. Fly thought, "I told him not to do that. Now he's gone and done it." Finally Coyote fell out some place and returned to the house. "I told you not to do that." Coyote said, "Ishavash,[1] I did not mean to do that. I thought I could get away with it."

---

1. Niece, sister's daughter. Coyote calls everyone ishavash, whether female or

Fly said, "You would [will] not live on deer meat. All you are going to live on is gophers. All you are going to eat is gophers."

II.23. COYOTE STORY

MARY IKE

a. Coyote was married once. He got a divorce. He would not go any place, because he went again with his wife after [the] divorce and he was afraid someone would make fun of him.

b. Coyote went upriver to look for a different woman. He came to a creek. He saw two girls coming down the trail. They both had baskets on their backs. The girls decided to bathe in the creek because it was so hot.

c. Coyote jumped into the water and turned into [a] steelhead (saap). The two girls were sitting in the water. One said, "There is a steelhead." One went downstream, the other upstream, to try to catch it. One said, "Let's use the basket to catch it." The steelhead swam up the stream and splashed around the girl. She tried in vain to catch it. Then it did the same with the downstream girl. It went back and forth, and the girls called to each other to head it off.

d. Steelhead jumped out of the water and became Coyote. Then he went up the hill and danced. When the girls got out of the water they were already fat. Coyote ran away. The girls went home, both pregnant. Kupanakanak.

II.24. COYOTE STORY

GEORGIA ORCUTT (1940)

a. Coyote [was] walking on [a] trail and looking up every little ways. He thought he saw someone, he thought. He asked, "Where (are you) going?" No answer, (so he) got mad (angry). As he got close he swung at the person with his elbow. However, it was not a

---

male. It is a term applied [to a child] following the death of the connecting relative. Thus, Mary calls Shan [Davis?] ishavash. Shan's mother was Mary's cousin-sister, and Mary called her sister.

person, but (a) stump. His elbow was embedded in the wood so he could not get away. The various people came around: Woodpecker, Crow, etc. Coyote beseeched someone to free him. He asked the Woodpeckers to chip away the wood. He said, "I'll make you all pretty if you free me."

b. The Woodpeckers chipped away the wood and finally freed him.[1] Coyote asked for a basket of water for a mirror so each could see how pretty he became [had become]. Crow wanted to be red, but Coyote had only black pigment [left]. When Crow looked in [the] basket mirror, he was surprised to find himself all black. Coyote had used up all his red on the Woodpecker head tops. Also on the Woodpecker women he [had] put three marks on (the) chin, so women today have three tattoo marks on (their) chins.[2]

II.25. COYOTE STORY

GEORGIA ORCUTT (1940)

[This is an exceptionally interesting story. In it Coyote creates five sons from syringa sticks, the wood from which arrows are made. It is one of the few Karok myths in which Coyote is shown as a creator, but, having brought his sons into existence, he loses them through folly, in typical Coyote fashion, by sending them into battle against hopeless odds. The grief of Coyote's accomplice Wolf, who also loses his sons, is powerfully expressed.

The first part of the plot is echoed in Kroeber's Yurok myth, A16x *g,* in which spent arrows are transformed into young men. The idea may have been transmitted through the Karok, as Kroeber's Yurok informant, Lame Billy of Weitspus, was an imaginative synthesizer of plot elements from Karok and Hupa myths as well as from his own people.—Ed.]

•

a. One man ixkareya named Xavnam (to mash; also means Wolf) living at Panamenik had five sons. Coyote knew that. Coyote

---

1. [Ellipsis. Coyote then painted the birds, as promised.—Ed.]
2. [Kroeber observes (Handbook, pp. 77–78) that "women had the entire chin, from the corners of the mouth downward, tattooed solidly except for two narrow blank lines. A beginning was made with three vertical stripes, which were broadened until they nearly met. Occasionally a row of points diversified the edges

went to visit the old man. He asked him, "Where is your wife?" The old man said, "I ain't got (have) no wife. Coyote said, "It is too bad I asked you. Maybe you lost your wife already." The man said, "I ain't got (have) no wife." Coyote said (asked), "How (did) you get those boys? You got (have) five boys." The man said, "I raised my boys. I ain't got (have) no wife. Just the same I raised them." Coyote said, "You better show me how you raised them (your) boys." The man said, "You can't do that. It's awfully hard." Coyote said, "I'm going to try it. I'm going to try it." And the man said, "All right. If you want to try it, you can try it. But I don't think you can do it anyway."

b. "You have to make fire in [the] sweathouse first for ten days," the man said. "You can make [take] five sticks from xawish (the syringa) tree[1] and stand them on one side of [the] sweathouse. Where you make fire in (the) sweathouse firebox you must put sand. You can lay (lie) down by the fire. Don't open your eyes when you lay (lie) down. I shall put hot sand on you and you must not cry 'Ouch!' Don't wake up when I put the hot sand on you. It will be so hot you can hardly stand it. If you can't stand it, you cannot make the boys."

c. Coyote tried it, but when the man put the hot sand on him, he exclaimed, "Anok (Ouch)!" and jumped up. The man said, "You can't stand it. You can't make that boy."

d. Coyote said, "I want to try it again." "I'm sure you can't stand it," said the man. "No, I want to try it again," insisted Coyote. The man said, "No use for you to try it again. You can't stand it." But Coyote insisted, "No, I'm going to try it again."

e. The man said, "If you try it again, you'll have to give a name to each of the five syringa sticks. The names are Ixmacharamixkyuvare (sweathouse poles put on), Aksipakwapitiv (roots of grass

---

of the area. This style is universal in northwestern California. A little familiarity makes it rather pleasing . . . . Certainly it is not long before a younger woman or half-breed who has escaped the tattoo strikes one with a sense of shock, as of something necessary missing."—Ed.]

---

1. A small tree with white flowers from which arrows and pipes are made; pith in center; cheap pipes only are made from it. [In Schenck and Gifford, Karok Ethnobotany, UC-AR 13:(no. 6):384–385, the plant is further identified as *Philadelphus lewisii* var. gordonianus, the syringa or mock orange. The young shoots were the major source of arrow shafts, which had tips made from Western serviceberry twigs rather than stone points.—Ed.]

coming up when one runs over the grass), Pariptutschara (. . . tree),[2] Ahedimchûk adihiv (tree-fall-over jumping over it), and Taharatishnam (ten places flat running over).''

f. Coyote tried it again. Coyote lay on the sweathouse floor. For ten days he had drunk no water. The man put the hot sand on Coyote. He lay still; he did not say ''Anok!'' this time. He never opened his eyes. He called one name, and one syringa stick answered. He called another name, and another syringa stick answered. He called the third name, and another syringa stick answered. He called the fourth name, and another syringa stick answered. He called the fifth name, and another syringa stick answered. Then Coyote opened his eyes. There were the five boys.

g. Then Coyote made a living house (ixlivram) for his five boys, [and] also a sweathouse (macharam). Coyote built the houses with the help of the boys. Also they fished and hunted, so Coyote was living high.

h. After a while, Coyote asked the man (Xavnam), ''You [have] been living here all alone? Have you no brother or folks?'' Wolf replied, ''I've had lots of [many] relatives living here, but they were all killed off by enemies from Kayuras. Awful bad people come from Kayuras.''[3]

i. Coyote said, ''I think your boys and my boys will go up to Kayuras and kill off all those people. Those people are awful mean. You['ve] got five boys and I've got five boys. They can kill anybody.'' Xavnam said, ''All right.'' So the ten boys started out, but Xavnam and Coyote remained at home.

j. Coyote after a time suggested to Xavnam that they clean up a place outside to hold the War Dance when their boys returned. So they went to work on it.

k. After a time they heard somebody holler (calling) some place. Coyote said, ''You better get ready. Now we are going to have the War Dance.'' Xavnam was staying in the house. He never came outside. Coyote heard somebody holler (shout) again and he said to Xavnam, ''You better come outside. We are going to have a War Dance.'' However, it was a messenger from Kayuras, who said all ten of the boys got (were) killed in Kayuras. Xavnam cried and it

2. [Omission in typescript.—Ed.]
3. If asked to pronounce the name slowly, Georgia said Kahayuras. [It is identified as the upstream ocean in I.5*e* and II.14*c*, above.—Ed.]

looked like everybody heard him. People came from all directions. They knew something had happened. Xavnam said to Coyote, "I told you those Kayuras people were mean. Nobody (is) going to kill those Kayuras people up there. You always spoil everything."

l. Everybody came when they heard Xavnam crying. They came from every place. Coyote went in and told Xavnam not to cry. "We'll have to talk about pisiwava (dentalium money) and sapruk (whole Olivella biplicata, spire-looped)."[4]

m. Coyote never make [made] boys again. Xavnam blamed Coyote: "If you had not suggested (that) our boys go up there, everything would be all right now." Coyote always wanted to talk about money, but he never had any. He was a nobody.

II.26. COYOTE SIGN

GEORGIA ORCUTT (1940)

a. Sun rose bright over (the) mountains, but it was cloudy. Coyote said to his wife, "It's going to be a nice day. Let's go somewhere." So his wife put (the) baby in (the) basket (cradle), and they set out. Pretty soon, while they were walking along, the rain commenced. (The) baby got wet, contracted a cold, and died.

b. Coyote was mad [angry]. He said, "I thought it was going to be a nice day, but that Sun fooled me."[1]

c. Next day, Coyote said, "I'm going to kill that Sun." So he climbed up Uchkamtim Mountain behind Pearch Creek, so as to catch the Sun when it came up in the morning. But he found that it was far off. So next time he tried on (a) peak further east. Again it was too far away when it came up. So he kept on trying it on (a) mountain further over each morning. "Well," he said, "I'm going back home." But he got lost in (the) sky and could not find his way home.

d. "How am I going to get down?" He was in [the] sky and

4. Pisiwava comes from Kayuras, sapruk from Yuras. [Yuras is the downstream ocean, according to I.2a, above.—Ed.] Olivella (sapruk) were not used as money but as dress ornaments. They had to be purchased with dentalia.

1. Moon is kadam kus; Sun is tubaha kus. Georgia used "sun" and "moon" alike for sun.

completely lost. He pondered on how to get down. "Maybe, if I have my head down when I come down, and (I'll) break my head. Or maybe my shoulder will get broken. Or maybe I'll break my back." He was only skin and bones now, for he had been lost a long time without food. Finally he dropped down feet first. He landed all right without breaking to pieces.

e. He said, "I lost my baby. I paid big money for my wife, so my children would be well off when they grew up. But now I lost my child. As long as this world lasts, it will be that way when (the) Sun comes up clear but (the) sky is cloudy. It will rain," said Coyote.[2]

II.27. How Coyote Wanted to Die

GEORGIA ORCUTT (1940)

Coyote done (did) something, and two ixkareya men were going to kill him. When they caught Coyote and prepared to kill him, he said, "If you are going to kill me, please do it some (so in a) nice way. I'm going to lay (lie) down, so you can kill me in a nice way. One time I always think (I always have thought) I am somebody. I'm going to lay (lie) down so you can kill me in a nice way. I can lay (shall lie) down so you can kill me." He lay down and shut his eyes. The men looked for a knife or something with which to kill him. While they were doing this, Coyote jumped up and ran off. Kupanakanak.

II.28. Coyote Story

GEORGIA ORCUTT

a. Coyote visits (visited) one old man. Coyote goes (went) into (the) sweathouse to visit him. After a while the old man suggested they go into (the) house.

2. People say, "If you have paid big money for your wife and she has a child who will be well off, don't go out with the child if the sun comes out clear but the sky is cloudy, because it is going to rain." People always say this, when the sun comes out bright and the sky is cloudy. People call it pinefisim cheha, "Coyote sign." [See Bright's interpretation in the Linguistic Index, below.—Ed.] One should take a deerhide raincape as rain protection.

b. After a while (Later) the old man took a round wooden bowl (like a chopping bowl) off of (the) house ledge. It contained grouse meat. The old man invited Coyote to eat it. After Coyote ate, he said, "My, that was so nice! How do you get it?" Looked like (It seemed) the old man did not want to tell him, but Coyote kept asking him where he got it.

c. At last the old man told him, "I go up on a mountain, way [far] up on a ridge. I make (a) fire on the ridge. When I make (the) big fire under a fir tree and (it) all burn(s) up that wood and (so that) nothing but coals (are left) on the fire, then I stand up, and I holler (shout), "You folks come over this way!" Then the grouse come and afterwards they fall into [the] fire. After (their) feathers (are) singed off, then (I) clean out (the) guts, then cook the grouse. Then I come home with the grouse already cooked."

d. Coyote said, "I'm going to try it." The old man said, "All right. You can try it."

e. Afterwards Coyote went up on the ridge. He made a fire, a big fire, under a fir tree. When all the wood [had] burned to coals, that was the time he hollered (shouted). When he hollered (shouted), all kinds of big things came from all directions. As he was looking down, the limbs of the fir tree fell down and knocked Coyote unconscious. Blood was all over his face. He lay there. In (the) evening, he came to and returned to the old man's place. He never got nothing [anything].

f. The old man said (asked), "What have you been doing?" "I pretty near(ly) got killed. All the limbs of the tree fell on me." The old man asked, "Why did you pretty near[ly] get killed? You must have said something." Coyote said, "I was afraid I would not get enough. I wanted to get more. That was why I hollered (shouted)."[1]

II.29. COYOTE STORY

GEORGIA ORCUTT (1940)

a. Coyote was walking up (the) trail. Looked like he hear (heard) something. He look[ed] up and saw lots of (many) fishers on

---

1. [Following this story, Gifford's typescript originally had this notation: "Woman supposed not to speak first to a man." The point of etiquette does not

a tree. Coyote stood and looked up. He counted how many (the number) on (the) tree. He said, "I can pack it (carry) one for my arrows. I can put one hanging (hang one) from my belt here in front, one on each side, two in back. I can put one around my neck."[1] He was carrying an old fisher skin quiver. He pack it [was carrying an] old one. He had some old ones hanging from his belt.

b. He took off the old ones, tore them, rolled them up, and pitched them down the hill. After a while he shot at (the) fishers in (the) tree with arrows. He missed the one he shot at, and it jumped off and went down the hill. Then he shot at another with (the) same result. He shot at each of [the] others with same (like) result(s).

c. Before he shot at (the) last one, he boasted, "I can pack it; I'll put it right here under my arm." However, he missed it, and it jumped off and went down the hill. He had missed every one of them.

d. Coyote stood there and sang about having nothing. After a while he walked downhill and picked up his old discarded fisher skins. He patched them up and put them on again.[2]

II.30. Coyote Story

GEORGIA ORCUTT (1940)

a. One man was staying at [the] place Afam (on the west side of the Klamath below Martin's Ferry). Afam (place) chafchava (jealous man) was [the] name of [the] man. Some people from here (Panamenik) went down to kill that man. Coyote went with them.

b. On the way they took [a] short cut over [the] hill at Bluff Creek. They were getting hungry. "Let's cook it acorns," they said. Steller's Jay woman was cooking whole acorns (biish) there.

c. While the whole acorns were cooking, Coyote tried to take (them) from [the] boiling water. He said, "I can't get enough." Jay said, "You'll get enough afterwards."

---

seem to relate to this story, and G. had crossed it out. Perhaps it was intended for II.31e—Ed.]

1. [The fine fur of the fisher, turned inside out, was highly prized for arrow quivers (Kroeber, Handbook, p. 90). The fisher is a member of the weasel family.—Ed.]
2. A smart-aleck person who talked about doing big things, but never did, was likened to or called Coyote.

d. After [the acorns had] finished cooking, Jay dumped them out. "Now," said Jay, "you can eat them all. I told you to wait, that there would be plenty, but you would not believe me. Now you can eat them all," she told Coyote. There were so many the whole party could not eat them all.[1]

e. When they were through eating, Coyote said to Swivyuburuhat (a bird seen in winter; bigger than a swallow, speckled), "You better sing so we can have [the] War Dance. We are going to go down to kill that man." The bird said, "No, I won't sing. I got [a] bad song." Coyote insisted he sing. After a while singing that bird.

f. After a while [the] wind blew hard, blew over Coyote. Coyote stand [stood] up again. Now he said, "You better stop singing." But [the] bird kept [on] singing. Coyote kept falling over and getting up again. He finally got blown all [the] way back to Panamenik.

g. The other people went on down. They had wanted to get rid of Coyote because he always spoiled everything. They did not kill that man because Coyote spoiled the expedition.

II.31. Coyote Story

GEORGIA ORCUTT

a. Lots of ixkareya [were] living by [the] river at Yuruksuf (at the mouth of Bluff Creek in Karok territory). Looks like they live[d] high. [The] boys [were] always hunting and killed lots of deer.

b. Coyote stayed a little further down in Yuruksuf with his mother's mother. The boys came back in [the] evening with lots of deer [meat], come [came] back and cook[ed] it. They heated rocks in [the] fire and boiled the backbone after mashing [it] on rock. It made nice soup. After a while in [the] evening one boy hollered to Coyote, "You better come for pitschipchiptane" (cooking stones with soup adhering).[1] Coyote come [came] in [the] evening and licked off the scraps on the stones.

c. The boys had one long pole outside their house. Woodpeckers climbed up this pole, playing on the pole. And after a while one

1. The acorns not eaten by Coyote and his companions turned into small stones. They are still to be seen in a hollow place on Bluff Creek hill across from Shelton Butte. These stones are now called fadamuche (boiled acorns). [Cf. II.2, n. 1.—Ed.]

1. When acorns adhere, they are called pakarhas.

man who stayed at Akbachuripa,[2] who had two daughters, said to his daughters, "Maybe you can go down there and marry those boys. Well off are those boys. You can see the long pole outside their house on which woodpeckers play. You can stay there. They are nice boys."

d. The girls carried their lunch down. [I] don't know how found out Coyote [how Coyote found out their plan]. Them [Those] boys went hunting in [the] morning, so nobody [was] home. Coyote went up and got the long pole and pack[ed] it to his house. When the girls came down they looked for [the] house with [the] pole, for their father had said [there were] several houses there and [they] could tell [the] right house by [the] pole. They went to [the] house their father [had] described, but [there was] no pole there. Further down they see [saw] the pole. One of them said, "Maybe we are lost." But [the] other said, "The old man said there was [a] pole at [the] house. That must be the place down there."

e. They went into Coyote's house, which had the pole in front of it. When they went in they saw Coyote's grandma sitting there. The old lady was kind of surprised to see those girls coming in. She said, "Maybe you folks got lost."[3] The girls said, "[We] don't think we're lost because they tell [told] us to go to [the] house with [the] pole, and we see that pole outside."

f. After a while Coyote coming [came] back. Them girls had brought nice dried deer meat in their baskets and gave some to [the] old lady. After a while Coyote said to [his] grandma, "You better give them the best fish from the creek under the falls (hooknose salmon)." Coyote kept asking her. Finally she said, "I ain't got nothing." Meantime Coyote ate all the dried deer meat the girls [had] brought.

g. Finally Grandma said, "I got [a] dead fish found in [the] sand on [the] river bank.[4] That is [the] only kind I got." Coyote said, "Don't say that any more," for he did not want the girls to know what poor fare they ate.

h. In the evening them boys are coming [came] back from hunting. And after a while one said, "Who pack[ed] it down our

2. See Frog Story. [In III.3a, below, Akbachuripa is identified as a place on the long ridge below Bluff Creek.—Ed.]

3. [See II.28, n. 1, above.—Ed.]

4. Poor old women sometimes got these and cooked them on rocks and ate them with a spoon because they were so soft.

pole?'' Coyote never answered. He don't say [said] nothing. The girls stayed in the house.

i. Later in [the] evening, one of [the] boys called to Coyote to come and eat the scraps. Coyote said, "It looks like the only time they eat is when I wait on the table." He thought those girls could not understand what the boy had said. After a while Coyote went up there, saying to the girls, "The only time they can eat is when I wait on them people."

j. Afterwards them girls went outside and go [went] up there and peek[ed] in. They saw Coyote licking off the rocks. Then they went back to Coyote's house. One said to the other, "I told you we made a mistake." The other said, "The old man (their father) told us to look for the pole." Looked like them girls never sleep [slept]. They just lay there. Coyote spent [the] night in [the] sweathouse.

k. The girls left early in the morning and returned to their father. He asked, "Why did you folks come back?" The girls said, "We go [went] in [the] wrong house. We go [went] in Coyote's house." The father said, "I told you you could see that pole and that was [the] place to go in." "We go [went] in the same place we see [saw] that pole. But I don't know how, but Coyote must have packed it down that pole." After a while the old man said, "You two better try it some more." "No," they said, "we ain't going to try it no more. Look[s] like Coyote is in the way." They gave up. They never tried again. Kupanakanak.

II.32. Coyote (and Osprey) Story

GEORGIA ORCUTT

a. Coyote was fishing at Amaikiaram, and pack[ed] it down dry fish to his home at Panamenik. When he got close to Panamenik he see [saw] somebody fishing across the river.

b. After a while Coyote sit [sat] down at punwaram (any stopping or resting place). He take [took] it out that dry backbone of fish. And after a while he holler [shouted] to [the] fisherman, "I wish you [would] eat this one." The fisherman was working hard and getting nothing. Coyote was being [a] smart aleck.

c. The fisherman said, "I wish you would lie down and sleep." Coyote got very drowsy and said, "Oh, I am going to lay (lie) down for a little while. I am going to make a pillow of my dried fish.'' He made a pillow of it. ''I am going to sleep in a nice place and make a pillow of what I am packing,'' he said.

d. And after a while he was sound asleep. He never woke up. That fisherman came over and took his fish. Coyote slept so soundly, he never knew when the man took his sukrif[1] full of fish.

e. After a while Coyote opened his eyes. He said, ''Where did I lay (lie) down?'' It looked like he did not know where he lay down. After a while he looked over to the fisherman, who held up a backbone and said to him, ''I wish you would eat this one.''

Coyote said, ''Aw, you'd better give it back to me.'' The fisherman was Chukchuk (osprey bigger than vulture; carries fish with feet). When Coyote said, ''You better give it back to me,'' Osprey said, ''You can't eat salmon. You can eat gophers. I am going to be fishing all my life.'' And Osprey always eat[s] fish. Kupanakanak.

II.33. Coyote (and Water Dog) Story

GEORGIA ORCUTT (1940)

[For another version of this myth, by Mary Ike, see II.47, below.—Ed.]

•

a. Coyote went down by the river where somebody had a house, a man (named Pasnanwan, a small owl) and a woman (his wife). The man said, ''I always kill deer on a side hill. When I come back I just swim over this way. When I get ready to skin it that deer, somebody (Water Dog[1] or Sufsam) came [comes] around and took [takes] it away from me.'' Coyote said, ''Why don't you kill that man? I think I can kill him.'' The man [Owl] said, ''He is awful hard looking. You can't kill him.'' Coyote said, ''I think I can kill him.''

b. After a while, the man [Owl] said to Coyote, ''Let's go in the house,'' for Coyote was going to get ready to kill the thief. After a

---

1. [A sukrif (or sukriv) is a woven bag carried by men.—Ed.]

1. [Probably the harmless California newt, a small amphibian.—Ed.]

while Coyote was ready, and [then] he waited for his friend to bring another deer. When he brought it, Coyote waited for [the] thief to appear.

c. After a while that man [Water Dog] came and packed off the deer. Coyote was no place to be seen. No Coyote no [any] place. Coyote had dug a hole and was hiding in it so the man could not see him. After a while the hunter asked, "Where is Coyote? He never show[ed] up no [any] place." He knew Coyote had dug the hole. Then he looked for Coyote, who had said he was going to step out as soon as the deer was brought.

d. Then when the man looked in the hole, no Coyote. Only Coyote's feces were there. After a while go [went] home that man and found Coyote in his house. The man said, "You never showed up when the man stole my deer." Coyote said, "I jumped up and ran away because he looked awful tough." Coyote said, "Next time I am going to kill him." The man said, "You can't kill him. He is awfully tough."

e. Then Coyote asked for obsidian (sak) large flakes. The man said, "Yes, I got [have] that kind."

f. After a while the hunter was ready to go again. He brought in another deer. The thief (Water Dog) came to steal it after a while. Coyote jumped out, shouting, "I am going to eat you!" Coyote stepped out and hit the thief with a piece of obsidian. The thief had two heads. When Coyote hit him he cut off one head. After a while another one [blow] hit him and cut off [the] second head, but meantime the first one had grown up again. Again Coyote cut off the first head, and the second one grew up again. Then Coyote cut both heads off. Then the thief fall [fell] down. Coyote said to the thief, "You are never going to kill people any more. You are going to be Water Dog (sufsam)."

g. Coyote decided to go see where the double-headed man [had] packed the deer meat. Coyote, as he went, met a well-dressed woman. She had nice shoes, nice dress, and everything.

h. Coyote asked her, "Where are you going?" The woman: "I am going to meet my husband. Maybe you killed my husband." Coyote said, "No." "I think you killed my husband." Coyote kept saying, "No." It looked like that woman wanted to kill Coyote, and he was kind of afraid. So he killed the woman with a piece of obsidian.

i. Coyote said, "I'm going to look where she came from, that woman." He came to her house and went in. He saw all kinds of dried meat, just full that house. Coyote worked hard packing it to his own house.

j. Further upriver lived several boys who always hunted. Coyote never hunted; he was always bumming. He said, "I am living high." He told his wife, "You had better go up and see those boys and give them deer meat. Tell them I am shooting deer by using a deer mask—a new one which I just made—and they should not eat deer meat if they are dreaming about women."

k. The woman packed the deer meat to the boys and gave them Coyote's message. Coyote had fabricated the story, for he never killed the deer.

l. Went home that woman after packing the deer meat to the boys. The boys threw the meat out. "We don't want to eat Water Dog's meat."

II.34. COYOTE AND GREAT BLUE HERON

GEORGIA ORCUTT

a. Heron (akwai) was living here (at Panamenik) with his wife. He fished every day. After a while Coyote came to visit and stayed all night. In the morning Heron said he was going fishing.

b. Coyote said he was going down to [the sand]bar to eat milkweed seed. Coyote returned before Heron. After a while Heron came back. He said, "I lost my salmon harpoon." He felt badly because he had only one left.

c. Next day Heron went fishing again. Coyote said to himself, "I'm going into the river and get his harpoon." So Coyote got in the water and swam along like a fish. Heron saw a "salmon" after a while. He harpooned it, but it was Coyote. He [Coyote] took away Heron's [last] harpoon.

d. Heron went home because he had no harpoon. After a while Coyote came in. Heron and his wife were crying on account of the loss of their last harpoon.

Coyote said, "I found a harpoon down there." Heron felt better because he thought he was going to get back his harpoon. "How much shall I give you for you to give it back to me? I'll give you the smallest dentalia." Coyote said, "No." Heron offered more. Still

Coyote said, "No." Then Heron offered still more money. Coyote said, "No."

Then Coyote said, "You better give me your wife." Coyote like[d] her, for she was a pretty woman. Finally Heron said, "All right, I'll give you my wife." Then Heron left with his harpoon.

e. When Heron's wife offered Coyote dried fish, he said, "No, we never eat that kind. I'll go up on the hill and get all kinds of meat."

f. Next day Coyote went hunting, and he said he was going up on the hill. The woman remained at home making baskets by the river. In the evening the woman was coming up by the river. Coyote came back. Coyote said, "You had better make [a] big fire. We are going to cook it." Coyote burned up all the wood. Then he put his kill in the fire: snails (asipanak), lizards of various kinds, all kinds he put on the coals. He never kill[ed] deer. He picked up his kill on rotten logs.

g. After a while, when all [was] cooked, he took it out. He gave it to the woman to eat. They were eating acorns too. Coyote ate and ate, but the woman secreted her food in a hole beside her. After a while Coyote asked, "Do you want some more?" The woman said, "I'll [I've] got enough, "[and] yet at the same time (s)he never eat [ate]. S(he) put it in [the] hole.

h. Next day Coyote went hunting again. That woman [was] making baskets down by the river. In the evening Coyote came back. Coyote looked around. He never [did not] see no [any] place that woman. After a while he looked by [the] river. He saw her basket, but he could not see her. He looked around, and still he could see nobody. Again he looked around down by the river. It looked as though the basket were moving when he was looking at them [it]. They [It] moved into the water. Coyote hollered, "Your basket is floating away." No answer, no place.

i. After a while Coyote ran down. "I'm going to catch that basket because it is floating away." When he got there it had floated out into [the] middle. Coyote wanted to catch that basket, but he could not.

j. That was the way that woman got away. Both she and her husband got away, for he was in the basket too. The woman shouted to Coyote, "I won't (am not) going to stay with you; I can't eat what you feed me."

Coyote returned to the house laughing.

II.35. COYOTE STORY

GEORGIA ORCUTT (June 21, 1940)

Georgia learned this story from Red Cap Tom's father.

•

a. The people on [the] coast at Sufip [Rekwoi] had killed a whale (ip'at).[1] Coyote said, "I am going down to Sufip to get some whale meat." The folks at Sufip were ready to go "fishing" for [butcher the ?] whale in [the] morning. Coyote[2] had stayed all night with them. Coyote went down to the shore, but the people shoved off [in] the boat without him. Coyote said, "Maybe I can jump into that boat," and he ran along the ocean shore.

b. The men in the boat hooked something which they could not see, but which towed them along. There was a rock on the shore. The boat was headed toward it. After a while the boat came in close to the rock, and Coyote jumped in.

c. Coyote said, "Maybe you can do it this way and get fish in [the] boat." [The] boat kept going along, but they could not see what was towing them. Coyote said, "I can find out what it is towing us."

d. They were gone all day on the ocean, being towed continually. After a while the boat stopped. Then some kind of animal come [came] up under the boat. A lot of people were standing on the beach. This was on [the] other side of [the] ocean. The people shouted to the boatmen to come ashore. This was on the other side of the ocean. After a while when go [they went] ashore, Coyote went off by himself to a house where an old lady stayed alone. The other people all went together to one place; Coyote alone went elsewhere.

e. And after a while Coyote said to [the] old lady, "I [have] been thinking about my friends here for a long time, but I never had any way to come over before this." Then Coyote cried.

f. After a while five sons of the old lady came into the house.

1. Ipas = deer. [Kroeber, Handbook, p. 84, notes that the stranding of a whale was always a great occasion. The Yurok prized its flesh above all other food, but they did not attempt to hunt the animal.—Ed.]

2. Coyote = pinefish [three syllables] = ishamsondik ("on the flat sitting watching," in reference to its watching gopher holes). [See Bright's interpretation in the Linguistic Index, below.—Ed.]

The old lady told her sons, "Be careful. Don't step on Coyote. He is your father's brother." Coyote cried again and said to the boys, "I [have] been thinking about you a long time because I know you are my people. But I had no way of coming over."

g. After a while the boys said, "We can take you home tomorrow." Coyote knew he was going to get killed tomorrow; that is why he was crying. And them [those] folks said, "Come in [the] sweathouse with us tonight."

h. The five boys told some men from another house, "Don't kill any of these visitors. They are our people." Then Coyote felt better, and he did not cry all night. Before he heard this, he cried for fear he would be killed the next morning.

i. In the morning they all left the sweathouse and went into [the] dwelling house. In the morning when they were ready to return, Coyote said to [the] old lady, "I can come over any time now, because I know where you folks live now."

j. Then the voyagers all got into their boat. They voyaged across, the same thing towing it as on [the] preceding day. [They] arrived at Sufip. That is the time Coyote said how smart he was: "If I had not cried, we'd all [have] been killed in the morning." Kupanakanak.

II.36. COYOTE STORY

GEORGIA ORCUTT (1940)

a. One time Coyote went down to [the] ocean to eat whale meat. And he stayed all night down at Sufip [Rekwoi]. In the morning a boat was ready to go out to hunt whale. Coyote said, "I'll go too." The people never said, "No."

b. After a while they speared a whale, and the boat was capsized. When Coyote fell out, the whale's mouth was open and he was swallowed. After a while Coyote pondered, "How am I going to get out?" Looked like [the] whale was rolling about in [the] ocean, for he was already hooked by the harpoon. After a time the whale ceased rolling around and lay still.

c. After a time look like Coyote hear [heard] somebody talking. The whale was ashore at Sufip, and people were skinning it. Lots of people skin[ned] it. The people had cut only one side of [the] whale.

And after a while Coyote jumped out. Lots of people [were] there. They had gone to [the] other side of [the] whale to cut, and nobody saw Coyote jump out. Kupanakanak.

II.37. COYOTE STORY

GEORGIA ORCUTT (1940)

Georgia has heard this story many times.

•

a. Coyote said as he was staying at Panamenik, "I am going to go over to Hupa. What will I do when I go over there? I am going to walk a nice way. I'll come down over Bald Hill." Right below Bald Hill was [a] Hupa rancheria called Enhikiis. Coyote said, "When I walk down I'll be packing sweathouse wood." When he packed the sweathouse wood he talked Yurok, though his home tongue was Karok.

b. When he came to Enhikiis, he sang, "Ai yu kichikti" (=arareshpuk= dentalia). He sang about dentalia in Yurok. As he zigzagged down the hill with his load of sweathouse wood, the Enhikiis people were watching him and saying to one another, "Someone is coming. See you how prettily he walks."

c. After a while go [he went] into [the] sweathouse and make [made a] fire. Then he sweated, swam, and sat outside the sweathouse. After a time the people found out it was Coyote. Then Coyote found out the girls did not like him. After a while come [he went] back to Panamenik. Kupanakanak.

II.38. ANOTHER COYOTE STORY

GEORGIA ORCUTT (1940)

a. Coyote could not get along with his wife where he was living with her at Forks of Salmon. After a while he thought, "I am going to leave my wife. I am going to Tishram (near Etna)."[1]

1. [Etna is a small town near the Scott River in Shasta territory, about 25 air

When he started he said to his wife, "Maybe I'll be back in one year; maybe I never will come back." Then he left.

b. After three days he came back. When he came back he said, "If a man cannot get along with his wife, he can go over to Etna. When he come[s] back he always stay with his wife again. He will never leave her."[2]

II.39. COYOTE (AND ELK) STORY

GEORGIA ORCUTT (1940)

Georgia learned this story from Red Cap Tom's father. [This and the following two stories show Coyote as a monster-ridder.—Ed.]

•

a. Two sisters [were] living together. Coyote came to see them. "Why do you come around? Something is killing us off. Somebody comes outside, and as soon as someone goes out of [the] house he gets killed right away. Now there are only two of us left." Coyote asked, "What does it look like?"

The women replied, "It never comes in. It is just outside. It hooks people with its tongue. It can't go into [the] house because it is [a] big one; only its tongue could go in."

b. Coyote asked, "Have you got deer some [some deer] shin-bones?" After a while Coyote made four sharp long ones [points] from the bone they gave him. Every once in a while he said, "You folks better cook lots of acorns and fish, so I have enough. I'm going to kill that animal tonight. You will see." Then Coyote took out all his teeth. Then [he] got oak (not tan) bark and put it on [the] floor. He put all his teeth on the piece of bark, so he would not lose them. After a while he put the four sharp bone points in his mouth so they projected up and down like tusks at the corners of his mouth.

"In the evening the monster comes," the women told him. "We always hide." Coyote told them, "You folks better hide."

---

miles northeast of Forks of Salmon. The Karok called the Shasta Tishraw-arara (Kroeber, Handbook, p. 285). "Shasta civilization is a pallid, simplified copy of that of the Yurok and Karok," Kroeber comments (ibid., p. 288).—Ed.]

2. This story has been heard often by Georgia. She says it is a fact that many Karok who have marital difficulties do go to Etna.

c. Coyote sat down inside the door. After a while he heard the monster coming. He heard when it was coming. He was all ready for it. It looked like the monster was trying to come in, and Coyote growled like a dog. [It] tried to come in, that animal, and stuck his tongue inside. After trying several times to come, the monster finally stuck in his tongue. Then Coyote bit the monster's tongue with his four false teeth or tusks. After a while Coyote went outside because the [monster's] tongue [had been] pulled out.

d. Then Coyote pummeled the monster with a nodule of flint. He finally killed it by hitting on the head. Coyote said as he was killing the monster, "You can't kill people. You are going to be Elk." Kupanakanak.

II.40. Coyote (and Salamander) Story

GEORGIA ORCUTT

Georgia heard this story from Red Cap Tom's father.

●

a. Coyote went upriver beyond where he killed the monster that became Elk. After a while he saw two sisters at their house. "Do you two folks stay by yourselves?" They said, "No. Something comes around all the time in the evening." Coyote asked what it looked like, and they told him it was very thin bony person.[1]

Coyote asked, "What does he do?" They said, "When he comes in and sits down by the fire he says, 'My heart's burning because I'm hungry.' He has a yuhidim."[2]

Coyote said, "When he says, 'Suwaiten amfira' ('My heart's burning with hunger'), I am going to cut him open down the middle."

b. Coyote covered his front with pine bark which he then daubed it with pitch. After a while Coyote sat down and make [made] himself look small. He told the womenfolks to hide. "Heat a lot of small hot rocks (asamni)." They fixed them and then hid themselves behind the boards of the house pit, just below the acorn granary which sits on the house platform.

c. After a while that man came in. When he come [came] in, he

1. Ipivura is the Karok term for such a physique.
2. [A yuhidim is a flint knife (II.21*c*).—Ed.]

looked like he was interested in Coyote, for he [Coyote] looked like a nice fat man with all his bark padding. The thin man sat down by the fire. After a while he said, "My heart burns with hunger." Coyote said, "You can't eat nothing [anything]. Look at my front. I ain't got [have] no meat on me."

d. However, Coyote lay down and let the man cut off some of his bark armor. Then the thin man cooked it. After a while it looked like grease burning, but it was the pitch bubbling as the stuff cooked on the coals. When he chewed it, he found it was nothing but bark. However, he did not complain, for Coyote had warned him it was no good.

e. After a while Coyote said, "My heart burns with hunger (Suwaiten amfira)." Coyote got his yuhidim and cut the man's abdomen as he sat, just as Coyote had sat to be cut. Coyote cut him below the breastbone and suddenly pulled out his stomach. Then Coyote ran outside with it, the thin man after him. Coyote climbed on top of the house and threw his stomach into the fire. Coyote shouted for the women to cover the stomach with coals, which he had previously directed the women to build fire in a pit into which he would throw it [the stomach]. Shortly it burst open. Then fall [fell] down and die[d] that thin man.

f. Coyote said, "You are not going to kill people. You are going to be Suwait furahar" (a slamander that lives in water, is red underneath, black on back and 6-8 inches long). Kupanakanak.

II.41. COYOTE STORY[1]

GEORGIA ORCUTT (1940)

a. Two sisters [were] living at Panamenik. Coyote came into their house. He asked, "Why do you folks stay by yourselves, the two of you?" They replied, "All our people got killed off." "What kind kill[ed] it [them] off?" asked Coyote. "Something standing on [the] other side of [the] river said, 'You better come over and meet me.' Each time one went over, that monster pack[ed] it away." Ask[ed] them everything Coyote.

b. Coyote said, "You folks better cook for me tonight." After a

1. [Following this title Gifford's typescript had the word pik^{u}wa in parentheses. It is the Karok word for "myth"; see Gifford's Introduction, p. 107 above—Ed.]

while the two women cooked acorns. "What time in [the] evening does that monster come?" asked Coyote.

c. Coyote put on hard buckskin armor all over his body.[2] Coyote had obsidian, [a] round lump with sharp edges on it all around. After a while Coyote went down by [the] river. Pretty soon he saw the monster coming. After a while that animal stand [stood] up; it had [a] big belly. "You'd better come over and meet me," said the monster.

d. Coyote said, "You can come over here yourself." The monster said, "Why you never [won't you] come over and meet me?" Coyote said, "You'd better come over yourself." Coyote was all ready for him. He was going to kill that monster. After a while walked over that monster. Coyote stand [stood] up right there by the river. The monster approached. "Why did not you come over and meet me?" it asked.

e. The monster tried to grab Coyote, but Coyote dodged around. Look like Coyote is [was] all in when he jump[ed] around. After a while [he] used that obsidian lump to hit the monster. It had sharp edges. [Coyote] knock[ed] him down and he get [got] up again. Knock[ed] him down and he get [got] up again. Many times he knocked him down, and he got up each time. After a while [Coyote] kill[ed] him.

f. Coyote said, "You can't kill people. You are going to be Xachmom (a big-bellied "grasshopper"-like insect without wings, seen in woods).[3]

II.42. Coyote (and Owl) Story

GEORGIA ORCUTT

Georgia learned this story from Red Cap Tom's father. [The setting is in his natal village of Wuppam, or Red Cap.—Ed.]

•

2. This was made by "burning" buckskin somewhat to make it hard.

3. [The Xachmom may have been the Jerusalem cricket, which in its larval form was feared by the Yurok as a death symbol. See Kroeber, Yurok Myths, X1, n. 3, and elsewhere.—Ed.]

a. Coyote entered a house at Wuppam where a man lived alone. "Give me something to eat," Coyote requested. The man gave him some deer meat. The man was a small owl (bununuk). Afterward Coyote asked, "How do you get that deer meat?"

Owl said, "I killed myself that deer." "How did you kill it?" asked Coyote. Owl said, "I go up the canyon at Wuppam and go up on [the] hill. When I get there and come down, I see [a] big deer lying on [the] edge of [the] bluff above [the] river. I frighten him so he jump[s] in [the] river. Then I jump onto his back. When he swims down opposite my house, I cut his throat."

b. Coyote said, "I can wait on [at] the river when you come down." Owl said, "I don't want someone to see me when I'm coming down the river. Don't holler when you see me."

c. After a while when Owl come [came] downriver on [the] deer's back, Coyote hollered, "Deer coming down the river." When Owl got close he asked why he [had] hollered. Coyote say [said], "I thought only [a] deer [was] coming. I did not see you on his back." All the people came out to see, and Owl had to share the deer meat. Previously they had never seen him coming down with a deer. [This time] Owl had to give away most of his meat.

Coyote thought, "We got enough for both of us."

d. After a while Coyote missed Owl. He never knew [did not know] which way he went. He looked all over and can't [couldn't] find it [him] no [any] place. After a while he look[ed] up in [a] tree, and Owl was cooking deer meat up on [the] tree. Coyote can't [couldn't] get nothing [anything].

e. After a while Coyote said, "Chawash (brother's son), you'd better give me a piece." Coyote could not climb up, hard as he tried. Coyote begged, "You'd better give me a little piece. I thought we got enough for both of us." But Owl never answered.

f. After a while Coyote gave up. Then he decided to try to jump on [a] deer after frightening it into [the] river. He went up on the hill. He came down, saying, "I am going to find it some place so I can make it jump into [the] river." When he came down he never see [saw] nothing [anything]. Down by the river he never see [saw] no [any] deer or nothing [anything]. After a while he walked down by Wuppam again. He never see [saw] that Owl any more. Kupanakanak.

II.43. HOW PEOPLE GOT FIRE

MARY IKE (1940)

a. There was no fire. Coyote went all over looking for fire. Coyote discovered fire in the far north. He returned and told people he had seen fire, he had found it. They talked over the means of getting the fire. They lined up with Frog next to the river. Grouse said, "I'll be on top of the mountain. I am pretty slow, but I can fly down the hill."

The Bear said he could run down the hill, so they put him on the next mountaintop.

Turtle said, "I can run down too. I'll draw in my feet and head and roll down."

Aixlechton (a bird on A'u'ich which is white below, brown above, and calls like a seagull) said, "I can travel over two mountains, two ridges."

Fox said, "I'll take a hand in it, too."

Measuring Worm said, "I can go over about ten ridges and mountains and not have to run downhill."

b. Coyote went up north where the fire was. The girls there were Yellow Jackets. Coyote said to them, "You all sit around and I'll make you pretty." Coyote said, "Come on, girls. We'll all go into the house."

c. Coyote took black oak bark and put it in (the) fire to burn. To the girls, he said, "You all close your eyes. You will not be pretty if you open your eyes." While they had their eyes shut he pulled the bark out of the fire with his heel. "Keep your eyes closed. I've got to go outside for a minute. Don't open your eyes while I am gone."

d. Then he ran and ran and ran with the fire. He became exhausted and passed it to Fox.

e. After a time the girls opened their eyes and realized Coyote was gone. They set out in pursuit and finally spied Fox with the fire.

f. Fox ran until he came to Measuring Worm and passed the fire on to him. Measuring Worm wriggled around, as he reached from mountain to mountain. He went a long way. Then Measuring Worm passed it to Bear. Bear ran down the mountain, but was slow in climbing up the next mountain.

g. Bear passed it to Grouse. Grouse went a long way with it. Grouse passed it to the bird Aixlechton. He passed it to Turtle, and

Turtle rolled down the mountain to Frog, who had his mouth wide open to receive the fire.

h. The Yellow Jackets grabbed the Frog, but Frog jumped into the river with the fire in his mouth. The Yellow Jackets gave up. It was no use. They went back. Frog came up and spat out the fire to willow trees. Now you can get fire from willows. Willow roots are used for fire drills.[1]

II.44. TURTLE STORY (COYOTE TRIES TO MARRY HIS DAUGHTER)

MARY IKE (1940)

a. Coyote was telling his daughter Turtle she'd better get married. They were so poor, and then they'd (they would) have someone to take care of them. The girl said, "No, I'm too young."

"No, you go ahead and (you must) get married. How do you think you are going to live? You've got to (You must) have someone to take care of you. We'll eat eels after a while. I'm going to clean the eels. You go up and put (the) board back in place on top of (the) house."[1]

b. She went. She could not lift it (the board); Coyote was praying it would be [too] heavy. "I can't lift it." Coyote hollered (said), "Stretch your legs over so as to straddle the opening." She did. She knew no better. As he fixed eels he threw a clot of blood into her vagina. When she came down, he said, "You are old enough to be married now. I see you are bleeding."

c. "Look at this house. The man you are going to marry has a house that looks just like this. He has the same kind of a sweathouse."

He told her where to go to that man's house. "You take the shortcut this way. You must not go around. It is too far." "I never did see the man," the girl said. "Just look at me. He look[s] just the same as me. When you get there, put your load down and go to the

1. Cedar is used for the hearth. There are usually two sockets in the hearth, the reason being that if one does not yield fire, the other will.

___

1. ["The roof boards are as thin and wide as they can be made from 8 to 10 feet long. They are merely laid on in two overlapping thicknesses . . . . The smoke hole is made by laying aside a board in the middle" of the roof (Kroeber, Handbook, p. 78, describing Yurok houses).—Ed.]

sweathouse and tell the man to come out. Say, 'I am here now.' "

d. She went. She called the man. She made a fire in the house. "My, this looks just like our house."

e. Coyote had told her, "Tonight, when he wants to sleep with you, you must sleep with him."

The man said to her after supper, "You'd better make the bed." She said, "You'd better go to (the) sweathouse." "No," he said, "I'm going to sleep with you." He would not go to bed in (the) sweathouse. He stayed in the house and slept with her. She said, "I've got to go home. I don't feel well." She said this after two or three days.

f. He said, "If you don't feel well, you can go home, but leave everything. Don't take anything home."

g. Then she went home. As she walked along, she thought, "His house looked just like ours. Everything in it was the same."

h. When she entered, her father was sitting there. "My," he said, "I'm glad to see you. I've been lonesome. I'm so glad you came home."

i. She told him about the house. "(It is) just like ours. Everything (is) the same. (The) sweathouse (is) the same." After two or three days Coyote told her she'd (she had) better go back to her husband. "I know he's lonesome," he said. "Go back, but don't stay too long, for I'll be lonesome, as I was before."

j. She was suspicious. She went only a little way and sat and watched him. She saw Coyote carrying the dwelling, the sweathouse on top of it, the menstrual hut (yawuneixlivram) on top of that. She hollered (called to) him, "You are the one who married me!" Old Coyote left and went over to (the) Etna region.[2] "I don't ever want to see you again," his daughter said. Many coyotes (are) there now.

II.45. Coyote Wants to Marry His Daughter

GEORGIA ORCUTT (1940)

a. Coyote had (a) house (and) sweathouse. He had (a) nice daughter. After a while he said he was going upstream a little way to

2. [See II.38, n. 1, above.—Ed.]

visit some ixkareya friends. When he came home, he said, "Up
there is the same kind of house what (that) we got (have). (The)
sweathouse is (the) same way; (it) looks just like ours. That man that
stays up there looks like me." After a while Coyote said, "That man
wants you to marry him. Let's go up. We can stay up there. You can
marry that man."

After a while Coyote said, "We can go up there now. You go up
slow. I'll come up afterwards."

b. When (After) the girl start(ed) up, the Coyote picked up (his)
house (and) put (his) sweathouse on top. Coyote went up behind the
ridge, packing his house and sweathouse, while his daughter went up
along the river. The girl look[ed] back and never (but could not) see
him coming no [any] place (because he was behind the ridge). She
waited for her father, but he never showed up. After a while she
walked up (the) ridge and looked over. When she looked over,
Coyote was packing his house and sweathouse. She watched him
where he came out. Nobody was living there, nobody stay(ed) up
there. She saw Coyote set the house and sweathouse in place.

c. Now the girl knew that nobody was staying in that place, (that
there was) no house, nothing. When she got up there, Coyote just
stay(ed) in [the] house when she go in (entered). The girl never say
(said) nothing. Kupanakanak.

II.46. LIZARD STORY

GEORGIA ORCUTT (1940)

a. Lizard boy was staying with his mother at Wuppam. Below
was [were] two women named pinishkadim (Mountain Lion)[1] living
there. After a while the two Mountain Lion women went up on [the]
hill to dig potatoes. Lizard's mother went up there too. When she
came home, she said, "Looks like I'm kind of afraid. Looks like
those Mountain Lion women pick on me."

b. After a while Lizard his mother never come [came] home.
Lizard never know [knew] what become [became] of his mother. He
just stayed by himself. Afterward, Lizard he think [thought],

---

1. [Cf. III.18*a*, where the name is translated as "mean fellow." There the
epithet is applied to Grizzly Bear.—Ed.]

"Maybe they kill[ed] my mother." But he never did nothing [anything], just stay[ed] there alone. After a while one Mountain Lion woman come [came] and asked Lizard, "Where is your mother? Did she go up to dig potatoes?" Lizard never answered her.

c. After a while Coyote come [came] around looking for Lizard. He asked him, "What's become of your mother?" Lizard said, "I think she's [she had] been getting saiyis[2] (potatoes) on [the] hill, but she never come [came] home."

d. After a while Coyote visits [visited] with Mountain Lion women down the hill. After a while those two women sleeping [went to sleep] with [their] feet toward [the fire].[3] After a while Coyote told Lizard to get some pitchy wood. "You can cut their feet off. At the same time you cut their feet off, put the pitch[y] wood in the fire."

e. Coyote heard one woman cry when Lizard cut her legs off at [the] knees. Coyote said when he come [came] in, "What's the matter with you?" The woman said, "Lizard cut it off [cut off] my legs!"

f. Coyote said, "You look in [the] fire. The fire burn[ed] it off your legs. Lizard is too small; he cannot cut it off your legs." After a while the woman kept saying, "Lizard cut it off my legs!" After a while she die[d].

g. After a while Coyote say [said], "Of course, it [she has] got to be buried." Next day Lizard cut it off [the] other woman's legs. Coyote tell [told] Lizard, "You better chew alder bark."

h. Coyote went down to see [the] second woman with [her] legs cut off. The woman said, "Lizard cut off my legs!" "No," Coyote said, "Lizard is too small. He can't do nothing [anything]."

i. Coyote said, "Look up. Lizard is dancing on top of [the] house. I am afraid. I don't know what is [the] matter with him. Look at him. He has cut himself down the belly and the blood is all coming out."

j. The woman went out and look[ed] up at Lizard dancing. Coyote said, "Lizard cut himself and is all over blood." The woman

2. [Probably a typographical error in G.'s typescript. In Schenck and Gifford, Karok Ethnobotany, UC-AR 13:(no. 6):380, it is spelled tayish, meaning Brodiaea, the bulbs of which are dug, cleaned, put in a rock-lined pit, covered with leaves and rocks, and baked.—Ed.]

3. The usual way to sleep is alongside the fire.

cut herself open with [a] stone knife and fall [fell] down and die[d].

k. Lizard had not really cut himself. It was only the alder bark juice that made it look so. Afterwards when that woman died, Coyote said to Lizard, "Let's skin her."

l. Coyote went some place. Lizard cut up the Mountain Lion meat and packed into his house (a hole in rock) and cooked it. After a while Coyote came and tried to go in, but could [not] get into [the] small entrance. Lizard [had] made it small so Coyote could not enter. Coyote ran around outside trying to get in but could not make it. After a while he give [gave] up.

That's the way Coyote was working hard so he could eat that woman, but he never eat [ate] nothing [anything]. Lizard dried the meat.

II.47. STORY ABOUT BATSNAVAN (SCREECH OWL)

MARY IKE (1940)

[This story has elements of tales II.33 and II.42, told by Georgia Orcutt. See also Kroeber's A4, told by Mary Ike's husband with only minor differences in plot.—Ed.]

•

a. Screech Owl had a dog. He went hunting and took (the) dog with him. He took (the) dog up on (a) hill, and (the) dog would chase (the) deer down to where (the) man was waiting, down by [the] river. Then Owl would jump on the deer's horns and ride down to the river, and the deer swam [would swim] down the river. Then he pulls (pulled) the deer out.

b. Someone comes (came) out of the bushes singing a song. The person was Water Dog (ifvaifurdaxara). He told Owl, "Let me carry the deer." Owl went home without his deer. Water Dog took it away from him.

c. Every day it happened, the same way. He [Owl] did the same way again. He came down the river on the deer's horns. He pulled the deer out. When he got ready to butcher the deer, that man came out and told him to go away. "Let me have it," Water Dog said. He [Owl] goes (went) home without his deer. He done (did) that every day. The same thing he done (did). That man took his deer away. He was scared to death of Water Dog (yellow-bellied, brown-backed). That Water Dog came out singing that song, and Owl was dead scared of him.

d. Owl went hunting late in the fall when the deer are all fat. When he got home somebody (Pinef, Coyote) came to the house. Coyote said, "I came to eat some deer meat. I heard you were killing a lot of (many) deer." Coyote said, "You go up on the hill and do the same thing (i.e., ride down on the horns after the dog has driven the deer). I'll wait for you on the river bar. I'll wait for that man that comes out."

e. Owl pulled the deer out and Water Dog came out, but Coyote was waiting there. Coyote just looked at him, but he was scared of him too. "Why did not you grab him? Why did not you lick him?" Owl asked Coyote.

f. Coyote said, "You'd better go hunting again. This time I'm going to lick him." Owl took his dog up on the hill again. Coyote went down to the river bar and waited. "Coyote, come on now, grab him," Owl said. "You said you were going to do it." Coyote jumped on that Water Dog and stepped on his back. He stepped on him so hard his belly just got red and his back flat. Coyote picked up the deer and packed it home for Owl.

g. Coyote said to Owl, "Let's go look for that man's house." Coyote went into Water Dog's house. There was just room enough to turn around, as the house was full of dried deer meat. Coyote growled at Water Dog, "You are not going to eat deer meat. You are going to live in a swamp, mud hole. You are going to be Water Dog. You are not going to live on deer meat."

h. Owl packed all the meat out. They went home. Coyote could not get enough to eat. He ate and ate and ate. Owl got stingy. "Why does not this man get enough?" he asked. Coyote went to sleep, and while he was sleeping Owl moved all the meat up high. When Coyote woke up, there was nothing left in the house. He walked around there for a long time. Finally a piece of bark fell down. Then he saw Owl sitting up on a tree with all the deer meat.

i. "Throw a little piece of meat down. I'm getting hungry," Coyote said. Owl threw none down. He was stingy. Kupanakana.

II.48. STORY ABOUT RATTLESNAKE AND LIZARD

MARY IKE (1940)

a. Rattlesnake called Lizard his younger brother. He said to Lizard, "Let us winter together under the rock." "All right," said Lizard. "We'll go inside." Rattlesnake said, "We'll just make a fire that will keep us warm all winter." Lizard was scared to death of Rattlesnake.

b. After a time Lizard thought, "I'll go peek out." He saw sunshine, and he went back in and told the Snake (Rattlesnake), "There is a lot of snow yet." He told Rattlesnake (this) to deceive him.

c. Then Lizard pounded up a lot of white rock for imitation snow. "If you don't believe me," said Lizard, "you can look outside."

d. Snake (Rattlesnake) said, "Let me see you stick your tongue out," for he thought Lizard had been eating grass. Every time Lizard stuck out his tongue, he turned it so the other side showed. "Keep him in there as long as you can," the people told Lizard, for they were all afraid of him [Rattlesnake].

e. Snake (Rattlesnake) asked, "How is it outside?" Lizard said, "It is still just winter." "Are you sure it is winter yet?" "Go out and see for yourself. See the snow on the ground." Snake (Rattlesnake) saw green stuff around Lizard's mouth and he said, "You must be lying."

f. Snake (Rattlesnake) chased Lizard. Somebody was helping Lizard. "When Snake (Rattlesnake) chases you, run down the hill." The person had a big fire down at [the] foot of [the] hill. Snake (Rattlesnake) ran right into the fire. Snake (He) tried to get his younger brother Lizard to help him out. "Come and help me, little brother! Pull me out!"

g. Lizard heard someone calling to him to come over. He went over. It was Coyote that was calling him. Coyote told Lizard to lie down. "I want to fix you up so you'll look different because Snake (Rattlesnake) is going [trying] to kill you." Coyote marked him blue on (the) sides of (his) underparts. That is why Lizard is now so marked.[1]

1. [The description fits the common western fence lizard.—Ed.]

II.49. THE BROWN RACER

MARY IKE (1939)

[This is a somewhat bowdlerized version of Kroeber's B2, above, which Mary Ike told Kroeber in 1902. See also a shorter version, H3, above, told to Kroeber by Mrs. Bennett.—Ed.]

•

a. Absummunukich (racer snake) started out. Coyote asked, "Where are you going today?" "I am going up the river to visit around." "I went up that way," said Coyote, "and I nearly died of thirst."

b. Absummunukich put his pipe in his belt and set out. After time he came to a big resting place (ipunwaram). He sat down and rested and smoked. He blew his smoke out and made a big noise which was echoed from all the hollows and crevices in the mountains. Then he got up. "I guess I'd better go on." He took only about two steps when he slipped and fell. He tried again and fell. Then he went down the hill, then up the hill. He was angry because he fell down. He went to a big rock by the river and went under it. Then he looked out and up the hill. "It is too bad whatever happened to me. I have no more arms and [no] more legs, but just one straight body. I don't know how I'm going to walk, but I guess I'll try." He tried to walk up the hill but slid back down. Then he swam across the river. "Well, it is a good thing I lost my legs. Now I can slide around."

II.50. COYOTE DANCES WITH THE STARS

MAMIE OFFIELD (1939)

Told by Mamie Offield, as told to her by her mother (dead).

•

a. Coyote met two Fawn girls who were singing and dancing.

Coyote offered to teach them his song in return for learning theirs. They learned Coyote's first. Then he learned theirs. As he walked away, they said, "Forget it, forget it." Coyote forgot their song, so he returned and begged them to teach him again. They refused, but he persisted to no avail. They said they had to dance twice around the world in the sky every night. He immediately begged to be allowed to dance with them. They demurred, saying it was a long way. Coyote insisted he could do it, and they at last reluctantly assented, but said he must not stop, once he started. He would have to make the two circuits of the world with them.

b. Evening came and they started. After a time Coyote tired. He begged to be allowed to stop. They said, "No." Then he pleaded that he had to go to the toilet. He pleaded this excuse a number of times. They seized his arms to force him to continue. He struggled and his arms came off. Then they seized his legs and they were pulled off. He was limbless, so they finally left him.

c. He meditated about his condition and how he was to get down to earth again. He spat down and concluded from the sound that it was not far down to earth. "How shall I go down?" he thought. "If I go head first I may break my neck. If I fall sidewise I may break my ribs. If [I] drop rear end first, I may hurt myself there." Finally, he decided to close his eyes and just drop down. He did this, and when he struck the ground near Martin's Ferry he became a rock, Pinevifishisani.

II.51. PLEIADES STORY

MARY IKE (1939)

[There were] seven sisters who were singing and dancing at First Menses. Coyote heard them and wanted to trade his song for theirs. They refused, but he persisted. After a time they yielded and took Coyote's song. As they gave him theirs, they said, "Forget it, forget it." So Coyote lost his song, the girls had both songs, and Coyote nothing.[1] [Mary sings the songs.]

1. According to Mary, the girls were already in the sky and dancing there when Coyote heard them. According to Mamie's mother [II.50], this part of the story occurred on earth, and the girls ran up to the sky to escape Coyote.

II.52. TURTLE AND JACKRABBIT

MARY IKE (1940)

An old Karok man from upriver told Mary this story, so it belongs to the northern Karok. The man was from Hamburg; he was half Karok, half Scott Valley Shasta. Mary heard this story from him when she was only fifteen or sixteen years old.

•

a. Turtle (asakwu) and Large Squirrel (almost as big as a raccoon, called kahaksaai, and found out Etna way; longitudinal stripes on arms and legs; looks like ground squirrel but much bigger)[1] were talking about having a race. Jackrabbit was to be umpire and holder of the money. Jackrabbit was talking to Turtle and said, "Let's cheat the Squirrel." The Squirrel bet all kinds of nuts, every kind they eat he bet. Turtle bet dentalia.

b. Coyote came along. He said to Jackrabbit (sahēsyu), "Don't do that. You are relatives. You all belong here." They told Coyote to keep his mouth shut. "You are always doing something," they said. Squirrel said, "I'll beat Turtle because he can't walk." They were going to run around Mt. Shasta.

c. Turtle said to Jackrabbit, "Now you take my brother (another Turtle) and put him right where we are going to end the race." So they started out. Turtle did not go very far. His brother was already there [at the finish point]. "It will take us all night and all day to go around the mountain." One went in one direction, one in [the] opposite direction.

d. Squirrel ran all day and all night. When he arrived at (the) goal, Turtle was already there. Squirrel got (was) ashamed to think that Turtle beat him. He sat there with (a) long face, so ashamed that Turtle beat him, because he knew Turtle can't (couldn't) walk. He said, "I'm going to live right here. I am not going any place." That is why we do not have squirrels of that kind here (Ashanamkarak). Kupanakanak.

1. [Perhaps a marmot.—Ed.]

II.53. STORY ABOUT YUPSUKILA (PANTHER)
(RESCUING THE DEER GIRL FROM THE SKY)

GEORGIA ORCUTT (1940)

Georgia learned this story from Captain, her relative on her father's side, who used to sing for hunters for good luck. He was old and remained at home in Panamenik while younger men hunted, but he sang for them. This was in Georgia's time. She would sing the wildcat song herself.

•

a. Panther[1] was staying with his wife Deer. He was always hunting deer. After a while they had a little daughter. After a time Panther took Steller's Jay as second wife.

b. Deer was making [preparing] acorns. She told her daughter, "You had better go give your father the acorns." She took a basket of acorn mush to her father. Jay got up and pulled the basket away from the girl and threw the contents on the steps leading into [the] house pit.

c. The girl ran and told her mother that Jay had spilled the acorn mush. Deer never say nothing [said anything]. After a while Jay put a basket under the steps as a receptacle for acorn mush. After a while [the daughter] bring [brought] some more. Jay seized it and put it away under [the] steps, threw it into her basket hidden under [the] steps. Jay ate all the acorn mush by herself, it tasted so nice.

d. After a while Jay said to herself, "I am going to look it how she fix[es] that acorn when she cook[s] it." Then she climbed up on [the] roof to see what Deer was doing. Deer cut her elbow bone and took out marrow to mix with acorn mush. Jay had tasted it and said, "How does she make it so nice?"

e. After a while Jay said, "I'm going to cook it that way. It tastes so nice how they cook it." When she cooked acorn, she hit her elbow, but only blood came out. Never come out nothing. [No marrow came out.]

1. [Cf. II.46*a*. Panther, mountain lion, and cougar are American names for the same animal.—Ed.]

f. The little girl kept bringing her father that acorn. Deer told her daughter to tell her when the father got the acorns; but he never got them to eat. Jay always took it.

g. After a while when [the] girl pack[ed] it in that acorn, Jay get [got] up. About that time that man sit [sat] up. That man said, "I'm going to have that acorn," just as Jay was about to take it. That was first time that man got acorns to eat.

h. Jay started off right away because she was mad (angry). The acorns [had] tasted so nice she was afraid Panther would go back to his first wife. After a while Bluejay went down the river. She went down to Bluff Creek. She forded the creek. Somebody told her her dress was getting wet.[2] Jay never knew anything because she was so mad. When someone told her, she said, "That's all right, my friend!" She did not care about anything, she was so mad.

i. Deer said to her daughter, "Let's get ready to go." They took all the animals away from this place and went up to [the] sky (painanaavu'kam = on the flat up there).

j. Panther stayed alone and he hunted, but he never killed nothing [anything]. After a while he gave up hunting. He never climbed up the hill again. When packing sweathouse wood, he can't [could] hardly make it sometimes. Then pack it [he packed] down sweathouse wood and make [made a] fire. Then sit [he sat] outside. Nothing to eat; he can't [could] eat nothing. When go [he went] up and pack it [packed] down sweathouse wood, look like [he seemed to hear] a bird talking. When he sit [sat] down to rest, look like bird [the bird seemed to be] talking to him, saying, "I tell, I tell (senipiches, senipiches)."

k. After a while Panther got tired of hearing this, so he caught the bird when it came close to where he was sitting. The bird said, "Don't kill me! Don't kill me!" for Panther was going to kill the bird. The bird said, "I want to tell you that the folks are all having a good time in the sky. They are making [the] ihuk [First Menses] dance for your daughter, and your wife is singing."[3]

l. Panther coming [came] home. After a while never stay in [he no longer went to the] sweathouse. He just lay in [the] living house and never made a fire. After a while Coyote came, and he stayed all night with Panther in the dwelling house. Look like never open[ed] his eyes any more, Panther. After a while Akuwisi (small Wildcat)

2. It was bad to get a dress wet because if it was made of buckskin it became stiff when dry.
3. [For Kroeber's description of the adolescence dance, see the Editor's Preface, above.—Ed.]

came to [the] house and stay[ed] all night. Coyote stay[ed] all night too. They came to take care of Panther.

m. Sometime in the night, Wildcat was singing.[4] Coyote asked, "Your mother's brother is sick. Why do you sing?" Wildcat never answered.

n. After a time Wildcat said, "I was dreaming I was up in [the] sky. I see them having a good time up there. They stand in ten rows. In [the] first row are old bucks with horns. Look like further over, further over [in the other rows], get down to little ones." After a while Wildcat said, "I don't know how we going to get it back that girl. If they stay up there we won't have anything to eat down here. That woman [Deer], she take [took] it all up there." She had said, "Any time he eats that acorn I'm going to leave him, because I am angry because he took that Jay for wife and left me."

o. After a while Coyote said, "What are you going to do? This man is going to starve." Panther never open[ed] his eyes any more; [he] just lay beside the stone firebox. Coyote and Wildcat said, "We'll have to make string." Lots of people came in asking, "How are we going to get that girl?"

p. After a while [they] said, "Let's make lots of thread. Then after a while we can make [twist it into] string." They make [made] it that string. Coyote made one basketful [of] that string. Spider made string too. When Coyote made string, it looked like he wasted a lot of small pieces. Spider picked up what Coyote threw away. Coyote said, "Don't pick it up," as he [Spider?] made fun of it. Coyote made a basketful.

Coyote said, "Now we are ready. I've got lots of string," Coyote said.

q. "Who are [we] going to send up on the sky?" the people asked. Coyote had a big basket of string, so he said he would try. He got only halfway up and had to come down. Spider said he would try. Coyote said, "No use for you to try. You've only made a round and a half of string, and you can't go nowhere [anywhere]."

r. After a while try [tried] it that Spider. Everybody, everybody watched Spider. He keep [kept] on going, keep [kept] on going. After a while [they] never see [saw] him any more, he got up so high. He finally made it up on [the] sky. Then Bald Eagle shot [an] arrow to [the] sky to make it fast so they could climb up to [the] sky to rescue [the] girl. Somebody then had to climb up to make it tight up

---

4. The big wildcat is called akuwis; the small one is akuwisi. Both look the same.

there. Coyote said, "I can climb up." So he climbed up. He got up halfway and had to come down. He never got up there.

s. "Who is going to try next?" Measuring Worm (somkifkuswana) said he would try. Coyote said, "You can't climb up," for already he had tried and failed. As Worm tried he swayed from side to side and Coyote shouted that he was going to fall down, but he kept going. Keep [kept] on going, keep [kept] on going, and finally made it up there. Coyote never make [made] it.

t. Then Worm made the line tight up at the sky and he came down. Wildcat went up, but not Coyote. Coyote always fell down because Wildcat made medicine against him, saying, "You've got to fall, you've got to fall." The folks went up during [the] night.

u. The Deer were in the sweathouse dancing and holding up the girl (Panther's daughter). Looked like Panther can't [couldn't] open his eyes. He lay down. Fawns [were] playing outside, not at [the] dance. Wildcat grabbed one fawn and killed it. Then he returned to earth with it. He cooked it and rubbed some on Panther's lips where he lay under Coyote's care. After a while Panther tasted it. Then Wildcat went up again. When walking, nobody can [could] hear Wildcat when he is [was] walking. Look like nobody know [Nobody knew] it when he is [was] singing.[5] After a while Bald Eagle seized the girl while they were holding her in [the] air and brought her down to earth. All the deer followed her down.

v. About that time Panther was recovered because of the deer meat Wildcat had fed him. Panther said, "It will always be bad luck for a man if he does not treat his wife nice [well] and gets another one.[6] That woman (his first wife) will make bad luck for him."

II.54. MARY'S STORY ABOUT REGAINING DEER
(RESCUING DEER GIRL FROM THE SKY)

MARY IKE (1939)

a. Panther had two wives. One was Bluejay (Steller's Jay).[1] The

5. When men go hunting they sing the wildcat song because deer cannot hear a hunter walking when the song is sung. The hunter walks noiselessly like a wildcat.

6. The Karok use the name "jay" to refer to any woman who tries to steal another woman's husband. They also apply this name to a vain woman.

1. [The Steller's jay is crested; the California or scrub jay is not. Both are blue, but the myth is usually told about Steller's jay.—Ed.]

other was a doe. Panther had a daughter by the doe. Bluejay got jealous and said, "You'd better build me another dwelling." Panther said, "All right."

b. When night came they heard the noise of a little girl's dress decorated with deer hoofs. The little girl said to her father, "Here are your acorns." The mother [Doe had] told the Fawn, "You must stay there till your father gets through eating his acorns. Then we're going home. We're leaving."

c. Bluejay had tasted the acorns in the meantime that Doe had prepared for her husband. After that, whenever the little girl brought the acorns to her father, the Bluejay would take them and say they were not edible. This she told her husband. At (the) same time she dumped the acorn soup in a basket behind her. Thus she fooled her husband by saying the mush was bitter, but when he was gone she ate it herself. Then she said, "I guess I'll go see how Doe fixes the acorns." So she went and watched her.

d. Bluejay watched Doe. Doe had two warm rocks beside her, and with one [she] cracked her arm bone and let marrow run into the acorn mush with which she stirred it. Bluejay said to herself, "I'll go home and fix some acorns the same way." She got two stones at the river and heated them. Then she struck her leg, but she fainted. When she revived, she squeezed the break, but all she got was blood.

e. Her husband returned. The Fawn brought in acorns from her mother. Bluejay tried to take them from her, but Panther took them and ate them. He scolded Jay for always taking his mush, when it tasted so good. Fawn went back and told her Mother that Panther (her father) had eaten the acorns.

f. Doe told her daughter, "Let's leave." They left and went up into the sky.

g. Panther went around the world looking for his daughter. He was hungry; he was getting no food. He had left Jay because she had done wrong in taking acorns from the little girl.

h. Every now and then Wildcat (Panther's younger brother) would drag in a fawn he had killed. Panther was so weak he just lay by the fire, starving. Wildcat would say, "Older brother, you had better get up. I brought a fawn in." Panther would get up and eat nearly all of it alone.

i. Panther asked Wildcat, "Where do [did] you get it?" Wildcat said, "I got it up in the sky. Your daughter is big enough and they are

having the First Menses dance for her. The little fawns are playing
outside of the 'flower-dance' place, and I catch one now and then."
Panther asked, "What are they doing up there?" "When they are
dancing, the back row [of deer] has horns only [an] inch long, the
next row is of spike bucks, the (third) row is of forked horns, the
fourth row is of big bucks. They are tossing your daughter around on
top of their horns. Your wife is sitting down under the steps in the
dwelling house where they are dancing. She is doing the singing. She
says in her song: 'Toss her up high. They [Panther and Jay?] dislike
my daughter.' "

j. Panther asked, "How do you think we can get her back?"
Wildcat said, "There is a big hole on top of the house where they are
tossing her around. We can catch her there and bring her back."

k. Panther said, "Let's hear you sing that song again. I want to
learn it so I can sing it up there and they will think it is the girl's
mother singing." Panther said, "I'll learn the song."

l. So they said, "Let's make five bags (shidixcus) of tobacco."
They fixed them and they went, taking the bags of tobacco. When
almost there, they could hear singing and dancing.

m. They arrived. Wildcat told Panther to lie concealed on (the)
horizontal house beam, for there they tossed the girl. Wildcat said,
"Let's smoke first and pray ('spoil the tobacco') for luck." So they
scattered it as well as smoked it at a rest place.

n. Panther hid on the house beam. The bucks were tossing the
girl on their horns. Panther grabbed the girl. Wildcat had already
gone on [ahead] to relieve Panther if he got tired. Panther put her
under his arm.

o. The dancers did not miss her until Panther was halfway
home. They asked the children what had happened. They said
Panther had taken the girl. All the bucks with big horns followed.
Panther threw the girl in his house and locked her in. The big bucks
came, and all died because they felt so badly about the girl. The
younger bucks then came. Panther opened the door enough to let
them see the girl was there. They kept coming.

p. Pretty soon Coyote came and said, "I've come to eat some
meat." Panther told Wildcat not to show the girl to anyone when he
was away.

q. Coyote hung around with Wildcat to watch the girl. Pretty soon they heard a noise. He said to Wildcat, "Let's show (off) the girl off," even though Panther had ordered otherwise. Wildcat said, "No, my older brother said not to show her." Coyote said, "They can't take her away from us." Coyote pulled on the girl. Wildcat tried to restrain him by holding the girl too. But Coyote showed her off, and the other deer that were looking for her took her away from him. So that is how we came to have deer, when they brought that Fawn back from the sky.[2]

II.55. RESCUING THE DEER GIRL FROM THE SKY

MAMIE OFFIELD

This is a short version of the preceding story about Panther rescuing his daughter Deer from the sky. It was told to Mamie by her mother, a Karok woman of Saxvuram.

•

a. The Deer girl (from whom deer on earth were to come) had been taken to the sky. The people were instructed to spin string which was to be shot to the sky in order to allow someone to ascend to bring down the Deer girl. Each spun string. Coyote threw away half of his, saying he had too much. Each shot his arrow with attached string. The arrows were heard to strike the sky. Coyote's string was far too short. None of the strings were [was] satisfactory for climbing.

b. The people wondered what they should do to get the Deer girl back. Then a little Spider said he could do it. The people laughed at him because he was so tiny and his rope so thin. Nevertheless, they let him try. It was by means of his rope that the Deer girl was brought back to earth.

2. The above story is not a formula for luck in deer hunting.
    Mamie Offield's mother's version differs in having arrow shooting to the sky and in having all animals assist in carrying Fawn. Also there are details about cobwebs over the opening in Wildcat's house, through which deer meat was passed. [But see II.55, below.—Ed.]

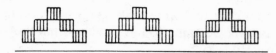

III. Animal Tales Without Coyote as a Character

III.1. Origin of Twine

MARY IKE (1940)

a. Ixkareya man said, "How are you going to live? You had better start making twine. You will have to use twine for snare for deer and you will use twine for fish. You will use twine for bird snare. You will use twine for bowstring sometimes."

b. Deer said, "Don't make the twine. I'll give you all my fat if you don't make it." Deer told big-bellied "Spider" (xachmubis), "You'll spoil iris if you pull it up. You must cut it to get (the) two (leaf) fibers out. Don't pull it up." The people on earth were making twine for deer snares.[1] Deer wanted Xachmubis to be on his side.

c. Yasara ixkareya (rich man) said, "This is the way human

---

1. [Schenck and Gifford, Karok Ethnobotany, UC-AR 13:(no. 6):381, say that ground iris *(Iris macrosiphon)* is one of the most important plants to the Karok "because fish nets and deer nets are made from it. The leaves are dried and then scraped with a musselshell scraper. Two holes are made in the shell and a thong is put through them. The first finger is then pushed through the thong loop, while the shell is held in the palm of the hand, or the shell may be held in the palm . . . without the thong. With this the two outer fibers of the leaf are separated and cleaned. The fibers are dried again, and then twisted together by being rolled along the front of the thigh. Cord of various sizes, according to the needs, is made."—Ed.]

beings are going to live. They will use the twine to catch the deer and to take salmon. They will have dogs to drive deer into the snares."

d. Xachmubis ate all the deer fat and became very corpulent. That is the reason he is so fat with that big stomach. Xachmubis and Big Spider worked together in storing iris for string.

e. Yasara ixkareya said, "The Indians will use twine for catching deer and salmon."

III.2. Story About Monte (?) Creek

MARY IKE

a. Down under the falls[1] was Ground Squirrel's (aksai) fishing place. The people living there were jealous over Ground Squirrel's possession of this fishing place. And there were some Dog Salmon (asawin) in the river. They [The people] told the women not to eat the Dog Salmon lest when they had their monthlies (menses) they would be protracted for three or four months. (The Ground Squirrels did not eat the Dog Salmon because they were people too.)

b. Woman Ground Squirrel said, "I bet you I can eat it." Vikaputunwei (bird? mammal?) asked Ground Squirrel woman, "Where are you going?" Ground Squirrel replied, "I am going down here a little way."

Pine Squirrel[2] (wininikich) man said, "I am going up on (the) hill."

They asked Dog Salmon where he was going. He replied, "I am going up the river a little way."

c. Vikaputunwei said, "I am going up the creek a little way. We are going to live right there. If you find flicker feathers, don't pick them up. That's (They are) ours; they belong to us. If you pick them up they'll make you sick. Don't drink this creek water. It belongs to me. Don't look at the falls, or you'll see a lot of things jumping in the water and you'll go crazy. You'll see all kinds of things jumping in the water, such as bows, arrows, baskets, (and) plates. If you see things like that, you'll want to look away because you'll know you are going crazy. It will be all [in] your imagination."

1. There is a waterfall in the creek (Kevkerishtu) opposite Oak Bottom, where the creek empties into the Salmon River. Mary was told not to look over there.
2. [This may be the golden-mantled ground squirrel.—Ed.]

d. Ixkareya told the Dog Salmon they should not go very far. So they didn't go beyond Salmon River bridge.

III.3. Frog Story

GEORGIA ORCUTT (1940)

a. Akbachuripa (a place on long ridge below Bluff Creek) was an ixkareya man living at [the] place with [the] same name. (Name means "elkhorn purse on ridge.") Another ixkareya man was living at Panamenik. Look like (He was) a nice-looking (young) man. And after a while somebody said, "If any women [woman] can find water she can marry that nice-looking man." And after a while them [those] girls tried to see if they could pack water and marry that man. And that girl tried, and another one tried and said, "I could not find that water." After a while she gave up because she could not get water. Then another one tried. After a while pretty near[ly] everybody give [gave] up, for there were no rivers or creeks or nothing [anything].

b. After a while Frog said, "I'm going to try. I think I can get water." And after a while she had looked all over and found no water. And after a while Frog pretty near[ly] give [gave] up packing that basket so she can get [in which she planned to carry] the water. After a while Frog think [thought], "Maybe I'll piss in [the] water basket," because she can't [couldn't] get no [any] water, every place she try [tried]. And after a while Frog give [gave] up.

c. After a while old man Akbachuripa said to a girl (not his daughter), "You'd better go down." The girl said, "No, we can't go down because we can't find that water."

d. After a while that old man said that people did not know where to cook that fish; they had no place to insert [the] spit because all [the ground was covered with] rocks. Old man said, "I always go down and visit those people. They can't find no [any] water. I can go down first. I am going to sit down near [the] fireplace and put my foot on [a] corner of it when I sit down. You can put the salmon stick right in front of my foot. When I sit there you can climb upstairs onto [the] platform and you can find water hidden in [the] wall." (The nice-looking young man had it hidden there.) "When you open it you can fill your water basket."

e. That man sit (sat) down, and the two girls (the one above and her sister, not hitherto mentioned) watched him. They knew how to put in the stick for cooking fish. And after a while the girl get (went) up and get (got) water. She could see it when she opened the rock wall (asanifa).

f. Lots of (Many) boys were in there. They look[ed] at each other when she was getting (the) water. They never say (said) nothing. They were just thinking, "How (did) she find that water?"

g. The girl married the nice-looking young man. The other girl and the old man went home. After that everybody (had) water. Before that nobody had water, because it was all impounded by the handsome young man.

III.4. STORY ABOUT ELK AND WOLF

MARY IKE (September 10, 1942)

a. This was in ixkareya times (i.e., before our time). The people were dancing the "flower dance" (ihuk) for (over) two girls.[1] The girls were sitting down. They [The people] danced ten days and nights for them.

b. Elk (isyuux) was the first one to sing. He sang the mukumuku song referring to the elk's horns breaking the branches as he went through the brush. Then Wolf (ixhavnamish) sang his song as they all danced.

c. The one who was going to give the word for the girls to run was standing there. Then they all ran. The girls ran to the water to bathe. The man who arrived at the water at the same time as a girl was the one who was going to marry her.

d. Wolf got in the lake first with a girl. Elk was way (far) behind, but he jumped in the water when he got there. When Elk came out of the water he looked very handsome, but when Wolf came out he looked untidy and he drew a long face. Wolf said, "Hereafter I am to kill you and eat you." Elk said, "Hereafter the young girls will like an (the) old man (men)." The Elk married the girl, and Wolf did not. Kupanakana.

1. [For Kroeber's description of the Adolescence or First Menses Dance, see the Editor's Preface, above. Tale II.19 is another version of the present tale, also told by Mary Ike.—Ed.]

III.5. LARGE BLACK ANT AND HUMMINGBIRD

MARY IKE (1940)

a. Asuwut (Large Black Ant) was a man, and Hummingbird (kanpuchiniswenach) was a woman. The people at . . . [1] were having trouble, and they had to call on someone for [as] go-between (ashipvaraivan) to settle the matter. "We better send Hummingbird because he can travel fast." They told Ant he had to go too. They told him he would have to wear a belt. "I don't need it. I won't wear any," Ant protested. "I have a good shape. I'm small around the waist. I don't have to have a belt."

b. They asked Ant, "Tell us what you are going to say when you get there." He said, "I'm going to say this: 'Karuimi (you, karuna'a (me), karuimi, karuna'a!" As he said this he held his hands on his hips, acting smart.

c. Hummingbird said, "You all be ready when I come back, so as to hear the news. Be waiting around the sweathouse door." Then Hummingbird went (departed), and they told Ant not to go because he could not walk fast.

d. Hummingbird wondered what they were going to feed her when she got back. She traveled so fast they could hardly see her. Then they all stood and watched for her. Pretty soon they seen (saw) her coming. She went from here to Etna.[2] They said to Ant, "You'd better say something. Let her hear what you are going to say." Ant said, "Karuimi, karuna'a (you, me)."

e. Hummingbird could not settle the quarrel. They told her, "All you are going to do [in future] is to eat flowers." They told Ant, "All you are going to do is to live on rotten logs."

III.6. STORY ABOUT BAT

MARY IKE (1940)

a. There was a big time going on. There were two girls there. There was a sugar pine tree with lots of nuts. Whoever climbed the

1. [Omission in typescript.—Ed.]
2. [See II.38, n. 1, above.—Ed.]

tree and got all the nuts would (was to) get the two girls as his wives.[1] They put (a) ladder (fudaki) against (the) trunk, and Bat said, "I'm going to be the first one to climb." The people said, "All right."

b. There was a fire under the big tree. It got so hot as Bat was climbing that he fell off into the big fire and burned his behind. The people pulled him out. His behind was all curled up from burning.

c. Many were sitting around watching. One fellow (Tree Squirrel, axru'u) was sitting there. He said, "I'll climb." He climbed without the ladder. He ran up the tree, talking. He went way up and cut off cones with nuts.

d. The people shouted for him to come down and let somebody else try. He came down. When he came down he brought the nuts down (with him).

e. Red Pine Squirrel tried next. He went way to the top and cut off cones on far-out ([the] tips of) limbs. He got lots (many). He cut one off, jumped down to another limb, cut one off, and so on. He was showing off. He had all of them, except one left far out on a limb. He went and got that. Then he came back down. After he got down, he rolled around in (the) ashes and got all the pitch off his body.

f. He married the two girls. The Bat did not get married, but (only) burned his behind (rump).

III.7. Story About (Bat and) Woodrat

MARY IKE (1940)

a. Woodrat's (asashnad) daughter married Bat's (timshukri) son.[1]

b. Old [Young?] Bat went hunting and was crazy after tobacco.

c. Woodrat's father said, "I'm going to see my son-in-law." Young Bat had killed a deer. The children were so (very) glad to see their grandfather. Old Woodrat had a lot of baskets of tobacco (tcirrixus, tobacco basket). He said, "I know my son-in-law likes tobacco."

1. [See Mary Ike's condensation of this episode in Kroeber's B1*a–b*, above.—Ed.]

---

1. [It was a marriage of convenience for Young Bat, according to Mary Ike's more detailed telling to Kroeber (B1, above).—Ed.]

d. Bat's wife (Woodrat's daughter) was cooking, but she would not give her father any deer meat. He fainted, he felt so badly because they would not give him something to eat.

e. Woodrat got up and put water on her father to revive him. The children were looking at their father (Young Bat), who was eating. The old man Woodrat came to (revived) and he smoked. Young Bat smelled the tobacco. He said, "I wonder if it is all gone. I smell something good." He ran outside and up on top of the house, where he could inhale the smoke from his father-in-law's smoking.

f. The old man Woodrat gave him a basket full of tobacco. He felt sorry for him, because he was on top of the house. Bat started smoking. He never quit. Toward morning he began eating tobacco. Kupanakana.

III.8. BIRD STORY

GEORGIA ORCUTT

Georgia learned this story[1] from Red Cap Tom, her brother-in-law. He was also Georgia's father's sister's son. Red Cap Tom's wife is Georgia's half-breed half-sister.[2]

●

a. Wingvīn (a bird with white breast, black cap, black marks on face, brown back; appears on river only when heavy snow; otherwise on mountains; comes only in winter)[3] had a sweathouse at Panamenik. His ten sons came back in [the] evening. One evening one failed to come home. Somebody told him, "Your son never [did not] come home." He never answered.

b. Next day the nine went hunting. One failed to come home. Somebody told Wingvīn one of his sons had failed to come home. He never answered.

c. Next day the eight went hunting. One failed to come home. Somebody told Wingvīn, but he never answered.

d. Next day the seven went hunting. One failed to come. Somebody told him, but he never answered.

1. [For another version of this giant-killing story, see Kroeber's F8.—Ed.]
2. [See G.'s section on "Informants," above.—Ed.]
3. [Perhaps a junco.—Ed.]

e. Each day [went] the same until none [was] left. Somebody told him each time, and he never answered. Finally his last son was gone, and still he did not answer. All [were] gone.

f. Afterwards in the morning, Wingvīn went into the dwelling house. He took a seed burden basket (atiki). In it he put in all kinds of things: sisegunva (belt), men's cap of buckskin called chonê, paranwa (wedge), taknuris (maul), tobacco, pipe of deer sinew called ipaporam (sinews from hind leg of deer), etc. Afterwards he went way [far] up on [the] hill with [the] lake called Uknamihich.

g. He sit (sat) down right by the lake. After a while he saw somebody coming up the hill. [He] looked like [a] long man when he come [came] up. He asked Wingvīn, "Are you looking for your boys?" Wingvīn never answered. After a while sit [sat] down that tall man (Marukara=On hill [maruk] man). After a while Marukara said, "You better smoke." Wingvīn had put pitch in his throat beforehand. When smoked, Marukara's pipe burned a hole in one's throat. In this way Marukara had killed Wingvīn's sons. Wingvīn knew this, so had prepared by protecting his throat with pitch. As Wingvīn smoked, Marukara was wishing he would fall over, as that is [was] the way he had killed Wingvīn's ten sons. But Wingvīn did not fall over.

h. Then Wingvīn said to Marukara: "You'd better smoke my pipe." When he gave it [to] Marukara, Marukara thought, "I'm going to chew it up and spoil it." Wingvīn knew he could not spoil the pipe. After a while, he gave up trying to mash the pipe and seized Wingvīn to throw him in [the] lake as he [had] done [with] Wingvīn's sons. After a while, Wingvīn called to his basket contents, saying, "You better come out," and he named each of the objects he had brought.

i. All came out. The belt got on Marukara's waist and squeezed him; the shoes got on his feet and took off his feet. The hook (takwukat, a wooden hook) hooked off Marukara's ribs; the cap took off all of Marukara's scalp. The gloves (tisakuara) got on his hands and took his fingers off. All these were in the atiki. Fall [Fell] down dead that Marukara.

j. "That's the way you have been killing off my boys. Now I know what you've been doing," said Wingvīn. Then he went to the lake. After a while he see (saw) all the hair of his sons. He picked it up. He put it all in the atiki. Then he packed it down to his home. He took it into [the] sweathouse. He separated it into the ten lots, the hair of each son separately. After a while he left (the) sweathouse and went into [the] dwelling house. After a long while he went outside. The ten boys came to life again. Each told how he had been killed by smoking Marukara's pipe, the smoke of which made a hole in the throat.

III.9. STORY ABOUT BUXHAAT, A SMALL BROWN BIRD

MARY IKE (1940)

Buxhaat is a small brown bird that lives at Katimin Yuutimits in the bushes.[1]

•

a. Buxhaat's house was at Yuutimits. A'at (spring salmon) was living at (the sacred living house) ixkareyaixlivram, or wenaram. There were two girls (Bobcat and Fox). Their mother and brother told them they'd better go up and live with A'at. Buxhaat heard the news that two girls were coming to live at A'at.

b. In front of A'at's house were two tall poles on which were two pileated woodpeckers, which were A'at's pets. Buxhaat sneaked up there and moved the poles to his house.

c. The girls' folks had told them they would recognize A'at's house by the pole(s) with the woodpeckers on it (them). One of the girls asked, "Where are we going to go?" The other said, "There is the house. They told us there would be a pole(s) and woodpeckers outside." They went into the house. An old lady (woman) had come to the door and told them to come in. "Come in. I have not a good home, but you can come in anyway."

d. They went in. Buxhaat came in. Buxhaat asked, "What are we going to have for supper?" Buxhaat built the fire. The girls were looking at him. Pretty soon they heard someone ask outside, "Who brought these poles here?"

e. Buxhaat said, "We will have the best salmon for supper. It is at the bottom of that basket of fish, at the very bottom." The girls had brought some acorns, which they were cooking. Buxhaat took the salmon out and spat on it to make it appear greasy. He prayed to it to be greasy.

f. He warmed it by the fire to make it flexible. He heard someone call from outside, "Buxhaat, come out here and lick the acorns

1. [Bright in the Linguistic Index, below, identifies it as the nighthawk.—Ed.]

off these rocks (stones)." He was so poor his neighbors let him lick the acorn mush off the cooking stones.

g. Buxhaat answered, "What is the matter with you guys (people)? Every time you want to make a dance you have to call on me first before you have it." He wanted the girls to think he was a big shot (an important person).

h. The girls ate their own food. They would not eat the salmon because they seen [saw] him spitting on it. Buxhaat came in and told the girls, "You all must go to bed early." Then they all went to bed. Buxhaat said, "I'm going to sleep in the middle." One girl said, "Something is eating on (biting) me. There must be a lot of (many) fleas." Buxhaat said, "It always is that way. Wherever I sleep there is a lot of (are many) ants."

i. The girls felt something big running around on their bodies. It was lizards and various bugs. One [girl] jumped up and said, "I'm not going to sleep here!" Then the other jumped up and said, "I'm not going to sleep here!" The last [second] one to get up left her dress.

j. Buxhaat had all kinds of vermin in his hair: lizards, lice, etc. The two girls ran away from him. They ran home. Their folks told them they had better try again. Next time they went to a different house where the poles were. When they got there they saw that fellow (A'at) sitting there. Then they knew it was the right house.

k. Buxhaat began to get jealous. A'at went up the hill to get some wood; back of Sugar Loaf [was] where he went after the (to get some) wood. Buxhaat said, "Now I am going to kill him." He was just (very) jealous. Then he grabbed A'at and cut him to pieces. He took his gills out and set them down there. He scattered his parts all over the hillside, the head too. These turned into rocks, to be seen today below the schoolhouse.

III.10. WHY CHIPMUNK IS PRETTY

MARY IKE (1939)

[For another version of this story, also told by Mary Ike, see III. 29.—Ed.]

•

a. They were all going to see the "flower dance" (First Menses

Dance): Woodrats, Mice, Moles, Gophers, etc. They all painted their faces.

b. After they were all painted, Woodrat asked the Mouse, "How do I look?" The Mouse said, "You look very pretty, and your hair is just right. All that is wrong with you is that your eyes are too small."

The Mouse asked, "How do I look?" "You look very nice, except that your eyes are too big." The Mouse said, "Oh, yes?"

c. The (little) Mole said to (asked) a big Mole, "How do I look?" The big one (Mole) told the little one (Mole), "You look all right, except that you have too long a face. The big Mole asked the little Mole, "How do I look?" "You look all right, but your hands are too wide and too short."

d. Chipmunk asked Wininkech,[1] "How do I look?" She replied, "You are the prettiest one here. Even your speech is pretty." Then Wininkech asked Chipmunk, "How do I look?" "You don't look good. You look as though you are too mean. Your body is nice." Wininkech told Chipmunk, "As long as you live people will always admire you." So now people say, "Oh, look at the little chipmunk! Isn't he cute?"

III.11. CHIPMUNK STORY

GEORGIA ORCUTT

[This tale of Jay as a greedy doctor closely parallels Kroeber's H.4.—Ed.]

•

a. Chipmunk woman (manowat=up on mountain) [was] making all kinds of food: pine nuts, hazelnuts, all kinds of nuts. Steller's Jay woman (pahanwan=eating peppernuts) came around. After a while Manowat got sick. All the doctors came after a while to cure her. Jay doctored her too. Hummingbird (xanpuchinis) woman was also doctoring Chipmunk.

b. After a while Bullhead Fish[1] (xangit) woman came to doctor Chipmunk. Bullhead said, "It looks like you folks can't pay me enough." Bullhead said, "You'd better pay me achpus[2] when I doctor."

1. [Wininikich is identified as the "pine squirrel" in III.2*b*.—Ed.]

---

1. [The bullhead, or sculpin, is a member of the genus *Cottus*.—Ed.]
2. On the underside of the fish, from the throat down, is a stringlike thing called achpus, which when removed carries with it the viscera.

c. After a while Jay got up and doctored Chipmunk again. Jay said, "She'll never get well, never get well." Then Hummingbird doctored. When singing she said, "I can't take out that pain; my mouth is too small." When singing Hummingbird said, "Jay, looks like Jay made her sick so she can [could] get all of Chipmunk's property."

d. And after a while Hummingbird took out the pain. When take (she took) it out (she) show(ed) it and said, "Now, this (is) Jay's work. Jay has deviled (apurowa) Chipmunk with cocoons" (which are called "Jay's devils"). Hummingbird had sucked out a cocoon. After that Chipmunk got well.

III.12. ANOTHER CHIPMUNK STORY

GEORGIA ORCUTT (1940)

a. Bullhead Fish [swam] at high river; river looked awfully high. Chipmunk way [far] up on [the] hill looked down and said, "Luhanish (friend), I looked down and I thought 'Where are you going with the river so high, even up into [the] woods?' " Bullhead said, "Lots of times when I look up that way, it looks as if there are no trees because all [is covered with] snow everywhere."

b. Bullhead said, "When I look up that way the trees look like feathers sticking up because they are all covered with snow." Chipmunk said, "Oh, I live high at that time. I always eat the chestnuts (sunyis) then. I cook them in [an] acorn cooking basket. When I take it to eat that chestnut, I always eat that kind when [during] snowy weather. All summer I work packing in nuts, so in winter I have plenty to eat." Bullhead said, "I have a good time eating all that floats down."[1]

III.13. STORY ABOUT CROW

MARY IKE (1940)

a. Crow (anaach) woman had (a) fishery at Amaikiaram.[1] Many

1. This story is for children particularly.

_____

1. [Women sometimes inherited fishing places, but they themselves did not

people were drying salmon during fishing. One young fellow (man named Cormorant=chufish) was always hanging around (visiting) at Crow's house, wanting to make a hit with (love to) her. His name was Chufish.[2]

b. A lot of (Many) people (were) living in Crow's house. One of them said to Chufish, "You'd better marry her." "That's what I think," said Chufish. "That's why I am hanging (staying) around here." They got married and had a baby.

c. Chufish went out fishing. He said to his wife, "You must give the baby a steam bath." He did this daily, and each day Crow steamed her baby for a long time. One day Crow thought she'd give her baby an extra good steam bath. So she went down to [the] river and got some good stones and made the bath real hot. She put all the hot rocks in the asip (acorn basket)[3] and got the water boiling furiously. She put her baby in the boiling water. She looked at it, and the baby was just falling to pieces. She went outside and got some black oak bark. She took her baby out and put it on the bark. It was falling to pieces.

d. Chufish came home. He found his wife crying outside. "Where is the baby?" he asked. She never answered (did not answer) him. Then she said, "You always tell me to give her a steam bath. She is already cooked. There she is."

e. "I did not tell you to cook it (her)! I told you to give her a bath!" Then Chufish beat his wife (and) then he left his wife (her). "I'm not staying here," he said. "She belongs here." The man went back down to Sufip [Rekwoi], whence he had come.

f. Somebody told Crow, "Your husband is back down at Sufip. He sits on a big rock fishing. He has a big nose and wears a big blanket." Crow then sang, "My husband sits on a rock with a big nose and a blanket around him." The reason Crow has a sort of funny walk is because her husband kicked her hips. Kupanakanak.

---

fish. Their sons or other males substituted for them (Kroeber and Barrett, Fishing in Northwestern California, UC-AR 21:[no. 1]:4).—Ed.]

2. [G.'s typescript had a deleted parenthetical description reading "A bird as large as vulture with knob of feathers on head; it is dark green in plumage, has some little white on head; seen sitting on rocks; has short legs—sounds like cormorant." Bright in the Linguistic Index, below, identifies Chufish as the bald eagle.—Ed.]

3. [Spelled aship by K. in G3c, and translated there as "cooking basket." —Ed.]

III.14. STORY ABOUT WHO SHALL ASCEND RIVER FIRST
TO FALLS OF KLAMATH

GEORGIA ORCUTT (1940)

At Sufip [Rekwoi] they were discussing who would go first up the river to the Klamath falls.[1] White Duck (kind?) said, "I am going to be the first one to go to Klamath falls." Spring Salmon said nothing. Duck flew up and thought he would be first, for he did not know that Salmon was going up the river. When Duck arrived at [a] nice flat rock below the falls, he saw salmon skins on the rock. He said, "I guess I got beat. Salmon has come first. I came afterwards."

III.15. ANOTHER FROG STORY

GEORGIA ORCUTT

a. Frog was married and staying with her husband, Frog. After while, they [the people] had all kinds of fun, but Frog woman would not go. Frog man had to go alone. After a while somebody said [to her], "Why do you always stay home? Why don't you go? Your husband always has a good time with the girls." When he come home Frog [would] never tell his wife he had [had] a good time or what he had been doing.

b. After a while Frog woman said, "I'm going [to] see. That man is going [has gone] already." After a while she put on all kinds of nice things, including a nice shell-decorated buckskin dress. When she came to her husband in the Brush Dance, he did not know her and he said, "Oh what a nice girl!" he said, as he held her arm under his.[1]

1. So called by Georgia. ["About a mile below the mouth of the Salmon the Klamath tumbles down a low fall, which was a famous fishing station. . . ." (Kroeber, Handbook, p. 99). The locale is to be distinguished from Klamath Falls, Oregon, a town at the head of the Klamath River.—Ed.]

1. In the Brush Dance, women put their arms under the men's arms. [Kroeber says the Brush Dance is a minor dance, "ostensibly held to cure an ailing child. As a matter of fact it is often made when the younger men are desirous of a holiday" (Kroeber, Handbook, p. 61).—Ed.]

c. After a while [they] danced again that Brush Dance. Different ones danced at different times, not always [the] same ones. After a while people seeing [saw] that Frog man [was] holding onto that nice-looking Frog women [woman]. He never knew it was his wife; he thought it was some other woman. She never say [said] nothing [anything] to him, just danced with him. Afterward sit [they sat] down outside. Look like he hang [hung] onto that woman. Then she talked to him.

d. After a while when [she] talk[ed] to him, he find [found] out it is [was] his wife. He know [knew] it [was] his wife when she talk[ed] to him. When he knew it was his wife, he asked, "Why did you come up here?" Then he held her and kicked her behind. All she said when he kicked her was "Kikkik." Frog has [a] flat behind now on account of [that] kick.

e. After [the] dance [was] over, they separated. The man was mad because his wife went to the dance. Kupanakanak.

III.16. STILL ANOTHER FROG STORY

GEORGIA ORCUTT

a. Frog woman got married up at Forks of Salmon. She came from Etna (Ishram).[1] They stayed at Forks of Salmon.[2] After a while sombody came down from Etna. And when come [he came] down look like he [he seemed to] holler, holler [shout]. Nobody could understand what he was saying. After a while one old man never said nothing [anything], but he heard and understood what the man was hollering [shouting]. Frog man said to his wife, "Listen [to] what he is saying. Maybe you can understand what he says. Listen outside."

b. And after a while, [when] Frog woman [was] outside, that man is hollering [shouting] when he is [was] coming. After a while

1. [Cf. II.38, n. 1.—Ed.]
2. Georgia's mother's mother was from there, and spoke a different language. (Mrs. Grant is related to Georgia; she is Carl Langford's mother-in-law.) [The Salmon flows into the Klamath from the southeast. About twelve air miles above its mouth, the Salmon forks. Just above the small village at the forks was the southeast boundary of Karok territory; beyond were the New River Shasta (Kroeber, Yurok Myths, map 1). In the story, Frog woman, being from Etna to the northeast, would also have spoken a Shastan language.—Ed.]

Frog [woman] came in. Her husband asked what [the] man was saying; it looked as though he was excited, for he was hollering [shouting] loud.

c. Frog woman said, "Somebody wants me up there. They want me to come up and fix them something." And after a while the one old man who said nothing kind of [almost] cried when he set [sat] down. Somebody asked him what was the matter. Frog woman said, "Somebody wants me up there." That old man never say nothing [said anything] that sit [who sat] down.

d. After a while somebody again asked [the] old man, "What's the matter?" He answered, "Yes. Lots of people die off, my own people. Got some kind of a sick(ness) up there." That is why he cry [cried] when he sit [sat] down.

e. Frog woman made believe she knew what that man hollered [shouted]. But she never knew what he said. She spoke a different language, but she made believe she understood.

f. Frog man got mad. He said, "You can't understand what he hollers [shouts]. You make believe you understand." Then he kicked her. Then Frog woman left.

III.17. FROG STORY

GEORGIA ORCUTT

The mice make nests in acorn storage baskets, and their young get thrown out into [the] fire when people find them. One day the old Mice in a house were crying because their babies had been burned. Frog came in, and she cried too. Then she talked to Mice: "Why [do] you always do this—go into somebody's house? I raise my family in the water, where nobody bothers them."[1]

III.18. HAWK OF A'U'ICH

MARY IKE

This hawk catches all kinds of birds—ducks on the wing, for instance. It is white underneath, brown on top, about the size of a wild pigeon. Aixnek-

1. Mouse = shiit, frog = hanchiv.

shan is its name; it means "living up high." It lives on A'u'ich (Sugar Loaf).[1] It leaves in the fall.

[Tales III.18 and III.19 form a pair, with the present telling, by Mary Ike, much more graphic than Georgia Orcutt's version.—Ed.]

•

a. Hawk man married Grizzly Bear woman (penishgardim= mean fellow).[2] Hawk went out Etna way in Scott's Valley. His wife Grizzly Bear did not know that Hawk had another wife over there.[3] Every time he went out there he stayed a long time. Every time he went out there he told his [first] wife, "You must take good care of my little brother, Water Ouzel" (asaxwanichamvanich="goes and eats things off dirty rock"=water ouzel).

b. The little brother went back into the house and saw his brother's wife making baskets. She always made tight burden baskets (arus).

c. When her husband came home, Grizzly Bear said, "What makes you stay so long? I get lonesome." "I like it out there because it is nice and warm. The sun is always shining," he replied. She said, "I don't believe you; I heard there is always snow there." "It is nice out there." At the same time he had two children there.

d. He stayed here at Katimin about a year; then he went away again. He told his little brother everything. "I've got two children there, but don't you dare tell her (Bear) or she'll just choke you to death." Then he went away again, saying to his brother, "Don't you tell my wife a thing."

e. When Hawk got over to Etna his children were so glad to see their father. He stayed there a year. On his way back, from the top of Etna Mountain, he could hear his falls at Katimin.

f. When he arrived at Katimin he looked over his falls. "I wonder if everything is all right." And he looked them over. He stayed here a long time and looked over everything he owned. He looked at his spring near Smith's store at Katimin, for he claimed that too. He got ready to go back to Etna again.

1. [A'u'ich is the mountain at Katimin; for more details, see Kroeber, E2, n. 1, above.—Ed.]

2. [Cf. II.46*a*, where the epithet penishgardim is applied to Mountain Lion.—Ed.]

3. Who this second wife was the story does not say.

g. He now had four children[4] out there. His wife at Katimin did not have any children. He stayed out there more than he did here (Katimin).

"What makes you stay out there so long?" Bear asked. "I get lonesome." He replied, "You are too mean to me. Nobody growls at me out there." She asked, "Have you got relations out there?" He answered, "Yes, I have."

h. Then he went back out there. Now he had six kids (children) there. Bear began to wonder: "I'd like to know what he is doing out there."

i. His little brother always went to the spring near Smith's store. He watched two little fishes swimming in there. Then he sings [sang]: "My brother went away. My brother is going over the hill now. He is going out to see his wife and kids (children). He has eight kids (children) now. He is going to bring them over."

j. Bear sneaked up on the little brother while he was at the spring. She was listening to what he sang. The younger brother said, "I'll bet they are halfway up the hill now. My brother is coming back, bringing his eight kids (children) home." Bear grabbed Ouzel and started to choke him. "Tell me what you are saying. I heard you." He had to tell her, "My brother is coming home, bring[ing] his kids (children) home."

k. Hawk went ahead of his children. He did not hear any sound. He did not hear his waterfall. Bear went [had gone] down and wrecked the fish dam, she was just mad [so angry].

l. Hawk turned around to his kids (children) and said, "You come behind me. I can't hear the waterfall. I think she has found out." He ran on ahead, leaving the kids (children) behind coming. His other wife (from Etna) was coming too.

m. When Hawk got behind A'u'ich (Sugar Loaf) he kneeled down and he seen (saw) his wife going up the hill packing (a) basket (arus) on her back. Then he took a shot at her, at his wife. Then she rolled down the hill; she rolled around in the flat of Evril's field[5] (above Smith's store).

n. His other wife and children were getting near the site of the schoolhouse between Somes Bar and Katimin. On the hill above the schoolhouse, where there is now a big row of rocks, Hawk said,

4. " 'Kids,' family always says."
5. [On Evril's field, see V.3, n. 3, below.—Ed.]

"Since she wrecked my dam, I'm going to live right here. This will be my home." He told his kids (children), "Since you've only got this far, just as long as hereafter everybody will give you something, a rock or tree or anything they want to give, hereafter from now on."

From that day to this day, people who go by there always put something out there and say, "May I live a long time." The trail is there now.

o. "After this when I go away I'll get Aswi bird (looks like Aixnekshan hawk, somewhat) to take care of the place," Hawk said. "The people will take care of the kids (children) and give them something each time they (go) by here."[6]

III.19. PIDISHKADIM STORY

GEORGIA ORCUTT (1940)

A Katimin woman told Georgia this story, so this is an exception to her statement that all her stories were from the father of Red Cap Tom. This Katimin woman was Doctor Nancy, an eim [shaman]. She told many stories. This same woman also told the story [I.8] about the Amaikiaram women who turned into two white stones.

•

a. [An] animal looking like [a] bear and called Pidishkadim[1] was married at Katimin in ixkareya times. After a while her husband (a bird called aidjēn) went over to Etna (Tishram).[2] He come [came] back that man, always come [came] back. He stay[ed] with his wife when he come [came] back. After a while go [he went] back again up there.

b. After a while he had lots of children in Tishram but none in Katimin. The Katimin wife never knew about the Etna wife and children.

6. There is now said to be an L-shaped pile of stones, about fifty feet long and three feet high. There used to be another pile near the powderhouse [powerhouse?] on the road around Sugar Loaf. This was removed when the Forest Service road was put in.

1. [Cf. III.18, n. 2.—Ed.]
2. [On Etna, see II.38, n. 1, above.—Ed.]

c. There used to be [a] nice falls at Katimin.[3] When the woman found her husband had children by another woman at Etna, she was furious and wrecked the Katimin falls, by jumbling up the rocks.

d. When the husband and his sons came down upon the hill, he said, "What's the matter? I can't hear my falls," he asked [said to] himself. And after a while he said to the boys, "What's the matter? I can't hear my falls. You boys better stand right here and I'll go down and see what has happened." All the ixkareya were excited because the falls had stopped. The boys were excited and stayed upon [the] hill and turned into [a] row of rock piles. They appear to be standing in a row looking down toward Katimin.[4]

The woman was mean, and the term pidishkadim is now applied to [a] mean woman. Kodisera ifapbi is the contrary term, meaning "nice woman."[5]

III.20. "MOCKINGBIRD" (TUUS) AND VARIED THRUSH (ACHKU)

MARY IKE (1939)

[This and the following two tales are versions of the same myth.—Ed.]

•

a. Tuus ("mockingbird") comes in spring and leaves in fall. Varied Thrush (achku) comes in late fall or early winter as Tuus leaves. Tuus met Achku arriving as he (Tuus) was leaving. They met on the mountain Tuusipumwaram.[1] Tuus was sitting down resting. Achku came up the hill. Tuus said to Achku, "The place where you pick up acorns, everybody is picking up acorns there." Namkiruk was [the] name of [the] place; it is uphill back of Ishipishi. Achku said, "That's all right. I'll make them spill their acorns."

b. When Achku went out in the spring, he met Tuus at the same place, coming in. Achku told Tuus, "At your fisheries they are

3. The falls at Amaikiaram are called Yutimin.
4. [G.'s typescript has the following note, crossed out: "The sacred ixkareya rocks at Amaikiaram were for the salmon ceremony only, not the July Jump Dance."—Ed.]
5. [In I.3, n. 2, ifabi is translated as girl or unmarried woman.—Ed.]

1. [Punwaram is any stopping or resting place (II.32*b*).—Ed.]

catching many salmon." Wurishiat was [the] name of [the] fishery. Basakirem was [the] name of [the] second fishery belonging to Tuus. Tuus said, "That's all right. Let them take lots of salmon. I'll throw their net in the river when I get there."

c. So when anyone spills their acorns, it is said Achku made them spill them. If anyone loses his net, it is said Tuus made him lose it.[2]

Tuus is a bird that sings daily at Mary's house now. Its song is said to be: "I have not said anything yet."

III.21. MOCKINGBIRD AND VARIED THRUSH

SAM BROWN, HUPA (1940)

[Sam Brown served as a Hupa informant and translator for Gifford when the latter was collecting data on the world renewal ceremonies (Kroeber and Gifford, World Renewal, UC-AR 13:[no. 1]:132). G. says there that Brown was a halfbreed, a bachelor, and an excellent informant and interpreter. This Hupa version appears to be a summary.—Ed.]

•

Mockingbird [comes] in summer, Swamp Robin[1] (Varied Thrush) in fall and winter. [They] meet on Redwood Ridge as Mockingbird (soxchox, Salmon's grandmother) is leaving for [the] south and Chakne (Varied Thrush) is coming to [the] country. [They] exchange news. Mockingbird tells Varied [Thrush] she has not said anything yet, even though she has talked night and day. She scolds the people because they pick berries and acorns. She tells Varied Thrush the people are getting her acorns on her acorn claims: "Your acorn claims are taken." Varied Thrush says she does not care because once the Indians have their burden baskets full of acorns she can tip them over anyway.

When a woman's basket full of acorns tips over, she says the Varied Thrush did it.

2. Tuus and Achku were not ixkareya. Coyote was an ixkareya, but a marplot. Tuus is probably Oriole, Mamie [Offield] says.

---

1. shweaK [?] (guttural k) = Robin proper.

III.22. STORY ABOUT TUUS AND ACHKU

GEORGIA ORCUTT (1940)

a. Tuus is Mockingbird and comes in summer. Achku comes in fall and is Varied Thrush. Both are women. When Tuus is ready to go home, on her back she packs [a] flat openwork basket (of the sort used for salmon when they are cut up or split for drying). When on Assavichi (=rock ridge) ridge (bordering headwaters of Camp and Wilder creeks), Tuus on her way home meets Achku.

Achku owns acorn places. Tuus tells Achku that people are in her acorn preserve. Achku says, "I am making people spill their acorns."[1] Tuus said, "I never say nothing [anything]." Yet all the time Tuus talked all day and all night.

b. In springtime these two meet in [the] same place. Achku tells Tuus, "Someone is fishing at your fishery in Katimin." Tuus said, "It is all right. If they fish with [a] net at my place they lose it." When [a] fisherman loses [a] net, he may say, "Tuus has taken my net."

III.23. STORY ABOUT MOUSE

MARY IKE (1940)

a. Two Mouse (shi'it) sisters were living at Takininam[1] on [the] Salmon River between Oak Bottom and Somes Bar. The two Mouse sisters went down toward Katimin. One had her menses. The old folks told them not to drink water.[2] There was a little spring at [the] site of Carl Langford's house. One of the girls drank the water anyhow. This was the one with [the] menses. She vanished from sight the instant she drank [it]. The other one ran back home and reported [what had happened].

1. pakulif=acorn time; pakuhedem=acorn place. *No* one camped in another's acorn place.

---

1. There is no village at Takininam, which means "where they soak acorns."
2. [For ten days a girl having her first menses was to eat no flesh and drink no water; she was forbidden to look at the sun or sky or to touch water to her face (Kroeber, Handbook, p. 106).—Ed.]

b. "We told you not to drink the water." They looked for the vanished girl but could not find her.

c. Two persons came from Panamenik and went up [the] west side of (the) river. They found a puberty visor near Lake Uk-ramisiriki on [the] west side of [the] river, below Brace's place. One of them said, "Maybe it belongs to that girl who disappeared." A girl in her condition was not supposed to drink water. "Hereafter," the girl who escaped said, "girls at puberty shall not drink water."

d. The Panamenik pair went up to Willow Creek (affluent of the Salmon River) in search of taiyis ("potatoes").[3] They went to Nik-likichihacham (near the bridge across the Salmon upstream from Somes Bar). There is a big rock [there] now. This person (since become a rock) said, "You must not touch," said Niklikichi-hacham, "or you will have warts." Then he turned to stone.

If you have (a) wart you nowadays go to the rock and making [make a] motion of picking off [the] wart and throwing [it] to the stone, saying, "Take back your wart."[4] Kupanakanak.

III.24. MOUSE BOY

GEORGIA ORCUTT (1940)

a. Two women stayed on a hill (oksistani = ok, here; sistani, hill). The menfolks (not their husbands) staying at [the] same place eating [ate] lots of deer meat, everything. They never gave the womenfolks any of their kill.

b. After a while the women heard somebody hollering [shouting] some place. Keep [They kept] on hearing it. [They] don't [didn't] know where [it came from], but [it] sound[ed] like somebody holler [shouting]. Afterwards, one woman said, "Sound [It sounds] like somebody holler [is shouting]. Let's go over." [The] two of them went. After a while see [they saw a] little bit of things on [the] ground; [it] looked like [a] baby mouse. [It] looked like this baby mouse had [a] tiny bow and arrows. "Let's take it home," one of the two women said to the other.

3. [See II.46, n. 2, above.—Ed.]
4. People refrain from touching this rock for fear of warts. No medicine is given to offset touching it, but if one gets warts then he gives them back to the rock as described.

c. The two women took it home. They keep [kept] it in [the] house. After a while they missed it. After a while it came in. It looked like [a] nice young man when come [it came] in. "I know it. I seen [saw] you folks ain't got [had] nothing to eat down here," he said. "Up in heaven (painana avaka) is my place. You can eat there all you want. Let's go up there. I know you folks are feeling too bad because those men never give you any deer meat. I know you folks never get nothing [anything]."

d. The two women asked, "How are we going to get up there?" The young man said, "You can go into your house. I can pack the house up." They went into [the] house. They never felt it when the house was moved up there. That's the way they went up there. When [they arrived] up there the young man said, "You'd better go outside and look around." The women look[ed] around outside and found they were in a nice place.

e. [The] women said, "They never treated us nice, though we were kindly disposed. It will always be this way for other people like us: If they are nice, ultimately someone will feel sorry for them and they will be lucky because they have a nice way (i.e., are kindly disposed even though neglected by others)." They stayed in heaven.

III.25. Story of Big Horned Owl (sufkirik)

MARY IKE (1939)

[For another version of this story, told as a formula, see V.10, by Georgia Orcutt.—Ed.]

•

a. They were gathering and drying acorns, and he [Big Horned Owl] tells (told) his wife, "We're going to gather and dry acorns and you must dry a lot of salmon and eels."

b. So he went up to find some fallen acorns. Then he came back and they went to pick up the acorns. And when they were dry, his wife pounded lots of (many) acorns. And she said, "We'll take the salmon and hide it and save it. We have plenty else [of other food] now." He said, "Don't give us anything only (but) acorns now." And after eating the acorns he lay down and snored. And this happened every day.

c. He would tell his children, "I'm going to pick up acorns," and they wanted to go too, but he said, "No, you better not go; you might get hurt." And when they were all asleep he would take out a piece of salmon and take it with him for lunch. And then the children got hungry.

d. And one night his wife heard a noise like a mouse eating, and she found the Owl eating the stored salmon and eels. In the morning he takes (took) a salmon skin and eels and puts (put them) in the bottom of a basket and covers (covered) them with acorn shells. He tells (told) his wife, "I'll take this out and throw it away." "No," she said, "I'll do it."

e. After he left she pulled up the rock used for pounding acorns where [under which] the salmon and eels were stored, and she found the half of it [them] gone. So she took a piece of salmon and some eels and put it (them) on the fire for the children.

f. She heard someone hollering (shouting) and it said (saying), "It looks like my rock is crooked." He (Owl) had used the pounding rock for a pillow. She took the children and rubbed the salmon grease off their faces with ashes. He (Owl) flew up on the house and said, "(It) looks like my rock is crooked." "Yes," said the woman, "(it) looks like your rock is crooked! Your children are starving! As long as you live, you'll never eat any good food, but only mice."

III.26. Story About Panther

MARY IKE (1940)

a. Panther and his wife were living at Willow Creek (in Karok country). His mother-in-law lived with them. The old woman would tell her son-in-law constantly not to go on top of the mountain, not to look over the ridge.

b. Panther's wife was going to have a baby. He thought, "I'm going to look on the other side of the ridge and see what is there and why she keeps telling me not to look over there."

c. He climbed the ridge and looked over. He saw a lot of (many) girls there with white hats and busy preparing acorns. He thought that was the reason the old lady always told him not to look over, on account of the girls. He went down to see the girls.

d. One of the girls asked, "Why did not you come down here long ago? I suppose you are afraid of that old lady." Panther stayed there. He did not go home to his wife. When night came the girls said, "Let us all go down to Katimin." They went.

e. Just before daylight they returned. Panther had not gone with them. They brought back peppernuts, salmon, hazelnuts, acorns, etc. One girl said, "I almost got drowned crossing that creek." Panther was taking in their conversation.

f. For many year[s] the girls went on their nightly excursions. Panther had married one of them and never (had not) returned to his first wife. One night he asked his [second] wife, "Where do they get all that food?" She replied, "They go out and steal it from people. That is what we live on, what we steal from people."

g. Panther lived there a long time. One of the girls said to him, "You've been here a long time. Your first wife has a baby boy. He is old enough to shoot a bow. Your wife is going to leave and take the boy with her, and the old lady is going to wreck the place."

h. Panther thought he'd (he had) better go home: "I don't want that old lady to spoil my place." Then he went home. He crossed the creek and looked up the trail. He saw his first wife coming with a basket on her back. He saw his son coming, and he thought what a nice-looking boy he was. He seized (tried to seize) the boy when he got close, but the boy eluded his grasp.

i. "Leave him alone!" his wife said. "You left me. You did not want my baby. My mother is going to spoil the place. She is going to wreck everything."

j. Panther took his quiver off and threw it down with his arrows and bow in it. He was anxious to get to the house before the old lady wrecked it. He saw the old lady leaving the house with a load on her back. He ran after her. She said, "I threw your basket plate in the creek." He took his stone knife and stabbed her. As he struck her, she turned into rock. Then he ran to look for his plate up the creek, but it turned to rock.

k. He turned and ran after his wife and son. He went far down the creek. He saw where the boy had bathed. He saw where he had followed the creek up the hill.

l. On top of the mountain he saw his wife and son going back on the ridge. He caught up with them. His wife had two baskets on her back. She took a basket and covered her boy with one. She got under the other, and they both turned to rock. She said, "Hereafter you can come here and see us." He went off a little way on the ridge and turned to rock.

If one wants a good hunting dog, he should throw the pup into the "basket plate" in the creek. This rock bowl is in Willow Creek. The transformed persons are on the ridge above Willow Creek.

III.27. PANTHER STORY

MARY IKE (1940)

a. Panther was always hunting. He was brought up that way, always hunting. He went to (a) neighbor's house and seen (saw) a lady (Fisher's daughter) in there. This lady was cooking deer meat. The meat was without fat, but had (the) appearance of having been soaked in water. He said to her, "Do you eat that kind of meat? Does it not make you sick?" He had heard already (that) this woman was married to Wolf. He took a piece of meat out of his sukrif.[1] "This is the kind of meat you should eat," he said. He cooked it. The meat was very fat. "This is the kind of meat I live on."

b. The lady said, "I'd like to go with you. I'd like to go home with you."[2] "You can't go with me this time, but I'll come back and see you again." Then Panther went home.

c. When Fisher's husband came home, he noticed someone had been cooking meat, rather fat meat, on the coals. "Where did you get that meat?" he asked his wife. She replied, "I got it here. We have a lot of meat." But still he did not believe her.

d. Panther got home and found his little younger brother Bobcat (akwich) sitting by the fire. They cooked the deer meat and ate together. Then he said, "I am going out hunting. I am not coming back this time. I shall stay for a long time."

e. He knew he had got the Fisher woman in trouble [impregnated her]. He went to her house and said, "Let me take my baby home."

1. [A sukrif or sukriv is a woven bag carried by men (II.1*b* and elsewhere).— Ed.]
2. [Among other favors, she gave Panther some of the deer meat, as appears later.—Ed.]

Nobody had seen it, for she had kept it hidden. So he took his baby away.

f. The younger brother was worrying about Panther because he had been gone for such a long time. Panther arrived home with (the) boy baby. He told his brother, "I brought your nephew." Bobcat said, "Hurry up, I want to see the baby."

g. Panther said, "Nobody can see my baby, but you can, because I stole the baby; (I) got it from somebody else's wife. Come on, you can look at my baby."

h. Bobcat look[ed] at the baby and made a face, and his face stayed that way and got small. "Nobody else is going to see the baby," Panther said, "for he is going to eat human beings." The baby was Mountain Lion.[3] That is the reason lions are mean, because of stealing (the) baby from another man's wife.

III.28. Story About Robin (chibakba)

GEORGIA ORCUTT (1940)

a. Robin (chibakba) was staying in [the] sweathouse. ([The] ixkareya made it that if a woman wanted to marry a man she [would] go and stay with him a while. If he liked her too, she stayed; if not, then [she would] go back home.) Robin's mother told him to come into [the] house because a nice girl had come to see him. "What kind of dress is she wearing?" Robin asked. "She has a dress with all kinds of shells." But Robin would not come in; he stayed in [the] sweathouse.

b. After a while another girl came around, and his mother told him another visitor had come. "What kind of dress is she wearing?" asked Robin. The mother said, "She is wearing [a] dress with uruksa (*Saxidomus nuttalli* disk beads).[1] Robin never went in to look at her. So she left for her home.

c. After a while a third came. His mother said, "You better come

3. [G.'s typescript has the following etymology, later crossed out: "Mountain lion=aaskanyuksukiara; aas=water; aaskan=in the water as=rock. Panther=yuksukiara; yuk=eyes; sukiara=yellow." Mountain lion and panther are different English names for the same animal.—Ed.]

1. These were rare in olden times.

in. Someone [is] here to see you.'' He asked, ''What kind of dress?''
he asked. His mother said, ''Sapru *(Olivella biplicata).*''[2] He never
said nothing [anything], don't [didn't] go in. That woman went
home.

d. Another one came. His mother told him to come in. ''Someone to see you.'' He asked, ''What kind of dress?'' She answered,
''Dress with ip beads'' (small black seed beads from Kayuras,
upstream ocean, region). He never go [went] in. [The] girl went
home.

e. A fifth girl came and went in [the] house. His mother told him
another girl had come to see him. After a while Robin asked, ''What
kind of dress?'' ''Axyuus'' (Digger pine nut). He never come [came]
out of [the] sweathouse. He stayed[ed] in [the] sweathouse. [The]
girl went back home after a while.

f. A sixth girl came and went in [the] house. His mother told him,
''Another girl to see you.'' ''What kind of dress?'' asked Robin. She
replied, ''Xusripi (madrone berries).'' After a while Robin came out
of [the] sweathouse and entered [the] dwelling house. Then he sat
down close to that woman. The berries were on strings hanging
loose over [her] buckskin dress, not sewed on [the] dress.[3]

g. After a while Robin ate off all the madrone berries and [until]
nothing but strings were left. She [the sixth girl] stayed and became
his wife. Kupanakanak.

III.29. SHREW STORY

MARY IKE (1940)

a. Axbūm or Shrew[1] said, ''There is (an) ihuk (First Menses)
dance going on.'' They [The girls] painted themselves and dressed
to go to (the) dance. House Mouse (siit) lived with Shrew. Shrew has

2. [These are small cylindrical shells, which Kroeber says were strung and used
for ornament rather than currency (Handbook, p. 25).—Ed.]
3. The Karok never wore madrone berries.

1. [G. originally entitled this story ''Field Mouse Story,'' and queried his use of
''Shrew'' each time in the first paragraph. Later he changed the title to its present
wording and crossed out the queries in the text. Bright identifies axbūm as the
meadow mouse in the Linguistic Index, below. For a different version of the tale,
see III.10, above.—Ed.]

(had) little eyes; House Mouse (had) large eyes. They were both girls. They got all dressed up. Shrew asked the other, "How do I look now?" "You are an awfully pretty girl, but you have such small eyes that they spoil your looks." House Mouse asked, "Now how do I look?" "You are good-looking, you are pretty—real pretty—but your eyes are too big."

b. Munapmanxana (Small Mole) was all dressed up. She asked, "How do I look after I am all dressed?" They said, "You are pretty good-looking, only your mouth is too long."

c. Big Mole (mul) asked, "How do I look?" "You are a very good-looking woman, only your arms are too short. You have not any arms, just hands."

d. Woodrat (ashnat) wanted to know how she looked. "You are pretty good-looking, you are a nice-looking woman. But you cannot go with us. You are such a big thief you might steal something." Kupanakanak.

III.30. Skunk's Scent Bags

MARY IKE (1939)

a. Skunk got married in Panamenik. He had a sister-in-law. When she came to his house, she said, "Phew, I smell him." He had his scent bags hanging on the wall. She took a stick and threw them out. Skunk came home and inquired, "Where are my playthings?" His wife did not tell him. So he brought them in and hung them up [again].

b. Skunk's wife asked her sister, "Why do you always go home so soon?" "Because I don't like your husband."

c. Skunk asked, "Who is it that always plays with my playthings?" His wife replied, "It's not because she wants to play, but she throws them out." Skunk asked, "Why doesn't she keep them?"

d. Skunk went into the sweathouse and found his sister-in-law there. Then he said, "If my sister-in-law comes in here again, tell her she can have those things, my playthings." When she went away she took down the playthings, but she threw them back into the house. They broke, and everyone in the house died.

III.31. Skunk Story

MARY IKE (1940)

a. Ground Squirrel (aksai) was gathering taiyiis (Indian potatoes).[1] Pretty soon he saw someone come dancing down the hill. It was Striped (common) Skunk (kuuf)[2] dancing down the hill. The Ground Squirrels all died from the odor.

b. Skunk took all the potatoes home to his maternal grandmother to cook. Then he went to where the Squirrels were lying and made medicine for them. He put earth on them. He put earth shoved up by gophers in water,[3] and rubbed it on the Squirrels to remove the odor.[4]

c. Skunk went day after day and took the potatoes the ground squirrels had dug. The Squirrels got home and said, "Somebody takes (is taking) all our potatoes." He [Skunk] did this day after day, the same thing.

d. Skunk invited the Squirrels to his sweathouse: "You folks are getting cold, so come into my sweathouse." One refused to accept, saying, "He must be up to something." Skunk said, "You folks all stay in here while I go out for a little while. When I come back, I'll have bad news to tell you." Then he went out and closed the exit door. He exuded his odor [at the entrance] and killed them all.

III.32. Story About Steller's Jay

MARY IKE (1939)

[The greed of Jay woman as a doctor is a favorite Karok theme. This narration has touches of wry humor.—Ed.]

•

a. There were many young girls making food to eat. They were Mouse, Woodrat, Chipmunk, Tree Squirrel, Ground Squirrel,

1. [See II.46, n. 2, above.—Ed.]
2. [Gifford's typescript also showed an alternative spelling: guuf.—Ed.]
3. [Probably: He put in water earth that had been shoved up by gophers. —Ed.]
4. This is still done today to remove skunk odor.

Larger Chipmunk (wininiki). One got sick; Mouse got sick. They said, "You'd better get the eim¹ doctor, Bullhead (a fish)."

b. They said to the doctor, "We'll give you some food to doctor this patient." Bullhead said, "I guess she must have stole[n] that food." Then they got Steller's Jay² also for [a] doctor and gave her a basket of chinquapin nuts and a big basket (atiki) full of acorns.

c. Jay took her children and went to doctor the sick person. She said to her kids [children], "You come with me. They might say something bad to me." So she took her children along. She sang her doctoring song. [Song] Then Bullhead sang her song. [Song] "Give me that that's hanging up. Add it to my pay." They wondered what it was she referred to. It was something that comes out of salmon—it is called achpus—it hangs on [the] inside of [the] salmon's throat—it is white and looks like sweetbreads.³

d. Jay sucked (out) the pain out. "She'll be all right. Let's go," she told her children. The children pretty nearly ate up what was paid their mother. Then they went home and they ate the rest. Jay said, "You children are getting awfully hungry. I think I'll go devil someone."

e. Jay "deviled" Woodrat. Woodrat fainted. She [Jay] threw dirt on Woodrat's house to scare her, then ran, but stuck a stick in her eye in her haste. She ran home, fell down, and told [her] kids to throw ashes on her.

f. She heard someone coming. "We've come after you," the person said. "We'll give you a basketful of shelled acorns, a bucketful of pinenuts." She had her children posted to tell her she'd better go. "All right. Give me some water and let me wash my face. I went to the corner to get some wood and poked my eye." The children began eating up her pay. "Why do children eat everything before I start to doctoring?"

g. Then she went to Woodrat's house with her children and started to [began] doctoring Woodrat. "She'll live. I took the pain out. I'll go home now. The patient will be all right." She went home with her children.

h. Then Jay deviled Chipmunk and Big Chipmunk. "I think they'll find me out this time," Jay said to herself. The sick ones sent for Bullhead too. Then they went after "Under the White Moun-

---

1. [Shaman (see headnote to I.8).—Ed.]
2. [See II.54, n. 1, above.—Ed.]
3. [See the explanation in III.11, n. 2.—Ed.]

tain" doctor. "We went for that doctor because she is a fortuneteller. Two of the prettiest girls are sick now, Chipmunk and her sister." Jay told her children, "I think they'll find me out this time. Put these little flints under your belts." Then she went.

i. Bullhead was doctoring. Bluejay doctored too. "Under White Mountain" doctor was there too. She was dancing and singing: "It looks [like] it's popping down by the ocean, and it looks like it's popping right here. Who do you suppose is doing it? It is Bluejay that is doing it. My mouth is too small to suck the pain out."

j. Bluejay asked, "What is she saying about me?" White Mountain Doctor was Hummingbird. Jay threw a flint at Hummingbird, but it missed and hit [the] wall. Jay said to Hummingbird, "I'll [I] suppose all you'll do is suck honey from flowers all your life." Hummingbird retorted, "I suppose you'll be stealing acorns along the creek all your life."

k. The patients got well.

III.33. TURKEY VULTURE STORY

GEORGIA ORCUTT (1940)

Georgia's mother's brother told her this.

•

After pikiawish time[1] [the] Vultures leave. During [the] summer [they] roost on [sand]bars with [their] backs to [the] river. Long ago that way [they were] living [leaving?] early. Vulture goes away because they [he does] not want to see hooked-bill salmon. Vulture leave[s] right away after pikiawish, so he will not see hook-nosed salmon, (as they) were (once) fighting. Hooknose grabbed Vulture and shoved him in [the] fire so he got burned around [his] head and neck.[2] For that reason Vulture never wants to see Hooknose, and keeps his back turned when on a bar.

1. [After the world renewal ceremonies, held in August by the upriver Karok, in September by those downriver (Kroeber and Gifford, World Renewal, AR 13:(no. 1):130).—Ed.]
2. [The turkey vulture, a summer visitor, has a red head (Storer and Usinger, Sierra Nevada Natural History, p. 257.—Ed.]

III.34. Story About Pine Roots and Water Ouzel

MARY IKE (1940)

[Kroeber has two versions of this story (A2 and H2), identifying the selfish father as Kingfisher, and Gifford has a variant (III.25, also by Mary Ike), with Big Horned Owl as the leading character.—Ed.]

•

a. Water Ouzel's (asaxwanichamvanich) family was living there and began to get hungry, as there was nothing to eat in the house. "I guess I'd better make a fishery and go fishing." He went down to the river and made a fishing platform. He caught a spring salmon (with red belly). Then he pulled it out. Then he cut it up right there. He cut the tail off and put it on a rock. He said, "This is for the kids (children)." Then he built a great big fire (and) then he cooked the whole fish and ate it all himself, all but the tail. Then he went home carrying the tail. He hollered (shouted) to his kids (children), "I've got a tail for you." They all hollered (shouted), "I'm glad! I'm glad!" His wife cooked it.

b. "Where is the rest of the fish?" his wife asked. "There were a lot of people there and I had to cut it up and give each one a little piece," he explained. "Don't give me any fish. Just give me acorns. I'll feel better when you folks eat." Next day he went fishing. He fished and got one again, the same kind. Then he cut it up. He cut the tail off and said, "This is for my kids (children)." He built a big fire. Then he ate it all. Then he went home carrying the tail. "I've got a tail for you." "Oh, I am glad!" and they danced around and were so happy. His wife cooked the tail. "Give me acorn soup. Don't give me any fish. You folks eat the fish," he said.

c. He did the same thing again the next day, went fishing. His wife told him, "Don't give it away. Bring it home. Just give a little bit away and bring the rest of it home."

d. Finally she thought, "I'd better go down and see what he is doing. He never would eat anything but acorn soup." So she followed him down. She watched him from (a) hiding place. He cut the tail off and made the fire while she was looking on. She watched him cook and eat it all. Then she ran home.

e. When she got home, she said to the kids (children), "We might as well leave. I see what he is doing. He eats it all by himself.

Let's go. We'll leave him. He has been doing this for a long time."

f. She lifted up the mortar slab, and they entered a tunnel and traveled through it. They all went up the hill.

g. He [Water Ouzel] came home and hollered (called out). No answer. Then he ran down to the river where they always soaked acorns, next to the river. He went back up to the house, but there was nobody there. When he got back in the house, he heard people laughing. "That's what she did for your eating alone. They all left you." These were Mice.

h. "You tell me where she went or I'll kill you all." They all laughed again. He got hold of one. "Don't kill us, and I'll tell you where they went. She lifted that mortar rock and they all went under there."

i. Then he went under carrying the tail. He went up the mountain calling to them. He finally caught up with them. "Here is a tail for you." They took it and threw it down the hill, saying, "You eat it yourself!" He went after it and got it and gave it to another of his children.

j. His wife said, "All right. You have been doing this for a long time. From now on, all you'll do is go up and down the creek and eat mud from off of the rocks. My kids (children) will go wherever people are dancing. They'll be in front, in the front row all the time." She meant they would be pine roots from which baskets are made for passing acorn soup. He looked around and saw bull pines (ishwidip) grow up all around. These were his kids (children). The roots are called sadum. He went to live in the creeks.

III.35. The Birds and Water

MARY IKE (1939)

a. All kinds of birds got together, and the [male] Condor says (said), "You better go find the water. Whoever finds the water will marry me."

b. So the birds told the Hawk, "You better go get the water," and she said, "No, it's too far." Then they sent the Bluejay (Jay). She was the first one to go for the water. They offered her to be (the privilege of being) like all kinds of birds if she would. And every bird went, and everyone who went was given a name, and that's how each bird got their (its) name. But no bird could find it.

c. So they finally sent the Frog. She said, "I know where the water is." So they sent her. So she brought the water back, and what it was (was) her pee (urine). And they said, "That isn't water. As long as you live, everytime anyone touches you, you'll do that."

d. Then they sent the Seagull because she said, "I know where the water is; I'll get the water." And she shoved (aside) the big bird that was sitting there aside, and there was a board, and under the board was the water. So they found the water.

e. And they said to the Hawk, "You'll have to wait until August now for the water because you refused to go look." And so now the Hawks cry "Piuh-piuh," and (as) [if] she is [they are] asking her [their] sister to give her [them] water. And the Sparrow Hawk has tears running down her face (the lines) because she is so dry. And all the hawks cry all the time [for] water.

f. Cooper's Hawk (ikchaxuwa) was a downriver woman. "You cannot drink water until August," the Yurok tell her. (She was also a Yurok.) So she comes upriver to the Karok to drink water, crying, "Hi-hi-wi."

III.36. STORY ABOUT STELLER'S JAY
(STELLER'S JAY GETS WATER)

MARY IKE (1940)

a. Steller's Jay woman wanted someone to go for water for her. Everybody wanted to drink. Frog said, "I know where the water is." All went after it, but searched in vain.

b. "Everybody give me your language and I'll get the water," said Jay. They gave her the bucket (water basket), and she went. She went over there and took the plate away from Frog, who was sitting there, and there was the water under it. Bluejay took out some water and gave it to the people. She would not let Mourning Dove have any, because she had declined to go originally. Dove said, "I did not want to go because I did not know where the water was." Jay said, "You can have water only once a year, in August (karugwakus-rar)."

c. Jay told Chicken Hawk, "You can't have water because you did not want to go. You can have water once a year, in August." (Chicken Hawk begged and cried.)

d. Bluejay had all their languages and can imitate different birds.

III.37. STORY ABOUT MOON (WEASEL AND MOON)

MARY IKE (1940)

[This myth has strong echoes of the Yurok Pulekukwerek and Wohpekumeu cycles.—Ed.]

•

a. Kusraxbini (Moon old man)[1] had two daughters. "I wish you had somebody to take care of you," he told his daughters. There was [a] young man around there, kind of a silly one. His name was Anhus (Weasel). "You'd better marry that fellow," Moon told one of his daughters. She married him and bore him two kids (children), [a] boy and [a] girl.

b. Moon told (asked) his son-in-law, "What are you going to live on? You'd better fish for salmon in the river." Weasel asked, "How am I going to get it?" Moon said, "I'll go look for a spear."

c. He was gone for a long time looking for it. After a time he came back and had a long pole. He showed his son-in-law how to fix the spear. He made a fire to show him how to fix the spear. He heated a long rock in the fire. He used this to smooth over (the) pitch on (the) toggle head. He got some cord and tied on the spear (harpoon) for him. Then he put some more pitch on there and fixed it again with (the) hot rock. Then Moon put pitch on the pole.

d. Weasel went fishing. He saw a big salmon swimming. He speared it. His hand stuck to the pole on account of the pitch. He could not get away from it, and the fish pulled him down over two big falls. He heard someone holler (shouting) and saw someone (a person) running down. Weasel was dragged under the water. When he came up he told this fellow (man), "Help me! Pull me out and I'll

1. Both Sun and Moon are males.

give you my beads!'' This man grabbed hold of the pole and pulled Weasel and the fish out. The fish was really a (the) big snake Absumxarak. ''I am glad you helped me out,'' said Weasel. Then he took his beads and put them around his rescuer's neck. It was Kingfisher (askupamva) who pulled him out (and he has a white necklace on today).

e. Weasel took the fish up to the house and told Moon to go ahead and eat it. ''I almost died,'' said Weasel. Weasel noticed his wife's hair was trimmed on the ends. Absumxarak was Moon's son, and Moon [had] wanted his son-in-law to die. Weasel's wife had her hair cut[2] on account of her brother. Moon said, ''Oh, my son-in-law, I am glad you got that fish!''

f. Moon said, ''There is a nest in that tree. You'd better climb up and get those young birds.'' ''How am I going to get up there?'' Weasel asked. ''I'll make a ladder,'' said Moon. Moon made a ladder (buranara) of a long pole with diagonal piece[s] lashed on for hooking over limbs. The pole had stubs of branches left on it to serve as footholds.

g. Weasel suspected his father-in-law was trying to get rid of him. So he climbed up the ladder. Moon was praying for the tree to grow taller and taller. Moon ran off down the hill, dragging the ladder and leaving his son-in-law up the tree.

h. Weasel saw pitch gum on the tree. He chewed some of it. He came to the nest. He threw the young birds down. The wind began to blow, and he was about ready to fall. He thought, ''Well, I am going to sing my song.'' Then he sang. [Song]

i. Weasel had (a) bowstring with his belt. He killed the old birds with his bowstring, by striking them.

j. The tree grew to [the] sky, where Weasel found himself. ''How am I going to get back down?'' he pondered. He thought of the gum in his mouth. He took it and stretched it and let one end reach down to earth. Then he descended on the gum. On the ground, he picked up the birds and gave them to Moon. ''Here, eat them now. I almost died.''

k. Moon was dancing around before Weasel got back, thinking he was dead. ''I am glad he is dead. He killed all my kids (children).'' The birds were Moon's children also.

l. Moon had a long pole. He put it so it kind of stuck out into the

2. [In mourning.—Ed.]

ocean. He made a seesaw of it. He asked Weasel to get on (the) ocean end of it. Moon said, "I'll lift you up and down." Moon's intention was to raise Weasel very high.

m. Weasel said, "All right, go ahead and lift the pole," but at same time Weasel ran under it instead of getting on it. Weasel said, "I pretty near died that time. Now you get on and let me do the pushing. Get way out on the end like I did." Moon did so, and then Weasel pushed the pole and threw Moon against the sky.

n. Weasel heard someone laughing. It was Moon. He said, "I've got a good son-in-law. You've done me so much good. I'm going to live up here. Every day I'll go across the sky." Kupanakana.[3]

III.38. Story About Anixus (Weasel)

GEORGIA ORCUTT

[This myth contains most of the elements of the Yurok Pulekukwerek monster-ridding cycle.—Ed.]

•

a. Weasel stayed down at [the] ocean (Yuras). In [a] corner of his house he made a sand pile. That Weasel, he know [knew] everything. Look like [It seemed] he can [could] tell anything. He knew that lots of [many] animals want[ed] to kill people; he want[ed] to kill those animals so people [would] not get killed.

b. And he took his hair [head] feather and put it in the sand pile. He said to his mother's mother, "I set up my feather right here. If I get killed it will fall over; if it come[s] up again you will know I am all right again, not killed yet." And he got ready to go and put his quiver on, ready to go.

c. The first one[s] he saw coming [as he came] upriver were two old women sitting outside their house. Anixus stood up and watched those old women. They had no eyes [sight], no fire. They cooked their food in their armpits. They were cooking Indian potatoes. One took some from under her armpit and handed to [the] other, saying,

---

3. [G.'s typescript had this notation, crossed off: "ipanich = end of object such as rat's tail, etc." It perhaps relates to parts *l* and *m*.—Ed.]

"It is cooked already." Weasel took the food as she handed it. [The] other one said, "Is it cooked already?" The first one said, "Yes, I gave it to you." Other one said, "I did not take it." Anixus watched it a long time. He felt sorry for those old ladies who did not have any eyes or nothing [anything].

d. After a while he opened his quiver and took out some kind of sharp bone. He talked to that [those] old ladies and said, "Too bad you have no eyes and no fire." "Yes," they said, "we [were] raised that way, with no eyes and no fire." Then after a while Weasel said, "I'm going to fix you." After a while Weasel opened their eyes with his fingers and the bone implement. The [first] old lady said, "I can see." The other one said the same: "I can see."

e. After a while Weasel made fire for them. He said. "That is [the] kind of fire to cook potatoes." "Thank you, thank you, we can see now," they said. "I wish you never have bad luck," for they knew he was going to do something when he went up there. "I wish you always come out just right."

f. Weasel, as he came upriver, saw [a] dwelling house. He heard someone pounding acorns. When he got to [the] house he found [the] door shut. After a while Weasel went up on [the] roof and looked in. He see [saw an] old lady pounding something. The old lady saw his shadow and knew someone was looking down at her. The old lady went outside; she want[ed] to look. When she looked up, Weasel went under the [roof]boards, so she could not see him.

g. After a while she went back to her pounding. After a while Weasel looked down again. Went outside again, that woman, and looked. She thought somebody was looking in, but she never [could not] see it [anyone]. And when Weasel looked down he see [saw] some kind of bone in [the] mortar; she was mashing that bone. From [the] old lady's [ears] some kind of stone earrings hung.

h. Then Weasel went in the house. He asked her, "What have you been doing?" That old lady said, "Let's play cards (many-stick game)." Anixus found out that [the] old lady kill[ed] people. When playing "cards" Weasel was singing; look like he was [he seemed to be] making fun of [the] old lady when he was singing. And Anixus make [had made] his medicine already. And that old lady said, "Why do you make fun of me when you are singing?" And Anixus [was] just singing.

i. [The] old lady get [got] up. She want[ed] to kill Anixus. That was [the] way [the] old lady did; she hit people with her stone earrings when she want[ed] to kill them. And Anixus just jump[ed] out of reach, and that old lady can't [couldn't] catch Anixus. After a while Anixus holds [held] that old lady. He said, "You can't kill people, you can't kill people." The house had [a] wooden wall (sivriva = wall) around [the] pit. After a while Anixus hold [held] that old lady. Then he shoved her into the pit wall. He said, "You will always be right here, behind the wall. You [will] always stay right here. You are going to be Yonakaiyi" (= behind the pit wall).

j. Anixus had found that [the] old lady killed and ate people and pounded their bones for food.[1] That Anixus got good medicine, and no one going [would be able] to kill that Anixus.

k. Weasel started off. Further up he see [saw] two little boys. They got sticks and were throwing them as darts at [a] gray squirrel. And after a while Weasel watching those boys saw they could not get that gray squirrel. Weasel, he make [made] them bow and arrows. And when he finished he said, "Now you can try it this way." And he showed them how to shoot it. "Now you can shoot that squirrel." And when he shoot him [shot it], it coming [came] down. And pick[ed] it up them [those] boys. "How nice we can get it this way!" they said.

l. Weasel [got] ready to start off again. And to the two boys he said [And the two boys said], "Anytime if you need help—maybe somebody want[s] to kill you—we can help you out," the boys said.

m. Further up he see [saw] two girls and one old man staying. That old man said, "You are going to be my son-in-law. Up on that hill is Jackrabbit. I want you to go up and kill him tomorrow morning. I can go up with you. I [will] show you the way." In the morning that [those] girls say [said], "Don't go up there, don't go up there." Weasel was a nice man, kind of slim. Weasel went up. The old man went up with him to show him the way. The old man stood up and said, "You can look over. That's where he is coming out." The old man ran home. After a while jump[ed] out some kind of big animal (askanyipsuker was its name, a real animal that used to be here and sometimes killed people). Look like [It seemed] he wanted to kill Weasel. And Weasel shoot [shot] him. [The] arrow would not go in. Look like [It seemed that] Weasel just jump[ed] around, dodge[d]

---

1. Children were warned not to steal something, lest Yonakaiyi mash them up and eat them.

around. After a while [it] looked as though Weasel was all in. He shoot [shot] that animal every place, but can't [couldn't] kill him. Weasel thought, "I am going to holler to those boys." He pretty near give up because he can't do nothing. Afterwards them [those] two boys coming [came]. Them [Those] two boys said, "You can't kill that animal. No matter where you shoot him, you can't kill him, [but] you can shoot [kill] him right at [the] base of [his] toes." Weasel shot him there, and he just fall [fell] over right away. Weasel said, "You can't kill people," he said to [the] dead animal.

The two boys said, "Now we can kill anything anytime because Weasel made us that bow and arrows." The boys were named Abuishone (small Chicken Hawk).

n. An old man had two daughters. Anixus entered the house. The old man said, "It is a good thing you [have] come. You are going to be my son-in-law. I like to get fish out of [the] river. I see lots of fish but got [have] no way to catch it. You can catch it tomorrow morning."

In the morning, the old man said, "Let's go." So they went down by the river. And the old man show[ed] him: "I always see that fish right there. There is that fish." And when Anixus spear[ed] that fish and they hold [held] it, he kept trying but he can't [couldn't] pull it out. Look like [It looked as if] Anixus just go [was going to fall] in [the] river. He can't [couldn't] hold it. He got dragged into [the] river. Anixus was all in [exhausted]. [He] pretty near[ly] fall [fell] down in[to the] river. Lots of [Many] times he got up again. And after a while the bird Askupamva (=eats kup fish, trout)[2] said to Anixus, "You can hook it right there. It is not a fish you hooked. It is [the] big snake Absumxarak." The old man knew it was not [a] fish. He just (Everybody) wanted to get Anixus killed because Anixus was too smart. Anixus had come up to kill off all the animals that were preying on people. He wanted to kill all. Then Anixus speared Absumxarak where Askupamva [had] told him. He said to [the] old man, "You better eat that fish." [The] old man never answered him.

o. Weasel went on up the Klamath River, for he knew that bad animals were killing people who were beginning to come (i.e., Indians). He walk[ed] further up. He came to one old man and two girls again. The old man said, "Oh, you are going to be my son-in-

2. Kingfisher probably, as it has a white collar in front. [So identified in the previous myth, III.37*d*.—Ed.]

law." He said, "Up there on [the] hill I got [have a] big bird's nest. Maybe tomorrow you can get it and I'm going to raise [that] big bird."

p. In the morning the old man said, "Let's go up." "Don't go up," the two girls said to Weasel. "They'll kill you." Weasel never say nothing [said anything]. He went with [the] old man way up on [the] hill. "Now you climb up the tree," the old man said. "We fix [have fixed the] ladder so you can go up." Climb[ed] up after them, that Weasel. When he climb[ed] up, the old man take it off [took away] that ladder. Weasel knew he took it off [away]. [The] old man stood looking up and said to Weasel, "Further up, climb further up."

q. [The] wind was blowing. After a while it look[ed] like all the leaves [had] blow[n] off, it blew so hard. And after a while the old man run [ran] away and said, "He is going to get killed now." The old man knew Weasel was a smart man and knew everything, and that is why he wanted to kill him. And after a while it looks [looked] as though all the limbs blow [had blown] off. Only one limb [was] left, and Anixus was on it.

r. Weasel said, "I always figured I was somebody. Now I am going to sing [my] medicine song so I don't get killed." When he singing [sang the] song, so quit the wind ablowing. It stopped the wind right away. After a while he commenced coming down. After come [he came] back down to [the] ground, he went further upriver.

s. He see [saw an] old man and two girls. The old man said, "You [are] going to be my son-in-law." The old man said, "I got [have] wood I want to split into board[s]. I want to make [a] sweathouse." Next morning [the] old man said, "Let's go." Anixus was smart. He knew [the] old man was going to do something with the wood. He [The old man] had [a] wooden wedge in [a] log. The old man said, "Maybe you can get inside and force it apart, for it already got [has a] hole in it." When Anixus go [went] into [the] log, the old man stand [stood] there helping Anixus. After a while, when Anixus [was] in, that old man pulled out the wedge. The log closed on Anixus, but he had already split it to [the] bottom. The old man said, "Good thing you get [were] killed." But Anixus [had] escaped at [the] bottom. Anixus said, "Why, old man, [do] you want to kill me?" [The] old man said, "I'm crying because I missed it. I wanted to split it a little further down and [but] that wedge come [came] out."

t. Anixus said, "You'd better get in and I'll drive that wedge in some more." [The] old man said, "No, just push in." Anixus grabbed him and made him go in. After [the] old man get [got] in, Anixus pulled out that wedge. The old man holler[ed], "I am going to be right here all the time." It killed him. Anixus said, "You wanted to kill me. You think you can kill anybody, but you can't kill anybody. When you see white rotten wood in [the] center of [a] log, it is that old man." Anixus said, "You are going to be that kind" (ahopamva = white rotten center of log).[3] "You can't kill people."

u. After a while, as he kept on upriver, he saw [another] old man and two girls. "You are going to be my son-in-law," said the old man. He said, "I'm [I've] got [a] swing with [a] bent-over sapling to ride.[4] You can swing on it tomorrow morning." In [the] morning, [the] old man said, "Let's go." "Don't go," the girls said. "You'll get killed."

v. The old man said, "You better get on." Weasel was packing his quiver. Inside it he had [a] woodrat. When the old man was swinging the tree, Weasel put the woodrat on the tree. The old man let go that sapling. Anixus jumped out and went behind the tree. Woodrat got thrown up to [the] sky. After a while, the old man saw blood coming down and he said, "Good thing he is killed."

w. After a while Anixus said to [the] old man, "Why [did] you want to kill me?" [The] old man said, "I just lost my grip." But Anixus had heard what the old man said about being glad he was killed. [The] old man said, "I was just crying because I thought you were killed." And Anixus said, "You better get on" "No, I don't want to get on," said the old man. After a while Anixus pushed the old man onto the tree. Then Anixus bent it down and up, and when he let go, hit the sky the old man. He never did come down. [The] old man said, "Good thing. I am going to live up here. This is my home."

x. When Anixus went to [the] house where [the] girls were staying, after a while he picked up one of the girls and threw her up on the sky. He said, "You are going to be [the] morning star." After a while [the] other girl he pick[ed] it [her] up and threw that one onto

3. [In one of the Yurok accounts, the scheming old man turns into a white grub in the wood; see Kroeber, *Yurok Myths*, A15x*e*. See the Linguistic Index, below, on the etymology of the Karok name.—Ed.]

4. This type of swing = kunachkuna. The Karok played on such but did not let it fly up. They bent it up and down, and children played on it.

the sky in [the] opposite direction. Anixus said, "You are going to be the evening star."[5] She said, "I like you. I thought I was going to marry you. But you don't like me. I hope you are going to always have bad luck with woman [women]." But Anixus never heard when she said that. [The] old man turned into [the] moon.

    y. After a while Anixus got married. He don't [didn't] like that woman after a while. After a while he come [came] back to Panamenik. It looked like he was [He seemed to be] thinking about that girl he threw up into [the] sky to be [the] evening star. He said, "I'm going to go down to see that woman." He had left his wife. When [Then] he go [went] down to see that woman. When he got down there, that woman said, "Don't come around here. Why [do] you come down to see me? I like[d] you once and thought I'd marry you, but you did not like me."

    z. Anixus returned to [the] ocean shore because that woman did not like him. That Evening Star woman said, "It will always be that way when [a] man does not marry [a] woman who wants him. He will always have bad luck when he marries someone else."

    aa. After a while Anixus give [gave] up and go [went] home to his grandmother. The old woman said, "I watched that feather. Sometimes it went down. Sometimes it stood up."

III.39. ANIXUS AND KITAXARIHAR

GEORGIA ORCUTT (1940)

This Anixus and Kitaxarihar (kitaxari = wings) story is part of the Anixus long tale recorded earlier and should be fitted into it.[1]

•

    a. Anixus (Weasel) knew everything. Anixus went into [a] house where two ixkareya women were staying. The women said, "Too bad you came in." Anixus asked, "Why?" [The] women answered,

---

5. Supahas = morning star; kunanahas = evening star.

---

1. [This headnote probably refers to the previous tale. The myths have been left in G.'s original arrangement, as he did not indicate where the insertion was to be made.—Ed.]

"There are awful bad people around here. Always someone walk[s] over here." "What does it look like?" asked Anixus. They said, "When he comes over, he always kills one person." "What does it look like?" again asked Anixus. "It is awfully hard looking. On one side of his head grows ferns. On [the] other side grow live oaks."

Anixus said, "I think I can kill that animal." The women said, "[I] don't think so. It is awfully hard." Then they described the monster's habits.

"After a while we always hide under the house in the evening because we are afraid," the women said. "You'd better hide now," said Anixus.

b. Then after a while came the monster. He said, "I am hungry." That was the time usually when the monster killed people and ate them. He killed them with a yuhidim (knife). Anixus also had a knife.

Kitaxarihar said, "I am going to eat Anixus also." Then Anixus jumped up and slashed the monster across the belly with his knife. Looked like [It seemed that] Kitaxarihar came to life again, but Anixus kept on fighting him. After a while he lay dead. That's the time Anixus said, "You can't eat people. The only thing you can do is to go live under the rock. You can't eat people." Kitaxarihar has been living under rocks ever since.[2]

III.40. WOODRAT (ASHNAT) STORY

MARY IKE (1940)

a. The whole family went up in [the] hills to camp and gather acorns. Woodrat woman (ashnat) was always sick and lying down. She had sore eyes. She had two stones she warmed and laid over her eyes (a treatment used by Karok). They fed her only the acorn soup that stuck to the cooking stones. They gave her the stones to lick off. Her mother took care of her.

b. They all went to bed. One thought, "I'm not going to sleep. I am going to stay awake and see what she is doing." This one listening could hear acorns rattling. This one who stayed awake was a visitor who had been with them from a neighboring family. She

2. This story is about the Kitaxarihar that lives at Hebenafi, below Georgia's.

went home to her family and reported (that) she thought sore-eyed Woodrat was the one who was stealing their acorns nightly.

c. The whole family then went over to visit [the] family of the sore-eyed one to see what they could learn. They found the house clear full of acorns. The children of the sore-eyed one said, "She does not go out because she has sore eyes." She was only making believe she had sore eyes. They [The visitors] told her, "That's just the way you are going to be: stealing all the time from other people." She turned into Woodrat, and all of her family likewise, and they scuttled away into the bushes.[1]

1. [The dusky-footed woodrat, or pack rat, is mainly nocturnal, eating a variety of foods and carrying objects about. Its rounded or conical house, constructed of twigs and leaves, may be two or three feet high (Storer and Usinger, Sierra Nevada Natural History, p. 343).—Ed.]

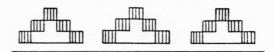

IV. Plant Story

IV.1. Story of Oaks

MARY IKE (1939)

a. The White Oak (ahuwham) had her cap all finished nicely. The Live Oak (kan'put) had her cap all finished too. Hansiip[1] was making ashiphanahitch (a long water-packing basket), and when they said, "Let's go," she put her hat on. That's (That is) why (it is) long. Tanbark (Oak) was making Indian (a basket) cap (ap'xan) and hers wasn't (was not) finished, but she put it on, and that's (that is) why the (tanbark) acorns look so rough.

Ixkareya were the beings before they became trees, (and) rocks.

b. They [White Oak and Live Oak] laughed at Tanbark (Oak) and Black Oak, (but they retorted), "As long as people live, they will always have us first, and you—they won't think much about you." And that is why, when people are together, they always have (tanbark) acorn soup,[2] and the next they use is black oak.

They laughed at Tanbark (Oak) because her cap looked so rough, and at Black Oak because her cap was so long.[3]

1. [Black Oak, from what follows.—Ed.]
2. [On the northwest Californian preference for tanbark acorns, see II.8, n. 3, above.—Ed.]
3. [The acorns of the tanbark oak have woolly surfaces and rough "caps." The caps of the black oak acorns are quite deep in proportion to the total length of the nut.—Ed.]

FORMULAS

INTRODUCTION

[The following introduction to the subject of formulas and formulists seems to have been compiled directly from Gifford's field notes. It was probably intended to serve as the basis for a generalized discussion. I have silently added pronouns and articles for greater reading ease, but I have not reorganized the material.—Ed.]

•

Shan [Davis] has three formulas, using madrone leaves, a fir sprig from the top of a tree, and tishwu (incense root).[1] All three formulas are made for curing. Sometimes he uses all three together. They are good for any kind of sickness. He talks to the plant while holding it in his hand. Shan got the formulas from Louis Tom's mother, who was an anekiavan.[2] She was a good friend, so he paid only a little, about $6 or $7. When he uses all three plants together, he talks to each separately as he collects them. [They are put in water that is] heated with hot stones and [is used] to steam the sick person.[3]

1. [These are V.43 to V.45, below. Tishwuf is identified as wild celery root by Dora Davis later in this Introduction. However, two of the three formulas from Shan Davis call for madrone leaves, and the third for a fir sprig.—Ed.]

2. [An anekiavan (or anekiava) is defined later in this Introduction as a praying doctor or medicine maker, who uses plants (i.e., leaves and roots) for medicines. Such a doctor is distinct from the fatawenan, the priest officiating at the New Year or world renewal ceremonies.—Ed.]

3. [For more on steaming, see p. 263.—Ed.]

One formula refers to Astexewa mountain at Clear Creek, one refers to Katimin (divide between two parts of Mt. Offield), the third to a mountain at the east end of the world called Ixkaramkem. Wakanwekareya is the ixkareya of Mt. Ixkaramkem; this ixkareya is a black rock. Astexewa goes with madrone leaves. Ixkaramkem goes with the fir top. Uichi[4] also goes with madrone leaves. Tishwu root goes with Katimin.

Georgia Orcutt says that for five days after reciting a formula no water is drunk. The ixkareya whose experience is discussed in the formula is mentioned at the beginning and end of the formula. (Anava means medicine; pik^{u}wa means story.)

Georgia verifies that if nothing is paid when a formula is said for someone, the result will be nil. A formula is wholly ineffective without payment even if it is recited by a near and dear relative. Anava transmitted within a family are not paid for, but if they are obtained from an outsider, they are usually paid for.

Formulas (most of them) mention the middle of the world at their beginning. Whenever a formula is recited, it is introduced by the statement, "Ixkareya did this."

Fir leaves were rubbed on a hunter's dog for luck, as well as on the deer hunter's hands when the formula was spoken (as given by Mary Ike). The hunter may sing a charm song (mentioned in connection with the formula).[5] Deer are called ixhareya mukuninan today (mukuninan means pet).

There are no ghost stories, but there is a formula for those who dream about the dead.[6]

For a mother whose milk ceases to come, a medicine is made from a plant which yields white juice; it is not the milkweed used for chewing gum. A formula is spoken over it. Georgia does not know the formula spoken by the anekiava.

A formula must be recited without missing a word. If a word is missed, then one must go back and start it over again. The patient drinks the water from the cup with madrone leaves in it. When he is through drinking, the anekiava puts hot rocks in a bucket of water with the madrone leaves and has the patient inhale steam. The patient is covered with a blanket, just like a sweathouse.

4. [Uichi is not identified, but see the discussion of the term ui, meaning a high place, in V.45, n. 1, below. Bright, in the Linguistic Index, below, suggests that Uichi is a variant spelling of A'u'ich.—Ed.]

5. [Probably a reference to V.32, below.—Ed.]

6. [This is V.38, below—Ed.]

Louis Tom's mother (deceased), from whom Shan learned a medicine, knew many of them. Mrs. Mamie McClellan in Eureka, with whom her daughter lives, also knows many. The daughter is named Alice; she is living with a man, but is not married. Mrs. McClellan lives out near Redwood Acres, which is across from the horse racetrack, out toward Myrtle Avenue. She lives across from the grandstand in a little house. She is not as old as Mary Ike. Blackburn is the name of the man Alice lives with. He sells wood for fuel. Mrs. McClellan is a Panamenik woman, probably not related to Georgia Henry [Orcutt].

Mrs. Bessie Tripp, of Oak Bottom, knows Amaikiara salmon medicines, but wants $5 to tell them. She was a woodpacker (ikiyawan).[7]

There was no medicine to shorten the period of exclusion at menstruation. The menstruant stayed in a separate house (yawuneixlivram = menstruant's house). (This was also the house in which a new mother was confined following childbirth, which took place in the dwelling.) No meat was allowed the menstruant.

Ten days after childbirth the new mother and infant were placed in the menstrual hut. The new father was not confined, but he did not eat with his wife because [they?] did not want to have bad luck. A mother with a baby never attended a funeral lest it make the baby sick and cause him to cry all the time. No medicine was made to purify the dwelling house after the new mother was removed. Moreover, the Karok never made medicine in the house while the new mother was there. It would have spoiled the medicine.

No medicine was made to make the baby grow fast.

At Forks of Salmon the Karok make medicine for a girl at her first menses. The girl lies down, and they don't want her to go to sleep. Beside her pillow is a basket hopper, which is supposed to keep her from dreaming in case she sleeps. It is believed that her dreams would come true if she did not have the basket.

The medicine is in the form of a song sung to the girl. While singing, the performers beat time with sticks on anything handy; they do not carry something to strike on. They sing two songs daily until the tenth night, when they sing another song. These songs are in Tisravar[8] language, not Karok. The informant did not know of

7. [An ikiyawan was a girl assistant in the world renewal ceremony; see I.15, n. 2, above.—Ed.]
   8. [See II.38, n. 1, above.—Ed.]

medicine recited for the burial of stillborn baby. But childbirth medicine is recited for the expectant mother whether the infant is to be born alive or dead. Of course it cannot be foreseen which the infant will be, alive or dead.

Bidisha kuyash is "love medicine." Bidish is a plant used as medicine for any purpose. As I understand it, bidish is the physical plant, anava a spoken formula.

Absumxarak[9] travels between lakes and river. Anixus[10] is not like Coyote. Anixus has good medicines, all kinds of medicines. Many medicines deal with Anixus.

Georgia got medicine once from an Amaikiaram old woman, Mrs. Mary(?) Wilder, married to a white man, Wilder. Two sisters married two brothers Wilder. She gave Georgia medicine out of kindness of heart. She said to Georgia, "I can't use medicine, but you got two boys. Maybe it will help them."

Pixuwa[11] means story; anava means medicine. Medicine must be recited from start to finish; otherwise it is not a medicine. It may be made at any time of day. For five days after making medicine, the anekiava does not drink water or eat fresh or dry salmon or deer meat, or eels. Eels are not dried, but eaten fresh only.[12]

Medicine was recited for a baby eating acorns for the first time, so it would grow up healthy. Also a love medicine was recited over salmon by a woman so that a man would be attracted to her. Salmon was fed to the man wanted. The woman did not eat supper nor drink water for five days after, but she might eat anything after the skipped supper of the first day. Sometimes love medicine [was held?] over water, which was given to the man to drink.

The bitch formula for childbirth[13] was bought by Little Ike's father from a Yurok downriver. He learned it originally in Yurok.

9. [Absumxarak is a big snake or water monster, probably the equivalent of the Yurok Knewollek, or "Long One." See III.37*d*, above, and Kroeber, Yurok Myths, Index, "Characteristic Stories and Themes," entries under "Monsters and harmful spirits."—Ed.]

10. [Anixus is Weasel, who is shown as helpful to humans, as in III.38—Ed.]

11. [Spelled pikuava in Gifford's general Introduction, p. 107, above.—Ed.]

12. [Kroeber, in Handbook, p. 85, says that "lampreys, customarily known as eels," ascended the Klamath in great numbers and were much prized "for their rich greasiness."—Ed.]

13. [Immediately preceding this sentence, G.'s typescript contained this question to himself: "Is the bitch formula attributed to Mary Ike as it should be, or to Georgia Orcutt? This is already in typist's hands." The query seems to refer to V. 15, which is correctly attributed to Mary Ike.—Ed.]

When he taught it to Mary, he did so in Karok. He paid the Yurok man one string of twelve dentalia for it. Mary got it from her father-in-law without payment.

If the formula is for curing, then it is anav tokyav. Singing =chiwit. It now develops that bidish tokyav and anav tokyav mean the same thing. Virtually all medicine formulas employ a plant or medicine which is called bidish. The words spoken to the bidish to make it effective constitute the anava or formula. Fuivaoru is a sort of "whistling" down in the throat which occurs in some medicine songs and is scarcely audible. When one says that another has no fuivaoru and is consequently unmarried, it means the person has no songs, no love medicine.

Mary Ike (1942) recently made medicine for Fred Johnson's son of twelve years who was sick. He could not retain food on his stomach. She has not yet learned the result (Sept. 3).

In introducing a medicine, the person says, "Here in the middle of the world . . . ." This statement was made in response to a question about Katimin being the middle of the world, which Mary seemed not to have heard of (sivsinenachip=middle of world). No one place was so designated, but any place was so referred to when an anava was begun.

The anekiavan is a praying doctor, using plants (i.e., leaves and roots) for medicines. The formulist has nothing to do with New Year ceremonies. Anekiavan means medicine maker. Tomorrow [in 1940], the purification of Jimmy Johnson's family will take place. The formulist is an anekiavan. Fir boughs in water will be used; the infusion will be drunk.

When Georgia's mother made medicines she did not speak for five days and ate by herself in the living house, refraining from meat and salmon. After medicine [the patient?] may eat anything and converse. No one was allowed to enter while Georgia's mother was making medicine. She made medicine for sickness. She was an eim. (Like Maggie George, she was evidently both a shaman [eim] and a formulist.)

The anekiava is supposed to eat out of special dishes and to go into retreat for two days after making medicine, so that the medicine will be effective. If the formulist mixed with people right away, the medicine would not work. Before making medicine, the formulist is supposed to abstain from water and meat for a couple of hours before getting the plant and speaking the formula. Also he or she must not make medicine when the sun is sinking behind a hill, as the person for whom the medicine is being made will die.

Question: Is it possible to cause death by a formula recited at sundown? Mary does not know, but says an eim may cause a person's continued illness and death by putting back a pain sucked out.

Louis Tom's mother from whom Shan Davis obtained the three above formulas[14] was a "doctor" (i.e., anekiava, not eim). She lived at Inuxtakats across from Ivīratiri.

Dora Davis knows medicine employing tishwuf, wild celery root. She confirms that the formulist must be paid something by the patient or the formula will not be effective. So even from a close and dear relative, the formulist must receive something as payment (pik-va = story; anava = medicine formula). The patient pays the anekiava before the medicine is made, just as he pays an eim.

Georgia says the anekiava sometimes have second sight also, like the eim. She mentions one case at Happy Camp of a halfbreed man whose children died. The anekiava who was called in insisted she saw a fire every time she closed her eyes. She interpreted this as meaning the man had medicine that was causing the deaths. She thought he had tishwuf root at the place she saw the fire.

On June 19, 1940, Georgia Orcutt continued: In making medicine, the anekiava abstains from water and eats alone for five days thereafter. If someone comes around, it will spoil that medicine.

June 24, 1940: A former son-in-law of Mary's visited her today, having learned of her illness. He suggested that perhaps the cause of her nose-bleeding was (1) that she had told medicines and (2) that she had subsequently eaten from dishes which her menstruant grand-daughters had used. Mary insisted she used her own dishes, not theirs.

Georgia's mother warned her not to look into or enter a house when she [the mother] was making medicine lest she too would have to go without water. Georgia never went in.

Apparently there is no soul theft; but if an aged or a sick person is neglected by a relative, then after death, the one who neglected the person may become ill or fall in the fire. If the person becomes ill, no eim can help. The illness is caused by the soul of the deceased

14. [See the second paragraph of this Introduction.—Ed.]

thinking about how he was neglected in life by the person responsible for his care. The only help for a person sick from this cause is to be derived from an anekiava who recites the necessary formula.

Georgia tells of the case of a blind old man at Tishannik,[15] who, following death of his wife, was neglected by his son. The son accepted the old man's earnings as an anekiava, but never so much as thanked him for the money. One day the old man fell from a cliff made by hydraulic mining and died. He was out gathering firewood at the time. Subsequently, the neglectful son became ill as a result of being conscience-stricken. He was cured by Sandy Bar Bob, who recited the necessary anava. It is bad luck to neglect the aged. If they are properly cared for, then "everything come out just nice" for the dutiful younger relative or relatives. The Sandy Bar Bob mentioned is the Bob discussed earlier in connection with dances.[16] He was Mamie McClellan's father. Georgia thinks Mamie's mind is failing. Her father was a very good anekiava.

The soul of a dead anekiava carries a taripan basket in going to the other world. All of his medicines (plants) are believed to be in the basket. He takes them with him. Plate 5e of O'Neale[17] illustrates a taripan basket, which is a plain dipper or cup used for drinking, for dipping water for acorn leaching, or for medicine leaves.

Most anekiava taught some or all of their formulas to members of their families; but now and then some did not. The blind old man discussed above taught none of his anava to his son; the son never spoke to his father in later years, never even thanked him for money.[18]

Anekiava, formulist, is a contraction of anava-kiawan; anav is formula.

Ben Tom, Sept. 17, 1942: Anava is medicine for sickness, while bidish is for other purposes, e.g., love medicine. Ben knows medicines for love, songs for deer, but he will not tell. Has heard

15. [Tishannik was at the mouth of Camp Creek (Kroeber, Karok Towns, UC-PAAE 35:[no. 4]:33).—Ed.]

16. [I find no other mention of Sandy Bar Bob.—Ed.]

17. [Lila M. O'Neale, Yurok-Karok Basket Weavers, UC-PAAE 32:(no. 1):pl. 5e, shows a plain, shallow, woven dipper without a handle.—Ed.]

18. [At this point G.'s typescript had a handwritten notation: "1942. Mrs. Ellen Allen: Georgia's half-sister, Mrs. Red Cap Tom, was anekiavan, but not eim." An eim is a shaman; see headnote to I.8, above.—Ed.]

name pidishkarem, but does not know what creature is like.[19] Maybe grizzly bear, he thinks.

Mary Ike, Sept. 18, 1942: Bidish=plant talked to in making medicine. Anava=medicine, after the talking to the bidish. Anava is also the formula spoken. Bidish is also used of a love medicine; anava is used of a curing medicine.

Medicine for rattlesnake: "Get out of my way, get out of my way. I have the hawk with me." (Mary Ike, 1939)

Medicine recited when seeing a person capsize a boat: "Kakanapmanach,[20] throw me back on the yasara's river bar."[21] (Mary Ike, 1940)

19. [See III.18*a*, above.—Ed.]
20. Kakanapmanach=double-header.
21. [Elsewhere a yasara is variously defined as a human being and as a rich man by G.—Ed.]

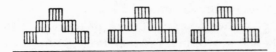

V. Formulas

V.1. Ixkareya Story (Love Medicine)

GEORGIA ORCUTT (June 22, 1940)

Georgia learned this story from Red Cap Tom.

•

a. Two womenfolks [were] staying together in one house at Panamenik. After a while the older sister made [prepared] acorns. Every day she made acorns. Even though they did not eat much, every day she made acorns. The younger sister was always packing wood. Every once in a while she wondered about what her older sister did with all the acorns she prepared.

b. Finally the younger sister decided to watch her older sister and see what she did with the acorns. After a while the younger sister made baskets while the older sister packed wood. Then the younger sister decided to look around and see if she could discover what her older sister did with the acorns.

c. She searched the house, and behind the woodpile on the house platform she saw something that looked like a baby. "Ah," she said, "it's you folks who eat the acorns. She continally makes acorns, but we have only a little to eat." After a while she killed these two babies with a stick. Then she pounded acorns. After a while look like [it seemed] the wind is [was] blowing. It blew harder and harder and finally blew off the roof. Next the walls blew away. The acorns all blew away, and finally the younger sister was blown away.

d. When the older sister on the hill heard the wind blowing, she ran down. She said, "I think sister (she) is doing something." When she ran down she found nothing left. The younger one got blown to [the] ocean and onto a sand beach across the ocean.

e. She pondered on how she would get home; she cried when she realized there was no way to get home. After a time somebody came around and found her sitting on [the] sand and asked, "How did you get here?" She replied, "My sister has some kind of an animal which I killed, and then the wind blew me down here." He said, "You killed the wind children. That is why you were blown here."

f. After a while the man asked her, "How are you going to get back up there?" The woman said, "I think I am going to stay right here. There is no way to go home." The man said, "I can take you home if you want to go home. If you marry me I can go home with you." She married him and they came to Panamenik. When the woman cried, that man [had] heard her and felt sorry for her. When they arrived at Panamenik, the woman said, "I never know [knew] I [had] been singing. I thought I was crying; I know now I [had] been singing." The man said, "I heard you when you were singing." The woman said, "I was not singing, I was crying, because I had no way to come home across the ocean. Now I find out I got [have a] good song, but before I never knew I had [a] good song." After a while she said, "If anybody with [having a] hard time stay[s] alone, somebody will come around and ask you [her] to marry him if you [she] know[s] my song." Kupanakanak.

The above is a love medicine without [a] plant, not anava.
Yuraskeruafishi = Across-Ocean young man is the man who married the younger sister. All in this story were ixkareya.

V.2 LOVE MEDICINE

GEORGIA ORCUTT (1940)

This is a Yurukvar medicine, but told to Georgia in Karok by a Yurok donor. She paid nothing for it. Georgia has never made it for anyone.

●

a. One man named Chumīweixkareya (Bald Eagle) [was] living down by the ocean (Yuras) with his wife. After a while somebody took his wife. He never knew [who did] it.

b. After a while someone asked the thief, "Why did you steal his wife?"

c. The thief saw Eagle on [the] mountain and thought he was looking for his wife.

d. The woman sat outside the thief's house. The thief lay on [the] floor inside. The woman was always crying [that] she wanted to go home. And after a while Mouse dug [a] hole under the woman. Mouse told the woman, "Your husband is coming after you. When your husband comes down, you must hold him tight." When Eagle came down and seized his wife, she held him tight and he flew away with her. The thief could do nothing.

This formula is said over water. The man who has lost his wife bathes all over with water; he does not drink it.

V.3. Love Medicine for Man to Use

GEORGIA ORCUTT

a. Two ixkareya sisters [were] staying at Machammischip (best sweathouse) at Katimin. Both were staying in this sweathouse (site of the present pikiawish[1] sweathouse). These two never went out, except to sit on [the] outside when [the] men sweated within. They were aiming to be somebody. (Yasara[2] women sometimes went in [the] sweathouse. [The] ixkareya made it that way that women raised as good women could use [the] sweathouse for their luck.) After a while for a long time nobody came around. They (two women) make [made] it that way, so nobody come [came] around. After a while the two women went up on the hill. When they came back they knew that somebody had come around. "We don't like (want) anybody to come around here," they said to each other.

b. After a while they said, "Let's look who came here." So they went around trying to find out who had come in. They knew it was a

1. [World renewal. This sweathouse is illustrated in Kroeber and Gifford, World Renewal, UC-AR 13:(no. 1):pl. 3*c* and *d*.—Ed.]
2. [Wealthy.—Ed.]

man. So they looked everywhere around Katimin to determine by the tracks who the man was. After a while they just go [went] around every place. Pretty soon they found one place with the poorest kind of a man. "Maybe we better go see that man," one said. The other objected, "No, I don't think it is that man. He is poor and does not go any place."

c. Pretty soon they both went to where he stayed. After a while they found out that that was the man who had been in their sweat-house. Then they decided to go and live in another place. They said, "We are going up in the heaven (paianuava)." They made a ladder from a fir tree by which to ascend to [the] sky. They wanted to get away from that man who was interested in them. They were both spinsters. After a while they went up to [the] ridge behind Everett's (see Evril's) field above Katimin.[3] From there they climbed up on their ladder to [the] sky. When they got up there they got ready to throw over the ladder so no one could follow them. But when they looked down they found that man was climbing up behind them.

d. The two women had planned to go to Kayuras[4] by a sky route, but when they saw the man the older sister said, "We better stay here tonight." The man sat between them. They said nothing.

e. When the women lay down, that man stayed in [the] middle with [the] women on each side. In the night it looked like [seemed] he had one woman on each arm. The women slept good, and never even moved that man. Pretty near daylight they woke up. After a while they looked. The man wanted to move but could not because the women were lying on his arms. When he looked he found it was two logs lying on his arms. The womenfolks had got up while the man slept soundly, put logs in their places, and then departed. When the man got up, he said, "It is too bad. What am I going to do?"

f. Then he said, "I am going to follow to the same place those two women went." After a while the women were traveling through tall grass and leaving a plain trail. The man followed their tracks. The women arrived at Kayuras. The man arrived after them. "When Indians come, if someone knows my medicine (bidish),[5] it is going to be [the] same way."

3. [Evril's field was near some of the places visited by the world renewal priest during the ten-day ceremony at Katimin (Kroeber and Gifford, World Renewal, UC-AR 13:[no. 1]:23–24.—Ed.]
4. [The upstream ocean.—Ed.]
5. Georgia never learned the plant used with this formula, which she learned

g. When the man arrived at Kayuras, the two women were already there ahead of him. They were already on the ocean beach. When that man [was] coming the women saw him. It look like [seemed] they were laughing when they saw him, and they asked, "Are you coming too?" He said, "I've come for just a little while."

h. The younger woman asked him, "Why do you come for just a little while? Which way are you going?" He replied, "I am going to the other ocean (Yuras)." He turned around right away and set out. He traveled on the ridges; he did not travel along the river. Ixkareya kaminstap (=poorest ixkareya) was his name.

i. As he came along [the] ridges he heard something. It looked like [seemed] he heard somebody cry some place. After a while he know [knew] that them [those] girls were coming along after him, following him. That man thought, "I am going to run away; I don't want them to see me. It is too bad that they treat[ed] me like that. They put logs on my arms too."

j. He ran away, and they never catch [caught] up with him. "If someone (yasara) knows my song and knows my medicine, the girls will run after him. If they don't like him at first they [will] change their minds and run after him."[6]

The above is a bidish tokyav, that is, "medicine talk to." This term is applied to love medicine.

V.4. LOVE MEDICINE FOR A MAN TO USE

MARY IKE (1942)

a. Dog sings [sang the] medicine song (which Mary sings). Dog was fooling around where the girls were. They all ran into the house when they saw him coming. Djishshii (male dog) was his name.

---

from a man of Aiyis. [Kroeber, Karok Towns, UC-PAAE 35:(no. 4):31 and 34, gives Aiyis as a middle Karok town on the west bank of the Klamath.—Ed.]

6. Tashe[?] is a kind of situation described in some tales, which makes bad luck for someone who originally turned you down. Thus the two women did not want the man at first, then later went to the opposite extreme of being crazy about him. Thus he made bad luck for them (from Georgia Orcutt, 1940). [Gifford's typescript had this note following I.2, but it seems more appropriate here, and so I have moved it.—Ed.]

b. One of the girls said, "He is outside. I am going out to see him." She went out. The rest followed her. (This is what the song says, which Mary was singing.)

V.5. DOG MEDICINE

MARY IKE (1942)

a. The old dog was lying by the fire. He was cold and freezing. The young fellows (dogs) would come to him and tell him about a certain girl. He said, "No, I'll have nothing to do with her. I'm getting too old."

b. Finally he said, "All right then." Then he sang the song (Mary sings it): "I was nothing but a dog, an old, old one. I can't get to the place where the girls are." Then he lay down again.

c. The next day he heard a noise outside. It was one of the boys. He said to the old dog, "The girls wanted me to come here and see you." There are [were] five girls with him.

d. One of the girls asked the old dog, "Are you asleep?" "No, I am not. I am just getting old," he replied. "Hereafter, if anyone knows my song, the girls will come to him. He will not have to run after them."

V.6. LOVE MEDICINE SO GIRLS WILL LIKE A MAN

MARY IKE (May 30, 1940)

This story is about Seiad.[1] Sayad was a village in which some people spoke Karok, some spoke Scott's Valley language. Some Karok moved to Scott's Valley in recent times, but it formerly belonged to the Scott's Valley Shasta.

•

a. A young man was living at [the] upper end of [the] flat. There were five girls living in [the] lower end of [the] flat. He went down

1. [Kroeber, G2*a*, above, identifies Seiad as Shammai, above Happy Camp.—Ed.]

there to see the girls. Every time they see [saw] him coming, they all run [ran] into [the] house. He sang that love song (love medicine) every time he went down to see the girls. "Here comes that young fellow. Let's all run and hide."

Day after day he did the same thing. "They don't like me, but I'll keep on until they do like me."

b. Every time he go [went] back home he kind of feel [felt] sorry for himself. Day after day he done [did] the same thing. "I'll try once more. I'll go down once more. This is the last time I'm going down there. The ixkareya are going to grow up [be transformed?] because [the] Indians are coming. I'll have to begin to look around [to see] where I am going to live when [the] Indians come."

c. The girls in the house all began to get lonesome. "I know that young fellow must be coming," each said.

d. The youngest girl said, "I'm going out to see if he is coming." She looked up the road and saw him going back up. "I'm going to run after him," she said. The older ones said to her, "Don't go. Don't run after him."

e. The youngest girl said to the young man, "Let us live together." He sang in reply, "No, I will not live with you. You did not like me. You did not want me." He was crying as he sang. Pretty soon he cried so much that his tears made little streams of water. He was walking up the creek, and the girl was right behind him. She kept telling him to wait for her.

f. He went way up on top of a big mountain. His tears made [turned] into a big creek. He sat down there, and the girl was a little way up [down?] the hill. She asked him, "Can I set [sit] down by you?" He said, "No, you did not want me. Don't get near me. I'm going to live right here," he said, "for the rest of my life."

"If anyone has trouble like I did and they know about me, they can use my song. Even if he [a man] is not good-looking, if he knows my song, the girls will run after him." He turned into a big mountain called Keishishyan (=big mountain)[2] at [the] head of Seiad Creek.

No plant is used with the above formula for a man's love medicine.

2. [Bright, in the Linguistic Index, below, identifies the mountain as Preston Peak.—Ed.]

V.7. Ixkareya Story (Anava for Love Medicine)

GEORGIA ORCUTT (1940)

a. Kusraafishi (Sun young man)[1] lived at Panamenik. Everyday he went to [the] ocean. His wife, Frog, always stayed home. After a while it look like [seemed that] that man never come [came] home. He stayed all night across the ocean. Every day that man went down to [the] ocean.

b. After a while his wife said, "I'd like to go down with you." He never answered his wife. But she persisted in asking to go with him. After a while that man came home [for] just a little while and then went out again every day.

c. The woman said again one day, "I am going to go down with you." After a while she got up and went with him. When they got up to [the] sky (painanaava), that man said, "We are going to stay all night here," but they never did so.

d. After that the man made a big fire. That woman sit [sat] down by the fire. After a while Sun picked up his wife and threw her into the fire. The man went on. The woman was all consumed by the fire. Only her hair was not consumed.

e. The hair assembled the bones. After a while got up that woman. Frog looked down, and she could see her husband walking down across the ocean. After a time the man looked back and thought, "Why did I kill my wife?"

f. After a time the man was coming back and he see [saw] his wife. He said, "I feel too badly when [that] I do [did] that."

g. That man had been married across the ocean. That is why he stayed home for only a little while. Yurasixyeru-ifapbi (Across-the-Ocean young girl) was name of his [second] wife across the ocean. He never went to see her any more. He stayed with his first wife again.

"After a while if [a] man don't [doesn't] like his wife and want[s] to get another woman, then if that wife knows my song her husband will come back to her," Frog said.

1. [Cf. Kusraxbini, translated as Moon old man in III.37*a*, above. See also II.26, n. 1.—Ed.]

V.8. LOVE MEDICINE FOR A MAN, SO WOMAN WOULD LIKE HIM

MARY IKE (June 15, 1940)

a. First the song is sung by the man (Mary sings it). Inam-weixkareya (Ixkareya from [we] Inam) was from Inam. He went across the river; then he went downriver along the river bar. Then he looked back. He heard the girls laughing at him. They laughed behind his back.

b. He looked up toward the hill and he said, "I wonder where I am going. I've got to find a place to live." Then he started singing his song (as mentioned above). Then he went up the hill onto the ridge. He looked back from the ridge toward the place he had come from. Then he seen [saw] a lot of [many] girls; all had white caps on. They all made fun of him. He was feeling badly for himself.

c. Then he went back down the hill by the girls, and they did not even notice him. They would not notice him nor take the boat over for him[1].

d. Then he stuck his hand in the river and threw some water over. Then they all looked over toward him. They said, "Take the boat over. Let him come." They brought him over.

e. Then the girls all said, "Let us go with you. Where are you going?" He would not even look at them.

f. The youngest girl said, "I'm going to go with him. I am going to follow him. Where are you going? I am going to go with you."

g. The man went up the hill. He was crying. He said, "They make fun of me. Nobody likes me." The youngest girl followed him. She said, "Wait for me!" But he would not even look back. He went way up to Astexewa, the big mountain near Clear Creek.

h. He arrived on top of the mountain. The girl said, "Let me sit by you. Let me live with you."

i. He said to the girl, "Sit down there. Don't get too close to me. You all made fun of me." He was still crying. Then he looked down from the mountain. And he seen [saw] a stream of water running down toward the river. His tears had turned into a creek.

j. He said to the girl, "I'll stay here and you can stay here, and

1. [The height of inhospitality. Kroeber, Handbook, p. 35, says that in the old days "even an enemy with whom one did not speak had to be taken as passenger."—Ed.]

we'll live together. Every year they will call on us during pikiawish at Inam. I am Astexewa we ixkareya."[2] Then he looked down and seen [saw] the river. It was his tears too. Kupanakanak.

No kind of plant is used with the above medicine, and no water. A man coming to a formulist must learn the songs and prose of this formula and then use both when seeking a girl. However, he repeats them out of earshot of the girl. Some medicines make girls "crazy" for a man.

V.9. MEDICINE (BIDISH) STORY

GEORGIA ORCUTT (1940)

Georgia got this story from a Chinas woman[1] named Yaveh (=good woman), or Clara.

•

a. This river (Klamath) never came down here originally. When it started to flow, the course was over bedrock. There was no sand or gravel. Look like it [It seemed to] make sandbars later as it flowed.

b. After a while asapip (cottonwood) began to grow on bars along the river.[2] After a while came two girls from Kayuras. They were sisters, both ixkareya. After a while [they] turn[ed] around and go [went] back to Kayuras. On the way home two boys caught up with them. "We [have] been hearing what you [have] been singing," the boys said. "We want to go up with you and stay up there." The girls said when they got back that they never thought they were

2. [Astexewa is the most powerful ixkareya, according to Gifford in Kroeber and Gifford, World Renewal, UC-AR 13:(no. 1):16–18. The priest during the Inam world renewal ceremony impersonates him and prays to him that there will be no more sickness in the world and that there will be more game and fish during the coming year. Near the end of the eight-day ceremony the priest also impersonates Takayu ifapbi (Young woman unmarried)—a spirit who gives good luck in hunting and fishing—as he rakes the ashes of his fire into a heap and covers it with earth.—Ed.]

1. [Chinas was a Karok village on the east side of the Klamath just above the Orleans bridge (Kroeber and Gifford, World Renewal, UC-AR 13:[no. 1]: 45.—Ed.]
2. K!i (guttural k) is a young tree or shrub in general.

going to get husbands as they sang when they were going down. "If somebody knows [women know] our song, they will always keep their husbands, never lose them."

The song tells of rock first, then sand, then cottonwood. There are cottonwood trees in Kayuras country. Cottonwood foliage is used for this medicine. It is not put in water but is talked to by the anekiava and turned over to the customer, who pays. Without pay it would not work. The same statement is applied to treatments by eim and anekiava: without pay their ministrations are worthless.

V.10. ANAVA (HATE MEDICINE)

GEORGIA ORCUTT

Georgia learned this from a Tishannik woman while she was staying at Happy Camp. [See Mary Ike's version, told as a myth, in III.26, above.—Ed.]

•

a. Nowirakan ixhareya and [his] wife [were] living at Nowirakan[1] (upstream from Happy Camp on same side of river). He always hunted ixkareya mukininas.[2] After a while his wife said, "Don't go way up on [the] hill." Then he never went far up, but went only partway and came back. After a while he thought, "I think I will go up there and look over, so as to find out why she always tells me not to go up there."

b. When he climbed up on the ridge, he looked over. When he looked over he saw a nice flat, with lots of nice green grass. Then he saw many nice girls digging potatoes on that flat. "That's why she did not want me to look over," he said to himself. Then he took his bow and arrow, intending to shoot an arrow. When he was ready to shoot he kneeled (bakatīs). The place where he knelt is indicated by a depression in the ridge. He dropped an arrow among them. The girls wondered where it came from. One young girl picked up the arrow.

1. [Nowirakan and Impurak on the opposite bank were the furthest upstream of the Karok settlements (Kroeber, Karok Towns, UC-PAAE 35:[no. 4]: 30).—Ed.]
2. [Deer. See Introduction to Formulas, p. 263, above.—Ed.]

c. Another girl asked her, "Why do you pick it up?" After a time the man ran down and stayed there. His wife knew about the girls and was [had been] afraid her husband would go down when he saw lots of girls. His wife was going to have a baby.

d. Never come [came] home that man. In time his son grew up. The woman got her father to stay with her. After a time her father made him a toy bow and arrows. The woman told her son, "If somebody tells you you are a big boy now, don't answer him."

e. After a while that little boy came into his mother's house. "Somebody, a man outside, said to me, 'You are a big boy.' " After a time the woman got her arus burden basket for seeds. She put (it) by the door inside the house.

f. That man came into (the) house. When he came in he said, "I have come back now." His wife never answered him. After a while got up and went outside that woman. She said to her son, "Let's go." They went down to the river and got into their boat. They went ashore on [the] east side. The boat and paddles turned into rock (the two "paddles" are still to be seen).

g. The boy shot at marks as he went up the mountain. The mother followed packing the arus basket. Some distance up, his mother said, "Let's camp right here." After a time the man swam across the river. He came to their camp. "Why do you come after me?" the woman asked. "You left me long ago." The woman said, "I think it is going to be that way that a man will leave his wife when he sees a young girl, but he will always come back later."

h. Then the woman picked up the arus basket and put it down over her head, turning into rock at [the] same time. The man started to cry and said, "I'm going to be something around here." The boy turned into a rock as he aimed his bow and arrow. He is there now. The man said, "I'm going to be Xavnam (wolf)[3] and be here all the time."

No plant is used with the above hate formula. The rocks are on the mountain today.

The purpose of this medicine is to make bad luck for the man and his new fancy, not to get him back. The formula is spoken to water, such as the river. It is not necessary for the object of hate to drink the water.[4]

3. [Wolf loses his children under other circumstances in II.25, above.—Ed.]
4. [For another version of this formula, see V.41, below, also by Georgia Orcutt.—Ed.]

V.11. MEDICINE TO MAKE FETUS SMALL

MARY IKE (1940)

When a woman is pregnant, they may make medicine for her so that the child will be small. Mary knows two medicines for this purpose. For the first one they use hazel buds for the medicine. These buds are put in water, which the patient drinks. The buds are addressed first as below. The medicine belongs to Mink.

•

a. "As soon as it gets dark you start out. You go to the head of this river. You just barely make it. You eat everything you come to, all the fish. Then you come out of the water and are just so fat, so heavy, you can't [can] hardly move. Then you look around and you find your medicine, bidish (medicine), and you eat it.

b. "When the night comes you start back down. Then you go to the mouth of the river. You are almost flying, you feel so good. Then when night comes you start back for the head of the river again. Then you just barely crawl out of the water, you are so fat. Then you find your bidish (and) again eat it. When night comes you start back down and go to the mouth of the river again. You feel so good. When you get there, you feel so light you can just fly.

"If anybody know[s] about me they can do the same, eat all they want. If anybody get[s] in trouble like I did, just call on me. You, Mink, did it that way."

The above medicine was made when a woman was seven months pregnant. It was obtained by Mary from Little Ike's mother; Mary paid nothing for it.[1]

V.12. ANOTHER MEDICINE TO MAKE THE FETUS SMALL

MARY IKE (1940)

In this formula sand is used. The sand may come from any place along the

1. [Little Ike's mother was Mary's mother-in-law. She was Kroeber's Informant C (above).—Ed.]

river. It is put into a cup of water and talked to when a woman is about seven months pregnant. The pregnant one drinks the cold water.

•

a. Absunkarax,[1] when you get fat, you eat up all the sand and little rocks. Then you go on a sandbar. Then you eat sand and you never get full. When you get back in the water you fill up the eddy. You are so fat. For two days you done [did] this: you went out on the sandbar and ate sand and little rocks.

b. Then you thought, "I'll make medicine for myself." Then you make medicine for yourself. You go on [the] river bar looking around for the medicine. Then you find a little black rock. Then you swim out to the eddy again. Then you feel fine. Then you thought [think] your medicine was [is] the best.

c. Absunkarax said, "You call on me if anybody knows about me. It makes no difference how fat you get, you call on me. I am Absunkarax."

Someone gave Mary this formula long ago. She paid nothing for it.

V.13. MEDICINE TO PREVENT CHILD BEING BIG AT BIRTH (IN CASE MOTHER EATS ALL THE TIME)

MARY IKE (1940)

Wild oat leaves are put in water. Mary made it for Bruce's wife and for Verdena[1] when they were pregnant. The woman drinks the water, which the anekiava has spoken over after the leaves are added. The water is not rubbed on the body. Dogs also eat wild oat leaves.

•

a. [The] anekiava says to [the] grass, "Old bitch, you just eat and never get full. You eat everything that is given to you. When you

---

1. [Identified as a big snake or water monster in III.37*d*.—Ed.]

1. [Bruce Donahue and Verdina (Donahue) Anderson, both now deceased, were children of Emily Donahue and thus grandchildren of Mary Ike (letter from Violet Tripp, also a daughter of Emily Donahue, dated August 3, 1978).—Ed.]

get through you go outside and pick up everything you see, everything that's dirty. You never get full, old bitch, no matter how they
feed you, you never get full. And nothing will hurt you.

b. "You get thin and your babies get small. When you know
about my medicine, the grass, you will never have any pains, you'll
never have any trouble in childbirth. I am the djishikevi (old
bitch)."[2]

V.14. MEDICINE FORMULA TO EASE LABOR PAINS

MARY IKE (1940)

The anekiava gets a plant with little pink flowers at the end of the stem
called imtarasuxbirish (=child-without-father plant).[1] The anekiava ad-
dresses the formula to the plant when she picks it. (All medicines are done
this way.)

•

a. The girl was walking around beginning to wonder, "What is
wrong with me, I am getting so heavy?" She went back in the house.
Pretty soon she got sick. She just got so sick. She felt around as she
was lying there. Pretty soon she put her hand on a plant (imtarasuxbirish). When she looked the other way she saw a basket full of
water. Then she took the flowers and put them in that water. She was
just sick, just suffering. She was all alone. "I am going to drink this
water." She was just sick when she drank this water with imtarasuxbirish.

b. Then she heard a noise outside. Someone opened the door.
She turned her head and seen [saw] a person (man). She was glad
someone had come to see her.

The person said, "What is the matter with you?" He spoke in a

2. Mary has a medicine for difficult birth used for her own daughter, who died in
childbirth, and for Mrs. Wilder, who had a side presentation. Mary does not want to
tell the medicine because it reminds her of her own daughter, for whom it was
recited in vain. [Mary's daughter who died in childbirth was Jessie Johnny, wife of
Edward Johnny (letter from Violet Tripp, August 3, 1978)—Ed.]

1. [Identified as *Lotus humistratus,* or hill lotus, in Schenck and Gifford,
Karok Ethnobotany, UC-AR 13:(no. 6):385.—Ed.]

mean voice. He never said another word. He just went back outside.

c. Then she cried, "That person did not even speak to me." When that person got outside he heard a baby crying outside[?]. The girl said, "Ixkareya must call on me when anyone suffers labor pains. My birish (plant) is the best, imtarasuxbirish."

The formulist has the parturient drink the water, and rubs it on her body. If it is a man anekiava who makes the medicine, he has another woman apply it to the parturient's body. Why?

V.15. CHILDBIRTH MEDICINE

MARY IKE (1940)

Little Ike's mother bought this medicine from a Wuppam man. She paid one string of twelve dentalia for it. After it was sold the original owner could go on using it also. Wild oats are used as the medicine—just the blades of grass, not the seeds or flowers. The formula is spoken to the grass when it is plucked. The medicine is administered when a woman has labor pains. The formula follows.

•

a. Asawufamweixkareya,[1] you lived there with your bitch. You always packed wood. You always made sweathouse wood. (This ixkareya was a man.) Day after day you went after wood. You used [a] long pole as [a] fire poker in [the] sweathouse.

b. Your bitch lay outside the sweathouse door. Next day you went after the wood again. Every day you went after wood. Your bitch watched you. Then you wondered, "What is the matter with my dog (bitch)? She never did do that before." Then you looked up the hill and you saw water coming out on the hillside everywhere. "The world is coming to an end! My dog looked at me." Then you closed the sweathouse entrance door. Your bitch jumped around. Then you and the bitch went back of the hill. There you found a big hollow tree. You both went into it. You closed the opening.

c. You were in there a long time and the water began to drip

1. Asawufam or Aswufam is below Martin's Ferry on the east side of the river [I.1*a*, above.—Ed.].

down [inside]. You were in there five nights and five days. The water was dripping worse. You were in there ten days and the water quit dripping. Then you thought you had better go [out]. Then you looked around. There was nothing but mud. Then you and your bitch went home.

d. You looked at your house and sweathouse, and they were covered with mud. Then you cleaned the house and the sweathouse. You fixed them the way they had been. You took your bitch into the house. Then you went after wood.

e. You lay in the sweathouse thinking how people would come into existence. You thought, "Well, I guess I'll have to go with my dog." Then you went out. (Then you) went back in [the] sweathouse. Then you went out and got wood. When you were back again in your sweathouse, you heard your dog (bitch) howling. "I feel sorry for my dog (bitch). I guess I'll go to the living house and see her."

f. When you looked in the door, you saw your dog (bitch) rolling around on the floor. She was so fat she could hardly move. "I feel sorry for my dog (bitch). I don't know how she is going to get well."

g. Then you went outside to look for medicine, but you found none. The earth was smooth; no grass or other plant was growing. There [Then] you looked right by your door and saw wild oats growing. Then you picked it, and you looked around and found a basket cut [cup] already with water in it. Then you put your medicine right in there.

h. You heard your bitch groaning. Then you took it and gave it to your dog (her) and rubbed it all over her. Then you went outside again and went back to the sweathouse door and stood there. You did not hear your bitch any more. Then you went back into the living house.

i. Your bitch gave birth to ten human beings (yasara), five dead and five alive. "If anyone knows about my medicine he will call on me. It does not make any difference what pain you have, if you know my medicine. You call [on] Asawufamweixkareya."

The human beings borne by the dog were not ixkareya but Indians. Mary made this medicine for Binoni Harris's[2] wife and was paid ten dollars for it. This was before Binoni became a doctor himself.

2. [The name should be spelled Benoni Harrie, according to William Bright (letter, September 26, 1978).—Ed.]

V.16. MEDICINE FORMULA TO ENABLE BABY TO EAT DEER MEAT JUICE

MARY IKE (1940)

In this formula "myrtle" leaves are used. The sprig of leaves is prayed to. Juice from cooked deer meat is squeezed out and mixed with pulverized myrtle leaves. This is given to the baby, that is, put in the baby's mouth.

•

a. Ixkareya, you have done this. (This is [the] way each formula starts.)

b. An ixkareya couple had a little son. They did not know what to do with him. He was crying. Then she [the wife] went to the sweathouse to call her husband. Toward morning they were handing the baby to one another. They did not know what to do with it. The woman tried to suckle it, but the baby refused the breast.

c. In the morning the baby went to sleep a little bit. Then it cried all day. Next day it could hardly be heard to cry, it had cried so much. The woman said to her husband, "We'd better make medicine for it."

d. The man went out to look for a deer. And he got one. Then he came home with [the] deer and the medicine plant (bidish). Then he cooked the meat. Then he squeezed some meat juice into a woman's spoon (i.e., a mussel shell).[1] He pounded the myrtle foliage. He mixed the deer juice and the pounded myrtle. He gave it to the baby to drink. He rubbed it all over the baby.

e. Next day the baby was running around all over the earth, it felt so good. "My medicine is the best," [the] ixkareya said. "Even if you can't swallow nothing [anything], you will call on me. My medicine (bidish) is the best."

After this the baby was given deer juice [alone] and finally meat. Mary got this medicine from her father's folks.

V.17. MEDICINE TO EASE SUFFERING WHEN CHOKING ON FISH BONES

MARY IKE (1940)

a. "Axtushuruktevni   (old-woman-living-where-they-sweep-

1. [Men used spoons carved from elk horns (Kroeber, *Handbook*, p. 93).—Ed.]

the-dirt-facing-downriver), where are you? You make the yasara[1] to choke with bone in the throat. Whey they sweep in front of the house, you eat the sweepings. If they do not feed you, you get mad. Where are you now? I am calling on you. I guess you made the yasara to choke because we did not feed you. I am Axtushuruk-tevni.''

This was said over a cup of plain water. No plant was used. The water was given to the sufferer by the formulist. Mary got this medicine from her family. Axtushuruktevni was an ixkareya.[2]

V.18. MEDICINE TO EASE SUFFERING WHEN CHOKING ON DEER BONE

MARY IKE

This formula was learned from Mary's folks. Only water is used.

•

a. Inamsufweixhavnam (wolf [havnam] of Inam), where are you? When you run after ixkareya mukininas (deer), you do not go very far before you get him. When he is still running you commence eating on him. When you get him down you eat him, bones and all. You do not digest the bones. They come out whole and (do) not even hurt you.

b. I am Inamsufweixhavnam. I eat bones and all of ixkareya mukininas. They do not harm me. You can call on me if you know any medicine, and nothing will harm you.

Mary says Inamsufweixhavnam is classed as an ixkareya.

V.19. MEDICINE FOR THIN PERSON WHO DOES NOT FEEL LIKE EATING, TO RESTORE APPETITE (AN ANAVA)

MARY IKE (June 25, 1940)

Thimbleberry roots are used. They are soaked in water which is drunk in the morning before eating.

1. [Translated as "human beings" in V.15*i* and as "rich men" in V.35*f*.—Ed.]
2. Mary relates the incident of a boy of fifteen, Ivan Charlie, to whom she taught the formula. When his mother's sister, Effie Charlie, had a fishbone stuck in her throat for three days, he made this medicine and the bone went down with the water.

•

a. Where are you,[1] Ixyarubixii (Widower-from-Across-Ocean)?[2] You had ten wives. You went to the sweathouse. All your wives were in the living house. You heard your wives laughing and having a lot of fun. Then you went into [the] house and lay with one. Towards morning you lay with the other nine, making ten in all. Some of your wives had their menses, some were pregnant, some had lost their newborn babies, some had [had] stillborn infants. Yet you lay with all of them in those conditions. Then you returned to the sweathouse and made [a] fire and sweated yourself. Then your wives called you to eat. You did not wash. You were dirty and ate without washing.

b. You did this way for a long time,[3] lying with all of them nightly. Then you returned to the sweathouse each morning, and they called you to eat. And you ate each morning without washing.[4] You listened and heard your wives laughing. Every night you did this for a long time.

c. Once when you went into [the] sweathouse you noted that you were getting thin, especially your knees, where the bones stuck out.

d. "Where are you?" your wives called. "Let's eat." You were about to leave the sweathouse, but you could not get out because you were too weak. Then they called you again. You said, "I do not feel good." When you looked across the river, all the trees looked blurred. You could not see well, because you were dizzy and weak.

e. Then your wives told you to drink water. You said, "I cannot get out. Bring the water to me." Then you crawled out the end exit of the sweathouse. You felt around and you put your hand on your medicine (bidish), which was already growing up.

f. Then you said to yourself, "People should not do as I have been doing. I lay with women who were unclean. I did not wash. If you know my medicine you can call on me. If yasara does not like to

1. All medicine formulas begin with "Where are you, So-and-So?" and all are in the second person. [This statement seems too sweeping. It probably should be amended to "many."—Ed.]
2. [See I.1 to I.4, above.—Ed.]
3. The formula has been shortened in telling me by combining the repeated episodes of night and morning events. The episodes should be spoken ten times in all. This formula was learned by Mary from her husband Ike's family.
4. If one eats after intercourse without washing, he will become thin.

eat, you can call on me. Hereafter you can call on me. You will find my medicine wherever it is growing. I am Ixyaruxbi'i.''

V.20. MEDICINE FOR SPOILED (UPSET) STOMACH

MARY IKE

This concerns Yeruxbihii (Across-Ocean Widower).[1] Mary got the formula from her father without payment.

•

a. You thought you would go way [far] upriver. You did not go very far before you seen [saw] a house. They said, ''You'd better come in and have something to eat.'' They fed you frog meat and lizard (long slender lizard, long head, brown, called xavramtiisveis) meat. Then you went out. You went on and you came to another house. They said, ''Come in. Have something to eat.'' You went in, and they put some dog meat in your plate. You ate it all and picked up the leavings that you dropped. Then you went out.

b. You came to another house, and they invited you in to have something to eat. They served you with gopher snake and rattlesnake.[2] You ate all that and went on.

c. Then you came to another house. They invited you in and gave you human flesh to eat. You almost fell down but you ate it. You were nearly blind.

d. Then you went on. You were looking around for bidish (medicine). ''I know they want to kill me,'' you said. You were halfway up the river. Then you looked down and saw the trees growing up. They were alders, your medicine.

e. You had a belt with a basket cup hanging from it. Then you made your medicine. You put it in your cup with water. You drank some and put it all over your body. After you drank it, you could see across the river.

f. ''Yasara will do the same if they know my medicine. Yasara

1. [See the spellings in I.1 to I.4 and V.19, above.—Ed.]
2. [All reptiles and dogs were considered extremely poisonous to eat, according to Kroeber, Handbook, p. 84.—Ed.]

will call upon me. If yasara does not feel like eating, he shall call upon me. I am Yeruxbihii."[3]

MARY IKE (1940)

Mary learned this medicine from her mother's folks. It makes use of willow roots exposed on a bank and usually red in color. After "praying" to the roots, the anekiava puts them in water. The water is drunk by the patient, not sprinkled on him.

●

a. Asta (small "duck") ixkareya went far upriver. She (He) took his medicine with him. He heard everybody was down on [disliked] him. She (He) came to two houses, one little house and one big house. They told him to come in. "Come in and have something to eat."

b. He asked, "What house am I going in, the little one or the big one?" They said, "The little house." He went in. Everything was all ready for her (him) to eat. They said, "Here, eat this." He looked at it a long time. Then they gave him a spoon. He asked them, "Do you eat this kind?" "Yes, we eat it." It was rattlesnake meat.[1]

c. There was some water in a cup. They told him to drink it. Then he drank the water. He got up and went out. He began to feel dizzy. Then he got his medicine (bidish) and put a little in his mouth. Then he went on.

d. He went a long way and came again to two houses, a little one and a big one. They said, "Come in and have something to eat." "Which house?" he asked. They said to enter the big house. They gave him menstrual blood to drink. He took one swallow and vomited. Then he went out. "I'm going now." He could not see across the river, he was that sick. Then he chewed his medicine (willow roots). When he got through he could see across the river.

3. It was taboo to eat with anyone after sexual intercourse. It might give the third party stomach trouble, for which the above formula is intended.

---

1. [See V.20, n. 2, above.—Ed.]

e. He went halfway to where he was going. Then he came to another house. The occupants told him to come in. Then he thought, "I know now they want to kill me." "Come on, have something to eat," they said. They gave him human semen to drink. When he took it, it almost knocked him down. He said to himself, "I've taken all kinds of dirty things."

"You call on me hereafter. I have taken everything, but nothing would kill me. My medicine is the best. You will call on me hereafter. I am Asta ixkareya."

V.22. Medicine Formula for One Who Has Been Ill, So He or She Can Again Eat Deer Meat

MARY IKE (1940)

Mary got this medicine from her father's family.

•

a. An ixkareya man and wife lived together a long time. The woman began to have pains; she was sick. She could not move. She couldn't eat nothing [anything]. He asked his wife if she would eat deer meat if he went out and hunted ixkareya mukininas (ixhareya's pets [=deer]). She was so sick he could not even turn her over. Then he went out to hunt. He did not go very far before he killed one. He cooked it on the coals.

b. The woman asked him to make medicine for her before she ate deer meat. He got some fir boughs. He told her to chew a little piece of the foliage and swallow the juice. Then he chewed a little piece and rubbed it on her legs, arms, and head. Then he chewed a bit of the leaf and cooked meat together [with it].

c. Next morning the woman was almost able to turn over herself. Then he cooked some more. Again she put a little piece in her mouth and swallowed both it and [the] fir foliage. Next morning she jumped up and ran on top of the house. She went on the other side of the hill. She tried to pull up a tree by the roots, she felt so good.

d. "I am ixkareya. If you know my medicine you will feel so good that you will run up the hill onto the ridge and try to pull up a tree by the roots. Hereafter you will call upon me. I leave my medicine behind for others to use. I am the ixkareya from halfway from either side (i.e., [from] the middle of the world)."

A fir sprig from the tip of a small tree is chewed and used with meat as described in the formula. No basket of water is used.

V.23. MEDICINE FOR GOOD LUCK

GEORGIA ORCUTT (1940)

a. Across-Ocean Widower (Yeruxbihi) had [a] daughter and five sons living at Amaikiaram. The girl had been cleaning eels. She went up to open [the] roof to give more light, as [it was] kind of [rather] dark. After a while that old man threw up some eel blood as the girl was moving [the] roofboards. The old man said, "You are yedihim (first menstruant)." The girl just cried. "Too bad it is going to be that way. I am going to eat with my brothers. My brothers [are] going to be nobodies if I eat with them." After a while she said, "Too bad. I think I'm going to make medicine." Then she cooked the eels. She said, "As long as this world be [is] here, always [will] come bad luck if [a man?] eat[s] from [the] same dishes as [a] first menstruant. I am going to make medicine now."

b. All the brothers come in to eat the eels. The boys did not know their sister's condition. Only the girl knew it. The old man did not know the girl had made medicine. She never told anybody when she made [the] medicine.

c. Next morning all [the brothers] going [went] hunting. When coming [they came] back in [the] evening, pack it all [they brought in many] skins and deer. Next day go [they went] up again and come [came] home in [the] evening, got [with] all kinds of things. After a while knew it that girl: "My brothers have got all kinds of things. My medicine is working all right. They got all kinds of nice things."

d. After a while the girl thought, "If anyone know[s] my medicine, [he is] going to be lucky. People who don't have my medicine [are] always going to have bad luck. If they know my medicine they [are] going to be all right. They will always come out lucky (ishtiits). People that ain't got [don't have] my medicine are going to be poor (kanim)."

The medicine told above by Georgia was made by Georgia for her sons when they were small. Eels are the medicine. No plant is used with the formula, which is said over the eels before cooking or drying them. Georgia has never told anyone [else] she knows this medicine.

V.24. MEDICINE FOR GAMBLING SUCCESS

GEORGIA ORCUTT (1940)

a. "What am I going to do? I ain't got nothing" (kohenmechko = "ain't got nothing" = poor person). "I am the poorest one. I ain't got nothing." After a while he said, "I'm going to try. Maybe I can play 'cards' after a while." After a while he said, "I won't have to eat anything. I won't have to eat fish. Anything fresh I won't going to [plan to] eat. I am going to eat only the Indian potatoes (taiyīs).[1] That's all I can eat."[2] [For a] long time he eat [ate] only taiyīs, nothing else.

b. After a while he said, "Now I'm going to try." [For] many months he had eaten only taiyīs and acorns. After a while he said, "I'm going to try playing 'cards' now." After a while he was playing "cards." After a while [he was] winning. And every day [he was] playing "cards." After a while he won all kinds of just everything. "Now I'm all right, now."

c. After a while he said, "If anyone know[s] how to sing my song, he will always be lucky if anyone sing[s] my song. If anybody knows he is poor and ain't got nothing, he will know how I feel. To be lucky he will eat nothing but acorns and taiyīs for about three months. When he is singing he will tell about what he is doing, how he goes without food. When first singing he will tell how poor he is. If anybody knows my song he will be lucky. He will know my song when singing. When singing he will never drink water."

The above is a medicine for game success. It is sung while playing. Bechkanwich is the name of this many-stick "card" game, a gambling game played only by men.[3]

1. [Taiyīs or taiyiis are Brodiaea bulbs. See II.46, n. 2.—Ed.]
2. "Always eat acorns anyway."
3. [The game is called stidjwuni in I.10e, above. It is described by Kroeber in Yurok Myths, BB2, n. 5, as a game in which one guesses which hand of the opponent "holds the marked one of fifty or more slender rods that are shuffled and divided into two lots with only their undifferentiated ends showing."—Ed.]

V.25. MEDICINE FOR LUCK,

GEORGIA ORCUTT (1940)

Georgia learned this formula from a female cousin of her husband, without charge.

•

a. [An] ixkareya woman [was] living at Suwufus (a flat below Katimin, now washed out by the river). She think [thought] when [the] ixkareya [were] leaving this world [that] she would go [stay] with man [humans]. After a while the woman was "fishing"[1] and praying for money, using [a] hazel stick. As she "fished," she prayed: "I am going to get the money." She fished a little above Katimin.

b. After a while she looked down and saw that the ixkareya were all going away, getting ready to leave. And the first one leaving the woman said she was going with. But she did not.

c. The woman said, "It is too bad I am going to be alone." After a while she broke to pieces her hazel "fish" pole. After a while she said, "I am going to make a basket of the pieces of the pole."[2] And she said, "That's all right if I am going to be alone. I am going to go up to Kayuras (upstream ocean)." Then she went to Kayuras. "I am going to be that kind of woman that always has money" (awastayahiki; probably means "wealth").

d. When she got up to Kayuras she scooped out dentalia with a basket plate (warûm). After a while she said, "I've got enough money now." She had fished for money a little above Katimin falls. Because of her fishing there, she became lucky and got money at Kayuras.

e. Then she thought, "I am going down, to go down to the ocean (Yuras) and get kanwās (*Glycymeris migueliana*) that the womenfolks use on the dress."[3]

f. At the ocean she got all kinds of valuable shells. She said,

---

1. [Women did not ordinarily fish. See III.13, n. 1, above.—Ed.]

2. [Hazel sticks were the preferred basketry material along the Klamath (Lila O'Neale, Yurok-Karok Basket Weavers, UC-PAAE 32:[no. 1]:15).—Ed.]

3. These cannot be found unless one makes medicine and prays first, and the same with *Olivella biplicata* (sapruk).

"Now I've got enough. It will be awfully hard for anybody to do what I have shown [done] (she never drink [drank] water for [a] long time). As long as the world is here, if somebody just ask[s] me and do [does] the same way I do—if they know [she knows] what I am doing—she will be [a] lucky woman if she do [does] the same way. If somebody knows my medicine and does just what I have done, it will come out nice. I am Kosoknamweixkareya."[4] Kosoknam is [a] flat close to [the] river above Katimin.

In using the above formula for a person, the anekiava gets a hazel stick denuded of leaves and also makes a basket plate. The buyer keeps the hazel stick and basket hidden away, lest an unclean person come in contact with it and ruin the medicine. Such a person would be a menstruant, a new mother, a person who had just had sexual intercourse, or a mourner not yet purified by the fifth-day ceremony.[5]

V.26. ANOTHER LUCK MEDICINE

GEORGIA ORCUTT (1940)

Georgia's father's sister taught her this formula without charge.

•

a. After a while the ixkareya found out that a certain spinster ixkareya was aiming to become a wealthy woman. After a while a man went into her house to spoil what she was doing. He sat down close beside the woman and talked to her. She said, "It is too bad. He is going to give me bad luck." She cut off the portion of her dress he had touched and threw it away. She had been working a long time to bring wealth to herself, but now she knew she was going to have bad luck.

b. After a while she knew it and she said, "I won't [I'm not] going to be somebody." She know it [knew that] that man spoiled her luck when he came in. That man look like he [seemed to] stand way off and say, "Now I am making bad luck."

c. Look like after a while that woman was not thinking about money anymore, but was thinking about that man and where he

4. The above ixkareya woman was ifabikevi (=old maid). There were very few old maids among the Karok.
5. [For the purification formulas, see V.36 and V.37, below.—Ed.]

was going. After a while it became apparent that she was going to be nobody, and she said, "When Indians come into existence it will be this way. If a spinster tries to become wealthy and then goes with a man it will spoil her luck. If womanfolks don't think about men and intercourse they will have good luck. They will always be lucky. Very few women will be that way, but they will be lucky.[1] I am Numenweixkareya."

The above luck medicine is made for a woman who has bad luck financially. The formulist sprinkles medicine water with her fingers on the person's head. No plant is used.

V.27. FORMULA FOR MEDICINE TO PROTECT ONE AFTER HE HAS COMMITTED A THEFT OR MURDER OR OTHER WRONG

MARY IKE (1940)

a. Monatmankana (shrew? a "mouse" with a long nose; a tiny animal living in grass) looked up the river. He saw men all lined up, waiting for him. One of the men spoke up and said, "I'm glad I'm going to eat that fellow that's coming up; I'm just mad [very angry] at him." Shrew went up and dodged them by going under the ground and coming out again upriver. Another spoke and said, "I guess you will eat him. Look at him running up the river bank!"

b. Then Shrew went way [far] up and he saw some more men standing in the trail waiting for him. One of them said, "Here he comes. I'm going to eat him." Then he dodge[d] under. He done [did] the same thing [as before]. Another said, "I guess you will eat him. There he goes, way up."

c. Then Shrew went on. He went way up and he saw some more men standing in the trail waiting for him. "When he comes, I'm going to eat him," one said. He done [Shrew did] the same thing again. Then he went on. One of them spoke up and said, "I guess we can't kill him. We don't even know when he passed us."

"As long as there are people on earth, if they know about me, [they may] call on me. Nobody knows where I travel. I am Monatmankanahanhich" (hanhich=long nose).

This formula was recited by a fugitive before going somewhere or before going to bed. No plant or water was used.

1. In Georgia's mother's family were two such old maids who became wealthy.

V.28. STORY ABOUT OLD WOMAN (A RAIN FORMULA)

MARY IKE (1940)

a. The old lady lived with her two daughters' [her daughter's two?] sons. She would tell her grandson, "We are getting hungry. We are going to starve." The old lady told the grandson (a young man), "I seen (saw) deer tracks. I guess you'll have to go and track the deer. You had better make some twine." The boy said, "It takes too long. You go down to the river and stretch the net for salmon."

b. It was cold. The rocks were all covered with ice. One grandson fell in the river and drowned.

c. That (The other) boy told his grandmother, "You had better build a fire. It is too cold." She told her grandson, "When I make fire here you go up on [the] hill and stay there. When you get on top of [the] hill, sing, 'Kastahak, kastahak, kastahak, etc.' " (Meaning of kastahak is unknown.)

d. She made a big fire to thaw the ice off the rocks. Ice said, "Old lady, don't be mean!" The old lady made more fire and more fire. She was mad (angry) because one of them was drowned. She melted off all the ice. She called to her grandson, "Come on down here. I killed them (the ice) all off." Kupanakanak.

Anyone who wished to have rain come in frosty weather told this story.

V.29. FLOOD STORY

MARY IKE (1940)

This is a medicine for crossing the river in a boat. Willow with red bark (kusfipfurak)[1] is broken off and fastened at the bow of the boat. It is talked to after it is broken off and before it is put on the boat.

●

a. Mink (xansunamwan) said, "There is going to be a flood." Ground Squirrel (axgai) was (the) one he was talking to. Mink said,

1. [G.'s typescript also showed an alternative pronunciation: the first letter *g* rather than *k*.—Ed.]

"We'll pair everything, a male and female of every kind in the boat."

b. (The) ixkareya said, "The world is going to come to an end. The ixkareya are not using their medicine right. Put [a] pair of every kind in the boat; then after the world comes to an end, we'll do it all over again. It will be a different world then, with different people."

c. They looked around and they seen (saw) the water. It was getting big, a flood. Ground Squirrel said, "Don't put me in the boat. I can swim to the highest peak. I'll save the fire. Put it on my back."

d. Mink went in the boat. He told the willow sprig when he put (it) in the bow, "Save me. Take care of me." With all the people in the boat they went around the world. Mink never got tired. They could see no land. There was nothing but water.

e. Squirrel swam to the highest peak, Mt. Shasta (Keishish-yam).[2] That was the only land not covered by water. Mink's boat arrived at the same time. Squirrel said, "I told you I could swim out."

f. Then they looked around and there was no more water. There was nothing but mud. Trees began to grow. Different people, a different generation, began to grow up. Squirrel has a kind of burnt spot on his back from carrying the fire.

V.30. MEDICINE FORMULA FOR KILLING BEAR

MARY IKE (1940)

This is spoken to hazel leaves at the end of a sprig, which are put in a big seed gathering basket (arus). After the talking is finished, the leaves are rubbed on the hands of the hunter and on his gun (bow and arrows).

•

a. [A] yasara woman was wondering, "Where am I going to live? I guess I'll live at the foot of a mountain. Then I'll not hear anyone crying for the dead. If I live there I'll hear no crying and no sorrow." You stayed all night, and the first night you heard some-body crying. "Now I can't stay here; I must go." Then you went up high, on a high ridge, and you stayed on this side of the ridge.

b. [The] first night [there] you heard somebody crying. "I am not going to hear anybody crying. I must move."

2. [Bright, in the Linguistic Index, below, identifies it as Preston Peak.—Ed.]

c. Then you went up the highest mountain; you went on the other side. "Now I am going to stay right here." Then you heard someone crying. "I think I'd better move. I can't [bear to] hear someone crying."

d. Then you went over another ridge. When you got on top of the ridge you put your basket down, so its opening pointed down [the] ridge. You looked down the trail and saw a black bear[1] coming. You placed the basket with the opening up [the] ridge and you saw [a] white (=takur) bear coming. Each time the bear fell in[to] your basket. Then you went on.

e. You said, "I am going to make my home at the foot of this mountain. People can still kill bears even if they hear crying, if they know about me. They can call ixkareya asistava (ixkareya woman). I am going to live right here hereafter. Whoever makes my medicine will name the white bear and the black bear. Even if they hear people crying they can still kill the bear, because my medicine is the best."

V.31. Ixkareya Story for Hunting Luck

GEORGIA ORCUTT (1940)

a. Lots of boys staying (lived) in one house, all of one family. People never knew when they went out hunting. The boys had two sisters. The boys stayed all night in [the] sweathouse. The girls never knew when the boys went out hunting.

b. Some men thought maybe they could marry the girls if they stayed in that place.

c. The boys came back in the evening, packing home all kinds of game. Lots of people found out about the boys, but nobody knew where they went. Looked like they [They seemed to] hide their destination.

d. After a while a man came down from way [far] upstream (Imtamwara, a place up on the mountains, not on the Klamath River). He stayed all night. They told him to sleep in [the] house instead of [the] sweathouse, so he would not discover where they went for deer. He had come down especially to find out if he could.

e. In the morning the Imtamwara man woke up. The brothers of

1. Widushur karamkunish (widushur=bear; karam=black).

the girls had already left long before. After a while the guest went outside and looked up toward [the] hill and discerned where they had gone up. Then he followed [them] up. He went way [far] up on [the] hill some place. That was [the] time he catch [caught] up with them [those] boys. The boys were waiting at just one place where they could shoot deer as they went over on [the] ridge.

f. After a while they told the Imtamwara man he had better watch the deer. At that time fog covered the ridge and the deer went over, but the visitor could not see the deer. They asked him when he was going to shoot, but at same time they had made the fog so [thick that] he could not see [them]. The Imtamwara man sat down and just watched. The boys knew the deer had all gone over in the fog. They made it that way so their visitor could not see [them].

g. After a while the Imtamwara man knelt and shot an arrow at a deer. When he go [went] over to see he found he had killed ten white deer with one shot. The ten boys had been working hard. They had seen nothing. [The] ixkareya had made it that way, so they could not see nothing [anything].

h. The boys wondered how he found out, but no one could find out how he killed the ten white deer. He had been singing as he walked up. After a while he think [thought], "If somebody know[s] my song he [will] always find good deer." When singing he talks [talked] about where he comes [had come] from. "If anyone singing calls my name, I'll hear it because I am going to stay in one place, the place where I came from, Imtamwara. I don't care if anybody make[s] bad luck, such as the boys making fog come over; just the same [even so], the one who knows my song will have good luck."

The above tale is neither pikuwa [myth] nor anava [formula], but mahanich (imitation). Songs sung by a hunter will bring good luck without repetition of the story itself. It [the story?] might be told in hunters' camp or in the sweathouse. It is not used for any purpose other than the deer hunt.

V.32. FORMULA FOR DEER HUNTER'S MEDICINE

MARY IKE (1940)

In this medicine the hunter rubs his hands with the medicine, and also his bow or gun, fir leaves being the medicine. The pufikanava (deer medicine) is made by an anekiava (formulist). No preliminary sweating is required. If woman and man have intercourse and then eat deer meat, they will sicken.

•

a. Woman ixkareya says [said], "I'm only a woman, but I'm going to be an ixkareya." She was menstruating while she was making this medicine. She got her fine woven burden basket (arus). She put her medicine (fir sprigs) in [the] bottom of this basket. She went way [far] up on top of the mountains to the highest peak. She took her basket off her back and laid it down so [that the] orifice [was] upriver. She never heard any noise. Then she turned it with [the] orifice downriver. Then she heard all sorts of noises in the basket.

b. Four deer fell into her basket. "Whatever unclean person eats this meat will be sick." She picked up the load and put it on her back. She started out. She went a long ways. It was all she could do to walk. She was trying to walk. Her dress was covered with blood—her blood and deer blood mixed together. She was so dirty she could hardly walk. She thought her name would be Woman ixkareya. "Whoever learns my medicine will call on me. I am Woman ixkareya. Whoever learns my medicine and goes out hunting will call on me hereafter. I am Woman ixkareya. If you do not use my medicine, you can sing my song."

V.33. Ixkareya Story (Pik[u]wa or Tobacco Anava)

GEORGIA ORCUTT (1940)

This story (pik[u]wa) is anava for rapid tobacco growth, and is recited at the time of tobacco planting. It can also be used as a formula to hasten tree felling by fire. Georgia learned it from Red Cap Tom's father.

•

a. Oriv ixkareya [o=tobacco with seeds][1] was living with his small boy brother Oriv mucha (=Oriv younger brother). The small

1. Georgia's mother's brother's father-in-law was named Oriv.

boy stayed in [the] living house [and] never went into [the] sweathouse. They were living at Panamenik.

b. Every morning Oriv [the elder] went hunting. When he come [came] back bringing deer, looked like [it seemed the] deer never had any fat on it. After a while the [younger] boy said [to himself], "I don't know why that deer never has fat. I am going to watch him [Oriv]."

c. One morning Oriv went hunting and his younger brother trailed him. Oriv killed a deer, and when that deer lay there Oriv chopped off the antlers. When he was chopping off [the] horns on one side, his younger brother hollered at him, "What for you [Why are you] doing that way, cutting off the horns?" He desisted, leaving [the] horns on one side of [the] head. He did not answer his younger brother's question.

d. When skinning [he skinned] that deer, one side only had fat on it; [the] other side had no fat. The boy was watching his brother. After a while the boy ate that fat.

e. One day Oriv went way [far] up on [the] hill and went to [the downstream] ocean (Yuras) shore. On the hill is a big lake toward the ocean. Yuarari (=downriver lake) is name of this lake. For a long time Oriv watched the lake. After a time he saw something shining come out of the lake. He took [a] hook [tawuka, compound bone fishhook made with pitch and string] and line and pole, and fished for it. After a while he hooked it. When he hooked it, it looked like [seemed that the] lake waters rose up. After a while it look like all mud [all seemed to be mud] where he is [was] standing. He began to sink in it. After a while he landed the creature, which was a big snake, Absunxarak.

f. He killed and skinned the snake. After a while go [he went] home. When he come [arrived], he put wood shavings on the skin, which he [then] put in [the] sweathouse. His younger brother asked, "Anix (older brother), where have you been? I missed you." Oriv never answered.

g. After a time he prepared the skin and head. He had only the anterior half of the snake. He had left [the] posterior half behind.

h. During the night the boy peeked into the sweathouse. He called, "Anix!" The older brother never answered. The boy continued, "Something when I lay down was right on my sternum. I picked it up and it was [a] nice little thing." The older brother never answered him.

i. After a while the boy came again to [the] sweathouse door and said, "Anix, I spit on my hand and that nice little thing licked up my spit." Oriv never answered him.

j. Again the boy came back to [the] sweathouse door and said, "Anix, [it] look[s] awful [very]nice now. [It] look[s] like [a] mouse." Oriv say [said] nothing.

k. Again the boy came back and said, "Anix, I feed [fed] him deer meat." Oriv never answered him. Looked like [It seemed] that thing [was] growing awful fast.

l. After a while come [he came] back again and said, "Anix, now he can feed himself deer meat. I don't have to feed him now. He's awful nice." Oriv never answered.

m. Come [He came] back again and said, "Anix, he is helping himself to the bales of dried deer meat!"[2] Oriv said nothing.

n. After a while come [he came] back again and said, "Anix, it looks like he has eaten all of our dried deer meat!" Oriv said nothing.

o. Come [He came] back again and said, "Anix, I'm afraid! Look like he [He seemed to] growl at me when I tried to stop him." Oriv said nothing.

p. The boy ran out of the house with the animal after him. The animal chased him around. After a while Oriv came out and told his younger brother, "You'd better come into [the] sweathouse." The boy went in.

q. Oriv put [the] snakeskin over his head and looked out at the animal that was running around outside seeking the boy. The animal kept running around all night outside. Oriv watched him all night long from [the] sweathouse door. In [the] morning Oriv fell asleep at [the] sweathouse door.

r. When he woke up he saw nothing of the animal. Then he went down into [the] sweathouse, but his brother had disappeared. He felt badly that he had lost his brother. He cried about his brother.

s. Oriv walked around on the flat at Panamenik. He carried a cane as he walked. When he sat down to take a rest, a bird [came and] sat on his cane and said to him, "Somebody took Oriv's younger brother." Oriv thought the bird was "swearing" at him and said to himself, "I am going to kill that bird for 'swearing' at me." He don't [didn't] like what the bird kept saying. He put pitch on the

---

2. Xanuwish is a bundle of dried deer meat tied with hazel shoots. Wutax is a single piece of the dried meat.

top of his cane. When the bird alighted on it again, it was held fast. Oriv grabbed him, saying he was going to kill him.

t. Churukwichi, the bird (bigger than robin, chibakbak), cried, "Don't kill me! I know where your brother is. I want to tell you where he is now." Oriv wanted to learn where his brother was, so he did not kill the bird. "All right," said Oriv, "you can tell me." "You can go right now, for it look[s] like they are going to cook your brother."

u. Oriv said, "That's the way I lost my brother, because he ate the fat meat of that deer I killed."[3] "Now is [a] good time to go after him, right now," said the bird.

v. They were going to cook Oriv's brother across the ocean (pananaava).[4] Across the ocean in [the] land there, people fell trees by burning them down and carry[ing] away whole tree[s]. The land across the ocean can be reached by the sky route, coming down over there, but Oriv did not go that way. He came down to earth and went by boat.[5]

w. The bird told Oriv to pack lots of tobacco. "When you go up in heaven," the bird told Oriv, "you must make fire. The Day-moon (Sun) will stop if you give him tobacco. He likes it. He will tell you where your brother is and tell you what to do."

x. Oriv went to [the] sky and planted tobacco all over the heavens, and it sprouted and blossomed right away. He broke off blossoms so it would grow better. He made fire, and after a time the Day-moon came down. When Oriv smoked his pipe, the Sun stopped. "I want you to tell me if you see my brother some place, and I'll give you tobacco."

y. Day-moon said, "Right now you can go after your brother across [the] ocean. They are going to cook him. When [the] last tree is felled by burning, they will take the wood for fire to cook your younger brother. Your brother is tied inside the top of the sweat-house. When you go there, you will kill the old woman who sits

3. Women were warned not to cook any fat meat in the hills lest the smell attract wild animals. If men with bows or guns were along, it did not matter. [G.'s typescript showed this note following paragraph *y*, but it seems more closely related to Oriv's remorse, expressed here.—Ed.]

4. [The word is translated as "up in the heaven" in V.3*c*, which seems to be the sense here.—Ed.]

5. [A summary of the action that follows in paragraphs *x-z*, after Oriv and the bird have finished their conversation.—Ed.]

by the fire that is burning down the tree, and don her clothing and cap. Throw her body in[to the] fire to burn."

z. Oriv returned to earth and then went by boat across the ocean, taking Moles and Mice with him to scuttle [his enemies'] boats. He found the old woman[6] and killed her, and burned her body. When the tree fell, a man came to get the wood, and he said to Oriv [who was] in disguise, "Oriv, you [are] already here! You [have] come to get your brother." Oriv sat crouched like the old woman. Oriv said, "Do you think Oriv is going to [would] put on this kind of dress?" Then Oriv killed the man and burned his body. He took off his disguise. Then he packed over the big tree with one hand, jumping from rock to rock with it.

aa. Whenever Oriv's brother heard a tree fall, he cried because he knew they were getting wood to cook him. Now this was the last tree, and he knew when that burned down to coals they would cook him. So he cried out.

bb. The people thought Oriv was the regular woodpacker.[7] "Oh, I've been looking for you, Anix!" "Don't say anything," said Oriv. "We don't want those [these] people to find out." Then he released his brother, who was tied at [the] top of [the] inside of [the] sweathouse.

cc. The people chased them as they fled to shore and jumped into Oriv's boat. The pursuers jumped in their boats, but Oriv had arranged for the Mice to bore holes in them, so they would not float, and underneath Moles had burrowed so the boats sank in the earth where [they were] pulled up on [the] beach.

dd. Later Mole swam across [the] ocean and got his hands turned into their present position from so much swimming.

Kemish or aruam (cannibal) was name of the monster that developed from what the boy found on his sternum in the story. This monster is from the ocean and eats people. The old woman who was poking fire under the tree to fell it and the man who came to carry away the whole tree were later forms of the monster that appeared first as a tiny thing on the boy's sternum.

6. When burning down a tree, the Karok poked the fire against or into the tree with a poker. That is what the old woman was doing. Usually dead or very dry trees were so felled. No large bonfire was built, but only a small fire.

7. [Ellipsis. And so they admitted him to the sweathouse where his brother was being held.—Ed.]

V.34. ORIGIN OF DOUBLE-BALL SHINNY AT ASWUFAM (SCABBY BOY)

GEORGIA ORCUTT (1940)

a. At Aswufam[1] were two ixkareya girls. The people were going to have a stick game (double-ball shinny/imsatwa). The girls were going to marry the man who won the stick game. Everybody (was) working hard, coming from every place, hoping to win the game.

b. Every day they played and nobody won. (The) girls watched the playing. It looked as though the players were going to give up. The father of the two girls said, "You two girls go up the hill to Numi where five boys are living." One of them (a sixth boy) was sickly and covered with scabs. Numi was on Orleans (the west) side of (the) river, back of Martin's Ferry. "You two girls see if you can get those boys to come down here and play." The girls went up. (Numi was the place where [the] bird ixnumen comes in winter.)[2]

c. (The) girls went to the boys' house. When they entered they found that (the) five boys were away hunting. Only one boy was at home, and he was crouched near (the) steps leading down into (the) house pit. After a while the others came in from hunting. They jumped into (the) pit, not walking down them (steps). The girls said, "Our father sent us up here to get you boys to come down and play the stick game." The five big boys declined to go but urged the scabby younger brother to go.

d. Lying by the Scabby Boy was a scabby dog which was emaciated too, so (it) looked like [a] bag of bones. The oldest boy told his younger brother to go.

e. Went out, the youngest girl (As the youngest girl went out, she) thought to herself that (the) scabby lad would not be much good to play. The Scabby Boy and his dog got up to go. The younger girl held back; she did not like it. "Why did you take that boy?" But (the) older girl went with the Scabby Boy. After a while (they) got down by (the) river and entered (a) boat to cross to (the) east side of [the] river. They waited a little while for the younger sister, but she did

1. [G.'s typescript had this note, later deleted: "Aswufum is across river from Martin's Ferry. Georgia thinks Kenek is the Yurok name of Aswufum, but she is not wholly certain." Kroeber, Handbook, p. 11, confirms these names for the Yurok town.—Ed.]

2. [See the Linguistic Index, below, on the two Karok names.—Ed.]

not come. She did not like that boy. She walked way (far) behind. But they waited for her, and she crossed with them.

f. The playing ground was a flat, high up above [the] river. When they looked up it looked like lots of (many) people (were) waiting for them. When they go up (arrived), the girls went into their house, taking Scabby Boy and scabby dog with them.

g. The boy asked if they had an atiki (burden) basket,[3] a basket which could be inverted as (a) cover. "Yes," they said. Scabby Boy said, "Let's take (the) basket up to (the) spring where there is water." (It) looked like everybody (was) watching. The boy could hardly walk there, he was so sickly. The older girl packed up the atiki.

h. The boy sat down on [the] ground by (the) spring. The older girl made (a) fire. She put rocks (stones) in (the) fire. She put (the) hot rocks (stones) in (the) basket of water. After heating [After she heated] (the) water, (the) boy and dog got inside, and she covered [them] with (the) atiki basket.

i. When (later) she removed the atiki, the boy and dog were different. The dog had (a) collar of woodpecker scalps and (a) leash of same for holding him. The boy's hair was tied in (a) pug at back of (his) head with woodpecker scalp ties. His eyebrows were woodpecker color (scarlet). His face look[ed] all red from alder bark which had been placed in (the) water. He was now the sixth brother, for he was never counted before because he was scabby. The five boys at Numi cut down the small trees which interfered with their view across the river to the stick-game ground.

j. When the boy came down everybody watched him and saw that they were going to have a big game. Already the boy carried a stick with which to play. (The stick has a curved striking end.) The older girl came down with him. He looked altogether different, and the young(er) girl watched him now. He looked so different and handsome now.

k. In playing (the) game, two opponents strike at [the] ball, each trying to drive it toward his goal of [a] bush set in [the] ground. No one wanted to play with the winner. But the Scabby Boy from Numi was ready to play with them. Then they both [boy and dog] stood up.

3. See Lila O'Neale, Yurok-Karok Basket Weavers, UC-PAAE 32:(no. 1):pl. 54, lower. The atiki is a burden basket for seeds. [Illustrated is a large, flared basket described as being used for seed gathering or as a cover for a storage basket.—Ed.]

The five brothers up at Numi stood looking down, watching. When [he was] ready to play, the brothers on (the) hill gave (the) victory call because they knew their brother was going to win.

l. When Scabby fellow (Boy) hit the ball, he knocked it over [the] goal, and the dog ran and brought it back to the center. But the opponent, who was (the) local champion, never got [a] chance to hit the ball. He was feeling so bad(ly that) he held (the) handle end of (the shinny) stick to his mouth at (the) end of game. He had been (the) unbeaten champion for a long time.[4]

m. The Scabby Boy married the older sister.

Prospective players used this story as a formula for medicine to win the stick game. The formula is used over water with which the prospective player bathes to have good luck. No plant was used, so far as Georgia knows. This game was played in summer.[5]

V.35. Story About Fox (apadāx)

MARY IKE (1940)

a. [The] ixkareya said, "When you dance you are going to use the hides off of fox as (an) apron, six of them sewn together. When you go to get them you are going to trap for them, using a snare. When the Amaikiara(m) smoke is made for salmon,[1] you are going to get a fragment of unburned wood to make medicine."

b. When they went to trap Fox they set (a) trap on each end of (a) log which Fox usually crossed on. They took (a) piece of wood from [the] sacred fire, put (it) on (the) log, and put (a) rock over it.

4. Aswufam kanachifi ("at Aswufam I was beaten") is the name applied to a long-billed bird seen along the river at times, because of the resemblance of its long beak to the shinny stick held to the mouth by the defeated and shamed champion. Perhaps the bird is the curlew. [G.'s typescript also had this note, deleted: "Maybe this is dowitcher."—Ed.]

The Aswufum man whom Scabby Boy defeated had long been the champion against whom all were afraid to play. The girls had been offered as the prize for anyone who could beat him.

5. [For more on the game, see V.46, below.—Ed.]

1. [A reference to the Karok First Salmon ceremony, held only at Amaikiaram. The smoke of the First Salmon fire was the most sacred of all ceremonial smokes, Gifford says in Kroeber and Gifford, *World Renewal*, UC-AR 13:(no. 1):36.—Ed.]

c. Fox said, "I'm afraid of that person (rock) sitting there. I am afraid he might throw me in the water." Fox sat a long time singing (a) song with (the) above words. Then he thought, "I am going to run across." So he went up on (the) hill a little way to get (a) better running start. Then he ran down and got caught with a rope around his neck and fell in the water.

d. Another Fox on (the) opposite side sang his song, [and] ran for it. He got caught too.

e. The ixkareya who was doing (the) trapping went into (the) sweathouse to sweat himself. Every day he went to look at (the) trap. He trapped till he had enough for one apron. Then he trapped enough more to equip each of (the) dancers for [the] Deerskin Dance.[2]

f. The yasara (rich man) uses this medicine if he knows it. Kupanakanak.

V.36. FORMULA FOR PURIFICATION OF PEOPLE ATTENDING FUNERAL

MARY IKE (1940)

Madrone leaves are used in this formula.

•

a. Spider[1] was born "down across the ocean." You [Spider] thought you would go up the river. You growed [grew] up to handle the dead. Then you came up the river. Then you got on this side of [the] river and they invited you in. And you looked in and you said, "No." "You had better eat." You said, "No, my hands are dirty. I always handle the dead."

b. Then you went on. You went a long ways until you came to another house. They invited you in to eat and you said, "No, my hands are dirty. I always handle the dead. I'll come in if I [may] make the medicine. Then I'll eat deer meat." They said, "All right, go ahead and make the medicine."

2. [The Deerskin Dance was not made at Amaikiaram but at Inam, Katimin, and Panamenik. I find no specific mention of fox skins as dance regalia.—Ed.]

1. Spider = Kahaviswantiniha. Spider in general = Kah. The spider of the formula is a small species.

c. Then you looked all over and could not find it growing. Then you looked again and saw the madrone leaves. Then you started and made the medicine. Then you ate the deer meat. Then you said, "Let us all go out hunting."

d. They did not go very far. Then they killed a deer. They packed the deer home on their bare heads, and it gave them [a] headache. They went again, taking hats. Then they brought more deer meat home. They packed so many deer home that their head(s) became calloused from the tied deer legs across the forehead. The hats were just covered with blood.

e. Again they said, "Let us go out." They did not go far before they saw all kinds of tracks. They saw no deer, only the tracks. Day after day they went out and saw no deer, but only deer tracks. They looked all over and never saw anything.

f. "I guess the reason we have no luck is because I've been handling the dead," Spider said. "You had better make that medicine again," [they said]. Spider made it.

g. "Let's go out again and try our luck." They had not gone far when they saw deer. "My medicine is the best. From now on you call on me when you lose a relative. After five days you call me. Mention my name. Then you all take [a] drink[2] because my medicine is the best."

The formula is recited when the madrone leaves are collected. The leaves are held in the hand when spoken to. They are plucked from the tree—any madrone, any place. Mary remarks that the leaves alone are not medicine. They become medicine only after they have been "talked to," that is, after the formula has been recited.

V.37. ANOTHER FORMULA FOR PURIFYING PERSON WHO HAS BEEN TO FUNERAL

MARY IKE (1940)

Mary knows only this and the one told yesterday [V.36]. This medicine is made with fir boughs—two or three sprigs.

•

2. Anava (medicine) covers both the drink and the spoken words. One who makes medicine is an anekiava.

a. Where are you, hunter? You, hunter? You went out to hunt. You did not go very far and you got one deer. Before you got to the house you heard people crying, rolling around on the ground. Then you throw [threw] your load in the house. Then you went over there where they were rolling around. "What is the matter with you?" you asked the people who were rolling around. One answered, "We don't feel good." "What is wrong? What happened?" "We lost a newborn baby." You helped them to bury the baby without washing your hands. Your hands were bloody with deer blood. Then you went back in the house. You did not even wash your face. You started cooking the deer meat. Then you put it in your mouth. Your hands were all dirty from handling the dead.[1]

b. You went out hunting the next day early in the morning. You did not go very far when you got a deer. Then you came back to the house and saw them crying and rolling around. You did the same thing. You took the deer meat in the house and helped bury the woman who [had] died in childbirth. Then you went back in the house and did not put water on your face. You went to cooking again. Your hands were dirty. You had not even washed.

c. Next day you did the same thing. You left early in the morning and went hunting. You did not go very far and you saw five deer with horns. Then you had a big load. You took five on your back, every one of them. When you got back to the house you saw the same thing—people rolling around and crying. You went over there and asked, "Now, what has happened?" "This time we had trouble with the water. The water took one of us." You went back in the house and started cooking again. When you ate, your hands were dirty from handling the dead. You washed your hands with juice from the cooking deer meat.

d. Next day you went out again. You had not gone very far when you saw five. All had big horns. You came back packing the

1. [After a Yurok funeral, Kroeber says, "all who have looked upon the dead bathe. Those of the mourners who have touched the corpse rub themselves with the grapevine with which the body has been lowered into the grave and hand it from one to the other, thereby passing on the contamination to the last one. This man for five days shuns all intercourse with human kind . . . and finally returns to communion with people by undergoing a washing purification of which the cardinal feature is a long formula" (Handbook, p. 46).

Deer meat was esteemed and was served on special rectangular wooden platters. After the repast the hands were washed in huge wooden finger bowls (ibid., pp. 84 and 92). The hunter in this story has broken two taboos.—Ed.]

load, and you put the deer in the house. You saw the same thing, the people crying and rolling around there. "Now, what happened?" "One of us had pains (aratanva) and we lost one [who] (died)." Then you went over there and helped them with bloody hands, and then went back in the house. You did not even wash your face. You threw the meat on the coals. You ate without washing. You washed your hands with deer juice after handling the dead.

e. You went out again the next morning. You got back and saw the same thing, crying and rolling around. "What happened?" you asked. "We lost one with [by an] arrow." Then you went over there and helped them with bloody hands—deer blood. Then you went back in the house, never even washed, started cooking, throwing the deer meat on the coals. You put it in your mouth, ate it. Then you washed your hands with the deer juice.

f. Next morning you did the same thing, hunting deer (ixkareyas mukuninas, ixkareya's pets). You did not go very far when you got ixkareya's pets (deer). When you returned you heard them crying, rolling around. "What is the matter? What happened?" "We lost one. A tree fell on him." Then you went over and helped to handle the dead and bury him with bloody hands. Then you went back in the house; you did not even wash and started putting the meat on the coals and cooking. You washed your hands with the deer juice.

g. Next morning you did the same thing. This time you seen [saw] the tracks and you started following the tracks. You followed them a long way. The tracks got old and had spider webs over them. When you returned to the house, this time you did not get [have] any [deer].

h. Next day you thought you would go out and try your luck again. Then you seen [saw] tracks. Then you went all over the world. You never saw any more deer tracks. That night you did not sleep. You began to wonder why. "I guess what I've been doing [has caused the trouble]. I did not wash my hands or my face. I ate without washing after handling the dead." You thought you would make medicine. You looked around. You see [saw] your medicine. Then you broke off a piece of it. Then you made your medicine. Then you washed your hands with this medicine. Then you went out again.

i. You had not gone very far when you saw five. All had big horns. You [also] saw five little spotted ones. "From now on after this, they must think of me, because my medicine is the best. I feel good after I drink my medicine. I feel clean."

Throughout the deer are called ixkareyas mukuninas, ixkareya's pets. The formula is said by the anekiava while holding the fir sprigs; it is not repeated when the medicine is administered. A mouthful is drunk by each person [who has been to the funeral].

V.38. MEDICINE FOR PERSON WHO DREAMS ABOUT THE DEAD

MARY IKE (September 10, 1942)

Solidago occidentalis (ᶦᶜʰwuhanahiich) is the name of the plant that is used for this medicine. [It is a species of goldenrod.—Ed.]

•

a. She was (You were) an old woman, the mother of ten children. (She was an ixkareya named Puyahanakemich=poor dead person.) She was (You were) lying down ready to die. She (You) could not make her (your) own fire. She (You) had no water to drink. All of the children had run out and would not wait on her (you). They gave her (you) no food or drink or fire.

b. They all came home in the evening. She (You) would think to herself (yourself), "I hope you will all do the same as I am doing [be in similar circumstances] when you get old." Then she (you) would cover up her (your) head. The oldest one would say, "How is she, the one who raised us?"

c. The next day it was the same way. They would not even talk to her (you). They made her (you) no fire, gave her (you) no food or water before they all went out. She (You) said, "I hope you all do the same when you get old. You do not even pour water in my mouth. You do not treat me right. I am going (outside to rest/to die) without a drink of water. I am cold." She was (You were) feeling badly and was (were) wishing her (your) children bad luck. "I am going outside to rest now. I am going out without a drink of water, cold and hungry." She died.[1] "That's all right. I'll come back and stand

---

1. [Sentence later deleted. Gifford left this and the next four formulas in handwriting rather than in typescript.—Ed.]

outside of your door." She (You) jumped up then and fell by her (your) door. She (You) had her (your) blanket on. Then she (you) jumped up again and fell down again outside in her (your) yard. Then she (you) died.

d. Then she (you) went on. Then you reached the forks of the road where the old man was sitting. The old man said, "Take the righthand road. Do not go over on the other side." There was a bull pine standing right at the forks of the road. It had no branches or limbs.

e. You ran down the road. As you were going down, you heard many people shouting and shooting arrows because they were glad that they were to have one more person with them. You looked up the road and saw the place to which you were going, where you were going to live. Halfway before you got there, you heard all of your children hollering [shouting] behind you. They all fell down.

f. The oldest one said, "I think our mother must be standing outside of our door. She died without water or fire, and she was cold and hungry. She said she was going to stand outside our door."

g. The children who were lying down heard the boards outside rattle. They heard bones rattling, legs and arm bones, skull, etc. The oldest one said, "Let me make medicine." He (You) went and got an acorn soup bowl (assip). Then he (you) went out and made medicine. "Our mother said she wished we would suffer the same because we would give her nothing to drink." Then he (you) returned and poured the medicine into the mouths of his (your) brothers and sisters and bathed them with the water. Pretty soon they all got up. "If anyone knows my medicine, he can take a bath in it and drink it. You (He) may call on me. Our mother died without water, food, or fire. I am going to leave my medicine here in the middle of the world. People will use my medicine hereafter."

V.39. MEDICINE TO GIVE SELF-ASSURANCE

GEORGIA ORCUTT (August 27, 1942)[1]

Chamkāt (pennyroyal, *Monardella odoratissima ovata*) is lucky. One rubs

1. [G.'s manuscript has the additional information that this formula was recorded at 9:15 A.M. at Orleans, California.—Ed.]

the hands with it or carries it in the belt for good luck. But it is lucky only if one knows the medicine (bidish).[2] When this plant first comes up in the spring, Georgia breaks it up and rubs it on her hands. If she makes medicine with it she does not drink water for five days, as it would spoil the medicine. When Georgia rubs in on her hands she does so just because she likes the smell and hopes to be lucky. That is not actually making medicine. The bidish follows.

●

a. "I am going to live alongside the road,[3] so all the money that travels at night will touch me. I'll always be lucky. If people know my medicine, they will always be lucky." This is from an ixkareya.

b. Either [a] man or [a] woman, who feels that he [or she] is nobody at a gathering and from whom people run away because he [or she] seems to be a poor person, may acquire popularity by making medicine with this plant. Thus a person who had been shunned might, after making the medicine, be invited to join in [a] dance. Everybody looks at you when you approach because you no longer look like a poor person.

c. When making medicine with bidish dogiup (the medicine name for any plant),[4] the person must not drink water for five days and says, "I'll be like the sunset glow, which everybody looks at because it is nice and red." This was originated by a woman ixkareya who had been ignored by people as though she were a poor person. She felt badly about it, so she look[ed] around until she found her medicine. She said, "My medicine has already grown up." Then she talked to a piece of the plant which she held and spoke to.[5]

V.40. LOVE MEDICINE

GEORGIA ORCUTT

a. [An] ixkareya woman, Oxsistanenifapbi (in the middle between the oceans) lived at Panamenik. After a while she missed her

---

2. Bidish dogiup = to make medicine.
3. Impaak = road or trail.
4. [Cf. n. 2, above.—Ed.]
5. Chamkātumweish[?] used by Mary means "Chamkāt small leaves."

husband. She thought, "Everybody is nearly ready to go, so I'll have to remain behind alone." The ixkareya went away.

b. After a while the woman went to Baumwitaturipa (on the ridge leading to Orleans Mountain lookout). When she stood up to look around, she saw her husband in the ocean.[1] "So that is where my husband stays." She could see him paddling his canoe. After a while she said, "That is the place my husband has gone [to]." She picked up a stone pestle. She found the chamkaat[2] and talked to it: "My husband is leaving me. No matter how nice a place he goes to, he will want to come home." She threw the pestle at him. Then he knew his wife had spied him. He beached his boat. He returned to his wife, but she said, "Don't come back. You can stay away. The ixkareya have all left, but I shall remain here alone." She had tried the medicine plant and found that it worked.

c. Then she said, "If anyone knows my medicine, one [she can] get her husband to return." She threw the medicine toward Panamenik so it will [would] grow there. "If anyone calls my name, Panamenik ifapbi, and use[s] my medicine, she can always cause her husband to return if he has left her, no matter how nice a place he has gone to. I shall stay right here." She became a rock.[3]

V.41. Love Medicine with Sausikahas

GEORGIA ORCUTT (1942)

Sausikahas *(Mentha arvensis)*, another small pungent plant with flowers growing from the stem, is carried by men and women in the belt for good luck.[1] Georgia's mother taught her this medicine.

•

a. [An] ixkareya couple [were] living on [the] ridge above Happy Camp. Nuhidok was [the] name of [the] place [where] they

1. Now the ocean is no longer visible from the place where this woman saw her husband because the brush has grown up. At sunset the ocean glistened.
2. [See the previous formula, V.39.—Ed.]
3. [See also the "hate" medicines, V.10, above, and V.41, below.—Ed.]

1. [Chamkāt or pennyroyal, used in the two preceding formulas, is also a member of the mint family. Referring to the present plant, G. has the notation "See specimen."—Ed.]

lived. After a while she said to her husband, "Don't go high on the hill when you go hunting." Every day that man went hunting. He never go [went] further up because his wife [had] told him not to. The man was Wolf.

b. After a while the man thought, "I don't know why she tells me that. I'm going further up and find out." He looked over the ridge down to a fine placed called Asistutishram (Minaree's ranch). There he saw many girls digging Indian potatoes. He knelt down and shot his arrow down among the girls. They all stopped to look at it. One young girl went to touch the arrow, but the older ones warned her not to, since they did not know whence the arrow came.

c. After a while the girl picked it up. The man came down to get his arrow. He stayed there and married that girl. He left his wife.

d. After a while the [first] woman knew her husband had deserted her. She bore a baby boy after a bit. She stayed at her place and the boy grew up, but the man did not return. Where the man had knelt there is a hole in the ground.

e. The woman told her son, "If someone says, 'My, what a big boy!' do not answer him."

f. The boy came running in after a while and said to his mother, "Somebody is outside. He said to me, 'You are a big boy.' I did not answer him, but came in." From dahumka (= storage place back of [above] the pit in the house) the woman took an arus basket (close-woven burden basket for seed and manzanita berries).

g. After a while the man came in. He had been away many years. He said, "I have come back," but his wife did not answer him. The woman got up and went outside, taking her arus basket. She said to her son, "Let us go." The boy had a bow and arrows. He [They] went down by the river.

h. His mother got into a boat, taking the boy with her. They crossed the river and ascended a ridge. The boy shot at marks as he ascended the mountain. Far up the mountain the woman said, "Let's camp right here." There she made a fire.

i. The man crossed the river and followed them. When he came to their camp, the woman hid under the arus basket. After a while she turned into a rock. The man cried when he saw his wife turn into this rock. The man was Wolf. The boy turned into a rock too, which looks like a person holding a bow and arrow.

j. The man said, "Why do you do this?" he said to his wife. She said, "Because you left me. I do not want to see you again. This is my medicine," she said. "Husbands will always come back if the wife uses this, my medicine." But she did not want her husband. He was Wolf. He did not turn into a rock.

V.42. Deer Medicine Story (An Anava)

GEORGIA ORCUTT (September 15, 1942)

a. At Imtamvarakasurakam (high in the mountains on the east side of the river) lived a rich ixkareya man with his daughter. The ixkareya man was Imtamvarakasurakam ixkareya. He had all the deer hidden somewhere.

b. He said anyone who could kill a deer might have the hand of his daughter in marriage. He knew no one could kill deer. Men had tried and tried without avail. No one knew how they were going to kill deer.

c. Many young men [had] tried to kill (find) deer, staying all night in the sweathouse. Next day each one went deer hunting without success. They never even saw a deer. Everyone gave up.

d. Finally a poor young man tried. He was singing a song before he went into [the] sweathouse. When he woke up in [the] morning, the girl's father had disappeared from the sweathouse. It was he who [had] made it so no one could kill a deer.

e. The young man went outside. He knelt down and prayed. After a while he knew which way to go. After a while when he went on [the] hills he could not see because of foggy weather. Nevertheless he knew where to go to find [a] deer trail. The trail led him up over [a] ridge.

f. Again he knelt down ready to shoot. He fired two arrows and they went over the ridge. Then he crossed over the ridge and found two white deer that he had killed.[1] He packed them down to the sweathouse. The old man (girl's father) was surprised to see him coming in with two white deer. Then the poor young man married

1. [White deerskins were of course the most valuable of all (see Kroeber, Handbook, p. 26).—Ed.]

(was given) the girl, but he did not stay with her. He went away and he said, "If anyone knows my song he will be lucky in killing deer and getting married to any girl he wants."[2]

The hunter who uses this song must not drink water after singing, until he gets deer. The poor young man who had the song was Imtamvarakasura-kam afishi. He is mentioned by the hunter when singing.

V.43. MEDICINE FOR CURING ANY SICKNESS

SHAN DAVIS (1940)

[This formula came] from Astexewa ixkareya at Clear Creek.[1] Madrone leaves, fresh, are used. The formulist talks to the leaves, held in the right hand.

•

a. When raised first time there were ten ixkareya brothers. Nine of them is [were] going [hunting] all the time. Ixkareya mukuninas (Deer) were the nine, for they were looking for deer all the time. The tenth one (youngest) sat right here and just looked one way. He don't [didn't] go with his brothers. They were gone about ten days. The youngest one never ate.

b. The youngest one finally came down to see the ixkareya living at Katimin. He[2] wanted to be smart and kill everybody. That's why he was setting [sitting] there for.[3] This fellow was setting [sitting] right there; he don't [didn't] like these ixkareya at Katimin. He [the youngest brother] returned to Astexewa. He sat down again. The other nine were working all the time looking for deer, packing it in, and cooking it.

c. After later on again, they say [said] to [the] youngest, "Another bunch of ixkareya they raise [are living] down there, way down

2. [For a longer variant of this story, see V.31, above, also by Georgia Orcutt.—Ed.]

---

1. [See V.8, n. 2. For more discussion of Shan Davis's formulas, see Gifford's Introduction to the formulas, p. 262-263, above.—Ed.]
2. [The youngest brother?—Ed.]
3. [That's why he had been sitting at Astexewa?—Ed.]

at Asfam.[4] The youngest one stirred around again when he heard him (this).

d. After his nine brothers left, he went downriver. He wanted to see the ixkareya they had mentioned. When he got up at Asfam karoom (uphill above Asfam), he looked down. He was pretty close to [the] ocean. He saw where those ixkareya lived. He see [saw] the air coming out just like smoke standing up. He went down. He got there. He jumped right in the center. The blood flew as he bumped against them, both from them and himself. They were dancing around there quite a while, just playing. After a while he said, "Let's go." Then he took all that bunch [group] and came upriver. He and they killed all the ixkareya they came across. He killed them all.

e. Then he said, "I think that will be enough." Then he walked up [the] ridge with his partners. When he got on top of [the] ridge, he broke off madrone leaves. Then he threw it [them] behind him. A bunch of ixkareya were ahead of him. He threw it [the madrone leaves] back of him right into [the] middle of the world (isivtanenav-chip). When he threw it back, he thought, "This madrone leaf is mine. I throw it back in[to] this world so people can use my medicine." Then he went over the ridge, down the hill.

f. He went back to Asfamsu (Asfam creek). This youngest one went back with his bunch to Asfamsu.

V.44. MEDICINE FROM UPSTREAM IMMORTAL

SHAN DAVIS (1940)

[This formula came from] Karamkenistukam weixkareya (other-side-of-mountain-at-upstream-end-of-world ixkareya). This ixkareya said, "Anyone who knows me and knows my medicine, he can have it." Madrone leaves were also used with this formula.

•

a. When he left Karamkenistukam he came down the Klamath River, where lots of ixkareya had been raised. He looked around all the time, looking for trouble. Every place ixkareya were living he

4. "Pretty near mouth of river, but not right there, which is Sufip [Rekwoi]." [Asfam may be Yurok Kenek, home of many of the Yurok immortals.—Ed.]

went in there and looked around. He kept on going, way down below
Panamenik. Before he got there he stand [stood] on top of [the] huge
rock Timnukwaram (opposite Ike's place). From there he looked
around. Then he went on down.

b. He can't [couldn't] see nothing [anything] around, so he keep
[kept] on going. He went right down on top of Asfam karoom (see
ante).[1] He stand [stood] on top of that mountain Asfam karoom and
he see [saw] that camping ground below. He saw lots of ixkareya
there. They had come from every place. Then he went halfway
down the hill. Then he sees [saw] somebody coming; he is [this
person was] living right there. Then this fellow asked Karamkenistukam weixkareya where he was going. "Don't go through there,"
he warned. "There are bad people there. You'd better go around
another way."

c. Then Karamkenistukam replied, "No, I won't go around. I
want to see this [these] people here. I want to see it [them]. Which is
the oldest one in the bunch [group] camping there?" The fellow said,
"You can look down this way. See that highest house. That is where
the oldest one lives." "That's what I want to see," said Karamkenistukam. Then he went.

d. When he got there he saw that the door was open. He looked in
and walked right in. He see [saw] that [that] ixkareya was looking
into a large deep basket and feeling around for something. Then
Karamkenistukam spoke to him, "Hey, what [are] you doing? Are
you tearing up your things?" The man did not answer. So he spoke
to him again. Then the man looked up and looked at Karamkenistukam. When he did so, the sparks came flying out of the basket in
all directions.

e. Karamkenistukam then turned around and went outside. He
dropped on the ground on the hill. He fell down and died there. He
must have been laying [lying] there for about half a day. He don't
[didn't] know nothing [anything]. When he came to, he sat up. He
kept looking around. Then he thought, "I think I've done wrong. I
don't think I can go back to Karamkenistukam. I think I am going to
die." Then he crawled on his knees in trying to get away from there.

f. As far as he could go was on top of Asfam karoom. There he
died again and lay for about one day. Then he came to again. He was
lying around; he could not sit up. Then he thought, "I am ixkareya

1. [V.43*d*.—Ed.]

from Karamkenistukam. I am going to make medicine, I think."
When he looked around he could not see anything growing, no
brush, no trees, nothing. Then he fell back again and lay there.

   g. After a time he got up again. He saw a little madrone bush
growing over there. Then he started crawling over there. He picked
the leaves and chewed them and rubbed himself with them. After
that he was able to sit up, after he got through swallowing that brush.
And after a while he stand [stood] right up. Then he walked over and
picked some more of that [those] madrone leaves. Then he turned
around and come back up this way.[2]

   h. He came running to the center of this world. Then he thought,
"I am ixkareya too. I am going back to Karamkenistukam." He
arrived there. Then he threw the madrone brush he had back into
[the] center of [the] world (Katimin). Then he thought, "This
medicine, my medicine, is for yasara (Indians).[3] They will use [it] if
they know it and know my medicine. If [a] yasara is raised good
[well] he will know me. If he is not raised good [well] he will not
know me and will not use my medicine."

The anekiava heats the medicine water a little with a hot stone and has the
sick person drink it. Then the anekiava picks a leaf out of the basket and
taps the patient on the head and elsewhere, redipping as necessary to
sprinkle the patient lightly all over. Then he puts the medicine leaves in a
large basket of water and heats it so as to steam the patient, who is covered
with a blanket of deerhide with the hair left on.[4]

V.45. MEDICINE FROM MT. OFFIELD IMMORTAL

SHAN DAVIS (1940)

When a fir sprig is used for medicine, it is taken from the top of a small
sapling. From madrone [V.43 and V.44] the sprig of leaves may be taken
from any part of the tree.

   A fir sprig is used for this medicine, [which comes from] Satimu

2. [From Yurok to Karok country.—Ed.]
3. [For other translations of yasara, see V.15*i* and V.35*f*—Ed.]
4. The blanket does not get stiff from the moisture of the steam because it has
been made soft with deer brains. It is put over the patient hair side out. The sick
person sits with the basket of medicine between his legs when being steamed.

weixkareya (Mt. Offield ixkareya). Satimu is the saddle between the two peaks of Mt. Offield.[1]

•

a. Satimu weixkareya had a wife. They had ten sons. Where he was sitting he was sitting back to back to his wife. They don't [didn't] like each other. When she gave her husband something she reached it around behind her. They did not speak.

b. Every morning the ten boys jumped into the river to swim. They stirred up the mud so [that] the river was muddy below.

c. Later on, they lost one boy. He died. Someone told Satimu weixkareya, who was in [the] sweathouse. "Your son is dying," the person said as he looked into [the] sweathouse.

d. After the mourning was over, the old couple sat back to back again.

e. When morning came, the boys ran down to the river and swam again, stirring up the mud. After later on, somebody told Satimu weixkareya, "Your son has dropped down again." Then the old man came out of the sweathouse and went to the dwelling house to see this second son who was stricken. Then the old man ran out and plucked a fir sprig from [the] top of [a] tree. He thought, "The best thing I can do is to make medicine." Then he made medicine in a basket cup with the sprig and gave his son a drink. Then he sprinkled him, using the fir sprig to dip the water and touch him with.

f. After a while the boy got all right, (and) the old man thought,

1. [G.'s typescript contained this handwritten note: "In Shan Davis's formula, a reference to Mt. Offield refers to Satimu. This differs from Mary Ike's attributions of names. However, Mary failed to mention Matimui peak. In Katimin pikiawish account she calls main peak Ixkareya tuiship instead of applying this to whole mountain and calling the individual peaks Matimui and Satimui." The Katimin pikiawish account refers to Kroeber and Gifford, World Renewal, UC-AR 13:(no. 1):19–34, in which G. has recorded both Mary Ike's and Shan Davis's information about the Katimin ceremonies. However, on p. 21 of that work Gifford says, "Mary Ike gave the following pertinent terms: . . . ixkareya tuiship, Mt. Offield; Matimui, higher peak; Satimui, lower peak. . . . "

G.'s typescript has this additional information on mountains, from Georgia Orcutt, recorded in 1940: "Summit of Mt. Offield and of mountain back of Orleans are both called ui. Summit of Shelton Butte is also called ui. Ui means high place. Shamakauui=Shelton Butte. Shaman is a flat place on Slate Creek (shaman=deer lick; kau = visible from). The whole name seems to mean that the deer lick on the west side is visible from Shelton Butte summit (ui) on the east side of the Klamath."—Ed.]

"Yasara, if he knows my medicine, will do the same way. Yasara must not live as I [have] lived with my wife, back to back. If he does that, everybody will do the same way like [as] I used to do. They must not do it. Yasara who knows my medicine will be OK, [will] be fine."

Living back to back with his wife and not speaking was what caused the son's death. People who do that will not have good luck.

V.46. Yurok Medicine Formula for "Stick" Game After Brush Dance or Deerskin Dance

MAMIE OFFIELD (1939)

This was told to Mamie's mother by [the mother's] sister's husband, a Yurok. Pakasnakanchiram was his name in Karok. In part the name means "where they stoop down." He was named for the place he came from: person (pa) from Kasnakanchiram. Mamie's mother taught the formula to her, saying she might have sons someday who could use it.

This shinny game was played with double balls connected with cord, which were struck with a stick. Imsatwa is the Karok name of the game. At Amaikiara was a flat where this game was played, down near the river. There was a little pond there and it was part of the course, so that players often wrestled in the water and one might be shoved under. Iptokpishwa ("he wins sometimes"), called Captain by the whites, was a noted player in his youth. He was Mamie's mother's mother's sister's husband. In old age, he tossed about one night as he dreamed. His wife wanted to know what made him move in his sleep. He told her he was dreaming he was playing the stick game on the Amaikiara course.

•

The medicine formula follows.

a. There were ten ixkareya at Iknumen (on mountains back of Weitspus) where they have the Jumping Dance. They are [were] called Iknumen ixkareya. They were ten brothers. The youngest was small and scabby. He sat there near the steps in the living house with his dog.[1] His eyes were nearly closed, and his hands were always clenched.

1. People who wished to be out of the way and unnoticed sat there.

b. The ixkareya said they were going to have a stick (shinny) game between [the] upstream end of [the] world and [the] downstream end of [the] world. The oldest brother went to play for the downstream end of [the] world. The young boy could hear the "tassels" (double ball) hit the upper end of the world and heard the hollering. Then he thought his brother was licked. When he heard them hit the lower end of the world, he knew his brother was licked.

c. Each brother then went in descending order of age, and each was worsted. Then the unsightly brother said to his sister, "Make me an arus wood-carrying basket (a tight-woven basket bigger than an atiki)." After she had finished it, he said to her, "I guess my brothers are licked. I'll go and try it." He told his sister, "Let's go." She went with him to the river. He dived into the river. When he came out, he told his sister to cover him with the arus basket. She did. Later when she uncovered him, he was a handsome young man whose hair ended in red woodpecker scalp feathers. Dentalia (ishpuk) were all over him. He opened his hands and revealed the double shinny balls, one in each hand, which had been there since his birth.

d. His dog jumped in [the] river. When he came out they put the basket over him. On uncovering him, they saw that he had red woodpecker scalp feathers on the ends of his hair.

e. He [youngest brother] and his dog went to the middle of the world. He arrived there and started to play by laying his "tassels" down. He swung his stick, and at once the pair of tassels struck at the upper end of the world. The dog retrieved it and laid it down, and he drove it to the lower end of the world.

f. Then [the] people shouted, "Iknumen ixkareya won the game, Iknumen ixkareya numen mistap! (Iknumen ixkareya, the smallest one!)" "He who knows about me will do the same."[2]

V.47. Story About Wuppam (Red Cap)

MARY IKE (1940)

This is classed as a bigishtu'u (confession) and is used as an anava (formula)

2. Karok women *for the first time* played double-ball shinny when the "crazy dance" (Ghost Dance) was here. The Shasta women played it regularly. [On the

to cure boils. Water is sprayed from the mouth of the anekiava onto the patient.[1]

•

a. There was a young ixkareya (immortal) girl at Wuppam. There was one old man there, the girl's mother's father. The old man told the girl to go out early in the morning and look around. The girl had a little basket cup of pine root weft. He said to her, "If you find a glowworm, pick it up and put it in this cup with some earth."

b. She found a glowworm and put it in the cup as her grandfather had directed. He told her to bring it in the house. He told her to put it in a hole to be dug in the ground of the house platform.

"What is my pet going to eat?" the girl asked. The old man said, "Every day you go down to the river and get a little sand and give it to him." She gave the glowworm water in a half of a wooden feather box (i.e., the lower part of it).[2]

c. The old man went fishing and caught trout for the glowworm. The glowworm kept growing bigger.

d. The old man told the girl, "When you begin to menstruate for (the) first time, don't come near the house." The glowworm was getting big and just ate everything, especially trout.

e. There was a Brush Dance at Chamikninich (village), and the girl wanted to go.[3]

f. The girl regularly made acorn meal, soaking it down by the

---

ephemeral influence of the Ghost Dance on the northwest California Indians of the 1870's, see Kroeber, Handbook, pp. 62–63.—Ed.]

1. [The present story, concerning the immortals and used as a formula, differs from the six stories of confessions made by Karok of historic times, which G. published in his article, Karok Confessions, in Miscellanea Paul Rivet (1958). In those accounts a parent acknowledged an earlier misdeed to try to save the life of his ailing newborn child.—Ed.]

2. [G.'s typescript has a deleted note reading "Wooden feather box with cover is called pahïch." The box referred to was probably a tapering cylinder, hollowed out and with a lashed-on lid, used to hold obsidians and other dance regalia such as feathers. See Kroeber, Handbook, p. 92 and pl. 15.—Ed.]

3. [Ellipsis. The old man forbade her to go. See paragraph *j*, below. Another deleted note in G.'s typescript reads: "There was a village at Chamikninich formerly, not merely a dance place only." Chamikninich is identified as a place on the east side of the river near Orleans (Panamenik) in G.'s II.14*j*, above, and is also mentioned in Kroeber's F6*e*.—Ed.]

river. Then she sold it to people passing in boats. That pet of hers was bringing her luck. Then she picked hazelnuts and sold them. She sold everything she gathered. She got woodpecker scalps for pay.

g. The old man told her not to drink water when she went up the hill, lest it spoil her luck for accumulating money. [The] old man (was) fishing on the other side of the river from Wuppam, and he packed it (his fish) up the hill (to her). People bought the fish from her.

h. They were having a dance at Amaikiaram. She wanted to go. He told her not [to] go because she would get hungry.

i. Her mother would feed the pet (kininas) when the girl had her menses and could not come near the house.

j. She [the girl] would look at her pet and begin to get scared [be frightened] because it was getting so big. Her folks [family] told her not to pay attention to any man. Her mother was making [made] an acorn storage basket (sipnūkis). The girl put her money in this basket that she obtained from sales of things.

k. The girl said about the Amaikiaram Jumping Dance, "I am going to go." She went up for one day and (came) right back again. Whatever she had she sell (sold) it; people begged to buy it.

l. While she was lying down one night she heard a noise. Then she went outside. At the door she stumbled [over] something [that] was lying there. In the morning she went to the sweathouse and told the old man she was scared [afraid] of (her) pet. It was just getting big. He was so big he filled the whole house platform all around inside.

m. The old man told her to dig a big hole back on a flat [prairie, and] then go to [the] river and get some sand and put it in the hole. She did. Then they opened the back end of the house and put the glowworm in an atiki (tight pack basket). Then she took it on her back and put the pet in the hole. Every day she would go up there and look at him. He would drink up the water quickly, [for] he was getting so big.

n. There was to be a pikiawish[4] at Panamenik, and she wanted to go. "If any man talks to you, don't pay any attention to him," counseled the old man. After she came back from Panamenik, she said she was going to get married, as one man wanted to marry her.

4. [See I.15, n. 1, above.—Ed.]

After she came back from Panamenik she went up to the flat to look at her pet.

o. Then she wanted to go to the irahiv[5] at Katimin. The old man warned her not to go with any man. She returned home from Katimin, where she had stayed only one night. She went to see her pet. She came running home, crying, "My pet is gone!" He had taken all the sand; not even (one grain of) sand (was) left. "We told you not to talk to a man."

p. The man came to the house and lived with her. After a time she had a baby. The baby was full of (had) boils all over its arms. Finally it died.

q. Then she had another baby. Then she confessed, "The reason (my) first baby died is perhaps because I had a pet—Absunkarax."[6] The second baby, a boy, lived.

5. [The irahiv was a term applied to the "climactic two days and night of the world renewal ceremonies at Panamenik, Katimin, and Inam" but not to Amaikiaram (Kroeber and Gifford, World Renewal, UC-AR 13:[no. 1]:8).—Ed.]

6. [The mythical big snake or water monster (III.37*d* and V.33*e*, above). —Ed.]

BIBLIOGRAPHY

ABBREVIATIONS USED IN BIBLIOGRAPHY AND FOOTNOTES

UC-AR   University of California Publications in
Anthropological Records

UC-PAAE   University of California Publications in
American Archaeology

[The works listed here are of two types: those cited directly in the texts, and other studies of the northwestern California Indians by Kroeber, Gifford, and their colleagues, especially those published in UC-PAAE and UC-AR. Complete volumes only of UC-PAAE may be ordered from Kraus Reprint Corporation, 16 E. 46th Street, New York 10017. At press time, the UC-AR volumes listed here were out of print, but current information may be obtained from the Sales Office of the University of California Press, Berkeley 94720.

For help in compiling this list I am indebted to Robert F. Heizer, emeritus professor of the Department of Anthropology, University of California, Berkeley.—Ed.]

•

Bright, W. O.

1954.   The Travels of Coyote: A Karok Myth. Kroeber Anthropological Society Papers, No. 11, pp. 1–16.

1957.   The Karok Language. University of California Publications in Linguistics 13:1–468.

1978.   Karok. *In* Handbook of North American Indians, Vol. 8, California, ed. Robert F. Heizer. Washington, D. C.: Smithsonian Institution, pp. 180–189.

Cook, S. F.

1955.   The Aboriginal Population of the North Coast of California. UC-AR 16:(no. 3):81–130, esp. 81–101.

332   *Bibliography*

Curtis, E. S.
1924.   The North American Indian, Vol. 13, ed. F. W. Hodge. Re-
               printed 1970 by Johnson Reprint Corp., New York.

De Angulo, Jaime, and L. S. Freeland
1931.   Karok Texts. International Journal of American Linguistics.
               6:(nos. 3-4):194–226.

Driver, H. E.
1939.   Culture Element Distributions: X. Northwest California.
               UC-AR 1:(no. 6):297–433.

Drucker, P.
1936.   A Karuk World-Renewal Ceremony at Panaminik. UC-PAAE
               35:(no. 3):23–28.
1937.   The Tolowa and Their Southwest Oregon Kin. UC-PAAE
               36:(no. 4):221–300.

Erikson, E. H.
1943.   Observations on the Yurok: Childhood and World Image.
               UC-PAAE 35:(no. 10):257–302.

Foster, G. M.
1960.   Edward Winslow Gifford, 1887-1959. American An-
               thropologist 62:(no. 2):327–329.

Gayton, A. H.
1935.   Areal Affiliations of California Folktales. American An-
               thropologist 37:(no. 4):582–599.

Gibbs, G.
1853.   Journal of the Expedition of Colonel Redick McKee, United
               States Indian Agent, Through North-Western California. Per-
               formed in the Summer and Fall of 1851. *In* H. R. Schoolcraft,
               Historical and Statistical Information Respecting the History,
               Condition and Prospects of the Indian Tribes of the United
               States. Philadelphia. Vol. 3, pp. 99–177. Photoreproduction,
               with annotations by R. F. Heizer, published 1972 by Ar-
               chaeological Research Facility, Department of Anthropology,
               University of California, Berkeley.
1973.   Observations on the Indians of the Klamath River and Hum-
               boldt Bay [in 1852]. Archaeological Research Facility, De-
               partment of Anthropology, University of California, Berkeley.

Gifford, E. W.
1922.   Karok. *In* Californian Kinship Terminologies. UC-PAAE
               18:(no. 1):1–285.
1926.   Californian Anthropometry. UC-PAAE 22:(no. 2):217–390.
1958.   Karok Confessions. *In* Miscellanea Paul Rivet Octogenario
               Dicata. XXXI Congreso Internacional de Americanistas,
               Universidad Nacional Autonoma de Mexico, Mexico City.
               Vol. I, pp. 245–55.

Goddard, P. E.
1903.   Life and Culture of the Hupa. UC-PAAE 1:(no. 1):1–88.
1904.   Hupa Texts. UC-PAAE 1:(no. 2):89–368.

Goldschmidt, W. R.
1951.   Ethics and the Structure of Society. American Anthropologist 53:(no. 4):506–524.

Harrington, J. P.
1930.   Karuk Texts. International Journal of American Linguistics 6:121–161.
1932a.   Karuk Indian Myths. Bureau of American Ethnology, Smithsonian Institution, Bulletin 107. US. Government Printing Office. 34 pp.
1932b.   Tobacco Among the Karuk Indians of California. Bureau of American Ethnology, Smithsonian Institution, Bulletin 94. U.S. Government Printing Office. 284 pp.

Heizer, R. F., and J. E. Mills.
1952.   The Four Ages of Tsurai: A Documentary History of the Indian Village on Trinidad Bay. Berkeley and Los Angeles: University of California Press. 218 pp.

Kelly, I. T.
1930.   The Carver's Art of the Indians of Northwestern California. UC-PAAE 24:(no. 7):343–360.

Klimek, S.
1935.   Culture Element Distributions: I. The Structure of California Indian Culture. UC-PAAE 37:(no. 1):1–70.

Kroeber, A. L.
1904.   Types of Indian Culture in California. UC-PAAE 2:(no. 3):81–103.
1905.   Basket Designs of the Indians of Northwestern California. UC-PAAE 2:(no. 4):105–164.
1907.   The Religion of the Indians of California. UC-PAAE 4:(no. 6):319–356.
1911.   The Languages of the Coast of California North of San Francisco. UC-PAAE 9:(no. 3):273–435, esp. 427–435.
1920.   California Culture Provinces. UC-PAAE 17:(no. 2):151–169.
1922.   Elements of Culture in Native California. UC-PAAE 13:(no. 8):259–328.
1923.   The History of Native Culture in California. UC-PAAE 20:125–142.
1925.   Handbook of the Indians of California. Bureau of American Ethnology, Smithsonian Institution, Bulletin 78:1–995, esp. 1–141. Reprinted 1972 by Scholarly Press, St. Clair Shores, Mich. Paperback ed. 1976 by Dover Publications, New York.
1926.   Law of the Yurok Indians. Proceedings of the 22nd International Congress of Americanists, Rome. Vol. 2, pp. 511–516.

1934.   Yurok and Neighboring Kin Term Systems. UC-PAAE
              35:(no. 2):15–22.
1936.   Karok Towns. UC-PAAE 35:(no. 4):29–38.
1937.   Culture Element Distributions: III. Area and Climax. UC-
              PAAE 37:(no. 3):101–115.
1939.   Cultural and Natural Areas of Native North America. UC-
              PAAE 38:1–242, esp. 1–31.
1945.   A Yurok War Reminiscence: The Use of Autobiographical
              Evidence. Southwestern Journal of Anthropology 1:(no.
              3):318–332.
1946.   A Karok Orpheus Myth. Journal of American Folklore
              59:13–19.
1957.   Ethnographic Interpretations, 1–6. UC-PAAE 47:(no.
              2):191–234, esp. 205–206.
1959.   Ethnographic Interpretations, 7–11. UC-PAAE 47:(no.
              3):235–309, esp. 235–240.
1960.   Yurok Speech Usages. *In* Culture in History: Essays in Honor
              of Paul Radin, ed. S. Diamond. New York: Columbia Univer-
              sity Press, pp. 993–999.
1976.   Yurok Myths. Berkeley and Los Angeles: University of
              California Press. 488 pp.

Kroeber, A. L., and S. A. Barrett.
1960.   Fishing Among the Indians of Northwestern California.
              UC-AR 21:(no. 1):1–210.

Kroeber, A. L., and E. W. Gifford.
1949.   World Renewal: A Cult System of Native Northwest Califor-
              nia. UC-AR 13:(no. 1):1–155.

Kroeber, T.
1960.   Alfred Kroeber: A Personal Configuration. Berkeley and Los
              Angeles: University of California Press.

Murdock, G. P., and T. J. O'Leary.
1975.   Ethnographic Bibliography of North America. New Haven:
              Human Relations Area Files Press. Vol. 3, pp. 82–84.

O'Neale, L. M.
1932.   Yurok-Karok Basket Weavers. UC-PAAE 32:(no. 1):1–184.

Pope, Saxton T.
1923.   A Study of Bows and Arrows. UC-PAAE 13:(no. 9):329–446.
              Reprinted 1974 by University of California Press, Berkeley and
              Los Angeles, with a Foreword by R. F. Heizer.

Posinsky, S. H.
1956.   Yurok Shell Money and "Pains": A Freudian Interpretation.
              Psychiatric Quarterly 30:598–632.
1957.   The Problem of Yurok Anality. American Imago 14:3–31.

Powers, S.
1877.   Tribes of California. Contributions to North American
                     Ethnology 3:44–64, 460–473. Reprinted 1976 by University of
                     California Press, Berkeley and Los Angeles, with an Introduc-
                     tion by R. F. Heizer.

Robins, R. H.
1958.   The Yurok Language: Grammar, Texts, Lexicon. University
                     of California Publications in Linguistics 15:1–300.

Sapir, E.
1928.   Yurok Tales. Journal of American Folklore 41:253–261.

Schenck, M., and E. W. Gifford.
1952.   Karok Ethnobotany. UC-AR 13:(no. 6):377–392.

Siskiyou County Museum, Yreka, California.
1971.   Mary Ike. Siskiyou Pioneer 4:(no. 4):31.

Spott, Robert, and A. L. Kroeber.
1942.   Yurok Narratives. UC-PAAE 35:(no. 9):143–256.

Steward, J. H.
1961.   Alfred Louis Kroeber, 1876-1960. American Anthropologist
                     63:(no. 5):1038–1060.

Storer, T. I., and R. L. Usinger.
1963.   Sierra Nevada Natural History. Berkeley and Los Angeles:
                     University of California Press.

Thompson L.
1916.   To the American Indian. Eureka, California.

Thompson, S.
1955.   Motif-Index of Folk Literature. Bloomington, Indiana: In-
                     diana University Press.

Waterman, T. T.
1920.   Yurok Geography. UC-PAAE 16:(no. 5):177–315.
1923.   Yurok Affixes. UC-PAAE 20:369–386.

Waterman, T. T., and A. L. Kroeber.
1934.   Yurok Marriages. UC-PAAE 35:(no. 1):1–14.
1938.   The Kepel Fish Dam. UC-PAAE 35:(no. 6):49–80.

INDEX

OF PARALLEL PLOT ELEMENTS IN FIVE COLLECTIONS OF KAROK AND YUROK MYTHS

GRACE BUZALJKO

[This index has been arranged in columns for greater readability. The first two columns index the myths in the present volume. The third column indexes Kroeber's Yurok Myths, published in 1976; the fourth column, J. P. Harrington's Karok collections of 1930 and 1932a; and the last column, William Bright's 1957 Karok collection.

Major themes of Californian folklore, as given in A. H. Gayton, Areal Affiliations of California Folktales, American Anthropologist 37:(no. 4): 582–599, have been incorporated into the index, with cross-references to my own more detailed entries where necessary.

Parentheses around an entry indicate a peripheral or related episode.

*The abbreviation YN refers to a numbered myth in Spott and Kroeber, Yurok Narratives, UC–PAAE 35:(no. 9):143–256.—Ed.]

•

Element	Kroeber, Karok Myths	Gifford, Karok Myths and Formulas	Kroeber, Yurok Myths	Harrington, Karuk Texts, Myths (1930, 1932a)	Bright, Karok Language 1957
Blood money instituted *see* Payments: origin of, for killings					
Bluejay *see* Jay					
Boat(s): mice bore holes in *see* Mice					
origin of			(A20*h*) C1*a* V1*g* X9		
tiny, stretched to normal size			A4*g*		
See also Bulb baby; Formulas: death purification; and Kewetspekw entries					
Bones of victims pounded *see* Monster-ridding cycle: blind women					
Bow, miniature. *See also* Owl, modest	F8		A16x *t* (P5) X1*e*		
Bows and arrows: origin of	A5*a* G3*e*	II.3*a–b* III.38*k*	A4*a–f*		
Breakers: Falcon fights angry			C3*b–c*		
Brush house turns to stone *see* Monster-ridding cycle: blind women					
Bulb baby dug from ground		1.3 (V.1*a–e*) (V.40)	A7 (F1*q*) F6 J8 Q3*b–c* (S3*f*) DD2		(50)
Buttocks, sharp: immortal (Pulekukwerek) cuts rock with			F1*i–j* P6*e*		
Buzzard: guides girl to land of dead					58
hair of; burnt off head by hooknosed salmon				1930:1b	
Cannibalism theme. *See also* Monster-ridding cycle: blind women	A8 E1	I.9	A23		
Childbirth medicine instituted *see* Across-Ocean-Widower: seduces girl					

Element	Kroeber, Karok Myths	Gifford, Karok Myths and Formulas	Kroeber, Yurok Myths	Harrington, Karuk Texts, Myths (1930, 1932a)	Bright, Karok Language 1957
Child-stealing ogre		I.14			
Confession for breaking taboo		V.47	U2		
Contest: beauty, among animals		III.10 III.29			
for bride *see* Woman: promised as bride of successful hunter					
in marksmanship *see* Owl: modest					
Cormorant/Shag: helps girls avoid missteps. *See also* Old man instructs husband-hunting girls			A12*j–k* B9*h*		
helps man avoid death at Pulekuk			B9*i*		
Corpse transport taboos *see* Formulas: death purification					
Courage, acquisition of	(C3*b–c*) F8		A13*b–h* G6 N1 T3 T5		
Coyote: creates sons from sticks, sends them to war		II.25		(1930:10) (from urine)	
dances with stars	A9	(II.50) II.51	I5 P7	(1930:4) (Turtle)	9.21–42 (22) (Turtle)
and daughter *see* Incest					
drowns, drifts downstream as log, attracts girls	(D2) F11*k–l*	II.14*c* II.15*g* 11.16*c–e*	(E2) G3 (J7)	(1930:3, 5)	1.76–118 3.77–121 4.106–117 5.55–75
eats sweathouse head-rests	F11*m*	II.14*e* 11.15*h* (11.22*b*)	J5*c*		(2.21–30) (2A.7–11) 3.122–140 4.118–143 5.110–127
fails as marksman	A6 B3*e–f* F5*f*	II.2*b, d* II.29	A8*c* C3*i* G2*a* K3 (Q1)		4.6–26 5.3–16 8.14–29
at first fearful, later succeeds as monster-killer	A4*c–d* H5*b*	II.33*a–f* (II.39) II.40 II.41 II.47	Q1*g–j*		

Element	Kroeber, Karok Myths	Gifford, Karok Myths and Formulas	Kroeber, Yurok Myths	Harrington, Karuk Texts, Myths (1930, 1932a)	Bright, Karok Language 1957
Coyote (*continued*)					
steals salmon for mankind. *See* Salmon: origin of					
steals water/juice from sweating man/Lizard, suffers thirst	D2 F11*f–k*	II.14*d* II.15*a–f*	E2 J7	1930:3	(1.1–81) (3.12–90) 4.50–105 5.32–60
strikes Sun, blaming him for children's death		(II.26*a–c, e*)	A14*e–h* (G3) J5*a–d* (DD13)		12
is swallowed by whale		II.36			
as swift runner			A12*b–e, n–v* A18		
trades harpoon for Heron's wife		II.34			
trades his song for another's		II.50 II.51			7 9.1–17
transported home by Ducks	F11*n–p*	II.14*e–j* II.15*i–n*			2 2A 3.122–177 4.132–178 5.110–145
travels upstream, seeking money		(I.7) II.17 II.18			1.1–81 3.1–90 4.1–105 5.1–60 (7)
tricks his intended executioners/pursuers		II.5*f–h* II.6 II.27			5.76–109
Upriver, secures water for mankind. *See also* Water: origin of			A18 T8		
as voyeur falls through living house roof				1930:12	
Crane			A8*d*		
leg-bridge drowns evil old woman			A9 K3*b–c* (Q2*c–d*) YN 29*		(18.52–74) 32.68–99
wears dance necklaces					42
Creation myths *see* Humans: origin of; River; Sky: woven by Sky Possessor; Water: origin of					
Cricket *see* Jerusalem cricket					

Element	Kroeber, Karok Myths	Gifford, Karok Myths and Formulas	Kroeber, Yurok Myths	Harrington, Karuk Texts, Myths (1930, 1932a)	Bright, Karok Language 1957
Crow: demands finery, is blackened with coals. *See also* Across-Ocean Widower: trapped sings in sacred sweathouse			A15x z A15y b–c E1b–c J1 S2	1930:11	
Dances; origin of. *See also* Coyote: dances with stars.	G4i–l		A1 A2a–h A3a–c, e–f A16x o–p A23l B1c B6i B12 C4c D2x, y D6x, y D7 T4 YN35*		
Dead: man/woman goes to underworld to bring lover back from	†	I.15 I.16	S3 (X2)	1932a:12	58
Death: man feigns *see* Sky Condor					
origin of. *See also* Formulas: death purification; Jerusalem cricket; Mole	C2l				
temporarily halted		I.15 I.16	X1b–c, g X8a Z3		
Deer: and dog *see* Dog: supplies/tracks deer invisible in Fog, *see* Fog: deer					
Deer brush (covert): young man establishes			B13 (K1b)		
Deer girl, taken to sky, is restored to earth		II.53i, o–v II.54f, h–p II.55		1930:2	(8) 33
Dentalium/Dentalia: caught on fishing line dress covered with, brought up from ocean floor	G4a–b, x	(V.25)	T1 D2x e		

†See also Kroeber, A Karok Orpheus Myth, Journal of American Folklore 59:13–19, with accounts by Informants A and F.

Element	Kroeber, Karok Myths	Gifford, Karok Myths and Formulas	Kroeber, Yurok Myths	Harrington, Karuk Texts, Myths (1930, 1932a)	Bright, Karok Language 1957
Dentalium (*continued*)					
eats flesh from young man, gives him power			T3*f–h*		
eats the sky			(J4)		
			Y1		
			Z5		
institutes basketry, cradles, clothing, money, etc.	(D8) G4		S5		
multiplies in hero's trunk *see* Courage, acquisition of					
and salmon caught with human bait			D6x *d–e, m* D6y *m*		
salvaged for mankind *see* Across-Ocean-Widower: pursues son					
secured by sweathouse practices/restraint. *See also* Formulas: money or love	G4*n, q*	I.19	A3 T1 T7 DD12		
travels and institutes money *See also* Coyote: steals dentalium; travels upstream, seeking money	F1 G4*a–g, w*		A16x *c* B14 D5x, y S5 T1 (DD12) YN36*		
Departure of the immortals		(I.4*e*) I.5 V.40*a*	A4*i* A14*o* A15x *p–aa* (A23*a*) B6 B10 D5x, y E1*h* F4*g–h* F5 H1*c–f* I2*a–b* J2*e* K2*b* K3 T3 V1*h* X1 X7 (X15) Y1 Z7 (CC2) (DD11)		

Element	Kroeber, Karok Myths	Gifford, Karok Myths and Formulas	Kroeber, Yurok Myths	Harrington, Karuk Texts, Myths (1930, 1932a)	Bright, Karok Language 1957
rocks; Jay: as greedy stepmother; Jealous wife			F1 F2 J3 Q1 T6 AA1*f–k*		
Duck Hawk *see* Falcon					
Ducks *see* Coyote: transported home by Ducks					
Dug-from-Ground *see* Bulb baby					
Earrings, gigantic, worn by evil one *see* Monster-ridding cycle: evil one with gigantic earrings/hooks					
Earthquake and Thunder shake the earth. *See also* Shinny game			B5 F1*o* J4 BB3 Z5		44 (Lightning)
Eel(s): formed from Across-Ocean-Widower's penis		I.4			41
loses bones to Sucker					33
Elk/deer: file of ten shot	A6*b* B3*a* F5*d–e*		I1		
given horns			X7*b*		
Envy expressed by one animal for another's looks		III.10 III.29			
Evil father-in-law *see* Across-Ocean-Widower: blinds grandson *and* sends son to fetch birds; Weasel entries					
Evil old woman *see* Crane leg-bridge					
Falcon: fights angry Breakers			C3*b–c*		
flies through bodies of others, killing them			C3*a*, (*g*)		
makes dam/fishing places. *See also* Bear: as jealous wife	E2 G1*a*		C3*d–e*		
Feather stands erect, leans over, as portent of distant owner's state	A10	III.38*a, aa*			20.6–65

Element	Kroeber, Karok Myths	Gifford, Karok Myths and Formulas	Kroeber, Yurok Myths	Harrington, Karuk Texts, Myths (1930, 1932a)	Bright, Karok Language 1957
Feces: eaten by Snake	B2*b*				14
impregnates woman	D7				
Fire: extinguished by rain					45
keepers of: Ants as			C1*o*		
			F1*l*		
Rattlesnakes as			C1*o*		
			F1*l*		
			J3*c–d*		
Squirrel as, in flood	F7	V.29			
woman/children as				1932a:4	10.20–37
Yellow Jackets as	A7		C1*o*		
			F1*l*		
origin of. *See also* Theft		III.38*c–e*	(A18*n*)		
of fire/light			P2		
Fishing: origin of. *See also*			A4		
Salmon: origin of			A15x *r–v*		
			(A16x *m*)		
			A20*g–h*		
			A21*a–f, l*		
			A22*f–i*		
			C2x *c–d*		
			(C3)		
			C4*a*		
			D4		
			R1		
			X14x, y		
Flood: hero rides out, in	F6*a–b*	I.3*c–e*	A14*o–p*		(56)
box/boat. *See also* Fire:		V.29	(F2*k–l*)		
keepers of; Mankind			X13		
sprung from dogs					
results from anger			B8		
			(G5)		
			L1*l*		
Flying: man flies on back			B4*e–g*		
of Sky-Condor. *See also*			M2*d–m*		
Coyote: transported					
home by Ducks					
man flies by means of			M2*a*		
Sky Blankets			T2		
			AA1		
Fog: dancers/ Across-	(C2*n*)		A2*k*		
Ocean-Widower's son			A15y *g*		
arrive(s) in			A23*h*		
			(G7*c*)		
			J2*g*		
			(K2*c*)		
			O1*k*		
			(T6*e*)		
			X6*d*		
			X7*e*		
			BB2 *c–f*		

Element	Kroeber, Karok Myths	Gifford, Karok Myths and Formulas	Kroeber, Yurok Myths	Harrington, Karuk Texts, Myths (1930, 1932a)	Bright, Karok Language 1957
Fog (*continued*)					
deer invisible to hunter in	F3*c–d* (F11*b*)	V.31*f–h* V.42			
Food: origin of. *See also* Salmon	D4 (F2) G3 G4*m*	II.1 II.8 II.9 (III.1) IV.1	A16x *f, k, r* V1*c–f* X1*h* X14 x, y BB3		(17)
Formulas: childbirth. *See also* Across-Ocean-Widower: seduces girl		V11–V.15		1932a:9	
curing		I.10 V.16–V.22 V.43 V.44	A23*c–d, g* B11 D3x, y I4 (U1) U2 U3		
death purification		V.36 V.37 V.38	F4 H2 K3*e–g* P4*d* X8 Z3		
drowning		V.29	X1*f* X3 X13		
hunting		I.12 V.23 V.30–V.32	B13 I1(?) Q11	53	
money or love		V.1–V.9 (V.10) (hate) V.25 V.26 V.39–V.41	C5 R2 S1 S4 S5 T1 T3 T6 T7 X14 BB2(?)	13 49–52 54	
rain		V.28			
salmon			A1 C2x, y D4 T4		
sterility		(I.4) (II.5) (II.6)	DD6		

Element	Kroeber, Karok Myths	Gifford, Karok Myths and Formulas	Kroeber, Yurok Myths	Harrington, Karuk Texts, Myths (1930, 1932a)	Bright, Karok Language 1957
Grizzly Bear driven from sweathouse by heat, songs. *See also* Bear entries; Sky Condor			(S2)	1930:1a	
Grown-in-a-Basket: grows magically			A14*b–d*		
plays shinny. *See also* Dog: scabby; Shinny game			A14*l–n* (D1x *a*) (D1y *a*)		54.28–40
restores Sun to sky			A14*j*–k J5*e* (with Raccoon)		
shoots giant bird on Shelton Butte			X1*e*		
steals fire			D1y *d, i*		
Hair: transformed into people	(F8*i*) G4*c*		A15y *b–c*		
two men's, tied together as trick			B8 G5		
Hate formula		V.10 (V.40) (V.41)			
Hawk *see* Falcon					
Heart as life force removed from own body	A4*e* A8*i–j*	(II.39) (teeth)	A15x *m–n* A23*k* C1*m* F1*k* J3*c*		(34)
Hills, mountains, rocks: origin of	F2		BB3		
Hook, magnetlike, attracts victims			A15x *b, i–j* B15*a, c*		
Horsefly paints face with human blood			X3		44
Houses, origin of	G4*n*		A16x *b*		
Humans, origin of. *See also* Arrows: transformed into men; Coyote: creates sons; Feces: impregnates woman; Hair: transformed into people; Lice: children grow from; Mankind sprung from dogs; Rattlesnake: as mate of human; Spirit impregnates woman	G4*a*		V1*a*		
Husband *see* Jealous husband of Merip					

Element	Kroeber, Karok Myths	Gifford, Karok Myths and Formulas	Kroeber, Yurok Myths	Harrington, Karuk Texts, Myths (1930, 1932a)	Bright, Karok Language 1957
Ice melted by fire			V.28		
Ikhareya (Karok) *see* Immortal(s)					
Immortal(s): departure of *see* Departure of the immortals					
grow from ground. *See also* Bulb baby			F2*q*		
smoke on seastack. *See also* Across-Ocean-Widower; Giant; Monster-ridding cycle			B6*e*		
Implements, origin of	G3*b–e* G4*h*				
Incest: brother-sister	A8	I.9	B3 B9 BB2		
Coyote-daughter/ grandmother		II.44 II.45	G4*c*	1930:5, 13	16
mother-daughter			E4		
Ixkareya (Karok) *see* Immortal(s)					
Jay (Steller's and Bluejay): finds water		III.36			
as greedy doctor	H4	III.11 III.32		1932a:6, 11	28 29
as greedy stepmother		II.53*a–h* II.54*a–e*		1930:2	(32) (Bear) 33.1–22
multiplies acorns		II.2	(F6*e*)		
takes language of other birds		III.36			
Jealous brothers shoot at sister's suitors			A15x *y*		
Jealous husband of Merip shoots immortal, fails to kill him	A8*j*		A15x *n* C1*l–m* F1*k* J3*c*		
Jealous wife: destroys husband's dam	E2	III.18	C3*k–n*		
takes daughter/other animals to sky		II.53*i–v* II.54*f–q*		1930:2	
turns to stone *see* Deserted wife and son					
Jerusalem cricket, larval: causes death and destruction. *See also* Mole		II.41(?)	A6 F4*b* P4*d* (X1*g*) (X8*a*) Z3*a–d*		

Element	Kroeber, Karok Myths	Gifford, Karok Myths and Formulas	Kroeber, Yurok Myths	Harrington, Karuk Texts, Myths (1930, 1932a)	Bright, Karok Language 1957
Mankind sprung from dogs: flood and. *See also* Humans, origin of	F6*d–e*	V.15	A14*p* J4 K4 X12 X13 (Z4*a*) YN27*		
Marksman, modest *see* Owl: modest					
Married at Rumai *see* Crane-leg-bridge					
Marrow, deer: human flesh restored by being rubbed with	A8*h*		A3*d* T3*f* T5*d*	1930a:12	59.15–40
Mauls, stone, as earrings, weapons *see* Monster-ridding cycle: evil one with gigantic earrings					
Medicine *see* Formulas					
Menstruation, first: and father's deception of daughter		II.44*a–b* (Coyote) V.23*a* (Widower)			
Mice: and frogs travel nightly by boat across ocean			(A2*k*) D7		
bore holes in boat to prevent pursuit	B3*g, k*	(V.2*d*) V.33*z–cc*	A14*g*		5.99–109
mourn for their children		III.17			
Mole: causes death and destruction. *See also* Jerusalem cricket			A6		
forced to remain in ground			F3 P1*a*		
as sister of Across-Ocean-Widower			F2*q*		
Money *see* Dentalium/ Dentalia					
Monster: as pet		(V.1*a–e*) V.47	All B2 T5 U2 U3 CC1 DD8 YN7*	1932a:5	
carries hero across ocean			A3*c* T5		
nearly drowns hero *see* Drowning, escape from					
steals/swallows child/man	B3	V.33	T5 DD4	1932a:2, 5	

Element	Kroeber, Karok Myths	Gifford, Karok Myths and Formulas	Kroeber, Yurok Myths	Harrington, Karuk Texts, Myths (1930, 1932a)	Bright, Karok Language 1957
Monster (*continued*)					
young man steals arrow from			DD9		
See also Monster-ridding cycle					
Monster-ridding cycle:	A8*i–j*	(I.9*i–j*)	A15x *b, g–h*		
blind women pound	(A10*b–c*)	(I.14*d–h*)	(A16x *s*)		
bones of victims	(D3*a, c*)	(III.38*c–j*)	C1*r*		
			F1*g*		
cannibal killed by having abdomen cut/ tongue pulled out		II.39–II.40 (by Coyote) III.39 (by Weasel)			
canoemaker tricks victims into split log	A10*i*	III.38*s–t*	A15x *b, e* (A16x *s*) C1*b, f* F1*a–c* J3*a*		
deadly ball game			(A16x *s*) C1*c* F1*d–e*		
deadly seesaw	A10*l*	III.37*l–n* III.38*u–w*	A15x *b, f*	20.39– 53	
evil one with gigantic earrings/hooks	A10*f* D3*a, c*	I.9*j* III.38*f–j*	A15x *b, i–j* B15*a, c* X3	19	
evil one feeds hot stones to victims	(B3*i*)		A15x *o* C1*q, r*		
horned serpent causes drowning. *See also* Drowning, escape from			A15x *b–c* A16x *i, s–u* C1*e* F1*f* X3*a–d*		
jealous husband who kills with arrows	A8*j*		A15x *b, n* C1*l–n* F1*k* J3*c*		
poisoned food/tobacco given to victims		III.8*g–j* V.20 V.21	A15x *b, d, l–m* A23*b–g, j* C1*g–k* F1*h–i* J3*b* P6		
woman with toothed vagina			F1*n–p*	(18.54– 71)	
Yellow Jackets, Spiders, Rattlesnakes in	A10*d–e, h*		J3*d*		
See also Coyote: at first fearful; Giant					

Element	Kroeber, Karok Myths	Gifford, Karok Myths and Formulas	Kroeber, Yurok Myths	Harrington, Karuk Texts, Myths (1930, 1932a)	Bright, Karok Language 1957
Payments: origin of, for killings	G4*t*	A19 F2*q* (F5) J4 P3 P4*a* X3*c* X10*b* Y1*b* Z4*b* (Z5) Z7*b*			
for wives, children	G4*e, s*	F2*e, q* X3*b* X10*a* Z4*a* Z7*b* (YN26)*			
Pestle: woman throws, at fleeing foster son *see* Bulb baby					
Pet brings luck to owner: deer as		B6			
Dentalium as		T1			
dog as *see* Dog: supplies/tracks deer for man					
monster as *see* Monster: as pet					
mythical bird as		U2			
Pipe case/tobacco pouch helps owner *see* Weasel: helps man					
Pipe rolls to signal taken by immortal		A15x *a* (T6*g*)			
Pitch, sea of		M2*a–c* T2 DD7			
Plank, burning: immortal rides across water on, kills monster(s)		A15x *b–c, o* A16x *i, s–u* C1*e* (F1*f*) X3*a, d*			
Pleiades *see* Coyote: dances with stars					
Porpoises: fight with immortals for possession of houses			C5*d–gl* (F2*k–l*)		

Element	Kroeber, Karok Myths	Gifford, Karok Myths and Formulas	Kroeber, Yurok Myths	Harrington, Karuk Texts, Myths (1930, 1932a)	Bright, Karok Language 1957
as poison smokers *see* Monster-ridding cycle: poisoned food/ tobacco			X1*f* (X7*a*)		
Pulekukwerek (Yurok immortal) *see* Monster- ridding cycle *and* under specific exploits					
Quiver for arrows eats poison food			A23*f–g, j*		
Rabbit desires horns			X7*b*		
Raccoon(s): helps Moon when attacked	F9*b*	(D3*f*)			
restores Sun to sky		(A14*h, j–k*) J5*e* DD13 II.52			
Race: Turtle cheats Squir- rel in. *See also* Woman: promised as bride					
Rattlesnake(s): as keeper(s) of fire			C1*o* F1*l*		
as mate of human			U1		
as wife of Moon	F9*b*				
Redwood: origin of			X9		
refuses to go beyond Kepel			T6		
Return of son/daughter to visit grieving parents	C1*g–h* C3	I.18*j–n*	B6*g* G6*f* (T3*h*)		(61)
River: origin of. *See also* Water: origin of		V.9	V1*a* X14x, y DD3		
Robin disdains all girl suitors except one wear- ing edible berries		III.28		1932a:3	
Rock(s): deserted wife and son transformed into *see* Deserted wife and son immortals as *see* Depar- ture of the immortals; Formulas: death purificaton man enters *see* Dripped on twice					
Rolling head, disem- bodied: attempts to seize brother/others		I.17	(A16x *s*)		

Element	Kroeber, Karok Myths	Gifford, Karok Myths and Formulas	Kroeber, Yurok Myths	Harrington, Karuk Texts, Myths (1930, 1932a)	Bright, Karok Language 1957
Star(s) (*Continued*)					
made by immortal from tobacco smoke			A16x *y–aa*		
Stepping-stones: pebbles/ thongs thrown as			B9*e, g* AA1*i*		
Stolen brother *see* Abandonment: of younger brother					
Stolen daughter *see* Deer girl; Giant: kidnaps small girl					
Stolen wife		V.2			
Stone(s): dropped into sweathouse in attempt to kill immortal			C1*k* F1*i*		
hot: fed to victims by evil one	B3*i*		A15x *o* (A16x *s*)		
See also Stepping-stones			C1*q, r*		
Stools jump as portent of owners' return	C3*b*				
String/twine: origin of. *See also* Spider spins rope/ ladder	G4*a–b*	III.1	A16x *w–aa* A16y		
Sun: course of	F9*a*		A17*g* X10*c* Z1*c*		
falls from sky, is restored			A14*h, j–k* J5*e* DD13		
kills wife (Frog)		V.7			
Sweathouse: birds sing in hero moves		(III.24*d*)	S2 A2*h* D5x *d* D5y *d* D6x *u–v*		
man seizes pains in			C4*d–j*		
origin of	G4*n–o*	II.12	T7		
women excluded from	G4*n–o*	(V.3*a*)	C1*d*		
See also Formulas		(V.19)	F1*e*		
Theft of acorns *see* Food					
Theft of fire/light for mankind. *See also* Coyote: strikes Sun; Fire entries	A7 F10 F11*a–e* (G2b)	II.7 II.43	D1x, y G1*d–e* X11 Z1		(33.72–90)
Thunder(s): accept blood money. *See also* Payments: origin of, for killings			J4 P3 (Z5)		

Element	Kroeber, Karok Myths	Gifford, Karok Myths and Formulas	Kroeber, Yurok Myths	Harrington, Karuk Texts, Myths (1930, 1932a)	Bright, Karok Language 1957
and death purification formula			Z3d–e		
and Earthquake shake the earth *see* Earthquake and Thunder					
as source of hero's strength *see* Courage, acquisition of					
woman escapes from marriage to	C3b–e	I.18a–f	B3		
Tobacco: Bat craves	B1e–f	III.7			
grows out of immortal's hand			A16x y (DD1)		
poison *see* Monster-ridding cycle: poisoned food/tobacco					
snake smokes	B2 H3	II.49			
Towhee looks in fire, reddens eyes					36
Transformation to stone *see* Departure of the immortals; Deserted wife and son					
Treasure: hero finds, in his cylindrical trunk/basket. *See also* Formulas: money or love			A1d A2a–g A13f–i M2m		57.112– 131
Tree(s): origin of. *See also* Acorns; Food		IV.1	T4 X9 V1d, f		35
split apart by hero with bare hands	F8c		A13f		
Upriver-Ocean-Girl provides water for mankind			T8d–f YN37*		
Vagina dentata episode			F1n–p		18.54–71
Vulnerable spot	A8j	III.38m			20.55–70
Wasps *see* Yellow Jackets					
Water: drips twice on hero's head			A3c T3 X15b–d		
origin of. *See also* River	D9 F1 (from tears) F2 (F3g)	III.3 III.35 III.36 V6e–f, V.8i–j (from tears)	(A17a, d) A18 (B15c) (I2) T8d–f V1a–b (from urine) BB3 YN37*		

KAROK
LINGUISTIC INDEX

WILLIAM BRIGHT

The following is a list of the Karok words, phrases, and sentences as written by Kroeber and by Gifford. For each entry there is a gloss, an indication of where the form occurs in this book, and an attempt to re-transcribe it in more systematic notation. Citations are given only for the first occurrence of a form in a given collection.

The retranscriptions use the phonemic system described in Bright, Karok Language (1957). The vowels are *a e i o u,* with values approximately as in Spanish; a raised dot indicates that the preceding vowel is pronounced with double length. The consonants have the following values: *č* like English *ch* in *church, f* and *h* as in English, *k* like Span. *c* in *coco, m* and *n* as in English, *p* as in Span. *papa, r* as in Span. *toro, s* between Eng. *s* and *sh* (with the tongue-tip turned back), *š* like Eng. *sh* in *ship, t* as in Span. *tata, v* as in Span. *lava* (a bilabial fricative), *x* like the *ch* in German *Bach, y* as in English, and *θ* like Eng. *th* in *thin.* The symbol *ʔ* is a glottal stop, pronounced in the middle of English words like *oh-oh!*

There are two accents, acute (as in *ʔá·s* "water") and circumflex (as in *ʔâ·nxus* "weasel"). Where these contrast, the acute indicates a high pitch, the circumflex a falling pitch. Words with no accent mark are pronounced on a low-level pitch. Hyphens are occasionally used to indicate grammatical divisions; they have no relevance for pronunciation.

The phonemic writings used here reflect the way words are pronounced in running text; they are therefore not always identical with the somewhat abstract, "underlying" forms given in the Lexicon of Bright 1957.

Where a complete retranscription of Kroeber's and Gifford's forms was not possible, partial analysis has been suggested. Where a word was not recognizable, a question mark appears.

●

ABBREVIATIONS USED IN CITATIONS

K Ethno	Kroeber's Ethnographic Notes, pp. 87–103
G Intro	Gifford's Introduction, pp. 107–109
G Info	Gifford's section on Informants, pp. 110–112
G V Intro	Gifford's Introduction to the Formulas, pp. 262–269
end	end note following a myth or formula
fn.	footnote
hdn.	headnote preceding a myth or formula or a group of myths or formulas

Aanina kuvakiinya "song words" (K Fllƒ): ?

Aas "water" (G III.27 fn. 3): ?á·s

Aaskan "in the water" (G III.27 fn. 3): ?á·skan

Aaskanyuksukiara "mountain lion" (G III.27 fn. 3): ?askan-yupθúkkirar "water-panther, a mythical animal"

A'at "spring salmon" (G III.9): ?á·t

Aavunai "a place, Yurok Kepel" (K F6e): ?â·vnay

Absummunukich "racer snake" (G II.14a, II.49a): ?apsun-múnnukič "slippery snake"

Absumxarak, Absunkarax, Absunxarak "long snake" (G III.37d, III.38n, V.12a): ?apsun-xárah

Abuishone "small chicken hawk" (G III.38m): ?apvuy-íθyurar, lit. "tail-dragger"

Achku "a bird" (G III.20): ?áčku·n "swamp robin, varied thrush"

Achpus "part of a salmon" (G III.2c, III.11b): ?áčpuus

Afam "a place" (G II.5ƒ, II.30): prob. for ?asvúffam

Aftaram "a place" (K A6 fn. 1): ?aftáram

Aharat hushashit "gooseberry pudding" (K F11ƒ): cf. ?axra·t "gooseberry"

Ahayuush "pine nuts" (K G4r): ?axyu·s "digger pine nut"

Ahchunupich "a shell" (K G4j): ?

Ahedimchûk adihiv "tree-fall-over jump-

ing over it, a personal name" (G II.25e): cf. ?árih "to jump"

Ahichip ipumnish "Children, a tail!" (K A2a): ?axxí·č pipúnni·č (Bright 1972: 216) or ?axičapipúnni·šič (Bright 1972:218)

Ahoeptini "a place" (K A6a): perh. miscopying for ?ačípči·nkirak "Bluenose"

Ahopamva "white rotten center of log" (G III.38t): ?ahup-?ámva·n "wood-eater, i.e. wood worm"

Ahpuum "mole" (K A10c): ?áxpu·m "meadow mouse"

Ahsai "ground squirrel" (K F7): ?áxθa·y

Ahuram usaniirak "pipe-left-behind, a place" (K F3h): ?uhrá·m ?uθa·nî·rak "where a pipe lies"

Ahuwham "white oak" (G IV.la): ?axva·m

Ahvahahi wurukur "dentalia with pitch on them" (K G4ƒ): cf. ?axváhahar "pitchy"

Ahwa "crane" (K C1d): ?áxva·y "great blue heron"

Aidjēn, Aikiren, Aikneich, Aixnekshan, Aixlechton, Aixnexshan "falcon, duck hawk" (K A5a, E2a; K Ethno: Language; G II.1a, II.43a, III.18, III.19a): ?a-?ikrê·n, lit. "above-living", dim. ?a?iknê·čhan

Aiyis "a place" (G V.3 fn. 5): ?áyi·θ "Eyese Bar"

Ai yu kichikti "song words for dentalia"

(G II.37b): cf. ʔararé·špuk "Indian money"

Akavaki, Akawaki "quiver" (G I.9e, I.18d, II.16): ʔakvákkir

Akbachuripa "a place; a personal name" (G II.31c, III.3a): cf. -ripa· "uphill"

Akhapini "a place" (K A 8a): ?

Akich "friend" (G II.18c): ʔákkič

Akôra "axe" (K H5 fn. 2): ʔakô·r

Aksai "ground squirrel" (G III.2a, V.29 fn. 1): ʔáxθa·y

Aksimsaxsaxkwen "wren" (G II.2d): ʔasimčákčakve·nač

Aksipakwapitiv "roots of grass coming up, a name" (G II.25e): cf. ʔákθi·p "wild barley"

Akuwi(s) "wildcat" (G II.16e, II.53 fn. 4): ʔákvi·š

Akuwisi "small wildcat" (G II.53l): ʔakví·šič

Akwai "heron" (G II.34a): ʔáxva·y

Akwi(ch) "wildcat" (G II.16e, III.27): ʔákvi·š

Āma "salmon" (K G2c): ʔá·ma

Amaikiara(m) "a place, Ike's Falls" (K A5a, G, I.2h and passim): ʔame·kyá·ra·m, lit. "salmon-making place"

Anaach "crow" (G III.13a): ʔánna·č

Ananāmvan yupeiton "horsefly" (K F11a): ʔararamvan-yupsíttanač, lit. "baby man-eater"

Anava "medicine, magical formula" (G Intro and passim): ʔánnav

Anav tokyav "formula for curing" (G V Intro): ʔánnav tó·kyav "he makes medicine"

Anavukiyêhe "refers to herb or root doctor" (K Ethno: Valuations): ʔánnav "medicine", ʔikyav "to make"

Amayûp "this is good" (G II.8): ʔamáyav "delicious"

Anekiava(n) "herb doctor" (K Ethno: Valuations; G V Intro fn. 2): ʔane·kyá·va·n, lit. "medicine-maker"

Anhus(h) "weasel" (K A10, D3; G III.37a): ʔâ·nxus

Anhush itura tura "song words" (K A10f): ʔâ·nxus ʔitvaratvárat (no meaning)

Anix "older brother" (G V.33f): ʔárih, dim. ʔánnihič

Anixus "weasel" (K A10 fn. 2; G Intro and passim): ʔâ·n(a)xus

Anixus su kupanik "weasel did (it)" (G Intro): ʔâ·n(a)xus ʔukúpha·nik

Anok "ouch" (G II.25c): ʔano·

Ansafriki "a place, Yurok Weitspus, Eng. Weitchpec" (K A3a): ʔansáfri·k

Anshwufum "a place, Yurok Kenek" (K C2a): ʔasvúffam

Apadāx "fox" (G V.35): ʔapra·x

Apahaisuripa "name of a ridge" (G II.18a): cf. -ripa· "uphill"

Aphan "cap" (K G1b): ʔápxa·n

Apmaananich "smallest type of dentalium" (K G4a): perh. ʔapmá·nanič "little one having a mouth"

Apshunhara "long snake" (K A10j): ʔapsunxára

Apshun-mukuroo "he had rattlesnake for his wife" (K F9b): ʔápsu·n muhrô·ha "snake [was] his wife"

Apshun-munakich, -munukich "racer snake" (K B2a, H3): ʔapsun-múnnukič, lit. "slippery snake"

Apurowa "deviled" (G III.11): cf. ʔáppur "to bewitch"

Apurōn "disease object" (K H4 fn. 12, 16): ʔáppuro·n "sorcerer's charm"

Apuruwan "Indian devil, sorcerer" (K Ethno: Sickness): ʔapurúva·n

Apuvichiyuna "Cooper hawk" (K A5a): ʔapvuy-íθyurar, lit. "leg-dragger", dim. ʔapvuyíčyu·nanač

Ap'xan "tanbark oak" (G IV.la): xuntáppan "tan oak acorn"

Ara "person" (G II.3f): ʔára

Ara-ipamvanati "name of a lake" (G I.17a): ʔára ʔuʔipamvâ·natihirak "place where a person ate himself"

Arar(a) "person, human being" (Foreword; K G2b): ʔára·r

Arara ivwuna "brush dance" (G I.10a): ʔarara-ʔi·hvúna· "Indian brush dance"

Araraixsara "bread" (G II.8k): perh. ʔarara-sára "Indian bread"

Arara'op "Indian valuables" (K H4 fn. 5): ʔarará-ʔu·p

Arareiyunkuri "where they poke a person in, a place name" (G I.17e): ʔára·r "person", ʔiyú·nkurih "to stick into water"

Aratanva, Aratanwa "pain, i.e. supernatural disease object" (K: Ethno: Sickness; G V.37d): ʔarátta·nva

Aratanwa-tanakên "the pain moves" (K Ethno: Sickness): ʔarátta·nva tanakê·n "the pain moves in me"

Aratanwa-tôkên "the pain moves" (K Ethno: Sickness): ʔarátta·nva to·kê·n

Aruam "cannibal" (G V.33 end): perh.

Djishikevi "old bitch" (G V.13*b*): čiših-ké·vri·k

Djishshii "dog" (G V.4*a*): čiši·h

Eim "shaman" (G I.8 and passim): ʔê·m

Enhikiis "name of a Hupa town" (G II.37a):?

Faatyaha "be quiet!" (K F11*f*): fâ·t "what?", yáxxa "look!"

Fadamuche "boiled acorns" (G II.30 fn. 1): ?

Fatawenan "priest" (G I.15*b*, V Intro fn. 2): fatavê·na·n

Fudaki "ladder" (G III.6*a*): vurá·kir

Fuivaoru "whistling used in some medicine songs" (G V Intro): cf. ʔikfuy "to whistle"

Furah iruhap "headband with woodpecker scalps" (K G4*k*): cf. fúrax "woodpecker scalp," ʔiyruh "headdress"

Furah pikivash "headdress with woodpecker scalps" (K G4*k*): furax-píkvas

Gunashgunash "spring-pole, seesaw" (K A10*l*): kuna·skúnnas

Guuf "skunk" (G III.31 fn. 2): ku·f

Ha "spider" (K A10*e*): xah

Hakananap-mana(n) "small dentalium" (K D8, F1): cf. xákka·n "on both sides", ʔapma·n "mouth" (prob. = "a personal name," G I.2g)

Hanchifichi "frog" (K A7*a*): xančí·fič

Hanchiv "frog" (G III.17 fn. 1): xančí·fič

Hanhich "long nose" (G V.27*c*): prob. for yufiv-xánnahič "long nose" (dim.)

Hankit "bullhead" (K H4*b*): xánki·t

Hanpuchinishwe "hummingbird" (K A7*a*): xanpučíni·šve·nač

Hansiip "black oak" (G IV.1*a*): xánθi·p

Hasipnada "basket plate" (G I.18*c*): ?

Havnam "wolf" (G V.18*a*): ʔikxâ·vna-mič

Havuram-tīkivên "large lizard" (K F9*b*): xavrámti·kve·n

Ha-wishwantini "small spider" (K B3*e*): xah-višvantírih "flat-bellied spider", dim. xahvišvantínnihič

Hebenafi "a place" (G III.39 fn. 2): ?

Hohira "a place, Yurok Wahsek, Eng. Martin's Ferry" (K C2*e*): xô·xhirak

Hovena hanina, hadikman chimini "song words" (K F8*c*): ?

Ichaprimvar "buckskin decorated with woodpecker scalps" (K G4 fn. 5): ?

Ichitkin yufivihasip aan "Crooked Nose, my older brother" (K B3*a*): cf. yúffiv "nose"

Ichwuhanahiich "goldenrod" (G V.38): ?

Iduparaup "measles" (G I.4*a*): ?

Ifabi "young woman" (G I.3 fn 2): ʔifáp-pi·t

Ifabikevi "old maid" (G V.25 fn. 4): ʔifapit-ké·vri·k

Ifvaifurdaxara "water dog" (G II.47): ʔiθvay-fúraxar, lit. "breast-red"

Ihseira ahup "he carries wood" (K G 4*n*): cf. ʔáhup "wood"

Ihuk "First Menses Dance" (G II.19*a* and passim): ʔíhuk

Ikchahwan, Ikchaxuwa "a kind of hawk" (K A5*a*, G III.35*f*): ʔikčáxva·n "red-tailed hawk"

Ikeremia kemniikich "wind old woman" (K D3*b*): ʔikre·myaha-ké·vni·kič

Ikhareya "an immortal" (Foreword; K A5*a*, and passim): ʔikxaré·yav

Ikiyawan "girl assistant to priest" (G I.16*b*, V Intro fn. 7): ʔikyáv-a·n, lit. "maker"

Iknumen "name of a mountain" (G V.46*a*): ʔiknû·min "Burrill Peak"

Ikshupkire "a disease" (K Ethno: Sickness): ?

Ikurowak "a ridge" (G I.17*c*) ʔikurô·v-ak "on a ridge running upriver"

Ikūv "fox; a personal name" (K G hdn.): ʔiku·f

Ikxarey-arar "priest" (K G hdn.): ʔikxariya-ʔára·r, lit. "immortal-person"

Imahka "one whom nobody likes" (K F9*b*): ʔimá·hka "to despise"

Impā, Impaak "trail" (G II.17*a*, V.39 fn. 3): ʔimpa·h

Impurak "a place" (G V.10 fn. 1): ʔim-púrak

Imsatwa "shinny game" (G V.34*a*, V.46): ʔimθá·tva

Imtamvarakasurakam "a place" (G V.42): cf. súrukam "underneath"

Imtamvarakasurukam afishi "name of an immortal" (G V.42 end): cf. ʔafíšríhan "young man"

Imtamwara "a place" (G V.31*d*): ?

Imtarashun "bastard" (Foreword; K F9*a*): ʔimtarássu·n

Imtarasuxbirish "bastard plant, hill lotus" (G V.14): ʔimtarasun-píriš

Imvirakam "a place, Hamburg" (G I.2*j*): perh. ʔimvirá-kka·m "big fishing platform"

var "maul for driving wedges"
Pariptutschara "a personal name" (G
II.25e): ?
Pasnanwan "small owl" (G II.33):
ʔipasnáhva·n
Pasurak "upriver ocean" (K G4a): perh.
kah-yúras "upriver ocean"
Patapirihak "flat rocks on the ground, a
place" (K C1a): patapríhak (site opp.
Yurok Rekwoi at mouth of Klamath;
prob. Yurok Wełkwäu)
Patunukôt "refers to sucking doctors"
(K Ethno: Valuations): ʔupatumkô·ti
"he sucks at it"
Paura isha chupisrihesh "the water
would spread out here" (K F6a): cf. ʔíš-
ša(ha) "water", čupaθríhe·š "it will
spread"
Pavatanshununam "name of a rock" (G
II.5 fn. 1): ?
Penishgardim "mountain lion" (G
II.46a, III.18a): piriškâ·rim "grizzly
bear" (sometimes equated with the Afri-
can lion)
Pe'sara "Brush Dance doctor" (G
I.10a): ?
Pichvava afishni "a type of dentalia" (K
G4a): piθáva "a type of dentalia",
ʔafišríhan "young man"
Pidishkadim, Pidishkarem "grizzly
bear" (G III.19, V Intro): piriškâ·rim
Pikiawish "world renewal ceremony"
(G I.15b and passim): Eng. adaptation of
(ʔiθívθa·ne·n) ʔupikyâ·viš "he will re-
make it (the world)"
Pikuava, Pikᵘva, Pikᵘwa, Pikuwa, Pikva
"myth" (G Intro, II.41 fn. 1, V Intro,
V.31, V.33): pikvah
Pinef "coyote" (G II.2b, II.47d):
pihnê·fič
Pinefas "Coyote fix it, name of a rock"
(G II.6 hdn.): pihné·f-ʔas "coyote rock"
Pinefish "coyote" (K A1 fn. 1; G II.5 fn.
1): pihnê·fič
Pinefish su kupanik "Coyote did (it)" (G
Intro): pihnê·fič ʔukúpha·nik
Pinefisim cheha "Coyote sign" (G II.26
fn. 2): prob. pihne·fič-ʔímčax "coyote
(sun-)shine"
Pinefsui "a kind of bird" (G II.6h):
pihne·f-θúriv "coyote urine"
Pinevifishisani "name of a rock" (G
II.50c): cf. pihnê·fič "coyote", θá·niv
"to lie"
Pinishkadim "an animal" (G II.46):
piriškâ·rim "grizzly bear"
Pinits "old man" (G II.18b): pihnî·č

Pinnanih-tanakan "mourning dove" (K
G4w): pimnanih-tanákka·nič, lit. "little
summer-mourner"
Pirishkarim "grizzly bear" (K F9b):
piriškâ·rim
Pishpish "yellowjacket" (K A1a and
passim): pišpíšših
Pisivava, Pisiwava "dentalium shell" (K
G4a; G II.25l): piθváva
Pitschipchiptane "cooking stones with
soup adhering" (G II.31b): cf. pačípčip
"to suck"
Pixuwa "story, myth" (G V Intro):
piθvah
Pufikanava "deer medicine" (G V.32)?:
pufič-ʔánnav
Punwaram "resting place" (G II.32b):
ʔipu·nváram
Puyahanakemich "poor dead person, the
name of an immortal" (G V.38a):
puya·hara-kê·mič
Pūya pāiōmah "It's all right" (K H5 fn.
3): cf. púya "well, . . . "

Saap "steelhead" (K G2 fn. 1; G II.23c):
sá·p
Sadum "pine roots" (G III.34j): sárum
Sahēsyu "jackrabbit" (G II.52b):
sahíšyu·xač
Saiyis "Indian potatoes" (G II.46c):
tayi·θ "Brodiaea bulb"
Sak "obsidian" (G II.33e): sá·k
Samchaka "bar in river which divides it
into two streams; a place name; a per-
sonal name" (G I.19): cf. sav-, sam- "to
flow"
Samnannax "a place, Forks of Salmon"
(G I.4b): samnâ·nak
Sanhiluvra "name of an immortal" (G
I.9): ?
Sapru(k) "olivella shells" (G II.25l,
III.28c): sápru·k
Satimu "lower peak of Mt. Offield" (G
V.45): saʔtím-ʔu·y "downhill-edge
peak"
Satimu weixkareya "Mt. Offield im-
mortal" (G V.45): saʔtímʔu·y ve·kxaré·
yav
Sausikahas "a plant, Mentha arvensis"
(G V.41): ?
Saxvuram, Saxvurum "a place, Yurok
Operger" (G II.11, II.55): sahvúrum
Senipiches "I tell (song words)" (G II.53):
perh. nipasúppi·čva "I tell a secret"
Sha'ap "steelhead" (K G2c): sá·p
Shafnaikano "a place" (K D8): ?
Shahkunishamman "kingfisher" (K

A2*a*): sa?kuniš-?ámva·n "downhill eater"

Shahpīni "beaver" (K C1*d*): sah-píhri·v, lit. "downhill old-man"

Shamakauui "a place, Shelton Butte" (G V.45 fn. 1): ?išramaká-?u·y

Shaman "deer lick, a place name" (G V.45 fn. 1): ?išrá·mak, lit. "at a deer lick"

Shammai "a place, Seiad" (K G2, G V.6 fn. 1): sâ·may

Shapru "a type of shell' (K G4*m*): sápru·k "olivella shell"

Sharip "hazel" (K A2*e*): sárip

Sharuk-ashimnaun "down-by-the-river living long-haired, a personal name" (K C2*h*): cf. sáruk "downhill, by the river"

Shidixcus "tobacco bag" (G II.54*l*): cf. θiríxô·n "testicles, scrotum" (referring to an elk scrotum used to hold tobacco)

Shi(')it "mouse" (G III.17 fn. 1, III.23*a*): sí·t

Shipnuk "storage basket" (K F6*a*; G II.5*b*): sípnu·k

Shishareitiroopaop "a type of dentalium shell" (K G4*a*): cf. síššar "one who has a penis", ?itrô·p "five"

Shitūm "a place, Redding Rock" (K C1*c*): siytu·m

Shiv'ak "where the water flowed still" (K A10*j*): ?

Shridioni "bag net to catch woodpeckers" (G I.19 fn. 1): ?

Shunyisa "chinquapin nuts" (K H4 fn. 6): sunyíθθih

Shupā "light" (K F10*a*): súppa·h "day"

Shupa-hak-kuush "daylight-moon, i.e., sun" (K F9*a*): supahá-kku·sra

ShweaK "robin" (G III.21 fn. 1): ?

Shwufum "a place, Yurok Kenek" (K A10*a*): ?asvúffam

Sieruk-pihiriv "Across-Ocean-Widower, Across-the-Water Widower" (K A3, C.2, D.1): ?iθyaruk-píhri·v

Sihaviitka "a place" (K F1*b*): cf. sí·h "awl", ví·tkir "ridge"

Siit "mouse" (G III.29): sí·t

Sipnuk "storage basket" (K G4*h*): sípnu·k

Sipnūkis "acorn storage basket" (G V.47*j*): sípnu·k "acorn storage basket", sipnú·kiθ "basket for dentalia"

Sirihaon "testicle"(K D3*c*): θirixô·n

Sisegunva "belt" (G III.8*f*): síččakvutvar

Sistani "hill" (G III.24*a*): perh. ?iθívθa·ne·n "land"

Siv(i)chap "war dance" (G I.18*c*, II.6*a*): θivtap

Sivriva "wall" (G III.38*i*): θivrî·hvar

Sivsinenachip "middle of world" (G V Intro): ?iθivθane·n-?á·čip

Sivstap "war dance" (G II.5*c*): θivtap

Somkifkuswana "measuring worm" (G II.53*s*): ?

Spohokuran "name of a pond" (K F11*n*): ?aspahó·kra·m

Stidjwuni "gambling game" (G I.10*e*): cf. ?iθtit "to gamble"

Sufaim "a place" (K E1): ?

Sufip "a place, Yurok Rekwoi" (K F1*b*; G I.5*d* and passim): θúffip

Sufip ifapi "river-mouth girl, a name" (K F3*h*): θúffip "Rekwoi", ?ifáppi·t "young woman"

Sufkaro'om "a place" (K A6 fn. 1): θufkáro·m

Sufkirik "great horned owl" (K A5*a*; G III.25): θufkírik

Sufsa(a)m "water-dog, mud puppy" (K A4*d*; G II.33*a*): θúfθa·m

Suhurwish-kuru "a personal name" (K F2): ?

Suk "flicker, a bird" (G II.7*g*): θú·k

Sukiara "yellow" (G III.27 fn. 3): θúkkirar

Sukrif, -v "woven bag" (G I.7*a*, II.1*b*, and passim): θuxriv

Sukrivishkuruhan "name of an immortal" (G II.1*b*): θuxriv-?iškúruhan "he who carries a net bag by a loop"

Sununum "exit at floor level" (G II.15 fn. 1): cf. súru- "to make a hole"

Sunyis "chestnut" (G III.12*b*): sunyíθθih "chinquapin"

Supahas "morning star" (G.III.38 fn. 5): cf. súppa·h "day"

Suuk "flicker, a bird" (G II.19): θú·k

Suwaiten amfira "my heart's burning with hunger" (G II.40*a*): cf. ?iθva·y "heart", tanímfir "it feels hot to me"

Suwait furahar "salamander" (G II. 40*f*): ?iθvay-fúraxar "breast-red"

Suwufus "a place" (G V.25*a*): ?

Swivyuburuhat "a bird" (G II.30*e*): cf. ?ačvi·v "bird"

Taharatar "flint flaker" (K G3*b*): ?

Taharatishnam "ten places flat running over; a personal name" (G II.25): perh. ?itahara-tíšra·m "ten flat places"

Tahuravuripki chishi "I will cohabit with my dog" (K F6*d*): cf. čiši·h "dog"

Taichuka "lily bulbs" (G Intro): cf.

tayi·θ "Brodiaea"
Taiyiis, Taiyīs "Brodiaea bulbs" (G I.6 fn. 1, III.23*d*, V.24*a*): tayi·θ
Takayu ifapbi "young woman unmarried, name of an immortal" (G V.8 fn. 2): cf. ʔifáppi·t "young woman"
Takininam "where they soak acorns, a place name" (G III.23*a*): tákkiriram
Taknuris "stone maul" (K A10*f*; G III.8*b*): taknúriθ
Taknuris-tenvara "mauls-for-earrings, a name" (K A10*f*): taknuriθ-tê·nvar
Takur "white" (G V.30*d*): -ta·hko·
Takurada "hook" (G II.17*e*): tákkurar
Takwukat "hook" (G III.8*i*): taxvúkkar
Tamxanach "scorched, a place name" (G I.17*c*): ?
Tanapāsirip "a person who refused to heed the call to ferry" (K Ethno: Valuations): ?
Taniminok, Tanimuuh "kingfisher's song" (K A2*c*, H.2*a*): ?
Taprara "mat" (G II.15): taprára
Taripan "dipper basket" (G V Intro): taríppa·n
Tashe "situation which makes bad luck" (G V.3 fn. 6): ?
Tawuka "fish hook" (G V.33*e*): taxvuk
Taxasufkara "a place" (G I.2*d*): taxasufkára
Taxasufkarayuskam "a place, Sandy Bar" (G I.2*d*): taxasufkara-yú·θkam
Tayiis, Tayish "Broadiaea bulb" (K A10*c*; G II.46 fn. 2): tayi·θ
Tcirrixus "tobacco basket" (G III.7*c*): cf. θirixô·n "scrotum used for tobacco bag"
Telpak "entrance to sweathouse" (G II.15*a*): cf. čivčak "door"
Tetaxnehan "a brush" (G I.10*d*): ?
Ti'i "a place, Tea Bar" (K A2*a*): tí·h
Timkuru "grouse" (K A7*a*): timkúruh
Timnukwaram "name of a rock" (G V.44*a*): ?
Timshuk(u)ri "bat" (K B1*a*; G III.7*a*): timšúkri·h
Tinwaap "acorn winnower" (G I.9*g*): tínva·p
Tiptip "Woodwardia fern" (K A2*e*): típti·p
Tisakuara "gloves" (G III.8*i*): tikakvára·r
Tishannik "a place" (G V Intro, V.10): tišánni·k
Tishram "Scott Valley" (G II.38*a*, III.19*a*): tíšra·m

Tishraw-arara "Scott Valley Shasta" (G II.38 fn. 1): tišrávar
Tishwu(f) "incense root, wild celery" (G V Intro): kíšvu·f
Tisiram "lots of" (G III.8): prob. for tíšra·m "a clearing"
Tisravar "Scott Valley Shasta" (G V Intro): tišrávar
Tivaak "fingerlings" (K G2*a*): ?
Tubaha kus "sun" (G II.26 fn. 1): supahá-kku·sra "day-sun"
Tulukwichi "a kind of bird" (G I.6*c*): turuxvíθθin "meadowlark"
Tuus "mockingbird" (G III.20): tu·s
Tuusipumwaram "name of a mountain" (G III.20*a*): cf. tu·s "mockingbird", ʔipu·nváram "resting place"
Tuwahara "dry; name of an illness" (G Intro): tuváxrah "it's dry"

Uchkamtim "name of a mountain" (G II.26*c*): perh. ʔú·θkam "westward", tí·m "edge"
Uhuriv "a kind of bird" (K B3*d*): ?
Uhuriv "net sack" (K G1*b*): θuxriv
Ui "high place" (G V Intro fn. 4; V.45 fn. 1): ʔu·y "mountain"
Uichi "a place" (G V Intro): perh. ʔá-ʔu·yič "Sugar Loaf"
Uknamihich "a lake" (G III.8*f*): cf. ʔúkra·m "lake"
Uknamkana, Uknamxanak "name of a pond" (G II.14*f*, II.15*i*): ʔukram-xárah, lit. "long pond", dim. ʔuknam-xánnahič
Uknī, Ukni'i "word used to begin myths" (K H4*a*; G Intro): ʔuknî·
Ukramisiriki "name of a lake" (G III.23*c*): ʔukram-ʔiθríkkirak
Ukunamhanach "name of a lake" (K F11*n*): ʔuknam-xánnahič "long pond", dim.
Ukunii "word uttered by myth character" (K G1*a*): perh. ʔuknî· "word used to begin myths"
Uruksa "disk beads" (G III.28*b*): ʔúruhsa

Vikaputunwei "name of an immortal" (G III.2*b*): perh. vikapuh-túnvi·v "woven-quiver children"
Vunharuk "a place, Oak Bottom Flat" (K D hdn.): vunxárak

Wahar "eagle" (K F11*a*): vákka·r
Waiyat "Wiyot Indians" (K Ethno: Sickness): váyat

Wakanwekareya "name of an immortal" (GV Intro): cf. ve·kxaré·yav "its immortal"

Warûm "basket plate" (G V.25d): ?imváram

Washāratuva "people met without speaking" (K Ethno: Valuations): cf. vá·san "enemy"

Wenaram "sacred house" (K A5 fn. 2; G I.2c, III.9a): ve·ná-ram "praying place"

Widishur "bear" (G V.30 fn. 1): vírusur

Widishur karamkunish "black bear" (G V.30 fn. 1): virusur-?ikxáramkuniš

Wingvīn "a kind of bird" (G III.8a): ?

Wininiki(ch), Wininkech "pine squirrel" (G III.2b, III.10d, III.32a): vínninikič

Wirushur "bear" (K A1b): vírusur

Wīshini aweyishap "I am (fasting because I am) on my way to get money" (K F11h): cf. ni?áve·šap "I will not eat"

Wītcha "a place; a personal name (?)" (G I.12a): ?

Wuppam "a place, Red Cap" (G Intro and passim): vúppam

Wurishiat "a fishery" (G III.20b): cf. ?išyá·t "spring salmon"

Wutax "piece of dried deer meat" (G V.33 fn. 2): ?

Xachmom, Xachmubis "a kind of insect or spider" (G II.41f, III.1b): cf. xah "spider"

Xaipanipa "name of a bluff" (G I.7c): ?

Xāmnam "wolf" (K F11a): ?ikxâ·vnamič

Xangit "bullhead" (G III.11): xánki·t

Xanpuchinis "hummingbird" (G III.11): xanpučíni·šve·nač

Xansip "black oak" (G I.14g): xánθi·p

Xansunamwan "mink" (G V.29a): xanθun-?ámva·n, lit. "crawfish eater"

Xanuwish "bundle of dried deer meat" (G V.33 fn. 2): ?

Xatsipirak "a place" (G II.14j): kát-tiphirak

Xavin, Xavits "tiger lily" (G I.3a): xávin

Xavishtimi "a place" (G Info, fn. 5): xavíšti·m

Xavnam "to mash; wolf" (G II.25a, V.10h): ?ikxâ·vnamič

Xavramtiisveis "a kind of lizard" (G V.20a): xavrámti·kve·n

Xawich, -sh "syringa, arrowwood" (G II.3a, II.25b): xáviš

Xaxanan "go-with, girl companion" (G

I.10c): cf. xákka·n "together"

Xuparich "yew" (G II.3a): xupári·š

Xusripi "madrone berries" (G III.28f): kusríppiš

Yadubi'hi "Giant, Widower" (G I.1a): ?iθyaruk-píhri·v "Across-the-Water Widower"

Yarihivash "deerskin blanket" (K F11j): cf. va·s "blanket"

Yasara "human being, rich man" (G I.19 fn. 3 and passim): ya·s?ára

Yasara ixkareya "rich man immortal" (G III.1c): ya·s?ara-?ikxaré·yav

Yāsh-ara "rich person" (K F6e): ya·s?ára

Yaunakayeishch(i) "a personal name" (K A10f, D3a): ? (prob. = Yonakaiyi)

Yaveh "good woman, a personal name" (G V.9): cf. yav "good"

Yawuneixlivram "menstruant's house" (G II.44j): yahvure·krívra·m

Yedihim "first menstruant" (G V.23a): yê·riphar

Yeruxbihi(i) "Widower" (G II.8a, V.20): ?iθyaruk-píhri·v "Across-the-Water Widower"

Yonakaiyi "behind the pit wall, a personal name" (G III.38i): cf. yô·ram "back part of house"

Yuarari "name of a lake" (G V.33e): cf. yu- "downriver"; perh. yuh-?arári·k "Crescent City"

Yuduksov "Bluff Creek" (G II.18a): yurúk-θu·f, lit. "downriver creek"

Yufip "a place, Yurok Rekwoi" (K C1 fn. 1): prob. for θúffip "Rekwoi"

Yufivihasip "crooked nose, a personal name" (K B3a): cf. yúffiv "nose"

Yufkumuru "small salmon" (K G2c): ?

Yuhidim, Yuhirim "flint knife" (K G3b; G II. 21c): yuhírim

Yuhsarani "haliotis, abalone" (K G4m): yuxθáran

Yuhsaraniyu·nupus "haliotis ornaments" (K G4i): cf. yuxθáran "haliotis", ?iyur "to stick a long object"

Yuk "eye" (G III.27 fn. 3): yú·p

Yuksukiara "panther" (G III.27 fn. 3): yup-θúkkirar, lit. "eye-yellow"

Yuniyon "crazy" (G I.12b): yunyú·nha "to be crazy"

Yupashtaran "tears" (K F1a): yupastáran

Yupichnu "Deep-Eye" (K A4f): cf. yú·p "eye"

Yupsukila "panther" (G II.53): yup-θúkkirar, lit. "eye-yellow"

Yuras "ocean" (G I.2*a*, and passim): yúras

Yurashisiak "the other side of the ocean" (K C1*d*, F.1 fn. 3): cf. yúras "ocean", ?iθya- "across"

Yurasixyeru-ifapbi "Across-the-ocean young girl, a personal name" (G V.7*g*): yuras-?iθyaruk-?ifáppi·t

Yuraskeruafishi "a personal name" (G V.1): cf. yúras "ocean", ?afišríhan "young man"

Yuruk-i-siaruk "across the ocean" (K F1): yúruk ?iθyáruk

Yuruk-pasikiri "a personal name" (K C2*k*): yurúk-pa·θkir "downriver head-dress"

Yuruksuf "Bluff Creek" (G II.31): yurúk-θu·f, lit. "downriver creek"

Yurukvar, Yuruk-v-ārar, Yuruk-w-arara "downriver person, Yurok Indian" (Foreword; K Ethno: Language): G V.2): yúruk va?ára·r

Yuskam "across from" (G I.2 fn. 4): yú·θkam "across and downriver"

Yutimin "a place, Ike's Falls" (G III.19 fn. 3): yu?tim-?î·n, lit. "downriver edge falls"

Yūtwi "goody!" (K A.2a): yô·tva

Yuuh wītkiri kaura "endless sand hills" (K F6*b*): cf. yuh- "downriver", ví·tkir "ridge, horizon"

Yuutimits "a place" (G III.9): yuhtî·mič, lit. "little downriver edge"

Yuyeich "a place" (K Ethno:·Language): ?

THE LIBRARY
ST. MARY'S COLLEGE OF MARYLAND
ST. MARY'S CITY, MARYLAND 20686